THE SAME AGE AS THE STATE

'I would recommend it most strongly –
both for the beautiful writing, interspersed with some of Máire's poems,
many of them translated from the Irish, and for its tender and evocative
account of the Ireland of the first half of the last century ...
no one could doubt that this book is the work of
an accomplished poet.'
Garret FitzGerald, in *The Irish Times*

'She is, as she puts it, as old as the Irish state.
For much of that time, one suspects, the state
has lagged behind her, both emotionally
and intellectually.'
Gerry McCarthy, *Sunday Times*

'This is a moving story of an extended family
as much as it is the story of the life of one remarkable woman ...
A warm-hearted story that carries the reader along
with all the emotional
pull of a good novel.'
John Bruton TD

THE SAME AGE
AS THE STATE

MÁIRE CRUISE O'BRIEN

The University of Wisconsin Press

The University of Wisconsin Press
1930 Monroe Street
Madiscon, Wisconsin 53711

www.wisc.edu/wisconsinpress/

5   4   3   2   1

A Cataloging-in-Publication record for this book
is available from the Library of Congress
ISBN 0-299-21030-8 (cloth)

First published by The O'Brien Press Ltd., Dublin, Ireland

Editing, typesetting, layout and design: The O'Brien Press Ltd
Copyright for inside photographs © Máire Cruise O'Brien
Photograph of author on front cover and on back flap, top: Colman Doyle
Printing: Stamford Press Pte, Singapore

DEDICATION

For Milo

ACKNOWLEDGEMENTS

This book was Michael O'Brien's idea, and Íde ní Laoghaire of The O'Brien Press it was who finally persuaded me to write it. I owe them both a debt of gratitude. I loved actually writing the book and I feel that my father and mother and all the people from whom I came will be glad to have been remembered. My editor at The O'Brien Press, Rachel Pierce, turned what might have become a drudgery into a series of wonderfully refreshing social encounters without ever relaxing her perceptive efficiency. Thank you, Rachel.

As with all my literary undertakings for many years now, I could never have coped with the archival research involved without the constant, unstinting help of Máire Mhac Conghaíl, my dear friend who is also a professional genealogist – *Táim faoi chomaoin agat choíche, a Mháire.* I also owe a debt to Manus O'Riordan for correcting a serious error about Mrs Muriel MacSwiney.

My special thanks to Conor and the children and grandchildren who, in spite of their anxieties about the terrible things I might say, were endlessly loving and supportive. Many other dear friends are thanked in the course of the text.

Most importantly of all, may I thank the Military Archives staff at Cathal Brugha Barracks not only for facilitating my access to material about my mother, Margaret Browne, but also for their undisguised pleasure at the prospect of her plucky and picturesque career, from 1916 to the Truce in 1922, entering the public domain.

CONTENTS

INTRODUCTION

An American historian, Wright Morris, is credited with the dictum: 'Anything processed by memory is fiction.' Judged by that criterion, this narrative of mine is doubly fictitious, having been processed not only by my own memories but also by those of my parents' generation, on which I have drawn heavily in the important early episodes of this book. Paradoxically, I could claim that fictions can often be a better key to the understanding of actuality than strictly factual accounts. Be that as it may, I have made scrupulous efforts to prune these anecdotes of any conscious fictionalising and am in a position to declare that, as they stand, they are an honest attempt to set down my personal 'take' on the world that was Ireland in the last century.

I find, now that I have formulated my impressions and got them down on paper, I have become oddly detached from them, almost as if I had written a novel. It has been a cathartic experience. Old sorrows have surfaced and then ebbed; old joys have been articulated and have somehow lost their radiance; old animosities seem childish, or unworthy; only old affections remain constant.

This is not a textbook history of twentieth-century Ireland; it is a series of recollections and reminiscences, of personal experiences and of narratives recalled. It partakes of the nature of a stream of consciousness, and where I have reached conclusions the reader is not obliged to agree with them. I offer it as an aid to the understanding of our recent past, always the most difficult period of history to come to terms with. I hope it may also entertain.

Máire Cruise O'Brien
Dublin, 2003

CHAPTER I

'Those Mimes, the Elder Persons'

Part i: My Mother's People

Part ii: My Father's People

Part iii: Episode at Easter – 1916

PART I: MY MOTHER'S PEOPLE

My maternal grandmother, Kate Browne, died at the age of sixty-five, on 3 June 1923; I remember her from the waist down. We went together to feed the hens in the yard at the back of her house in the village of Grangemockler, County Tipperary, at the foot of Slievenamon in the Decies. They were very terrible hens, and I can remember looking at them, transfixed with fear, over a 'width' of her skirt. God rest her! Her story has been part of my consciousness from the beginning.

Kate Browne was born FitzGerald; the name is common throughout the old Desmond palatinate. Her brother, 'the Boss' FitzGerald of Balladuggan, was a strong farmer in the neighbourhood. The family had not always been so prosperous; in the 'Hungry Forties' (the Famine times) they had been evicted. My mother told me that, of a very 'long-tailed' (numerous) family, those born before the eviction were illiterate, Irish-speaking and did well in life; those born after they had resettled, this time in Balladuggan, were educated, English-speaking and never made any money. Presumably the Father FitzGerald who was chaplain to Charles Gavan Duffy in Australia belonged to the second clutch, as did my grandmother, or perhaps he was a clerical uncle from an earlier world.

Together with the sister nearest her in age, Kate FitzGerald was sent to board at the Loreto Convent in Kilkenny, where, as well as getting the sound secondary education of the period, she learnt many 'ladylike' accomplishments. I still cherish a fire-screen worked by her with a bird-of-paradise in crewel, and two gilt-framed watercolours – one by her sister, of Kilkenny Castle, and one a copy, by Kate herself, of Constable's Old Mill.

My mother remembered being sent on her bicycle, many years later, by her mother to visit a neighbouring parish priest and borrow (or return) the latest novel by Balzac, in the original French. With the innocent intellectual snobbery of the adolescent, she marvelled that French had been taught so well at the convent in Kilkenny. It was only after my grandmother's death that her family learnt that she and her sister had both been novices in the Loreto Convent in Gibraltar, and that she not only read French with ease but also Spanish. The convent's records, about which I enquired, do not show that the girls were intended to be choir sisters; perhaps they were lay pupil-teachers, or, even more lowly, lay sisters. (Lay sisters were servants, not professed nuns.) The family tradition says 'novices' and the passion for Balzac is well attested. My poor young great-aunt fell ill and died, and my grandmother's vocation did not survive her death. Kate FitzGerald returned to Balladuggan in the late 1870s to care for her ageing mother and to become, when her mother also died, the unpaid domestic of her brothers, the remaining family. That is my mother's version of the story; my Uncle Moss, in his thinly disguised record of the family, *The Big Sycamore*, gives a somewhat different one, but the essentials are the same.

Ↄ   Ↄ   Ↄ

Obviously, since, when I knew her, she was a matriarch in her own right and no longer lived in Balladuggan, Kate's then situation was not fated to continue. My grandfather, Maurice Browne, was the schoolmaster in Grangemockler, the neighbouring townland. I never knew him. The photograph I have of him,with a greying full beard, was the only one he ever had taken in his entire life. He was born in County Waterford, in Cappoquin, in 1844, the eighth and youngest child of a cooper in a prosperous way of business; the family employed as many as eighty seasonal labourers, men, women and children, when times were good. His parents, feeling that with their last little one they could relax a little from the grim grind of daily necessity, destined him for the priesthood and planned ahead for his education. His first language was Irish, and although my grandmother, mindful of her gentility (a legacy of the convent), always maintained that she had not spoken Irish 'from the cradle', but 'picked some up from the neighbours', the pair sometimes spoke it to each other in a, surely vain, attempt to keep something from five avidly curious children. Irish was not at that time a middle-class language; later the 'Revival' would render it fashionable.

When Maurice was a little lad, education for Irish Catholics was in transition from the hedge school to the State system, and the two frequently overlapped. The hedge school was initially a clandestine Catholic institution under the Penal Laws; such schools could be excellent. Cappoquin children were peculiarly lucky: their local school, initially hedge but later legalised, was run by two exceptionally gifted scholars, John Walshe and John Casey, both the products of hedge schools them- selves and both native speakers of Irish – one, John Walshe, a poet (his 'After Aughrim's Great Disaster' is sung to the air of 'Séan Ó Duibhir a' Ghleanna' to this day), and the other, John Casey, a mathematician of world stature. Of the two, Walshe's career was the more conventional: he died poor. Casey, on the other hand, became a scholar of Trinity College, Dublin, and never looked back. He had a further connection with the Browne family: in 1881 the Norwegian government presented Dr Casey, as a token of esteem, with the works of Norway's great mathematician, Niels Henrik Abel; in 1913 Patrick Browne, Maurice's son, was awarded his doctorate by the University of Paris *en Sorbonne*, for a thesis on a problem propounded by the same Dr Abel.

Meanwhile, disaster struck the ten-year-old Maurice. In the family coopering business, with its ancillary trade in wickerwork, nobody, how- ever young, was long idle. Maurice was sent one day, in sole charge of a donkey and cart, to collect a load of willow (sallies) that had come by boat up the Blackwater River. As one might have expected of someone his age, he was fool-acting, jumping from the cart to the back of the donkey and back again. He slipped, and the wheel went over his right shoulder and crushed his upper arm. Originally treated by a bone-setter, the arm be- came gangrenous and was subsequently amputated. Only a 'whole' man could be ordained a priest; the family's dreams of social advancement were in ruins. I think I can illustrate how deeply traumatic this was from my own memories.

An elderly relative of my grandmother's, Mrs Paddy Arrigan, whom the family called Ma Joe, was much loved by us all when my brother, sister and I were children. She was once telling me of a narrow escape my mother had had as a young girl: 'She was in the trap with your grandfather when the pony bolted and, of course, your grandfather had only one arm …' She saw my complete surprise and incomprehension – I had never been told – and begged me never to tell 'them' she had told me; I never did. Many years later when my poor mother was suffering a 'frozen' shoul- der, I was brushing her hair and she exclaimed, 'Now I realise what my poor father went through!' and I was told the whole story.

The Browne family got over their shock and it was decided to let the plucky Maurice continue his education with a view to making a teacher of him under the new national school system. He learned to write copper-plate with his left hand, became six feet tall and immensely strong, swam better than many boys who had both arms, cleared the grades of monitor and assistant teacher, benefiting no doubt from the instruction of both Walshe and Casey, and ended up, in 1869, as Master of the primary school in Grangemockler, where he courted and married my grandmother, the former Loreto novice.

CЗ   CЗ   CЗ

From old photographs that I saw of her, I had always thought my grandmother was plain, with strong features and her hair screwed back like Mrs Noah. Contemporaries of her children, however, notably the mathematician, Professor Michael Power, of University College, Galway, assure me that she was radiantly attractive, with a wonderful figure and complexion, ready laughter, an erect carriage and great lightness and swiftness of movement. Her children adored her, and I knew from them that she was endlessly loving, humorous and intelligent, while being in no way 'soft in the head'. I have a niece, Lucy, who is extremely pretty and genetically almost Kate's double, feature for feature, so I can imagine the Kate that Professor Power knew and her children remembered. The old sepia-tinted photographs, which required rigid immobility from the subject, did not suit my grandmother. My grandfather was a fine figure of a man, in spite of the lost arm, and, of course, both he and my grandmother were highly literate. A match, you might think, ordained by a wise providence, but the courtship did not run smoothly.

A local schoolmaster had status and respectability, but a strong farmer would know the schoolmaster's salary to the last farthing, might resent his book-learning and would not necessarily regard him as a good matrimo-nial prospect. Besides, in Tipperary a Waterfordman was something of an outsider, and my grandfather was known for his reserved nature. He liter-ally carried his head high, and neighbours remarked that 'if there was any money going astray on the ground, Mr Browne would not find it.' There was a further consideration: Kate's brothers – I'm not sure how many there were – felt that a young woman who had rejected a secure future, arranged for her at much expense, should be content to remain in decent quiet at home as an 'unmarried female relative, unemployed, resident on farm', as official census and other documents had it, and not go chasing after romance. They little knew my grandmother. A girl cousin of hers was a pupil on the female side in Maurice's school, and she acted as go-between. Her name was Joanna, and she became the Ma Joe whom I cite as a source above. It was three years before they could marry – money was tight and goodwill lacking – but by then Kate's youngest brother, James, had come round to the idea and subsequently became my mother's godfather. In 1883 the couple were wed – I assume in Grange-mockler; James and Joanna were their witnesses.

଼ଷ ଼ଷ ଼ଷ

It is possible that Kate brought with her a marriage portion because they were soon established in relative comfort in the house on the street in Grangemockler, which was to be their home for the rest of their days. It is still there; it stands beside the chapel, and next to the chapel is the school – is it not now a parish hall? Two small squares of walled garden screened it from the roadway; one was a traditional herbaceous garden, a riot of colour hedged with yew, in the other stood the family's pride and joy, a tall sycamore tree. It gave my Uncle Moss Browne the title for his lightly fictionalised account of the Brownes referred to earlier, *The Big Sycamore*, published by Gill and MacMillan in the 1950s. In the front room, behind the sycamore tree and permanently darkened in its shade, Kate opened a shop; the room opening back off it was a storeroom. It is difficult to imagine a product of the time that she did not stock, or, if not, was not prepared to order, from the everyday groceries, both farm-fresh and store-bought, to agricultural machinery, or a pair of lady's stays on the shop's account in Arnotts' Department Store in Dublin. Between their father's politics – although exceptionally pious, he was, even after Parnell's marriage to the divorced Mrs O'Shea, a fanatically loyal Parnellite, and had made a detailed study of the Land Acts in order to be able to advise his neighbours accordingly – and their mother's business enterprise – which also covered the advantageous acquisition of land and stock – the children to come were born into a microcosm of Irish rural life without leaving the confines of their home, and Brownes' became a tremendous centre for debate and gossip, much of it in Irish. Many of the older generation around were monoglot Irish-speakers, and everybody's English was literally laced with Irish syntax and vocabulary: 'The old *slugizje* (swallower) is looking *angish* (wretched)'; 'Lave your tay wesht' (meaning, Drink up your tea); 'Paatie, the craythur, is dark' (meaning bashful, incalculable, even sinister); 'I was working at him with a week', and innumerable others. It may be of interest that my grandmother was never a Parnellite; she believed firmly in women's rights, but she accounted the right to a secure marriage as among the most important of them, and saw Mrs O'Shea as a threat. In this she was typical of many of the strong-minded women of her time. My grandfather's views coincided with the initial position of the Irish Catholic hierarchy: a Protestant politician's private morals were irrelevant to his public policies.

Behind the flower garden was the parlour with cream walls and glass-fronted 'Gothic' shelved cabinets in each corner, picked out in gilt. The cabinets held china and books: Kickham, Shakespeare and Browning, Tom Moore, of course, and many devotional works, such as *The Devout Life of Saint Francis de Sales*. For many years my mother, who grew up with a splendid eye for furniture and décor, thought it the most beautiful room that ever was. My grandfather, and those of the children who were going through a studious phase, worked in the parlour. Back of the parlour, through a connecting door and down a short flight of steps, was the kitchen, the true heart of the house. I did not know I remembered that kitchen, but when, as a schoolgirl, I first revisited it after my grandmother's death, I knew at once where everything should be: the hearth, the stairs up to the bedrooms, the draught screen to the right of the fire, the paraffin lamp on the wall beside the back door to the yard and the haggard; I knew I had been there before, and I knew what had once been written on the wall under the lamp:

Haadie Browne
Muddie Browne
David Browne

Paatie Browne
Moss Browne
Baby Browne
John Browne
Majesty Brunoch   Honesty Tobin
Cows @ pounds
[This last was a gratuitous display of learning.]

There were five surviving children, as the eldest, David, had recorded on that wall in descending order of age (and importance); 'Haadie' was their version of Father, and 'Muddie' was clearly Mother; Majesty and Honesty were the two serving girls, Maggie and Honor. The first-born, little Margaret Bridget, is not listed; she died in infancy, but her siblings, even as adults, always spoke of her with love, often smiling indulgently as if they had actually known her. Baby was my mother, Margaret Mary.

⌇ ⌇ ⌇

No children were ever better cared for, or more loved. Their bedrooms opened off their parents' room; they had been added on as required. If somebody wept in the night they could be sure of being taken into the secure warmth of Haadie and Muddie's bed. Every Saturday all five were bathed in the big hip bath on the floor in front of the kitchen fire. Haadie stood by with a towel draped over his single arm and skilfully scooped up each in turn upstairs to bed. All grew up loving and physically warm and demonstrative, yet none of them ever heard a term of endearment exchanged between their parents. Nor were they at all conscious, as children, of their father's lost arm; Kate unobtrusively supplied it. She cut his meat at table, brushed his clothes and helped him on with his coat, anticipating his wishes intelligently and causing the entire household to do the same. As each child reached the age of two-and-a-half, they were dispatched off to school with him, where the big boys spoiled them and they regarded lessons as extended play, and all went smoothly until it came to Baby's turn. Baby would not go into the girls' school. She lay on the floor and kicked and roared and showed no remorse, but boasted later to her mother, 'First I kicked Miss Callinan and then I bit Miss Kennedy.'

She won a complete victory and for at least a year went happily to the boys' school. She was her father's pet; he called her 'poor womany' and always took her part. She finally compromised by agreeing to go to the girls' school if her brothers, Paatie (Paddy) and Moss (Maurice), would come and sit with her. This was simply terrible for them, but fortunately did not last long. My mother switched to 'little girl' mode and decided she didn't want 'any old boys anymore'. She remained something of a terror and collected her share of slaps. The first time, she ran up the road to Kate to complain. Kate was not sympathetic: 'That,' she said, 'was the slap that wasn't going astray.' Margaret Mary had met her match.

All the children absorbed knowledge like sponges, but Paatie (my beloved Uncle Paddy and a second father to me) was phenomenal. My grandfather's monitor (schoolboy assistant), Michael Bowers, whom I knew later as an old man and the last surviving native Irish-speaker in Grangemockler, put it this way: 'David is a good lad, what you tell him he remembers, but Paatie knows it before you tell him.' Paatie early calculated the rewards of scholarship – all the children could milk the cows and take a hand about the farm, but Paatie, when there was any onerous task in prospect, always had to do his Latin and, because he was his father's favourite of the boys, he got his way. On his deathbed he turned to my mother, who held his hand, and said, with a most wonderful smile, 'My father says I don't have to go for the cows.' Maurice, their father, taught them Latin at home and 'ground' them in maths; their mother taught them French and, later Irish, when it became fashionable after the founding of the Gaelic League (see James Joyce's *Dubliners*), using Father O'Growney's primers.

On the whole the young Brownes were respectful of authority and their learning was conventional, but in Religious Knowledge their ideas took an original turn. As each struggled, in preparation for First Confession, with the Examination of Conscience, their mother explained to them that 'adultery' was the sin of watering the milk, but they needed no help with the meaning of 'the opposite sex', so hedged around with prohibitions; they knew it meant Protestants! Because of this the three eldest refused sweets when offered them by the minister's wife, but my mother and John were allowed to accept because they had not yet reached the use of reason, '... generally,' as the Catechism said, 'believed to be about the age of seven years.' This age difference did not always work out well for them, however; in the 1890s came a year when a great comet was foretold to be about to destroy the world, and the two small ones were informed by their seniors that, as they had not made their First Confession, the best they could hope for in eternity was Limbo. Their only remedy would be to recite 'an Act of Perfect Contrition'. Now an Act of Perfect Contrition, they knew, was very difficult to make; perfection is never easy. A fictitious Pope once nearly succeeded, but at a crucial moment he was distracted by his shoe-buckle and failed. Margaret and John sat at the top of the stairs that led down into the kitchen and concentrated desperately on the words they knew by rote. Needless to say, they were constantly interrupted by their tormentors until, fortunately, the comet changed its mind. Similarly, the little ones longed to be able to climb the big sycamore tree in front of the house, from the tip of which, the big boys assured them, you could see America and talk to the neighbours who had emigrated.

All these stories and many more I heard from my mother, who never lost her rural gift for 'shortening' an evening (or a car-drive, or a childhood fever). When we were small we had no wireless – although my father and his brothers constantly tinkered with crystal sets in cigar boxes – and Mammy was an unrivalled source of entertainment. She sang too, all the songs of her childhood, and played the piano (courtesy of Miss Kennedy in the 'girls' school' and of the Dominican Convent in Eccles Street, Dublin) while we polkaed and reel-stepped around the room. Like her mother, Kate, she could teach French and Irish, and lessons with her were a glorious succession of mnemonics and jokes; she set the French irregular verbs to music for chanting and skipping along the roads to when we were in the country. Life in Grangemockler, as she recreated it, was part of the treat. As a little girl she had retained her baby lisp for a long time and told people about another little girl who had been 'soked with a sellystone' (choked with a cherry-stone), or assured them that she would not be 'sy over-right Samesy' (shy in the presence of Jamesy, her godfather, the gentle FitzGerald uncle). She was constantly corrected and taken up by her brothers with, 'Baby, speak 'stinctly', in imitation of the Religious Examiner who had visited the school, and who was a very pompous priest indeed, and began each session by intoning to the First Communion class, 'speak slowly and distinctly and very loud'.

CR   CR   CR

My grandfather loved small children. In his one-room school he encouraged the bigger boys to look after the little ones. Exceptionally, I would imagine, among headmasters of his day, he took members of the infant class, little boys still in petticoats, on his knee to listen to his watch, or to look for sweets in his pockets. We sense that adolescents were a different matter; he was a stern parent to his sons as they grew up, especially to David.

Maurice liked to encourage intelligent conversation at the dinner table and had the habit of dispensing small nuggets of useful information, as it might be: 'It is not generally known that the corncrake is a ventriloquist,' or, 'What a pleasant, useful, inoffensive creature is the sheep.' The young Brownes remembered these stock phrases, but not, perhaps, to the exact effect that their father intended – they thought them hilarious – and Kate, regrettably, sometimes also sabotaged the intelligent conversation by her laughter.

By the time he was twelve, my Uncle David was almost as tall as his father and terrifyingly strong. It was time for him to go to boarding school. Rockwell College, near Cashel, run by the Holy Ghost Fathers, was the obvious choice, as it was within easy range by pony and trap. Tom MacDonagh (who would be executed in 1916) and Eamon de Valera were teaching there at the time, but I doubt if this was a factor in the family's decision. David was accepted and invited to sit the scholarship examination on the first day of term. They set off early in the morning, Kate driving, David in his new suit and Eton collar with his bags packed. Kate took the eleven-year-old Paatie with her for company on the way home; he wore his country boy's gansey and hobnailed boots. Kate decided to wait till the exam was over, to have an idea how David had fared. She had friends among the staff and they persuaded her to let Paatie sit the exam as well as his brother: 'Better for him than being idle.' How Kate passed the time I do not know, but in due course she was asked to come and meet the Dean of Studies. 'Madam,' he said, 'your boy David will certainly qualify for a scholarship.' This was undoubtedly good news, for money was indeed a consideration. Then the Dean continued, 'But the little fellow is a genius, you must leave him with us right away.' Paatie had come first on every paper. Kate was overwhelmed, 'But he has no suit,' she said. 'The tailor here will fix him up.' 'And his boots?' 'We have a shoe-maker also.' Kate asked Paatie would he like to stay. His eyes shone; he would love to. She drove home alone and very uneasy as to what would be her reception, for she knew how much this particular pupil meant to his father and how he would be missed. She did not dare tell her husband what she had done, and when Maurice, in puzzlement, kept asking where Paatie was, she told him brusquely to stop annoying her; she had to see to the cows. Eventually, of course, the truth came out, and a sad Maurice accepted the *fait accompli*.

03   03   03

School years after that were a series of triumphs: David's at rugby; Paatie's at his books. Consequently the summer holidays were a series of treats. Maurice took his two eldest boys by special excursion train to Cork, to visit the Cork Exhibition of 1901. A straight-laced and innocent man, he was distressed that they should be exposed on the journey to the lurid language and drunken amorousness of the British Army privates and their girlfriends, bound on the same spree as themselves; he had chosen the Exhibition as an improving outing. He was further disconcerted when the first sight that met their eyes in the entrance hall was a replica of the *Venus de Milo*. He hurried his boys past it, but worse was to come. Right in front of them was a full-length portrait in oils of Queen Victoria. Maurice's pious and nationalist soul was disgusted; first a naked woman and then a foreign queen! Otherwise, the Exhibition was a success.

Some time later, Kate glanced one morning, at breakfast, at the *Waterford Star* and came upon a letter signed, 'Anxious Parent'. It deplored conditions where decent people and their families could not travel by rail without being subjected to 'the foul language and lewd conduct of the drunken soldiery of a foreign power'. She laughed and said to Maurice, 'That's the kind of letter an old show like you would write.' He was very angry and asked her how she dared? But she was not altogether surprised, when she was brushing and shaking out his good suit, to find a draft of the letter in one of the pockets.

In 1903 Race Week coincided with the family's annual holiday stay in Tramore, on their last such occasion. Paatie – now more decorously known as Paddy – had swept the decks in the Intermediate exams and had made headlines in all the local newspapers; David had done respectably well. Maurice was buoyed up with pride and joy and was persuaded by the young to take them to the races. There, the last race was a maiden and one of the runners was a horse called *Paddy Browne*. In a burst of happy exuberance Maurice, though very much not a betting man, laid a shilling each way on the lucky name, and the horse won. Maurice, however, had not the heart to collect his winnings for fear the bookmaker's wife and dependent children might suffer for his own good fortune. It was the last time he had all his brood of five safely under his wing, and he left them a brilliant example to remember, of principle, of celebration, of compromise and of the respective limitations of each, which was to last them the rest of their lives.

C3   C3   C3

The 'dark streak' that the neighbours discerned in all the Brownes, except Kate, had already surfaced and marked the end of their golden, common childhood. The 'Master', you will remember, was remote; the children could be arrogant. David was now an immensely strong young giant who had that year been caught smoking and been beaten by his father. Worse, in the face of his father's express and very reasonable prohibition, he had played rugby for Rockwell Past – grown men – against Garryowen and had broken his collarbone, so that he had had to do all that year's vitally important exams writing with his left hand. Of course, it had been unconscionable of the Holy Ghost Fathers to allow a child, to whom they stood *in loco parentis*, to take such risks, but it was David's disobedience, and the grim memory of his own loss of his right arm in childhood, that caused Maurice to have difficulty in becoming fully reconciled to his eldest son. On their return from Tramore, the boy announced baldly that he was leaving Rockwell to enter the novitiate of the Dominican Order. He was sixteen years of age. White woollen socks were required by the Tallaght Priory dress code. His mother knitted them under a white cloth bag, lest any gossip should spot them; white socks, in local experience, were worn only by inmates of the workhouse. According to my Uncle Moss's account in *The Big Sycamore*, which was admittedly fictionalised, neither she nor their father ever saw their son again, and he disappeared almost entirely from my mother's reminiscences. I myself was a teenager before I met him. David always maintained that, of all Kate's children, he was the only one to whom his mother had spoken Irish in babyhood. His own baby talk is recorded in English: 'Muddie deddle (girl), Muddie deddle, tum (come) to bed.' He cannot have liked sharing her with his siblings. When I think of him now I am reminded of WH Auden's poem:

> *'A penny life will give you all the facts*
> *How father beat him, how he ran away ...'*

Those lines seem to summarise David's break with his family. Here, then, are the remaining facts, taken from the card in memory of his death; Michael was his name in religion:

Card. Michele BROWNE
Grangemokler (Ireland) ✠ March 31 1971
    May 6, 1887   Rome

Sept. 14, 1904	Dominican Religious
May 21, 1910	Priest
1932–1941	Rector of "Angelicum" University (Rome)
1951–1955	Master of the Sacred Apost. Palace (Rome)
1955–1962	Master General of the Dominicans
March 19, 1962	Cardinal
April 19, 1962	Bishop

Meanwhile, Moss and Baby (Margaret) in their turn went to boarding school: Moss to Rockwell and my mother to the Dominican Convent in Eccles Street, in Dublin. Physically, of the children, Moss was the most like his father, but he had also inherited his mother's happy disposition. He had charm to burn and what can only be described as a talent for frivolity, which masked a deep inner seriousness. He was said to be a better Latinist than either of his older brothers, was very musical and never lost his countryboy's love of sport, particularly coursing and fowling, nor his green fingers for gardening, inherited from his mother. My mother was the only member of the family to take up Irish academically. As with all the family, it was taken for granted that she would win exhibitions and scholarships, and she duly did, including the Lord Mayor's prize for 'proficiency in the Irish language'. The youngest, John, remained at home with his parents to farm. He was asthmatic, and it was felt that the rough and tumble of Rockwell would not suit his health. He cycled, every day the weather allowed, to Carrick-on-Suir, to the Christian Brothers' school, and Kate kept a close eye on her 'Benjamin'. He grew up a strikingly handsome, life-loving young man who, in rapid succession, joined the GAA, Sinn Féin and the Volunteers, and was very much the man of the house.

It had by then become clear that both Paddy and Moss would follow David's example and embrace the priesthood. All three sons were un-doubtedly influenced by accounts of their father's childhood – his lost arm and frustrated vocation – but it was, of course, no longer true that the Church was the only path to a career for talented country boys, as witness, for example, the rise of Mr de Valera from a labourer's cottage. For Paddy and Moss, however, unlike David, there was no great break with home: they attended Clonliffe and Maynooth respectively, seminaries for the secular clergy, and University College, Dublin, and they kept in close touch always with Grangemockler. They were models of chivalry and fun towards their teenage sister and their girl cousins, and later became the adored uncles of Margaret's children, so that they will figure largely henceforward in the story of my personal memories, as John and his father were not destined to do.

 CR CR CR

As Maurice advanced towards retiring age as a teacher, clouds of 'dark' paranoia tended to descend on him increasingly. The young only became aware of this when he commanded the brilliant young student of mathematics, Paddy, home on holiday from Clonliffe and UCD, to audit the books of his mother's shop. Maurice was convinced that she was withholding money from him. Kate was in tears, Paddy passionately angry, but the accounts were inspected. As would have surprised nobody who knew her, Kate had not been salting away her takings for some nefarious purpose of her own; her accounts were, in fact, considerably in the red. Firstly, she was temperamentally incapable of refusing credit, and was far more likely to extend an interest-free loan than to foreclose on a bad debt; a great saying of hers was, 'Decent people are never exact.' Secondly, she was extravagant where quality was concerned: Margaret's stock-collars on her school uniform, for example, had to be the most expensive available, as had all Margaret's shoes and her corsets. Needless to say, Kate sold only the best tea. She considered her losses offset by incalculable benefits in goodwill, and the children had always been taught to be charitable. They were authorised to give coppers from the till to any 'poor person' who might drop in from among the beggars that went the roads. On one occasion my Uncle Paddy had emptied the entire till in his enthusiasm, and 'poor' was a term of endearment in their vocabulary, as it is to this day in mine.

The young Brownes loved their father, and with reason, but they realised he was ill. He had now shifted his ground from resentment at being, as he felt, cheated of monies due to him to a morbid fear of destitution. The family contrived to restore calm, by what means I never learnt exactly. My mother often told me of how, when she was very small, she first realised that not everyone was as comfortably off as they were. It was a Sunday, and a poor woman who had been taken ill in the chapel was brought into their kitchen. It was obviously more serious than the usual fainting spell brought on by the inanition of the fast before Holy Communion. The poor thing's little daughter was brought in with her, but was rapidly forgotten in the general concern for the mother. She stood forlornly on the outskirts of the action, with no one except my mother, another just such near-baby, to notice her. The Brownes had recently killed a pig, and bacon and black puddings hung from the kitchen rafters. The little girl was repeating to herself, without much hope, over and over again in a tiny voice, 'I loves puddings.' Nobody but my mother heard her, and my mother was so appalled at her plight that she could not do anything about it. That kind of hunger belonged in a grown-up world beyond her power to influence.

Maurice had always been very devout, but nothing to excess. Now, with no school timetable to structure his days, he took to spending long hours in the chapel, becoming more and more reclusive and solitary. Neighbours whispered that he was growing 'strange'. This particular evening, in December 1910, a great storm of wind arose, but Maurice went as usual to the chapel. He returned later, much agitated and holding his hand to his forehead, saying that the chapel gate had struck him in the head and that he was bleeding to death. When Kate persuaded him to take his hand away, there was no trace of blood, or a blow; some days after, Maurice suffered a serious stroke.

Moss and Margaret were due home for Christmas, and when John met them at the station in Carrick-on-Suir, he was in tears. 'Haadie,' he said, 'is not so well.' Next day, Paddy arrived from the Irish College in Paris, where he lived while a student at the Sorbonne. Maurice's mind was wandering, but he was not distressed. He knew them all and was happy they had come, but my mother was sad because he seemed fonder of Moss, Kate's pet, than of her, who had always been 'his little queen'. He sang his old songs – 'Siúl, a Ghrá' and 'By the Shannon's dancing waters' – I know all the words yet. At one point he saw that Our Lady had come to visit him to take him home. 'Set a chair for her, Moss,' he said, 'she has come a long way for me.' He died on 3 January 1911.

The grief of the household was terrible, in particular that of the old serving-man, Mick Stack, believed to be a by-blow of the Kickham family and nicknamed, to his fury, Mick Kick. Kate, in her own grief, was called on to console him. He would not, he told her, live long after the master. 'Where would you like to be buried so, Mick?' she asked, trying to raise a laugh. 'In Ooning [his home graveyard], if I live for it,' he replied. Long before, when asked by the landlord what year it was that he was born, he had answered, 'The year of Corrigshock [a notorious eviction], and a bad day for your breed.' The passing of my grandfather marked the end of an old world, the world of the Fenian Kickham's great rural novel *Knocknagow*, and new, eventful times were coming.

ଔ   ଔ   ଔ

How all the children, including David, became involved with Sinn Féin, I will leave for another chapter. One more sorrow lay in wait for my grandmother before she died on 3 June 1923, by which time the house in Grangemockler had, for many years, been a republican 'safe house' in loving memory of her youngest, John. John was heart and soul a Sinn Féiner, in the popular meaning of the word at the time, as it might be, an 'all-purpose' nationalist, not ruling out physical force. Twenty-two years old in 1916, he was incandescent with enthusiasm. In the 1918 election he worked around the clock to elect the nationalist Pierce McCann for his local constituency, Tipperary South Riding. Earlier, in the winter of 1917, when the men of the Rising were all still in jail, John had ridden the snowbound roads at night on horseback to be first with the news of Count George Plunkett's election in the North Roscommon by-election. By July 1919 John was dead, of a ruptured spleen received on the football pitch, so also was poor Pierce McCann, struck down by the Great 'Flu in Gloucester Jail, where my father was his fellow prisoner.

John was brought to Dublin for surgery – it might have been better could the surgeon have come earlier to him in Tipperary – but it was too late, and he died, cheerfully, playing cards with his brother, Paddy. David, who was also in the hospital, had left the ward in protest because the Prayers for the Dying were not being said. Paddy said, 'That boy does not need our prayers, he has gone straight to heaven.' John's fellow Volunteers met the coffin at Kilkenny and carried it, draped in the tricolour, through the city. From there a cycle corps of Volunteers escorted the hearse, which was met along the way to Grangemockler by relays of further contingents. Paddy sang the funeral Mass. My mother came back from the Glens of Antrim, where she had gone that summer to study East Ulster and North Leinster Irish. I found John's *In Memoriam* card in her Irish-language missal after her death.

Nor did John's comrades leave Kate alone in her grief. They saved the hay for her and kept her company in the evenings throughout the grim times to come. She thanked God that John had not lived to see the 'Tan War'. During the Civil War, in 1923, the house was raided by Free State troops while Kate lay dying, but they left when Moss, still her favourite, brought them to the door of her room. In fact, there were two 'Irregulars' hidden behind the head of the poor woman's bed. It is a story without a moral, but I doubt if it weighed on Moss's conscience.

And here I must say goodbye to Kate, whom I remember only 'from the waist down'; it is my earliest memory – I was a year old that April before she died. Her personality, whose memory was so cherished by her children, has influenced my entire life. I know she was pleased to know me and I am forever grateful for it. When my Uncle Moss published his book about the lives I have summarised here, I wrote a poem to preface it. I would like to reproduce it in their memory, if I may; it was written in English to match the language of the book.

> *This is the village; there you have the school,*
> *The little chapel, and the single street;*
> *Here at my feet the graves; and you can see*
> *Across the upland fields the fairy mountain.*
> *The black sky heavy with the summer's rain*
> *Bends threateningly above us as we kneel;*
> *My ears are ringing with unnumbered voices;*
> *I cannot raise my eyes, lest they should meet*
> *Their eyes that hem us in on every side;*
> *I shrink from their invisible vain hands –*
> *Schoolmaster of this Parish, there his wife,*
> *The youngest son, the little long-dead daughter;*
> *And all around the taut air leaps and sings*
> *Charged with unbidden presence that retrieves*
> *The instancy of childhood. Now the beat*
> *Is loud through chapel, school, and dwelling house,*
> *Wakens the slumberous vacant afternoon*
> *With thronging passage, and the street with feet*
> *To clamour round us kneeling at the cross.*

PART II: MY FATHER'S PEOPLE

I have just come from rereading my father's account of his experiences in 1916 in his lovely little book, *Episode at Easter*, and I am overcome once again by his remarkable personal charm. Not that we weren't well inoculated against it in childhood. Of course, we loved him – all good children love their daddies – and we were fiercely proud of him and took it for granted that when he was at home the whole household revolved around him, that his interests, personal, professional and political, took precedence over all other considerations, but we rarely saw him and hardly knew him. Let me fast-forward for a moment and give an example of how his public career influenced the entire microcosm of our young lives.

I was twelve years old; the 'Economic War' with Great Britain was at its height and all nationalist families were involved in an intensive 'Buy Irish' campaign to support Irish industry. My father was Minister for Finance in Mr de Valera's government, an office he held till the outbreak of the Second World War. One of the many patriotic women's organisations hosted a children's party in the Mansion House, in the Round Room. There were prizes for the best Irish-made party dresses. The winners were picked by a system of 'musical chairs': we all had numbers and marched around to the music and, when the music stopped, the numbers called out sat down. My little sister, Barbara, and I had dresses made of very fine Irish poplin, specially woven with a view to entering the contemporary ladies' fashion market. Hers was duck-egg blue with a short, flared skirt and matching pants and wired, cream-coloured, short lace 'wing' sleeves, the whole decorated with tiny pink rosebuds. She was an exceptionally pretty child, with honey-coloured 'sausage' curls, put in with rags and sugar-and-water; she looked good enough to eat. My own dress was floor-length, long-sleeved with a square neckline – it doubled as a Confirmation dress. It was cut from ankle-length, cream poplin on romantic, high-waisted, medieval lines. I loved it. It was our job to popularise the material for wear on gala occasions and hopefully so save the industry; we failed.

By this time the circling children had diminished in number to about twenty, of all ages, including me and Barbara. We saw my mother go up on the stage and talk briefly with the judges and, when next the music stopped, my number and Barbara's were called out. We later learnt that my mother had withdrawn us from the competition on the plea that our dancing pumps, covered with material to match our dresses, were of English origin. I cannot remember that we minded. Barbara knew she was by far the prettiest creature there and was getting tired of marching around and around anyway. She was only six years old and didn't much understand about prizes. It was explained to me that, if we won, people would think that Daddy had used 'influence' – a terrible crime. Further, if our special, custom-made-for-us-individually-in-the-factory dresses – we were celebrities in those days – won, it might discourage less fortunate children, in home-made, off-the-peg, or dressmaker-made outfits, and defeat the purpose of the exercise, besides 'hurting their feelings'. 'Hurting someone's feelings' was the worst possible offence in our catalogue and simply could not be contemplated, especially in a politician's daughter. I think I felt mostly a grown-up satisfaction, like a character in James Stephen's *Irish Fairy Tales*: 'I would do more than that for Fionn.' If it is not clear from this anecdote that I was conscious of being 'a politician's daughter' – although I don't remember it ever being put in exactly those words – I despair of ever being able to make it so.

Those dresses of mine and Barbara's were museum pieces, virtually the last products of a craft established in Dublin and environs since the expulsion of the Huguenot weavers from France under Louis XIV, and associated 'in the trade' ever since with Ireland. Poplin was woven on a warp of wool with a weft of silk, and was expensive and used mainly for upholstery. 'Irish Poplin' ranked with 'Belfast Linen' in the fashion world and, of course the Mansion House, where the 'Buy Irish' party was held, was a focal point in the fashionable Grafton Street shopping district. In those days every upmarket dress shop had its own workroom, where 'models' (brand-name goods) were copied to customers' requirements; my mother liked to wait till the sales and buy the 'model'. 'Buyers' from Switzers' and Brown Thomas' department stores would have been among the parents, watching the parading children. They would have been there to spot talent and check sources. We were doing the factory – in Balbriggan, I think – a favour in modelling for them. My dress and Barbara's went, in due course, as 'cast-offs' to younger friends and relatives, just as their wardrobes came down to us. That generation had nothing to learn from ours about 'thrift-shop *chic*'.

CR   CR   CR

Even as children we could see that my father was ridiculously handsome, and we knew him to be enormously fastidious about his appearance. We also knew him to be very devout and saw him, when he was at home, saying his prayers every morning, kneeling on the seat of the big armchair in his bedroom. He was the only adult in our experience to pray outside the chapel. (We did not say the family rosary; I think my mother would have found it bourgeois.) From a very early age, we recognised both the piety and the fastidiousness as being Northern. He was born at 42 Mill Street, Belfast, in 1889, the eldest son of James MacEntee, who came from Monaghan, and Mary Owens, also from Monaghan. My grandfather was a publican and, in his heyday, owned three public houses in Belfast, of which the famous Crown bar was one; its mahogany booths and porcelain beer handles figured, with James Mason, in the cult movie *Odd Man Out*. The initials 'MacE' can still be seen, worked into The Crown's mosaic floors. When I remember him, his three pubs had been reduced to one, since destroyed by a bomb. This was MacEntee's in King Street, near the railway station, where, in the 1920s, the family lived 'over the shop'; it was an old, many-storied building, very comfortable. When I was born, in April 1922, there was champagne on the house all night. Legend had it that my grandfather had lost his other two premises playing cards.

After my father in the family came: May, Jimmy, Eddie, Charlie, Meg and Joe, but there was never any doubt but that my father was the favourite and that this favouritism embraced us, his nuclear family. Indeed my grandfather's partiality towards this particular son's exotic Southern bride verged on the shameless, and caused my good-hearted mother some embarrassment, which was only finally overcome with much generosity all round. While my grandfather was happily squandering his family's future, he bought my mother expensive presents, such as a silver fox fur in which she was photographed with him. Like his pretty wife and all his children, he was small in stature and extremely dapper. He wore waxed moustaches, striped trousers with a dark waistcoat and jacket, a gold watch-chain, wing collar and bow-tie, or even a stock, and, of course, a bowler hat. We were told that he had two brothers, each over six-feet tall, both of whom emigrated to Canada and ended up owning the Biltmore Hotel in New York. If so, they have disappeared entirely from history as far as any of my generation knows. During the grim years of 1920–21 my grandmother worried that 'Granda' might be 'called before his Maker with the smell of drink on his breath.' He had been a Fenian, and then a Parnellite – before and after the split – and was an alderman on the Belfast Corporation. By the time I knew him at all well he had relinquished the management of his business to his sons and son-in-law, and had his betting money doled out to him in half-crowns by my grandmother. Nevertheless, he had style. I guess you could say he was a reformed rake.

My grandmother was an exquisite, white-haired, Edwardian doll with a whim of steel under a nervous, retiring exterior. She disapproved of the freedom with which Barbara and I were brought up. In her youth she went to one dance a year and her mother put her out the scullery window to go to that one. She used to say, 'Not that I lacked boys either. I could have thatched houses with them, and scolloped them with the wee ones!'

My father was christened John Francis and became, as did so many of his peers, Seán. (John Betjeman's little son, Paul, once asked if 'Seán' were 'an Irish title of nobility'.) He went to school at Saint Malachy's College in Belfast – a Catholic secondary school, of course – and then on to the Belfast Municipal College of Technology, to qualify as an electrical engineer. My mother always understood his bitterness at being denied a university education; she herself was aware that, had her own father lived, her mother would have had to fight very hard indeed to ensure one for herself, the only surviving girl. Middle-class materialistic families at that time did not necessarily value higher education – even less so for girls. I think myself, however, that my father may well have followed his proper bent. He was thoroughly a man of the twentieth century, and very gifted in modern design. The impressive lighting of the Basilica in Lough Derg is his work, and all the handcrafted metal components in it were made by Irish craftsmen, to his specifications. His literary side was always more of a hobby than a vocation, and his poetry was jettisoned after 1927 under the weight of his political responsibilities. In 1914 he was employed as assistant chief engineer by the ESB in Dundalk, and his initial reaction to this new community was not flattering:

'Coming from the stronghold of Ulster unionism where nationalists had to fight unitedly for their rights against odds of three to one, the political situation, as I found it in Dundalk, was somewhat dis-edifying. There it did not suffice to be an Irish nationalist, one had to be a nationalist of one or other of two rival dispensations: You either followed John Redmond and abhorred Tim Healy; or you followed Tim Healy and abhorred John Redmond. If you happened to be a follower of Arthur Griffith [founder of Sinn Féin], you were "an extremist", a visionary, a dreamer.'

My father was, at that stage, a member of James Connolly's Socialist Party of Ireland, which was distinctly to the left of Sinn Féin. Subsequently, again in his own words, uttered as recently as 1946, he declared: 'During the better part of a lifetime, that problem (*ie*, national unity) has been my first and greatest preoccupation. I joined, first, the National Volunteers, and subsequently, the Irish Volunteers in order to prevent Partition.'

Partition was, of course, already being envisaged in 1914 by, among others, King George V, in the context of Prime Minister Herbert Asquith's Home Rule Bill. From that point on, Part II of *Episode at Easter* tells the story. It is based on the manuscript account of events that my father wrote in the immediate aftermath of the 1916 Rising, while he was being held in solitary confinement in Stafford Jail, awaiting trial by court martial for 'the murder of a policeman in Castlebellingham [County Louth].' The prayer book his mother had given him, between the lines of which he wrote, is now in the Kilmainham Jail Museum.

ᘓ   ᘓ   ᘓ

I am conscious that my account of 'my father's people' has amounted rather to an account of my young father. That reflects actuality. His personality among his siblings was so outstanding, and his role in public affairs so momentous, that they tend to become shadowy figures, mere features of his original environment. They were essentially private people, repressed by the inherent puritanism, not to say bigotry of Belfast life, by an authoritarian and unreliable father and, it must be said, by an exceptionally self-assured and autocratic eldest brother, who evolved into a national hero. By the same token my father never spoke about his childhood; I gather it was stern and cold.

All his brothers 'drank too much'; Daddy drank a great deal, but never 'too much', and never stout. Charlie, who was intensely lovable, died young; neither he nor Joe married; Jimmy was my godfather and the widowed father of my cousin, Betty, who was the least repressed of her generation and married a British soldier. Eddie became a doctor and an alderman and, like my father, pulled free to some extent from the poisonous morass of his childhood and married a lovely, sane English girl. May, who shared a lot of my father's qualities, married well; her husband, my Uncle Ted, seemed then to us to own Coalisland in Tyrone – pharmacy, grocery, sand-pit, the lot – and to deprecate my father's politics; without my father the family would have been natural Redmondites – Irish Parliamentary Party. Sand from my Uncle Ted's sand-pit built Stormont! My Auntie May, his wife, irritated us whenever she saw us by saying that we were 'much improved'; we could not see any need for improvement. Her phrase is, in fact, Ulster dialect for 'coming on nicely'. My Auntie Meg was the gentlest, most innocent, most loving person possible and the most put-upon. She never married, was a mother to Betty, and saw to it that Betty escaped.

When, in due course of nature, our Northern grandfather died in 1939, Séamus and I travelled up by train to the funeral. (Séamus was, of course, named after both grandfathers, Séamus Maurice.) Our parents went by car, changing escorts at the border for security. We felt very sophisticated and grown-up, having lunch in the dining car, and we discovered that we got on very well on our own together. The North had always been something of a foreign land to us. We knew our own generation of Northern cousins quite well, but there were wastes of unexpressed non-comprehension between us. My father could not forget how solidly pro-Treaty all the Northern nationalists, led by Joe Devlin, had been, and was infuriated by the facile, reproachful, republican rhetoric with which even his close family now received him. This rubbed off on us. The Lord Mayor of Belfast and the Aldermen attended the funeral, *in the Church*, entering in state when the Mass was ended, and my aunts were in a frenzy of socialite excitement. We couldn't understand it – why wouldn't they attend? Our

Northern cousins understood. 'The toad beneath the harrow knows, exactly where each tooth-point goes!'

My Conor and I once stayed in the home of the President of a 'black' university, south of the Mason-and-Dixon. I had this overwhelming sense of familiarity: the sullen, barely suppressed aggro of the young, the *Deutsche Blick* of their elders, the quick glance over the shoulder to check who was in earshot, the implicit clash of cultures – I had known them all before, in my grandfather's house in Belfast.

PART III: *EPISODE AT EASTER – 1916*

Episode at Easter is a young man's book, all energy and enthusiasm. It is also remarkably frank and closely observed. Often it is humorous at the novice revolutionary's expense, as when, sitting exhausted on the stairs in Liberty Hall, he takes the time from a clock that 'everyone knows has been stopped since before anyone can remember', and misses his train back to Louth. It has been compared to the account of the Battle of Waterloo given by Stendhal's young hero, Julien Sorel, in *Le Rouge et le Noir*, for combining, as it does, romantic idealism with a brisk, practical verve. It is dedicated to the 'men and women of Louth --- who served through 1916 and in what followed.'

⚃   ⚃   ⚃

Over fifty years after 1916 I took part, on RTÉ, in a discussion on Irish nationalism. Among the participants was the Reverend Martin Smyth, sometime Grand Master of the Orange Order. In those days RTÉ, and most other television stations, offered hospitality *before* as well as after the show. Over his gin and tonic, Reverend Smyth said to me, 'Do yew know that the Raballion of 1916 began with the murder of a polissmon in Castlebellingham?' I replied, 'I do indeed, Mr Smyth, my father was tried for it and condemned to death.' He did not bring up the subject when we went live; I had talked my advantage away.

In fact, probably the most vivid childhood memory I retain of my father is that of being taken by him and my mother, when I was about four years old, to a tall, dark house on, I think, the Malone Road in Belfast, with a tall monkey-puzzle tree on the front lawn darkening its windows still further. There I was set on the knee of a very old gentleman in a plaid dressing gown, with a shawl around his shoulders and smelling faintly of age and illness. This was Dr Tom Alexander, the former City Coroner of Belfast – a Protestant, of course – who had given evidence at my father's court martial in his favour, and subsequently organised a petition to the Crown on his behalf among the liberal Protestants of Belfast, which had a strong persuasive effect, in the climate of popular revulsion succeeding the main executions, in saving my father's life. The death sentence was commuted to penal servitude for life and, in his despair, my twenty-seven-year-old father could have wished for death. Now it was explained to me that, only for Dr Alexander's intervention, 'there would be no me'. I put my arms around the old gentleman's wasted neck and kissed him several times; I thanked him with my whole heart. Imagine a world with 'no me'!

03   03   03

In August 1998, I read with some astonishment, in Kevin Myers' column in *The Irish Times*, that one 'John McEntee (*sic*) of Belfast had shot two named, unarmed captives ... in the back quite coldly and casually.' Myers was relying on the *1916 Rebellion Handbook*, a work by many hands, published immediately after the Rising by *The Irish Times* of the day. He did not, apparently, regard it as a hostile source. I wrote to him personally, pointing this out and directing his attention to my father's own published account of the incident, in *Episode at Easter*, based on the notes he had made in its immediate aftermath, which are also extant. I got a fairly dusty answer. In justice to my father, I now add this account of those happenings, in his own words, but somewhat condensed, below – this was Easter Monday and the Dundalk Volunteers (IRA) were following their original orders to converge on Dublin, despite being somewhat disconcerted by the 'Countermanding Order', of which more later:

'Two miles from Lurgan Green lies the village of Castlebellingham ... The main street is built along the Dublin road ... Along this street lie all the village shops, and in its centre is a little grass plot railed off from the roadway. The cars with the main body of our men were drawn up beside this enclosure and extended in a line down the street. [My father was an officer, but not the CO.] I was in the last car, which was on the opposite side of the roadway, close to the houses and the footpath. As the cars halted, a detachment of our men ... jumped out, entered the shops and commandeered whatever provisions were to be had ... Then the village police arrived ... and, like their confrères at Lurgan Green, were placed under arrest and searched, very superficially to be sure, for firearms ... [They] offered no resistance and were not molested in any way. I had just placed a guard over them when another constable rode into the village. The newcomer was a tall, fine looking man ... and he refused to obey when I ordered him to dismount. It was only under pressure from the other police that he complied. He was then placed under arrest, searched and put in the line with the other prisoners.

By this time we had procured all the supplies we could get; the men had resumed their places in the cars ... when another car drove into the village and, of course, was stopped by our picket. The occupant ... an officer in the Irish Guards, was exceedingly angry at being held up and refused to get out of his car, whereupon there arose something of an altercation ... in which some rough words passed. At length the officer got out, and with his driver was placed beside the other prisoners. Before there was time to search him for arms Hannigan [my father's CO] ordered us to get ready to move off.

To ensure as far as possible that no mishap would occur [which might impede the getaway], I now took charge of the prisoners myself and ordered the men who had been guarding them back to their cars. Keeping the prisoners covered, I then backed towards my own car, which was the last in the line. I had just turned to enter it ... when a shot rang out, I jumped back at once and looked towards the prisoners. The officer was standing quite steady and upright, two of the policemen were running across the road, while of the third policeman and of the officer's driver there was no sign. I thought that ... they too had run away. At the sound of the shot the cars had stopped. I ran to the leading car and told Hannigan that someone had fired on the prisoners.

"Have any of them been hit?" he asked.

"No," I replied, "I think not. I saw the police running across the road, but the officer is still standing there and apparently is uninjured."

"Very well," he said. "If there is no one hit, get back to your car." And [he] blew two blasts on his whistle, which was the signal to start.

The cars were moving off as I walked back, and mine was just starting as I reached it. I got into it as it moved and turned then to look back at the officer. He had been standing very bravely and steadily up to this moment; but, as I looked at him now, I saw him tremble and sway and sink to the ground. I realised then for the first time that he had been wounded. By now most of our cars had already left the village and were moving along towards Dunleer; I could not stop them, nor turn back to find out whether the officer had been seriously wounded or not. Every moment, we thought, was precious to us and we dared not risk the delay. Besides, so far as the wounded man was concerned, there was a doctor in the village who would be of much greater service to him than we could be. We followed the other now fast-moving cars; and it was not until nearly five weeks later, when I was brought back [by the British] from Stafford [Jail] to stand my court martial in Dublin, that I learned that the same shot that wounded the officer had killed Constable Magee as well.'

The officer survived to give strictly factual evidence at the court martial; I take it he was the second man *The Irish Times'* contemporary account listed as being shot dead. My father never disputed his primary responsibility, as officer in charge of the prisoners, for the death of the handsome and courageous Constable Magee, but, of course, denied that it was murder. Historians, generally, who record the incident have taken the killing as accidental. My father's narrative concludes with the words:

'Alone in the whole country, the Volunteers of Louth, under Dan Hannigan and Paddy Hughes, took the field on that Easter Sunday morning ... They remained under arms ... for days after every other post in the country had surrendered. Even then they did not surrender – they disbanded.'

My father had, by the time of that disbandment, reported to the GPO in Dublin, of whose garrison he believed himself to be the last surviving member at the time of his own death in 1983. His ultimate rank in the IRA, in 1922, was that of Staff Captain.

Land of War

PART I: MARGARET BROWNE

My father and mother were married, by my Uncle Paddy, in University Church, Saint Stephen's Green, Dublin, at eight o'clock in the evening of 18 May, 1921, behind locked doors, with £50,000 of 'blood money' in the congregation. That was a lot of money at the time. Both bride and groom were 'on the run'; Austin Stack was best man; Joe MacDonagh, Tom Cullen and Michael Collins were among the guests – a litany of the republican hierarchy since the 1916 Rising. The young couple spent the first night of their honeymoon in the Marine Hotel in Sutton, so as to be able to catch the Belfast train, undetected, next morning at Howth Junction (my father was on his way North for a spell of the pretty hopeless Belfast electioneering of the period), rather than risk arrest at Amiens Street station (now Connolly station) in the city, which, of course, was under close police surveillance. In this they succeeded, but not without being spotted at breakfast by a clerical golfing party of my Uncle Paddy's colleagues from Maynooth. My poor mother had no alternative but to introduce her new husband; with startling originality they had registered as Mr and Mrs John Smith! 'Why, Margaret, we had no idea you were getting married!' 'Paddy never said a word to us!' and so on and so on ... It was only too clear how these cheerful priests interpreted the situation. As for my parents, they were both on the run, and took happenings of this kind in their stride.

We left my mother a schoolgirl in Eccles Street in the last chapter; and my father facing a lifetime of penal servitude after the 1916 Rising, his death sentence having been commuted. The late Tod Andrews, the couple's close contemporary, political ally and friend, always insisted that the squalor of penal servitude was more terrible for lower middle-class boys, who had been waited on hand and foot by their mothers, than for the more privileged, who had faced the rigours of boarding school. In this chapter I will tell what I know of how my parents came together and what I know of the early years of their marriage.

ᘓ   ᘓ   ᘓ

My mother had been a brilliant but irreverent student at UCD. When the Literary and Historical Society, in order to exclude women members, substituted a 'smoking concert' – considered a strictly male event; women did not smoke in public then – for their annual 'Inaugural' meeting, she and several of her equally adventurous pals from the Dominican and Loreto Women's Halls of Residence bullied the unfortunate Dean of Women, a Mrs Greene, into chaperoning them to the event. All mixed gatherings were chaperoned in those days. She flirted openly, it was said, with the distinguished and reclusive, if youthful, Professor of Celtic Languages, Dr Osborne Bergin, and was understood to address him as 'Osby' when they met on holidays in the Irish-speaking district of Ballingeary. 'Count yourselves lucky,' she would say to us children, on the rare occasions when we criticised our father, 'that I didn't marry Osborne Bergin.' I still own a copy of his *Maidean i mBéara agus dánta eile* (Morning in Beare and other poems), inscribed by him, '*Do Phéarla na mBrúnach ón té do cheap*' (To the pearl of the Brownes from the author). She liked to think of herself as one of the daring young women in the famous limerick, popularly ascribed to James Joyce, about the old Royal University College in Dublin:

> *There was an old man named Delany*
> *Who remarked to the girls, 'Nota bene*
> *Before the Archbishop*
> *The way that you swish up*
> *Your skirts when the weather is rainy.'*

Dr Delany was the Rector of the Old Royal.

I do not think she gave much thought to the morrow; she knew she could always earn good money in the top rank of teachers, and she knew she could marry – well. Anyone my mother married was bound to succeed. In the meantime she was fun-loving, and young. I like to think of her like that. She took a double degree with first-class honours in Irish and Modern Languages – English and French. (So, when my turn came, did I.) She is someone I am proud and happy to identify with.

The Dominican Order in Ireland has always been nationalist, and Eccles Street was a Dominican school, so my mother's association with

Sinn Féin began early. Her politics developed organically as she grew and were an integral part of her personality. This is how she describes it in a statement she made to the Bureau of Military History in the late 1930s, for their archives, in relation to her involvement in the events of 1916:

'About 1910, when I was a small girl in Eccles Street, a cousin of mine [almost certainly Bee Doheny, later Mrs Matt Kissane] took me to the house of Miss Kit Ryan [afterwards (the first) Mrs Seán T O'Kelly], where she was staying. They took me out to St. Enda's where we were received by [Pádraig] Pearse. We met also Tom MacDonagh, Willie Pearse [both executed after the Rising] and Tomás McDomhnaill there. That was my first association with any of the revolutionary leaders. I remember Pearse and Connolly at a Gaelic League meeting at the Mansion House. Alfie Byrne [a famous Lord Mayor of Dublin – not a 'physical force' man] attempted to speak, but was howled down by the audience. Pearse made an appeal that Alfie Byrne should get a hearing. [This generosity was typical of Pearse.]'

As she continues her evidence – such communications were voluntary – you realise how young they all were; she was conferred with her degree at nineteen (So, again, was I):

'At an Aonach [Gaelic League term for an assembly] in the Abbey Theatre in December 1914 or 1915, I met Seán MacDermott [executed 1916]. I had previously known him. I met him on an earlier occasion when he was travelling to Kilkenny to a meeting and I was going to Bagenalstown, where I worked. My brother, Dr Paddy Browne, was a great friend of his. He used to come to our digs in Grove Park, Rathmines. We also met him a lot at Ryans' in 19 Ranelagh Road [the Ryan sisters' flat].

I used to meet Ned Daly [executed 1916] a lot at Céilís in the Banba Hall. He used to walk home with us, also Jim Ryan [later Mr de Valera's Minister for Health] who was in his battalion. Daly gave me the impression that he was in the Volunteers for the excitement. He seemed [to me] to keep great discipline, because one night in our digs, when it came to the time for some Volunteer meeting, he ordered Jim Ryan to go to it and remained on himself with us. I remember we had only three eggs left for tea, and Jim Ryan had to do without one. [At what point Jim Ryan had to undergo this deprivation she doesn't say.]'

Like my father, she was, when the time came, directly affected by the famous 'Countermanding Order' (see below) and its sequel. She was already a member of Cumann na mBan (the women's auxiliary of the IRA), but I do not know whether she had ever before acted as an IRA courier, or in this instance, more properly, IRB courier. This last is not generally known, but I have it on the authority of Gearóid O'Sullivan (later Michael Collins's 'right hand') that the messages she carried were not the general Volunteer orders, but a kind of advance counter-countermanding order from and for IRB men. O'Sullivan stated, on oath, before the Military Service Pensions Commission in September 1946:

'I don't think there is anybody alive would know this but myself: Seán MacDermott's despatches [those carried by my mother] were IRB despatches … MacNeill's was a Volunteer order; and the countermanding [order] by MacNeill really didn't countermand MacDermott's order.'

Irish readers, even quite young ones, if they have taken Leaving Cert. Honours History, will know that on the eve of the 1916 Rising the Commander-in-Chief, Eoin MacNeill, a scholarly rather than a military figure, tried to call off the whole thing and issued a Countermanding Order to that effect. The IRB – an inner, secret and oath-bound group within the movement – frustrated this. My mother's narrative continues:

'I came to Dublin [from Bagenalstown] on the Saturday before Palm Sunday as I was to spend part of my holidays in Galway with Professor Power's family. [This is Michael Power, who so admired my grandmother.] I used, in fact, to come to Dublin every weekend, as I was preparing for my MA and used to study in the Irish Academy. [She was editing a medieval saint's life from mss: *Betha* (Life of) *Mheic Creiche*.] I went on Holy Thursday morning to [the] Ryans' [flat], in Ranelagh Road. Father Hannon, S.J., was there and they were discussing the plans in the [infamous government 'Castle Order'] document [leaked to and] published [by the Volunteers] on Spy Wednesday for the arrest of the Volunteer leaders and the seizure of certain buildings by the British [a decisive factor in the decision to defy the Countermanding Order]. I was given two large sealed envelopes containing copies of the document for the Bishops of Galway and Tuam. I was taking the afternoon train

45

from the Broadstone for Galway and when I arrived at the Station, Seán MacDermott came and gave me two despatches, one for Laurence Lardner of Athenry and one for George Nicholls of Galway. He did not tell me what was in the messages, but he said they were very important and that I should not let them fall into anyone's [see below] hands. I was to eat them if necessary. [The contents would have been typed on flimsy paper with this in mind.] He then took an affectionate farewell of me. [This was the last time she saw him.]

When I got to Athenry it was getting dark. I went to the hotel and left my case. I found Lardner's – a public house – at the corner of the street. It was full of people drinking. [Surprisingly, it was probably the only time she was ever in a public house.] I walked through into a room at the back of the shop. Laurence was not there, but his brother and mother were. They told me he was in Dublin. They also mentioned that Mellowes [Liam Mellowes, a republican officer returned clandestinely from deportation] was in the neighbourhood, I think in Oranmore. The brother assured me I would be safe in giving the message to himself. [Presumably she did so; it was the right decision.] Athenry was full of police and the sergeant came in to inquire who was the young lady that had come in. Mrs Lardner told him I was her cousin who was working in Pim's. They asked me to have tea but I wouldn't. Mr Lardner brought me out the back through a vegetable garden which was very muddy, into which my high heels sank. My get-up was very unsuitable for that sort of expedition. [Clothes were my mother's weakness!] I reached the street and went to the hotel and had tea.

Shortly before 10 o'clock the hotel people asked me was I staying the night. I said no. Then they said that there was curfew and I would have to go to the Station. When I reached it I found it full of police. It became rather cold and I had a long time to wait, so I sat with the night watchman who had a fire. [She would!] I had sent a wire to Power's to say I was not coming until the night mail. Professor Power did not meet me in Galway as his motorbike had broken down on his way to the Station. I decided to stay in the Railway Hotel. I was not long in it when the Professor came to fetch me. I decided, as it was so late, not to leave the hotel till morning.

The following morning [Good Friday] Mrs Tina Power [a college friend who had married the professor] came and brought me to George Nicholls in his office. When I handed him the message he seemed very disturbed and excited. He asked did I know what was in it. I said no, and he said no more about it. Afterwards, I delivered the sealed document to the Bishop of Galway whom I knew, as his niece was in Eccles Street with me. He was worried about it and asked a lot about the contents. In the afternoon I went to Tuam by train and delivered the [second sealed] envelope to the Archbishop.'

In our family we never had any doubt but that our mother's message got safely to Liam Mellowes and that that was why Oranmore 'rose'. I know now that several couriers got through. On her circuitous route back to Dublin, my mother looked so pathetically tired and worn that a British officer brought her a cup of tea. She did not refuse it. I remember that round about the time these recollections were being recorded my mother cried a lot, which was not like her. So many of the young men whose names she remembered were so untimely dead. I witnessed her signature when she submitted them to the Pensions Commission – I was already a barrister by then – but I did not read the contents. They could have been confidential.

The work which kept her in Bagenalstown involved some type of inspectorate of convent schools and was a diocesan appointment, as far as I can deduce from memory at this point. She attributed her success in nailing it, at the ripe age of nineteen, to an excessively smart costume, purchased on the indispensable Arnotts' account, which she wore to her interview with the Bishop. That much I recall clearly. I wonder was it the 'unsuitable get-up' of her statement?

Meanwhile, on Easter Monday, the Ryan girls whom she mentions, Min and Phyllis, had reported as nurses to the GPO, where they were joined by their brother, Dr Jim, who set up a makeshift hospital in the building. When the girls were sent home by Pearse before the surrender, they returned to Loreto Hall on Saint Stephen's Green, a Hall of Residence for women students, where the eldest of their sisters was a nun, Sister Stanislaus, always known to them as Sister Stan. Understandably, they found themselves surrounded by students and community avid for news. When they reached the end of their story, the Reverend Mother, Mother Eucharia, spoke with her accustomed authority, 'Go straight back, girls,' she said, 'and tell Mr Pearse that he has done very well, but that this is quite enough!' Poor Mr Pearse had already come to the same conclusion …

PART II: THE YOUNG BROWNES

It is impossible to exaggerate the desolation that engulfed all these young people in the aftermath of the Rising. My Uncle Paddy's despair was so terrible that his friends feared for his reason. Through a benign(?) oversight, he had been locked in with his beloved friend, the prisoner, Seán MacDermott, whom he was visiting in his cell in Kilmainham Jail on what they both believed was to be MacDermott's last night on earth. His execution was fixed for 11 May. In the small hours of the morning came news of a stay of execution, but for one day only. The British Commanding Officer, an Irishman called Lynch, who seems to have been a humane man, within the parameters of his office, overlooked the earlier serious breach of prison regulations, which had resulted in the overnight stay, and permitted Paddy a further short farewell visit on the postponed actual eve. After Paddy had 'held him in a last embrace', poor Seán, whose personal effects had been taken from him on his arrest and not returned, gave Paddy four overcoat buttons, three to go to the MacDermott sisters in America, and one for my mother, Margaret. That button, in after years, when I was a baby, lived with the sovereigns I had been given at my christening, in a matchbox in my mother's desk. Our then flat in Pembroke Road was raided during the Civil War by the troops of the new government, and the matchbox, with its contents, disappeared.

It is not always remembered that Seán MacDermott's 'cover' as a Gaelic League *timthire* – 'an organiser (rec.)' according to Father Dineen's Irish-English Dictionary – was also the vocation of a genuine enthusiast. The *timthirí* (pl.) rode their bicycles, in all weathers, from town to town and village to village throughout Ireland, founding branches of the League, instituting Irish classes, encouraging Irish music and dancing, infecting young people with their enthusiasm for the rescue of a native cultural heritage that people had almost forgotten existed. Hitherto my Uncle Paddy's fascination with Irish had been a scholarly and romantic recreation. Now he swore on his friend's memory that henceforward it would constitute the main motivating force of his life and that, in this respect at least, the sacrifice of all that youth and courage would not be in vain. That summer he took his bicycle and travelled south and west till he came to the most westerly parish in Ireland, the Gaeltacht of Dunquin in County Kerry, on the Dingle Peninsula. There he came to terms with his loss and there he resolved to build the house that, for most of the remainder of his life, was to be his only home where, in due course, his sister's three children grew up Irish-speaking. Seán MacDermott's framed photograph, in colour, hung ever afterwards at the foot of my Uncle Paddy's bed, a testimony to my uncle's extraordinary capacity for loving friendship no less than to MacDermott's extraordinary capacity to inspire it.

In that same terrible month of May 1916, my unobtrusive Uncle David, in religion Father Michael, came from Tallaght Priory to attend the last hours of another of those executed, 'the boy-soldier', Seán Heuston. In that month also, my father, the man 'responsible for the Dundalk and Castlebellingham affairs', according to Prime Minister Asquith, faced his court martial, had his death sentence imposed and commuted to penal servitude for life, officially on account of his youth and 'previous good character', but most certainly in large degree consequent on Dr Alexander's petition and the popular revulsion against the executions, which had developed by then. He was imprisoned in Dartmoor; he was twenty-seven years old and he thought his life, insofar as life was tolerable, was over.

☙ ☙ ☙

I imagine my mother went back to Bagenalstown and resumed her work and her study. In 1917 she got her MA, and things took a decided turn for the better: the prisoners, including my father, were released and she went to a Sinn Féin fancy dress (!) *céilí*, held to welcome their return. She wore the Cú Chulainn costume that was used in the Yeats plays and which, characteristically, she had coaxed from the brothers Fay at the Abbey for the occasion. At that *céilí* she and Daddy, newly released from his nightmare, met for the first time. Those who remember my mother only as the imposingly stout lady she became will find it difficult to believe that, in her twenties, she was considered 'too thin' and could, in the appropriate clothes, pass as a boy; could and did when it was expedient for 'Miss Browne' to disappear. It must have helped to have had four brothers, but how did she manage her hair? Was it already 'bobbed', or 'shingled'? I simply do not know, although I remember my slim mother quite well, in the years before my brother Séamus was born; then she had a romantic cloud of curling dark hair.

On the euphoria of the 1917 releases followed, in short order, the Anti-Conscription campaign and the 'German Plot', so that my father – with the other surviving 1916 officers – was to find himself back in an English prison, this time in Gloucester Jail, but in much better spirits than the first time since by now public opinion in Ireland was fairly solidly behind Sinn Féin. When I was a teenager, I remember, the Anglican Dean of Gloucester came to lunch at our house. My father informed him, with a straight face, that he had spent many months in the shadow of the Dean's Cathedral! It was the last time I remember the 'when Daddy was in jail' ploy being used. By then it was socially accepted that anybody who was anybody had been at least interned 'shoulder to shoulder with the bravest of the brave', *mar dheadh!* (I don't think!) My brother and I, however, at our Protestant school (Alexandra) got great mileage out of the formula and used it to shock and horrify our sheltered classmates.

C3   C3   C3

My mother came back from Bagenalstown in 1917 to teach in the Dominican Convent in Cabra. She taught Irish and, her father's daughter, maths. She took a flat in Pembroke Road – these were the 'liberated' Great War years – which rapidly became a 'safe house' for 'the movement', as did every other home she ever had until Mr Aiken's ceasefire in 1923 signalled the waning of the Civil War. Desmond FitzGerald (Garret's father) and Pádraig Ó Máille stayed there, among others. She met Michael Collins at the Irish National Aid Fund, where he was secretary. 'We were all bowled over by him,' she said. Collins and Harry Boland, his *fidus Achates* (close friend), came often to Pembroke Road. They were not terribly popular visitors with the neighbours, and not only for political reasons; there was their horseplay and high spirits, too.

My Uncle Moss was ordained in the summer of that year and left for a stint of three years in New York on the 'American Mission', the same American Mission that was to impact so disastrously on the preservation of the Irish language, as it did subsequently on the Latin Liturgy. Americans distrust languages other than English, and the use of Irish clergy to the Vatican depends largely on their being English-speaking. Uncle Moss carried with him to America a message from Republican HQ to the old Fenian exile and rabid Irish-American nationalist, John Devoy. My Uncle Paddy had put Moss in touch with Diarmuid Lynch, the appropriate Volunteer officer, for the purpose; Moss considered it 'an honour to be asked'. The message was in a code devised by Paddy and based on a translation of his from the first book of Horace's *Odes*:

> *'Hear now the pretty laugh that tells*
> *In what dim corner lurks thy love;*
> *And snatch a bracelet or a glove*
> *From wrist or hand that scarce rebels.'*

The key depended on a piece of doggerel and five digits which Moss had to get by heart:

Bearing east you travel west
Limerick hams are the best – 73254

Moss was fairly rigorously searched, with scant respect for his collar – clerical dress was a common Volunteer disguise – and Paddy's translation was dismissed as 'sentimental rot', and its purpose was not suspected, or at least not detected. When he gave it to Devoy in New York, it was to find that Devoy had already received a duplicate; now we will never know what it was.

Meanwhile, in Dublin literary circles, my Uncle Paddy was becoming somewhat of a cult figure and he carried his spirited sister along with him. He was now Professor of Mathematics in Maynooth, tall and handsome with curling dark hair and deep-set, expressive eyes. His poems, in English, on 1916 were passed eagerly from republican hand to republican hand. His beautiful rural good manners, with the aura of sophistication he retained from his years in Europe, at the Sorbonne and at Göttingen University, made a winning combination. My mother remembered particularly *soirées* – it is the only possible word – spent with Dolly and Lucy Lynd, sisters of Robert Lynd (later the celebrated essayist, YY, of the *New*

Statesman), where she met Liam Ó Briain, afterwards Professor of Romance Languages in UCG, and the tragic Tom Kettle, whom she had known and admired when she went to his brilliant lectures in UCD. As children we were brought up almost to reverence Tom Kettle, as we were to reverence Mick Collins, and to mourn both their deaths as the deaths of 'great Irishmen', however mistaken they might each have been in the events that led immediately to those deaths. Other acquaintances were Oliver St John Gogarty, who speaks of Paddy in his autobiography as 'the man I loved', the writer Seámus O'Sullivan, founder of the *Dublin Magazine*, Pádraig Colum the poet and his wife, Mary, and that entire cast of characters. My mother had scant time for Mrs Colum, who had once been engaged to Seán MacDermott. The lady broke off the engagement – she did not think Seán was 'going anywhere' – and threw the ring in the fire. Poor Seán, who could have ill-afforded the outlay, went down on his knees and raked the coals to retrieve it. Mrs Colum frequently told the story afterwards – before 1916, that is – and spoke of her former lover with contempt for his 'materialism'.

CB   CB   CB

After the 'German Plot', Sinn Féin was denuded of male workers to fight a series of important by-election campaigns, orchestrated mainly by the famous Father Michael O'Flanagan, the archetypal 'republican priest', and in May 1918 my Uncle Paddy was asked by George Gavan Duffy, one of the founders of Sinn Féin, if he would go to East Cavan to help elect Arthur Griffith. Nothing loth, he went, and his headquarters were in Ballyjamesduff, which pleased him because of the song, 'Come back Paddy Reilly to Ballyjamesduff' – Percy French's. The Catholic hierarchy was certainly not, at that time, hostile to Arthur Griffith, who had become the respectable face of contemporary nationalism. They did not, however, countenance the actual participation of men of the cloth in electioneering; Father O'Flanagan was actually 'silenced' – a technical term in Church discipline – for his activities over these years, something which, when we were children, made him, paradoxically, holier in our eyes even than the norm. My Uncle Paddy received a command from the local Bishop, Dr Finegan, forbidding him from taking any further part in the election 'in my diocese'. Fortunately, the constituency straddled two dioceses and my uncle had only to move out of Dr Finegan's jurisdiction to continue his work within the law. Dr Finegan seems to have taken this rather well, but said, 'You obeyed the letter, not the spirit, of my order.' Paddy is reported to have replied, 'Had I obeyed the spirit, I would have been on the opposite platform.' That would have been the Irish Parliamentary Party platform. It was in East Cavan that my Uncle Paddy performed his first miracle – you've guessed it: the dead voted.

In 1918 the voting registers were out of date and inaccurate. A sizeable number of Sinn Féiners felt that here were opportunities not to be wasted. In his *Life of Michael Collins*, Tim Pat Coogan credits Harry Boland with 'political talent of the vote early, vote often variety'. This talent was certainly in the ascendant in the Volunteer element among the Sinn Féin election workers in the constituency of South-East Dublin. My mother remembered canvassing decorously for votes with Colonel Maurice Moore – George Moore's nationalist brother, who sent his sons to Saint Enda's, Pádraig Pearse's school for boys. However, the young men who turned her Pembroke Road flat into an *ad hoc* election headquarters and bear garden had another, less ladylike use for her. She had charge of the list of dead, or otherwise absent voters and directed her less scrupulous co-workers accordingly. She wasn't proud of engaging in personation, but neither did she ever deny it. Perhaps she shared with Mr de Valera the ability to wrestle with her conscience and win! She was, however, deeply shocked when one of her 'cohorts' came back to her saying he had been challenged and had 'sworn'. Personation, apparently, was one thing, perjury another. 'You didn't!' she protested. He was a realist. 'Jaysus, Margaret,' he replied, 'they'd have torn me apart else.' The number and nature of the visitors she entertained in her flat at that time found no favour with her landlord nor with her fellow tenants, and she was obliged to leave. She moved to 39 Parnell Square, over the Leinster College of Irish, and a whole new chapter in her life ensued.

PART III: ACTIVE SERVICE

It is not clear whether my mother's new choice of address was directed by someone other than herself, or, if so, by whom, but it seems fairly clear from what happened afterwards that Mick and Harry found it for her, with intent. Volunteer GHQ was on Parnell Square at an address variously given as 44 and 46; the Keating Branch of the Gaelic League had offices in the building, too. The famous Vaughan's Hotel – an alternative GHQ – was at one end of the street, and Liam Devlin (father of the poet, Denis Devlin) owned the pub, Devlin's, at the other end, where Collins was regularly to be found. In sworn evidence, given in 1946 in connection with the provisions of the Military Service Pensions Act, 1934, no less person than Liam Tobin – Michael Collins's Director of Intelligence during the 'Tan' war and the terror of successive subsequent governments, for obvious reasons – speaking of Margaret Browne's flat, put it like this, 'It had the same standing as Vaughan's Hotel.' Shortly after she moved in, she was asked by Mick Collins to put up a young Volunteer on the run: it was Tom Cullen, one of the 'Twelve Apostles' – gunmen who carried out Mick's execution orders – and for the next eighteen months or so he made it his home and was very much the man of the house, although technically he was my mother's guest. To quote Liam Tobin again, 'The History of Margaret Browne's flat is the history of Tom Cullen – QMG and Intelligence. That is so and that's the way of it.' Arms were stored there and distributed from there, confidential and dangerous documents were kept there – it was a veritable post office for couriers and despatches – she concealed codes in the band of her hat, and armed Volunteers were constantly billeted on her there. My Uncle Paddy also had a room there and he kept his skylight open at all times, having arranged with the musician Vincent O'Brien, Director of the Palestrina Choir, who owned the house next door and who was another cultural nationalist like himself, that the corresponding skylight would stay open there too, as an escape route. Paddy kept a suit of clothes and shaving things – cut-throat razor and razor-strop – there always, to provide cover for any untoward male presence that might be detected by unfriendly observers. Mick and/or his courier, Joe O'Reilly, were there most mornings, and Gearóid O'Sullivan regularly sent his courier, Paddy Howard, there with what he gallantly termed 'requests rather than orders'. Absolute secrecy was essential, and as a result my mother's part in all this is recorded only in subsequent oral testimony; so far as I know, there is no contemporary record of it in writing. She was not allowed to employ a cleaning lady, and her connection with Cumann na mBan – always fairly tenuous – was allowed to lapse; she was never a 'joiner'. Mick did not like his 'girls' drawing attention to themselves with uniforms, or drilling, or parades. She surfaces briefly and anonymously in Frank O'Connor's biography of Collins as the 'girl-next-door', who was not afraid to upbraid Mick for his disgraceful bullying of subordinates. O'Sullivan testifies to her direct contact with Headquarters staff and remembers that Collins 'called her Number One'. Thus it was that when, ultimately, in January 1921 the flat was raided and she had to leave, it became clear that the Square itself was no longer a safe haven. Gearóid O'Sullivan, in a sworn statement, tells it like this:

'I remember that night Collins and I were sleeping in the Congested Districts Board offices; and there was a great shoot-up in Parnell Square that night; and they searched nearly every house except the Congested Districts Board offices; and Collins said, "We're bet!" I said, "Why?" He said, "If we're beaten out of the Square, we're beaten out of Dublin, and if we're beaten out of Dublin, we're finished. They've hunted Margaret Browne out of the Square and she is our last stronghold here." That is an example of the status she held.'

My mother was in Grangemockler for Christmas when the raid took place. She was told that only an insignificant amount of ammunition, left in the flat 'by accident' after it was supposed to have been 'cleared', was found. We know, however, from Tim Pat Coogan that in or about this time, 'Tom Cullen had left a bag of Collins' papers with a friend who was raided and the papers seized.' If this friend was my mother, as I think it was, Tom wouldn't have felt the need to let her know this, or that he was in deep trouble. All that my mother said about the break was, 'It was at this time that we parted company.' I would not think she ever saw him again. They were on opposite sides during the Civil War.

When we were small we thought of these goings-on in my mother's flat as a sort of grown-up Teddy Bears' Picnic, with Piaras Beasley – then a Volunteer, subsequently a noted authority on Gaelic verse – as the bad bear, leaving his boots outside his bedroom door and expecting her to clean them, and Tom Cullen as the good bear, lying on the hearthrug in front of the gas fire, reading Wordsworth to 'improve himself'. Mick himself featured as a combination of Prince Charming and Demon King, which is why I never want to see and have never seen a movie about Mick Collins, for fear of overlaying the vivid impression I retain from my mother's splendid stories, which she related as far back as I can remember – certainly from the time I could talk.

As we grew older she made us aware of the grimmer aspects of her life at that time, although she never presented it as other than 'exciting and enjoyable': 'Danger I suppose there was, but ... I enjoyed doing it and I had a great time at it altogether.' Now, though, she explained to us how, when she saw Tom Cullen check over his gun before going out of an evening, she felt miserable, knowing that he might well have to kill someone and that he would certainly be entering the sub-Dickensian world of police informers and prostitutes in quest of 'Intelligence'. She seemed more distressed by his frequenting prostitutes than by his carrying out executions; that was certainly the morality of the day. What she never told us at all was that on one occasion at least she herself carried his gun for him, so that it would not be found on him if he were arrested, to and from the scene of a particularly notorious shooting – I prefer not to define it further. Like any good operative, she contrived to know as little as possible about what did not immediately concern her.

ઝ   ઝ   ઝ

About one terrible series of events, however – those of Bloody Sunday, 21 November 1920 – she was only too accurately informed, apart altogether from what she may have surmised about her flatmates' involvement therein. My Uncle Moss had returned from his three-year stint in the parish of Rockville Centre, Brooklyn, as curate to Monsignor Queely, carrying £27,000 of republican funds in the lining of his hat, which he conveyed directly to Mick Collins, and he was personally caught up in the happenings of that terrible day. He had been assigned to the parish of Valleymount near Blessington, often known by the less complimentary name of Black Ditches. 'There's no need,' said my grandmother, 'to say anything to the neighbours about Black Ditches.' It sounded to her like the name of a place where they might send disgraced priests.

One of my Uncle John's comrades before he died had been Mick Hogan, who had now become her surrogate son in John's place. Mick had always been in and out of the Brownes's house. As a little fellow he had been placed in Moss's care on his first day in school. He was in tears and would not be comforted, repeating over and over again, 'Go home, see Da,' until my grandfather packed himself and Moss back up the road to Kate's shop, where he was coaxed into better form with bullseyes. By now he was a member of the Tipperary football team due to play against Dublin in Croke Park on that November day. He and Moss – up in Dublin for the game – met briefly in Barry's Hotel. The atmosphere was tense and ominous after the morning's shooting of British secret service agents – the 'Cairo gang' – by Collins's men, and there were dark rumours of impending reprisals. It had been decided, however, to go ahead with the match, and Moss took his place on the sideline just as the teams came onto the field. The account of what happened then I give below in his own words; it is a third-person narrative under a fictitious name, 'Martin', otherwise it is as I heard it innumerable times; I have changed the name 'Martin' back to his own, Moss:

'Michael Sammon, the referee, looked at his watch, threw in the ball, and the game was on. There were some lively exchanges of play before a British aeroplane hovered over the field, like a murky vulture ... A feeling of apprehension passed through the crowd. A pistol shot rang out, sharp and clear. It was the signal for attack. Forthwith, a platoon of Black-and-Tans went 'over the top' as if into battle. Using trench ladders, they scaled the Canal Wall, enclosing the playing-pitch, dropped to the ground and sent volley after volley into the crowd.

There was a momentary pause and then there ensued the wildest panic. The spectators on the north side raced towards the railway wall, those on the south went in headlong flight towards the main exit. Occupiers of touchline seats ran onto the field and threw themselves flat on the ground. While they lay there, another wave of fugitives passed over them. On top of these surged another wave, until human mounds piled up on several parts of the pitch. Those underneath were almost suffocated. Many were shot and fell, wounded or dead, in their effort to reach safety. While they lay on the ground, breathless, bullets raked the grass close to their bodies.

... Moss made it to the dressing-room close to the main exit. Hundreds of men, women and children were packed together there ... machine-gun (*sic*) bullets beat a tattoo on the corrugated roof ... Moss and another young Tipperary priest attempted to calm the crowd. They told them to recite an Act of Contrition while they themselves gave a General Absolution ... Moss was just inside the door ... a Black and Tan came to the doorway ... brandishing a smoking revolver, he pointed it directly at Moss's forehead ... but instead of being fired at point-blank range, the gun was pointed upwards ... and the bullet whizzed through the roof.

The command was given, "All come out with hands up!" The occupants of the dressing-room poured out of the building. When they came into the open, they saw thousands marching on the field with hands held aloft. All were ordered to halt. The crowd was marshalled into ordered ranks. Field guns were wheeled into position directly in front of them. "Forward three paces!" The ranks moved forward. A counter-command was given, "Step backward three paces!" The crowd obeyed. The gunners swivelled their field-pieces back and forth in a menacing manner, now seeming to aim directly at one individual, now playfully switching to another position. While some were 'frisking' for arms, others were roaring in a besotted fashion, "Keep your hands higher, or by G— I'll blow your b—y heads off!" The strain was intolerable. A boy, who stood beside Moss, collapsed ... Moss lifted him in his arms and carried him toward the exit. He was not halted. To his intense relief he was allowed to pass through the cordon with his unconscious burden. He took him to a house on Jones's Road ... [Moss was told there that Mick Hogan was among the dead.]

[Still] he could not tear himself away. He found himself attached to a group that were looking down on Croke Park from a laneway that led off the North Circular Road. It was a glorious sunlit afternoon. They had a perfect view of the field. They saw groups of people being systematically searched. They had a clear view of men being beaten down to the ground with rifle butts. In an isolated part of the field a man was on his knees. A Black-and-Tan towered over him, waving his revolver. The man's head went lower and lower until at last he lay quite still ...

Moss was now seized with one fixed idea: to return to Croke Park and get Mick Hogan's body off the field. Memories of the past crowded into his mind: Mick's first day at school, crying 'Home, see Da'; Mick coming to help, after John's death, with the saving of the hay and the sowing of the crops; Mick laughing and joking in the kitchen at home.

When he reached the top of Jones's Road, he saw that a convoy of lorries extended for the full length of the highway. The Black-and-Tans were "roaring drunk", shouting and cursing ... They looked like demons that had taken a day's holiday from the underworld. They held their rifles at the ready. Not a civilian was in sight. For a moment, Moss hesitated. Then he decided to go through ... to find Mick Hogan's body ... A policeman [Dublin Metropolitan Police] shouted, "Come back, come back; you'll be shot"... Moss said resolutely, "I want to find Mick Hogan's body" ... [The policeman] said very calmly, "If you are so bent on going, I'll accompany you" ...

When Moss and the policeman entered Croke Park, the place looked like a battlefield that had been abandoned by the combatants. The ground was strewn with empty cartridge cases. Lifeless bodies were on the sideline and on the sward. Not a living soul was in sight. The silence of the tomb reigned supreme. After a brief interval, the whine of the Crossleys was heard as they moved off. All at once people began to appear on the field, like rabbits coming out of burrows on a summer evening. The danger was past. They went to inspect the dead. Moss did not know where to look for his friend. Suddenly, there was a cry, "Here is the footballer!" At the Railway end, about twenty-five yards from the north corner of the pitch, close to the cindertrack, his body lay, shrouded in a fawn overcoat. No one has ever identified the person who had so respectfully covered Mick Hogan's body. He was in his football togs and jersey of white and gold, the Tipperary colours. The grass was red with his blood. A bullet had entered under his left shoulder blade, another at the back of his ear. Death must have been instantaneous ... Moss got a seat in the ambulance that conveyed Mick Hogan's body to the morgue at Jervis Street hospital. He remained there for some time and met Mick's brother, Dan, who was Commandant of the IRA in the Monaghan area.

Mick is buried in Grangemockler beside his lifelong playmate, John Browne. Kate had one more fine young man to mourn and to pray for.'

ை   ை   ை

After the raid on my mother's flat in Parnell Square, it was inevitable that Eccles Street, where she was teaching, would be next. The raiders wanted a Miss Browne, but as none of the lay teachers, her colleagues, was prepared to give her name, six ladies were arrested and carted off to the Bridewell RIC Station. The Library steps had to be brought down, amid much laughter, into the street to enable the young women in their hobble skirts to mount the lorry. Meanwhile, Miss Browne, in her underwear, was safely in bed in the school infirmary. She could not, of course, risk bringing any further such inconvenience on the nuns and had to resign from her post and move right across the city to Norfolk Road. There she shared a flat with Joe MacDonagh, Tom's brother, who was Deputy Minister for Labour in the Sinn Féin government under the First Dáil and in charge of the Belfast Boycott Office, Countess Markievicz, the actual Minister, elected in 1918, being in jail. I feel that the Countess was no longer terribly relevant to the active Volunteers in the field – whose feminism was of an immediate and practical kind. My mother knew her, of course, slightly; Conor's mother, Kathleen, Hanna Sheehy Skeffington's sister, knew her much better. My mother liked the company of women, advanced and intellectual or not, but preferred that of men.

In no time at all, Joe had profited from the circumstances that provided him with an ideal deputy for his own work in the Boycott Office, in the person of Margaret Browne. Joe was a droll fellow and very good company. He had no patience with relatives of dead comrades who spoke of having 'given' them for 'the cause', as Mrs Pearse did of 'Pat and Willie'. Joe would say, 'I gave Tom, and I'd give Jack [his brother] and George Bingham [his brother-in-law] too!' There was nothing of the pseud about him. He would greet prim female members of staff returning from leave with a cheerful, 'Any immorality?'

My mother liked and admired him but was not happy in her work for his department. She felt guilty about dispatching Volunteer squads to break up small businesses in places like the Liberties, which might, for example, be accused of selling matches made in Belfast; this was the function of the Boycott Office. She stuck it out, however, until the immediate eve of the Civil War, when it was disbanded. The Office and all its staff, who were mostly women, were very much 'wanted' and on the run; service with the Boycott Office was equated with service in the Volunteers. They had frequently to change their premises and were remarkably successful in evading arrest. One of my mother's colleagues, my godmother, Maureen Power, was described by a well-known IRA man, the dentist Seán Dowling, as being 'high' in the movement. It is an interesting coincidence that among the people for whom my mother again found beds in her flat was the original proposer, in the Dáil, of the 'Belfast Boycott' motion – which was seconded by Ernest Blythe – this was my father, Seán MacEntee. I don't imagine they discussed it, they had happier things to talk about and, besides, being both on active service, discipline would have precluded their gossiping about 'the shop'. Another 'lodger' was Frank Gallagher, de Valera's press officer. One evening, when my father was leaving and my mother went with him to the front door to say goodbye, she came back to the common sitting room to find that a jumper she had been knitting had been unravelled and the wool wound around the legs of all the furniture to create a maze. It was Frank's protest against the length of time she had been absent and having finished it, he had gone to bed! I refrain from speculating on his motivation.

Mick dropped in often to visit, until one evening he found my Uncle Paddy there with Kit Ryan, the first Mrs Seán T O'Kelly. Kit was tall and thin, *jolie laide* (plain, but attractive) and supremely elegant. She had studied in Paris. She and my uncle made a spectacular pair. Too spectacular for Mick's taste. His fugitive's instinct was alerted and he did not approve. 'What time have you ordered the [arresting] lorry for?' he asked grimly and didn't come back again. He considered my mother's visitors too conspicuous.

ೞ   ೞ   ೞ

In the aftermath of his release from Gloucester Jail, my father became first Vice-Brigadier and then Acting Brigadier of the Belfast Brigade of the IRA. While in jail, he had been elected to the Dáil as Sinn Féin Deputy for South Monaghan. The 'war' in Belfast was a thankless horror. Tens of thousands of ferocious male working-class unionists lived packed into tiny streets, ready to engage in pitched battles at the first hint of 'Home Rule', or 'Papist' threat; the Catholic population of the city was a hostage community. In these circumstances IRA actions were impossibly dangerous, while there was little or no hope of protecting Catholics from ferocious reprisals. Nevertheless, the Belfast IRA reorganised and, as they saw it, 'held their own' during the 'heavy fighting' of 1920 and 1921. During the 'Partition' election, my father brokered the deal with 'wee' Joe Devlin, the Irish Party member at Westminster, which resulted in six Sinn Féin and six constitutional nationalist seats, all abstentionist, for the Stormont Parliament. He himself was nominated for West Belfast, a forlorn hope, and it was to his final election rally at Smithfield, in Belfast, that he and my mother slipped away on the first day of their oh-so-brief honeymoon.

My father at that time figured in the police publication, *The Hue-and-Cry*, with a reward posted for his capture, 'dead or alive'. The accompanying photograph showed a young thug with several days' growth of beard, a grubby muffler and a broken-peaked cloth cap; it had been stage-managed in Dartmoor Jail and defeated its own purpose, for my father was an intensely well-groomed and clothes-conscious person. When he was released from jail in 1917, my grandfather had travelled from Belfast to meet him off the boat-train at Westland Row, in Dublin, with a new three-piece suit, so that he could discard at once his horrible ticket-of-leave clothes. However, he distanced his natural appearance from the image even further by a very simple disguise: he grew a small toothbrush moustache, padded one shoulder of his respectable jacket and lowered one boot heel to create a 'natural' limp; a bowler hat and a cane completed the effect. He was never spotted. My mother did not like this protective colouring: 'It made him look like Charlie Chaplin.'

PART IV: COGADH NA GCARAD (THE WAR BETWEEN FRIENDS)

Now that I have come around again to my parents' wedding – my mother was twenty-eight and my father some years older, the same age as Paddy – it would be nice to write 'and they lived happily ever after', but of course the dates tell a different story. In December 1921 a woman and her husband cut Michael Collins dead in the street (see Tim Pat Coogan's biography of Michael Collins), just before the opening of the Dáil debates on the Anglo-Irish Treaty. I have reason to believe that that couple was my mother and father. It is hard to imagine the heartbreak this involved for all three. My father, of course, voted against the Treaty and explained his position in the only speech in those debates that concentrated on the issue of partition. I quote below:

'I have heard some say that they will vote for this "Treaty" because it is not a final settlement. But I am voting against it because I believe it will be a final settlement, and it is the terrible finality of the settlement that appals me. Under this Treaty, Ulster will become England's fortress in Ireland – a fortress as impregnable as Gibraltar. A vote for the "Treaty" is the betrayal of not only our own rights but of our pledge to our Ulster people – a people who, under conditions that those who have not endured them can have no conception of, have stood for us in the hope that ... we should not forget them ... I would not let them go. I would not traffic in my nation's independence without, at least, securing my nation's unity. I would not hand over my country as a protectorate to another country without, at least, securing the right to protect my countrymen ... and because I will not do these things, I will not vote for this "Treaty".'

My father was at this time Sinn Féin TD for South Monaghan – he was sharing my mother's current flat in Pembroke Road – and was involved with Aodh de Blacam, the noted Fianna Fáil journalist, and Séan Lester, later a distinguished League of Nations civil servant, in the production of a short-lived propaganda weekly newspaper, ambiguously titled *The Unionist* and addressed primarily to potential liberal unionist readers. It lasted about a month and my father was providentially able to close its bank account, which was in credit, before its office on Bachelor's Walk was raided. He had opened a short-lived office as a Consulting Engineer with Fergus O'Kelly, an old GPO comrade, in, I think, Dawson Street. My mother continued to work in the peripatetic Boycott Office. They must have pinned their hopes of some kind of return to normality on the Collins–de Valera pact election, due in June of 1922. The idea was that a united Sinn Féin should face the electorate and that the Treaty would not be an issue – some hope! Meanwhile, against a background of continuing horror in the North and lethal ambivalence in the South, the hopes of evading a civil war evaporated, and on 4 April 1922 I was born and christened for my Ulster and Munster grandmothers, Máire Caitríona (Mary Kate). My father said I looked 'like a Maori', which made my poor mother cry, until my Uncle Paddy reassured her that Maoris were 'very handsome people'.

The June election came and went, with a decisive plebiscitary majority in favour of the Treaty. It established the pro-Treaty wing of Sinn Féin as the party of government, and the Free State was established. Dissenting republicans quoted Mr de Valera: 'The people have no right to do wrong.' They considered their options, and the first shots of the Civil War were fired.

CƐ   CƐ   CƐ

On 14 April, Rory O'Connor and the anti-Treaty Volunteers had seized the Four Courts to hold for the 'Republic', as against the coming Free State; on Wednesday, 28 June the shelling of the Four Courts by the Provisional Government of the Free State began, and my father threw up his consultant engineer's practice for the third time since 1917 and reported for active service with the (anti-Treaty) Dublin Brigade. He presented himself to Oscar Traynor at his Headquarters in the Hammam Hotel in Upper O'Connell Street, now the Gresham Hotel.

It is well known that almost the entire cadre of the anti-Treaty leadership – Mr de Valera, Seán T O'Kelly, Austin Stack, Countess Markievicz, Bob Barton and, of course, Cathal Brugha – were gathered at Brigade HQ, for one reason or another, on the Monday after the Four Courts fell. My father, with a handful of men in the Marlborough Street Post Office, was charged with keeping open their lines of retreat. With one tragic exception he was successful in this, and the entire garrison – other than Cathal Brugha, who commanded the rearguard – of some seventeen men and three women was safely evacuated. Brugha's orders were to surrender when the building became untenable and, on Wednesday evening, he duly ordered the last remaining defenders out into the lane behind the hotel, where attackers, onlookers and members of the fire brigade jostled together, to surrender. Friends and enemies alike waited for the commanding officer to show. As we know, he did not surrender but came out fighting from the burning building and was fatally wounded. It is unlikely that Collins's troops intended to kill him – animosities had not yet ripened to hate – but it seems certain that he deliberately courted death, seeing any compromise with the Treaty or the Provisional government as dishonour. My father, his function discharged, escaped under fire.

In or about this time, my mother and the other employees of the Boycott Office got three months' pay instead of notice from Michael Staines, who had displaced Joe MacDonagh. She was teaching again by this time, maths and Irish as always, but money was very tight nonetheless. She was still living in Pembroke Road, but she now had help in the shape of the invaluable Cassie who, as well as cleaning, was prepared to babysit indefinitely and gave it as her opinion that the baby, myself, 'wasn't earthly'. To my mother then, no doubt anxious and unhappy, came an unlikely visitor. The Dublin correspondent of the *Morning Post* was a peculiarly poisonous English journalist called, I think, Bretherton. During the opening events of the Civil War in O'Connell Street, described above, he had been taken prisoner by Republican HQ. Nobody quite knew what to do with him, but my father had the bright idea of sending him out under a flag of truce to take a message to my mother, presumably to say that he was still alive. Years later, in Spain, at a cocktail party in the British Embassy, an amiable, white-haired gentleman approached me saying, 'You may not remember this, Miss MacEntee, but in July 1922, in Dublin, you received me graciously, sitting on the knee of your lady mother.' It was, of course, Bretherton (if I am right in thinking that was his name – I haven't checked).

છ છ છ

My father was not long left idle or free. He was approached by Mrs Tom Barry, wife of the legendary Cork 'column' commander, with a plan to tunnel into Mountjoy Jail to rescue Rory O'Connor and the other Four Courts leaders. A house close to the walls of Mountjoy was bought and operations were set going. In the nature of things, it was not easy to keep the work under wraps. Whether because of this, or for more sinister reasons, the operation lasted less than two days before it was discovered and the diggers arrested. The arresting officer was the same Joe O'Reilly, the courier, whom my mother had once defended from being bullied by Mick Collins. It is not surprising that my father never warmed to the narrator in Francis Stuart's quasi-fictional account (see Appendix 1, page 330) of a similar episode, where Stuart recounts how he fell asleep on his watch while his fellow prisoners were tunnelling out to meet the party tunnelling in, with the result that all were apprehended. My father was taken to Kilmainham Jail and later to Gormanstown Prison Camp, in County Meath, where he was supposed to be interned indefinitely. My mother took her baby and went to stay with her brother, Moss, the curate, in Valleymount (aka Black Ditches), in the mountains above Blessington village.

⚃   ⚃   ⚃

The district of Valleymount – 'up the Featherbed and towards the mountain' – was remote and beautiful; much of it is now under the waters of the reservoir. It was reached, if my memory has it right, from the Blessington end of the steam tramline, which had many traits in common with the West Clare Railway of Percy French. It was several miles on foot from the nearest stop. Moss's parishioners were mostly sheep farmers. Mass offerings were often: 'A half-crown for the Missus and a half-crown for the ewes.' Valleymount was, moreover, traditionally a 'hot-bed of disaffection' going back at least to the time of Fiach MacHugh O'Byrne, 'the Firebrand of the Mountains', in the first Elizabeth's day. Moss's 'boy' (servant), Jack Twomey, was reputed to be the local 'head centre' of the 'Irregulars'. Moss and he were comfortable together on a need-to-know basis. I remember myself that, in later years, whenever Jack drove us in Moss's car past Maryborough Jail in Portlaoise, he would intone grimly, 'Avoid evil and do good'; he had spent some time there. There was also a metal mined in the parish, lead, I think, but the miners were a breed apart and a law unto themselves.

My mother's visit must have been in August 1922, between my father's arrest, for which I do not have the date by me, and the start of the school year in early September. Some time after her arrival there, she was involved in a classical Irish, 1920s, trench-coat drama. Night had fallen when a heavy knocking came at the curacy door: a party of anti-Treaty Volunteers was seeking shelter. As the drill then was, everyone in the house got up to leave the beds to the men. I was sleeping on the inside of my mother's bed next the wall, and she went to lift me to let Mr de Valera, who was of the party, get a decent sleep. 'Leave her there,' he said. 'I have five of my own.' She did, but crept in again with the dawn to retrieve me, put her hand over my mouth and ran as hard as she could with me, down the road, out of earshot. We were always told, when we heard this story, that Mr de Valera was returning from the south and his efforts to avoid the Civil War. As an irreverent young woman in France after the Second World War, I made this incident a talking point. If ever I was asked, did I know '*ce de Valera?*', I would reply, '*Si je le connais. J'ai couché avec!*' It never failed of its effect. What is certain is that ever afterwards, Mr de Valera was very fond of me personally.

On a more sombre note, I think it may have been at this point that my mother learnt that Michael Collins had been killed. Poor, poor Margaret! Poor, poor Mammy! In her missal I find an *In Memoriam* card for Harry Boland – the first heartbreak; none for Michael. It is only now that I realise that there may be readers who will not know that Harry and Michael, who had been David and Jonathan, were on opposite sides during the Civil War, and that Michael's men shot and killed Harry during its course.

ᘓ   ᘓ   ᘓ

The litany of grief was to continue. In late November, Erskine Childers, the brilliant novelist who was the republican press officer, was shot dead by the forces of the Provisional government: another terrible blow for my Uncle Paddy, comparable to the execution of Seán MacDermott. Before he died, Erskine asked to be allowed to speak with Dr Patrick Browne of Maynooth, and was refused. One of the Childers biographers – I forget which – seems to think that this Dr *Brown*, as he has it, was a medical doctor. Then, in rapid succession, as most people (once it was everybody) know, came the executions, by the Free State, of the four comrades: Rory O'Connor, Liam Mellowes, Joseph McKelvey and Richard Barrett. My Uncle Paddy's poem used at one time to appear regularly in the *Irish Press* on the anniversary of their death, 8 December 1922. I quote it below in full:

Rory and Liam are dead and
    gone,
Star of the Morning, Mary,
    come,
Slain at the Eighth of December's
    dawn,
Mary Immaculate, guide them
    home.

Rory and Liam and Dick and
    Joe,
Star of the Morning, Mary,
    come,
Red is their hearts' blood, their
    souls like snow,
Mary Immaculate, guide them
    home.

Their slayers have rung no
    passing bell,
Star of the Morning, Mary,
    come,
But the rifles' crack is their
    funeral knell,
Mary Immaculate, guide them
    home.

Their eyes are steady in face
    of Death,
Star of the Morning, Mary,
    come,
For their minds are rapt by
    the vision of faith,
Mary Immaculate, guide them
    home.

For Winter will pass and
    Spring be born,
Star of the Morning, Mary,
    come,
And Freedom will waken the
    land at morn,
Mary Immaculate, guide them
    home.

And what is Death but an
    envoy sped,
Star of the Morning, Mary,
    come,
With a call from the Heaven
    of Ireland's dead?
Mary Immaculate, guide them
    home.

Why reckon the pangs that
    have sufficed,
Star of the Morning, Mary,
    come,
To bring free souls to their
    Captain, Christ?
Mary Immaculate, guide them
    home.

Rory and Liam are dead and
    gone,
Star of the Morning, Mary,
    come,
They have found the lights
    that go out at dawn,
Mary Immaculate, guide them
    home.

Rory and Liam and Dick and
    Joe,
Star of the Morning, Mary,
    come,
Our starlight fades, but the
    road they know,
Mary Immaculate, guide them
    home.

Another anecdote from those days involves the MacSwiney sisters, Mary and Annie. I am not sure exactly where it took place, but my Uncle Paddy and the two ladies were all arrested together. When Páidín O'Keefe, the famously plain-spoken Governor of Mountjoy Jail, saw Dr Paddy Browne brought before him, he was not at a loss for words: 'Christ, Paddy,' he exclaimed, 'they'll unfrock you for this!' Years after, some kind soul abstracted Dick Mulcahy's memorandum on this incident from the former minister's files and made a present of it to my uncle. It recounts that Dr Browne used language 'unbecoming to his cloth', and also that 'there were found on his person certain verses in the Irish language of indifferent merit ...' As he passed this document over to my father, my uncle exploded with indignation, 'Of indifferent merit, indeed! That from Dick Mulcahy! That master of anacoluthon!' The dictionary tells me that anacoluthon is 'a sentence or construction in which the expected grammatical construction is absent.'

PART V: GREY AREA

After my father's arrest in 1922, my mother's life became a desperate treadmill of wage-earning, teaching from nine in the morning till after nine at night. She paid the rent on my father's office and she paid his typist. She taught maths and Irish in Miss Louise Gavan Duffy's Irish-speaking primary school, Scoil Bhríde in Earlsfort Terrace, and Irish to adults in the Rathmines Tech. Cassie and the uncles, Moss and Paddy, and many of her woman friends from the Boycott days, like my godmother, Maureen Power, helped cope with the baby. The historian

Dr Dick Hayes, our family doctor and close friend always, who had fought with Tom Ashe at the Battle of Ashbourne in 1916, had espoused the pro-Treaty cause, but continued to be an ever-present help in time of trouble. Late one night, in response to an urgent call from my mother, he called to the flat to inspect a very sick baby. Sitting by the fire he found the two formidable Misses MacSwiney (see above), sisters of the late, revered Mayor of Cork who had died on hunger strike; they were sharing Mammy's vigil. My cot was in the sitting room. Ignoring the other occupants he went straight over to me, stuck his hand into his (inevitable) trench-coat pocket, drew out his revolver and addressed the baby: 'Did you ever see one of these before?' 'Dick,' cried my mother, 'what are you doing? Are you gone mad?' 'I want,' he replied grimly, with his eyes studiously avoiding the two ladies by the fire, 'those two harridans to know I am armed!' It was on the occasion of this illness of mine that a well-meaning neighbour was distressed to hear my mother and my Uncle Paddy 'talking to the poor little thing in Irish and she like to die.' She felt Irish was too cranky and difficult a language for a sick child. Manifestly, I did not die, and I cannot remember ever not knowing Irish, or English either for that matter.

℀   ℀   ℀

Some time before Christmas 1923, circumstances, and some human goodwill, contrived my father's escape from Gormanstown. My father had planned the new street-lighting scheme for Wexford town, which had now reached completion. The Mayor of Wexford, the father of Brendan Corish, later to become leader of the Irish Labour Party, refused to pay the contractors until the planning engineer had passed the work as satisfactory. He took this unexceptionable decision in the full knowledge that it would involve at least the temporary release of that planning engineer from internment, and he refused to be moved from it. Meanwhile Desmond FitzGerald, then a minister in the new Free State government (and whose wife, Mabel, was a close friend of my mother's, not to mention an ardent republican) backed Mayor Corish's stand, for old times' sake, so that my father was released, presumably on parole. I had always assumed he broke his parole and went on the run. Desmond's son

Garret now tells me that Desmond, as Foreign Minister, issued my father with a passport and told him to take my mother to Paris. The following August, on the twenty-fifth day, my brother Séamus was born. I am told that when my father first appeared in our flat, probably at Christmas, my reaction was to order his immediate expulsion: 'Put that horrid man out of my house.' Misguidedly he took up the challenge. 'I'll put you in the wastepaper-basket,' he said, whereupon I roared with outrage. The following paragraphs are my father's own account of subsequent political developments, as told to Michael McInerney of *The Irish Times* in 1974:

'The Civil War ended in May 1923, when Frank Aiken, as Chief of Staff, or-dered the Anti-Treaty forces to cease fire. De Valera endorsed the decision, and "once free he set himself to put things on a solider democratic foundation, and formed Sinn Féin on an ad hoc basis to fight the 1923 General Election."

In that May of 1923 all the evidence seemed to show a shattered, scattered Republican Movement, a poor shadow of the great Movement of 1918–21, with the Free State solidly established, but in August, the new political drive by de Valera won 44 seats in the general election and the hope was born that, perhaps, after all, real gains would be made through political action. "By November," Mr MacEntee says, "a Sinn Féin Ard Fheis of well over 1,000 delegates was held in Dublin." It elected de Valera as its President, though he was by then in jail, and Caitlín Brugha and Seán MacEntee were elected as treasurers. A year later Sinn Féin won some spectacular by-election victories, including one by Seán Lemass [in North Dublin]. That victory was so utterly unexpected that it startled even extreme Republicans. It was the end of one epoch, that of physical-force, and the beginning of a new, the era of Parlia-mentary politics combined with a mass extra-Parliamentary force, the mili-tant political party-organisation. The 1917 Sinn Féin was being reborn. The 1924 Ard Fheis even outshone that of 1923. People were beginning to see politics as the road forward.

The revived Party went on to further successes in the 1925 by-elections, but already the signs of a new, dividing issue were appearing both inside Sinn Féin and inside the I.R.A. First, the I.R.A. broke with Dev. and Sinn Féin in November 1925, and then came that March 1926 Ard Fheis when de Valera proposed a campaign to get rid of the Oath of Allegiance for Dáil Deputies, and, with that oath gone, to enter the Dáil and seek political power.

The Republicans were split again, for the third time in three years, and de

Valera, for the third time, had to rebuild a scattered team; as in 1917 after the Rising, as in 1923 after the Civil War, and now again. But within the week, the old team – de Valera, Lemass, O'Kelly, Aiken, Ryan, Boland, Ruttledge, Derrig, MacEntee, later to be joined by Mrs Pearse, Madame Markievicz and Mrs Clarke – were meeting in de Valera's home in Dublin's Sandymount, with the aim of launching a new Party. It was called Fianna Fáil [Soldiers of Destiny], and again Mr MacEntee was elected a Treasurer and Executive member.

He was a founder and executive of Fianna Fáil as he had been a founder of the 1917 Sinn Féin and the 1923 Sinn Féin. With him as Treasurer was Dr. Jim Ryan, who, like himself, was to become Minister for Finance in a Fianna Fáil Government. This time they founded a party which was to endure and prosper. Perhaps it was the only one to be built on reality.

Of the growth of Fianna Fáil, Mr MacEntee says: "For more than five years hardly any of us were at home for a single night or any week-end. Lemass bought up four or five second-hand Ford cars, 'old bangers', and with them we toured every parish in the country founding Fianna Fáil branches on the solid basis of Old I.R.A. and Sinn Féin members. They were all marvellous people.'"

❦ ❦ ❦

Meanwhile my mother's unrelenting struggle to fund the family continued. We had moved by now to a pleasant, semi-detached house at 42 Marlborough Road, and I had been taught to say, 'I am Máire MacEntee, 42 Marlborough (Mawbrill) Road, please take me home,' in case I wandered. I must have been about three. Opposite, on the northern side, down to our right and towards Herbert (Herbrill) Park, lived Mabel FitzGerald with her then three sons, Deimín, Pierce and Fergus; on the same side as the FitzGeralds but up towards Ranelagh, at number 39, lived the writer and indefatigable republican, left-wing activist, Peadar O'Donnell; on the same side as us, and again to our right, was a nest of Plunketts – I was never sure how many or which. Other neighbours were: Professor John Synge, the mathematician (nephew of JM Synge), and his Canadian wife Bessie, same side as us, up towards Ranelagh; same side again and down towards Herbert Park were Fred and Sheila May, musician and actress, brother and sister, teenagers when I knew them; next door to us was the O'Gorman family and Joan, technically my 'best friend' – everyone had to have one.

At that time Mrs FitzGerald's espousal of the republican cause was so intense that she would not let her husband, Desmond, a minister in the Free State government, come home to his own house. Garret, as yet unborn then – indeed uncontemplated – remembers hearing, when he was small, how during that time of stress his always-rebellious brother, Pierce, would, whenever their father was present, address him as 'you bloody traitor', as in, for example, 'Pass the salt, you bloody traitor.' The two grass widows, Margaret and Mabel, politically and personally close, were company for each other and crossed the road alternately every second night with their little families to spend the night under the one roof and ward off loneliness. When reconciliation was ultimately effected between the warring sides, domestic and military, and Garret was born, my mother was his godmother and my father, had he not been still to some degree *en clandestinité* (on his keeping), was to have been his godfather. Garret was always known in our family, with great affection, as 'the child of reconciliation'. That friendship, like that with Dick Hayes, survived, and was even strengthened by the Civil War. When my father was dying, the only politician, other than my Conor, he wished to see was Garret, to tell him how he regretted the Civil War and how proud Garret's godmother had always been of her godson. However, back in the ambiguous days at the close of civil hostilities, before he was born, Garret's godmother had renewed troubles to face.

The Treasonable Offences Act of 1925 meant that, although my father was materially at liberty, he could be arrested and reimprisoned at any moment. Further, the requirement that all Local Government employees make a declaration of loyalty to the new State lost my mother her post at the Rathmines Tech. and some similar regulation had her dismissed from Scoil Bhríde, which was a national school. All the while my father was mostly absent from home and certainly unable to contribute much to its upkeep. At this point, in her desperation, she saw in the newspaper that Alexandra School – Protestant and academically distinguished – was looking for someone to teach Irish. The headmistress at the time was the celebrated Dr Isabella Mulvaney, Trinity's first woman graduate to receive a doctorate. When she realised that my mother was competent to teach not only Irish, as required by the new dispensation, but also to teach maths to a fairly high standard, she was enchanted and exclaimed, 'Mrs MacEntee, you are an answer to prayer.' It was then that my poor mother summoned up all her courage and literally took hold of the edge of Dr Mulvaney's desk in front of her with both hands, to steady herself, and said, 'Dr Mulvaney, I must tell you that my husband has been in jail for his political opinions and that I share them.' Dr Mulvaney's reply was unhesitating, 'Mrs MacEntee, I am not employing your husband. If, however, you feel you could keep this situation from the parents, I should be deeply obliged.' From that moment on, the two women were firm friends, and Alexandra treated my mother with immense generosity.

೮೩   ೮೩   ೮೩

Three of my most vivid memories are related directly to those paradoxical times. Although our finances were as precarious as I have described them, we kept two maids: Mary O'Flanagan and Lydia Sermon, both of whom were remarkably devoted and remarkably gifted. Lydia was an expert tailoress who finally became head of the cutting room in Richard Allen's, one of Dublin's most fashionable dress shops, while Mary had immense poise and natural refinement and saw my parents' children, all three, safely through into their teens. One day, when I was about three years old, I was tagging up and down stairs after Mary when the front door-bell rang. We went to open it and there was a man outside, at the top of the steps up to our door, who said absolutely nothing but ran straight past us, down the back stairs to the basement and out the back door to the garden. We followed more slowly and watched from the return window. He swung himself over our back wall, into the lane and from there over another wall into Muckross Convent grounds. He was barely out of sight when the bell rang again, and we went back to open the door again. This time there were several men outside, in what I now know to have been Free State Army uniform. They asked Mary had anybody come to the door recently. She replied calmly that no one had. I, of course, knew that this was not true, but some inchoate instinct kept me silent, and the men went away. When, some years later, I reported the incident to my mother, she merely said, 'Oh, that was Peadar O'Donnell.'

In my second political memory I am, I think, somewhat older. I am in the kitchen, again with Mary, and I do not know why I am not at school. The milkman comes to the basement door below our front steps and asks me do I know that my 'Da' is now a TD (*Teachta Dála*, member of the Dáil, our parliament). I loftily ignore him, but it registers.

My third memory has high potential for drama. There are two unknown men in bowler hats in our hall in the early morning. There is also a very grand old lady in one of those hats, like a very large birthday cake smothered in veiling, that ladies of her generation still wore. She imperiously demands a chair and gets one. She is the Countess Plunkett, our landlady and the mother of the executed 1916 leader, Joseph Plunkett. Lydia and Mary are murmuring angrily about bailiffs, and about heroes who died for their country, and about Daddy, who would if he could. Countess Plunkett has come for her rent. My father comes running downstairs, pulling on his jacket. He pays no attention to anyone, but rushes out the front door, down the granite steps and into our car. We now have a little two-seater car, with solid wheels and two extra 'dicky' seats in the boot for me and Séamus. Was it a Trojan? Anyway, my father is off to the National Bank in Dame Street, the old Land Bank, where Tim Caffrey, the manager, is sympathetic to the republican cause. He is successful, and the Countess withdraws her Myrmidons, but a coolness has been created between Plunketts in general and MacEntees that is never properly resolved.

By this time I have two homes: Marlborough Road and Dunquin, which has a totally different flavour and demands a chapter to itself.

CHAPTER III

A Celebration of the Irish Language

Part i: *Alternative Lifestyle*

Part ii: *Cultural Controversy*

Part iii: *'A Cloud no bigger than a Man's Hand'*

PART I: ALTERNATIVE LIFESTYLE

I must now set down my personal memories of the 1920s and 1930s and, in particular, of the part played by the Irish language in the life of Ireland at that time, and I must admit to a feeling of some discomfort at the task. If I have understood its nature correctly, it is a peculiarly difficult one. It involves bringing to life a period of the past beyond the reach of memory for a substantial part of my readership, on the one hand, and yet too recent to have become fashionable, on the other. It involves doing this on a basis of personal recollections from childhood and early youth; this is a positive minefield of booby traps. Like all people whose talent it is to exploit their emotions, I prefer to do so under a decent veil of literary convention, and not in any immediate capacity as witness, or advocate. Yet this is the double role I am now called upon to assume. I may say that so profound was the conditioning in ancestral piety through which I, like all my generation, passed, that I can in no way refuse to take on this function, which has fallen to me through the ineluctable processes of time. I must grapple with it as best I can, and I must ask the reader to bear with me in the process. The era for which I speak was no mean era, and the people who inhabited it no mean people. Perhaps they deserve a better chronicler.

છ   છ   છ

By now you will want to know what all this soul-searching has to do with the Irish language and its celebration; I will explain. My parents and their circle, at the time of the foundation of the Republic, believed absolutely and unapologetically in the restoration of Irish to its rightful dignity as the national language of Ireland, and they believed in its preservation and restoration as a living language. This was on their part no joyless and xenophobic enterprise, but a great, life-enhancing undertaking that permeated and enriched their entire experience and was, without exaggeration, an influential factor in every quotidian decision they were called upon to take. They were part of that body of young people throughout the country, in their late twenties and early thirties – an intellectual leaven – many of them exceptionally gifted and imbued with a love of and an enthusiasm for art and culture in all their forms, a love and enthusiasm that (alas!) could only appear simplistic and naïve today. They were, above all, incandescent with fun and hope and self-confidence, which perhaps burnt all the brighter in that they were emerging from times of discouragement and very real grief.

The central inspirational figure of this group, as you will perhaps have gathered, was undoubtedly my mother's brother, Paddy, a linguist, classicist and humanist in the great tradition of Erasmus and More. As is so often the case in rural Ireland, the bond between brother and sister was very close. Their parents, as we saw, belonged to the last generation of native speakers in the Tipperary of Kickham and *Knocknagow*, and the triumphant establishment of Irish as an academic subject during their schooldays did the rest: I have never known any two people more effortlessly and completely bilingual. My father, on the other hand, was a theoretical revivalist only. He learnt Irish as an adult as he learnt German, but never spoke any language other than English with any ease. In this he was typical of his Northern, urban culture, which did not produce linguists, for want of the facility, essential to that end, for making a fool of oneself. His Irish, however, infiltrated his poetry, as it did all that generation's.

Those students who had the good fortune to attend my mother's lectures on the *Dánta Grá* (classical Irish love poetry), in University College, Dublin, will remember the extraordinary phenomenon of a warm and witty, twentieth-century, middle-aged, middle-class Irish lady entering completely into the mind of the medieval Gaelic poet in his lighter moments, and communicating her understanding and her enjoyment to her hearers. Here were two highly sophisticated and idiosyncratic cultures complementing and illuminating each other. That symbiosis has been a part of my life as far back as I can remember. People who experienced it still talk of it. Our present parish priest in Howth remembers her saying, 'You must not look at the seventeenth century through the spectacles of the present day.'

CR   CR   CR

In the troubled circumstances of those times, which I have tried to convey in the last chapter, my father was much away from home and his place was taken by my Uncle Paddy. Every Friday he came from Maynooth to stay the night and I went with him on the crossbar of his bicycle to his Mass on Saturday mornings in Loreto Hall. Our spare room was known as Pábú's room. 'Pabú' was my early realisation of Paddy Browne, which stuck to him for life. The two men, Paddy and my father, were very different in temperament but identical in ideals. Their friendship was profound and enduring, founded on trust, respect and mutual generosity. A lesser man than my father might have resented his children's education being taken over by his brother-in-law; a lesser man than my uncle might have insinuated into that education some disenchantment with the realities of pragmatic politics. It did not happen.

It is said that a too perfect childhood unfits you for life, but I would not barter my golden childhood for any possible alternative. The theory of the time was that if one adult in a household spoke consistently to the children only in a given language, the children would grow up speaking that language, irrespective of what other languages they might also learn. In our household my Uncle Paddy constituted himself that adult, and he never spoke to us except in Irish. He did this so successfully that, for a long time, I believed him to know no other tongue. I was an incurious, self-centred, unobservant child, a lot of whose life went on inside her head, but sometime after my First Communion, when I was interpreting for my uncle to a petrol-pump attendant on the road from Dublin to the Dingle Peninsula, it dawned on me that the exercise might not be entirely necessary; the adults were smiling in a peculiar way.

It was thanks to the constant presence of my Uncle Paddy that all my knowledge of the world of art and letters was mediated through Irish. At the age of four I played the boy that leads the blind prophet Tiresias on stage in my uncle's translation of the *Antigone* of Sophocles – performed in Loreto Hall by the students – and I was deeply conversant with the story, although in my secret heart I thought Antigone was too big a girl to be altogether interesting. At ten I created the part of Joas in the first production in Irish of Racine's *Athalie* – Pabú's translation again – and identified completely with the boy-king in his breathtaking exchange with the terrible queen. There is a part of my mind that still thinks of *Treasure Island* as a novel written in

Irish because my uncle read it to us in Irish, translating at sight from the English as he went along. It was the kind of party-piece, polymath that he was, that he could always perform with panache, and that we took for granted. He taught me my first Latin (through Irish) at six, my first, indeed my only Greek at ten. He taught my brother maths and physics, also through Irish – we never spoke any other language with him. He spoke English only to my father in the family. He taught my little sister to play Bridge; my lack of card sense he deplored. With him we read and memorised and recited reams of poetry in several languages; he himself retained from boyhood the wonderful, verbal memory of the Irish rural illiterate, now a thing of the past. We read omnivorously; the big eighteen-inch by twelve-inch edition of Shakespeare's historical plays was too heavy for us to handle and we crawled all over it on the floor. For many years afterwards I believed a 'bastard' to be an official of the English Royal Court, something like a *poursuivant*. Some of us, I'm afraid, also scribbled on some of the pages. We have that same book here in our house in Howth yet. These are trivial juvenile memories: I list them only to establish my credentials as a witness to an extraordinary experiment in what would now be called alternative lifestyles; to bear witness to its influence and effects at the time, or to its lack of them, then and thereafter.

03   03   03

Readers will remember that, after the execution of the leaders in 1916 – of whom Seán MacDermott had been his particular friend – my uncle's grief was so terrible that his reason was feared for, and even his life. He took refuge in the extreme southwest, in the Kerry Gaeltacht, and came to terms with his desolation, clawing his way back to sanity and hope by dedicating himself to the cause of creating in Ireland an Irish-speaking society of such sweetness and power that it would reverse the course of history and make the Irish language, in every field, a cultural medium of which not only Ireland but Europe could be proud. He made his home in the parish of Dunquin; he built his house there, within the boundaries of an old religious settlement founded by Saint Gobnait; it was, and remains, the most westerly dwelling on the mainland of Ireland, 'the nearest house in Ireland to America', as we would proudly assert as children. The house was built for us, his sister's children, so that we would grow up speaking Irish naturally, in completely Irish-speaking surroundings. That was more than seventy years ago. I have heard my uncle described in present-day Dunquin as 'the first of the affluent summer visitors'. Nothing could more thoroughly misrepresent the truth. The modest, red-roofed bungalow, clinker-built of creosoted timbers to a Scandinavian plan, was my uncle's *home*. He spent every Christmas there, every Easter, the strange ten-day recess that Maynooth took at Whit for what had once been political reasons (to allow students to vote in 1918), and the long summer of the academic holidays, from June to September inclusive. We three, my brother, my sister and I, spent most of that time – often including Christmas – with him there.

It was just after my third birthday (4 April 1925) that I first arrived at Tigh na Cille (the House on the Old Church site), in the townland of Cill Ghobnait, in the parish of Dunquin, County Kerry. We had been on the road, in a convoy of model-T Ford cars, for two days – Paddy, Moss and my father driving. We broke the journey at Limerick. Beyond Adare the roads were mostly unmetalled and passengers, drivers and baggage – bedding mostly – were covered in white dust. By the time we arrived dusk had set in, and the square timber house was quite dark inside. The kitchen ceiling wasn't yet in place, and you could look up into the shadowy rafters. The room seemed crowded with large, indistinct people – the neighbours. I stood in the doorway – no door as yet – rubbed my eyes and announced, '*Tá míogarnach im' shúile,*' literally, 'There is a dozing in my eyes.' The remark had a most gratifying reception; the Dublin child spoke Irish. It may be worth mentioning that the remark is baby-talk, it is not a recognised idiom and no adult would use it. My mother introduced my father. '*An é seo do chéile leapan, a Mháiréad?*' an old woman enquired forthrightly (Is this your bed-companion?) My brother Séamus, eight months old, was put to sleep in a dressing-table drawer, tea was brewed from the well-water buckets in the kitchen, the paraffin lamps were lit and the bedsteads (four double) set up: we were at home.

The house had been designed by the family's close friend, the architect Tom Cullen (not Mick Collins's aide, but none the less a convinced republican); his firm had been responsible for the design of the UCD building on Earlsfort Terrace (never completed). Our bungalow was creosoted black on the outside with a green front door and white framed windows; it had a brilliant red, felt, pyramid roof and was anchored to its foundations by two massive brick chimneys: it looked like a child's drawing of a very pretty house. There should have been a back door also, but a local wiseacre persuaded my uncle that this would make the house draughty and less of a *cúirt* (court), as all houses not on the traditional plan (see below) were called. From the slight elevation on which the fifth-century religious foundation, Cill Ghobnait (The Church of Gobnait), had stood, the house had a panoramic prospect of the entire parish to the south and east; from Marhin Hill (Cruach Mharthain) on the left-hand rim to Dunmore Head (An Dún Mór) on the right, jutting out to sea; to the north we looked out on the ruined convent church, the actual *cill*, a rock shelter construction, one wall of which was living rock while the remainder had been enclosed by several courses of mighty masonry, Cyclopean, and roofed over perhaps with thatch. A great stone cross, the focal point of the 'rounds' (*turas*) that were held annually on 11 February, as they are to this day, was sunk towards the centre of the building, and between it and the western cliff was a holy well (*Tobar Ghobnait*); other Stations were two cairns (*leachtáin*) to the east of the complex. My memories of the *turas* are early and confused – we were usually back in Dublin before then. My impression is of a purely religious occasion, with none of the recreational associations of the 'pattern' in other traditions. From the western windows of the new house you saw the Blasket Islands and the infinite Atlantic. On Sundays, when we were older, we were sent out to sit on our western wall and watch for the island boats (*naomhóga*) leaving the Great Blasket (An tOileán Tiar) in procession for my uncle's nine o'clock Mass. Only when the islanders had made the landing-cove (*an caladh*), would the celebrant (my uncle) leave for the chapel. You could always recognise an islander: the paths on the Island were so narrow that they walked in single file, like Red Indians, and they said 'a hyahin', not 'a hyawin', for '*a Shéain*'.

We knew the story of the foundation of the *cill* from way back. Its foundress, Saint Gobnait, was the patron saint of blacksmiths (*gaibhne*) – as also of bees – and consequently had the useful domestic gift of being able to carry live coals in her apron. When she was establishing her religious house in Dunquin, she went first to the forge for live coals to kindle the new convent's fire. As is often the case, the forge was a great meeting place for gossips and idlers, and a crowd of young men was gathered around the door when Gobnait arrived. She asked the smith for an apronful of coals – live, of course – and received them in her apron. As she was going out the door, however, holding her skirts high to carry the coals, she revealed her barefoot ankles to the watching audience. One of the young men remarked aloud, '*Nach néata an dá alt coise ata fúithi!*' (That's the neat pair of ankles!) The saint heard '*agus níor mhiste leí an chaint sin*' (she was not displeased by that speech), and immediately the coals burnt down through her apron! History does not relate whether or not she was ever able to employ this gift again.

The whole landscape of our childhood was landmarked by these stories, some foreign, some native. It seemed to us that the gentle husband of a churlish wife (*fear séimh ag bean bhorb*), who is evoked in the charm against bleeding and who put Our Lady and her infant to sleep in the prickly barley-straw (*colg*), had his stable in a lean-to against our eastern wall; we thought of direction automatically, as did the local children, in points of the compass. In the great sea-locked cave that broke the flank of Dunmore Head lived the Cyclops, and in my uncle's version of the tale, when Ulysses escaped from his terrible captivity he brought Séamus and Máire and Biddín (our housekeeper's daughter) with him, clinging to the undersides of the sheep; we did not as yet have Barbara.

My greatest hero, from the beginning, was Pierce Ferriter, the seventeenth-century poet-captain, whose name resounded through the district – Baile an Fheiritéirigh, Ceathrú an Fheiritéirigh (Ferriter's Town, or Ballyferriter, Ferriter's Quarter) – and resounded through our house, almost to the exclusion of any other, one particular summer when Father Dineen (he of the Dictionary) made us his headquarters and my uncle his chauffeur and amanuensis, while he combed the district for folklore about Ferriter for his new edition of the poems. The emerging personality enchanted us children; Ferriter, in the popular mind, is half hero and half rogue and his poetry, much of which survives in folklore, is riveting. This fascination continued into my adult years and, at the time of writing, has resolved itself into a substantial piece of prize-winning research in Irish, at present with my friend, Caoimhín Ó Marcaigh, the publisher, and, hopefully, due to appear shortly. May I give one lyric in translation as a foretaste:

An bhean dob' ansa liom fé'n ngréin
(from the Irish of Pierce Ferriter)

The woman whom I loved the most,
Did not suppose me worth a pin
But by the shoulder of my host
Sat --- wed! Harsh stroke! – and I within.

The little fallow field I broke,
Long labouring, for myself alone –
Came yesterday one from the road,
Harrowed and sowed it for his own.

My curse on him who breaks a clod
Nor leaves his green sod fallow lay –
For when that I was called abroad
My nest of eggs was robbed away.

If I were wont abroad to go
And leave my nest perforce behind,
About its edge a breath I'd blow
Would make it loathed of birdly kind.

Till love like coal go packed in sack
All pacts of love I do reprove;
My heart's turned cinder, burnt and black,
On the cold slack of women's love.

O pity him who must repent
A love misspent as I have done,
Pity the man who goes unwed –
Pity instead who loves but one.

As a child, my conception of these mighty figures was as being near-contemporaneous with each other and with ourselves. They included Gregory Ashe (Griaghair Ághas), whose son, Tom Ashe, had died on hunger strike in 1917. Gregory was a strong farmer in the area north of Dingle, to whom every year young men from Dunquin and district went as serving boys, and who typified for us power, mystery and distance. A similar legendary patriarch in our minds was Séathra 'ac Criomhthain (Geoffrey MacCrohan) who, once upon a time, farmed the Great Glen and the Common (*coimin*) of Baile na hAbha (Ballinahow), to the northeast of the parish. He was a man of enormous strength and personal authority, who became blind in his old age. I have not identified him historically, but Séathra's Field is called after him to this day. It is told that, when he was a sightless old man, his sons let a valuable colt go wild on the mountain and could not recapture it. Séathra told them to set his chair at a certain gap and drive the colt down towards it. This was done. As the colt surged through the gap, Séathra reached out blindly and grabbed his foreleg. Such was the strength of his grip, that the leg snapped and the beautiful young creature turned a cartwheel in the air, came down on his back and broke his neck! There seemed to be no end to such characters and their adventures: there was Gadaí Mór Gleanna Fleisce (the great thief of Glenflesk), who was an O'Donohue of the Glens and the ancestor of Daniel O'Connell's grandmother, and she was a witch; there was Lord Ventry, a bad landlord, and his formidable woman agent, Clara Hussey, who 'picked him out of the wet' – a mysterious phrase, heard only in English and never explained. There was, of course, Gearóid Iarla, Earl of Desmond, the wizard and poet, of whom the mocking quatrain, which I translate, was written:

A mharcaigh fá ndéantar fonóid Horseman, harassed by jesters,
Nó an gcuala tú scéal Ghearóid Iarla? Earl Gerald's story hear,
Gur éalaigh uaidh a Chontaois Of how his Countess left him
Le luaircín ar feadh bliana! With a midget for a year!

I hope one day to write a novel about him.

ℭ℘   ℭ℘   ℭ℘

My mother, herself being a teacher, regarded school primarily as a babysitting service and yanked us in and out as it suited her. In Dublin we attended Alexandra, for obvious reasons, of which more later; our attendance at Scoil Ghobnait in Dunquin was not unconnected with the need to keep up the numbers and ensure a two-teacher school. It was a typical Irish, two-roomed national school, with four classes, from infants up, in one large room under 'the Mistress' (An Mhaistreás), and four in the other, up to eighth class, under 'the Master' (An Máistir) – fifty or so pupils in each. I remember seeing the number one hundred and eleven chalked on the attendance-board (111), and catching a glimpse of the fascination of mathematics.

Alexandra and Dunquin were very different: no one got hit in Alexandra – everyone, sooner or later, except for a very few quiet and good girls, of whom I was one, got hit in Dunquin. Further, I must say that I never saw anyone hit for anything *other than* failure at lessons. We were all too docile and/or cowed for actual misbehaviour. It must also be said that the genetic pool of intelligence in those two classrooms was very high and that most of us were eager to learn. In those days young people stayed on at primary school up to fifteen or sixteen years of age, preparing for civil service and similar examinations. Our particular Master, Muiris Ó Dálaigh, a son of 'old' Master Daly, was very generous with his time and trouble to such pupils, taking them for extra classes after school hours and persuading their parents, where necessary, 'not to stand in their way'. I thought him very handsome – he was dark and olive-skinned; the other girls didn't – he was 'yellow' (*buí*), where the preferred type was fair. He had his own troubles: a cracked knee that caused him a lot of pain, and a doomed romance with the very pretty daughter of the only Protestant house in the district. I think he may have taken his worries out on his pupils; there was one very bright boy who came to school after an illness, jaundiced and listless, and that child got a terrible time and, very shortly afterwards, died. I think Muiris' exasperation with him may have been frustrated affection. It never occurred to any of us to tell tales out of school, and Muiris was not regarded as a *máistir mallaithe* (vicious master). He was a brilliant teacher; I certainly owe him any grasp I have of algebra, and there are interesting facts about the amoeba and the hedgehog (*gráinneog*) which I got from him and that I remember yet. I can also recite 'King Bruce of Scotland' and 'Rich and Rare were the Gems she Wore', raising the pitch at the end of every line like this:

> *'King Bruce of Scotland flung himself* down
> *In a lonely mood* to think'

I can still recite simple addition tables in the musical sing-song that used to make the schoolhouse hum restfully like a beehive. The Mistress, Mrs Lynch, taught me to sew, not very well, but to some practical purpose in later life. We knew the great Munster songs, such as 'Slán le Máighe', 'Casadh an tSúgáin' ('Farewell to Moy', 'The Twisting of the Rope'), and many more by heart, as well as entire passages from the works of Father Peadar Ó Laoghaire. English essays sometimes caused difficulties. For example, if the subject were *My Father*, the Master would chalk key sentences on the blackboard:

> 'My father is a farmer.
> In the Spring he ploughs and sows the seed.
> In the Autumn he reaps ...'

My little sister, Barbara, knew that none of these sentences applied to Daddy, so she wrote:

> 'My father is a Minister.
> He puts tax on things.'

We were, of course, comfortably well off compared to the subsistence farmers and fishermen of the area, but even in Dunquin parish there was at least one strong farmer who would have been substantially wealthier then we. I do not think our way of life was regarded as particularly ostentatious for a priest's household. There was a housekeeper from the place, our dearly loved Bríde, whose daughter, Biddín, became my friend and close companion, and there was a nurse-girl, originally from Ballinasloe, our irreplaceable, loving, ladylike Mary, who looked after us children and subsequently married the local postman. Biddín, in particular, adored Mary, who loved Irish and poetry and clothes and the West Kerry Gaeltacht to the extent that, in the end, she was unable to tear herself away from that heartbreakingly lovely shore. Biddín became a nurse and is now married and living in the Vale of Glamorgan in South Wales – I wonder how it compares in beauty with Dunquin?

СЗ   СЗ   СЗ

It is difficult to convey both the order and the freedom of our Dunquin lives; by contrast our Dublin lives were like boarding school – secure, loving and domestic, no doubt, but essentially restrictive. As anyone who has lived in the country will know, daily life there is far less uneventful for the individual than city life, and country children, of course, are infinitely less excluded. I have glorious memories of the widening of the boreen that led to our house, with cauldrons of pig's head, potatoes and cabbage simmering on our old-fashioned range, and the *meitheal* (working party) – probably not strictly voluntary in this case, as there was a ganger – coming in to eat in shifts. I remember repartee flying between our beloved Bríde, my uncle's marvellous housekeeper, with her willing assistants, our young and pretty woman neighbours, and the laughing husbands, brothers and lovers who were building the road. Peace to their ashes today! One famous 'Ireeshian' among them, Séamus beag Ó Lumhaing, engaged Bríde in a rhyming contest over second helpings:

Séamus:	*A bhean ó Ghleann Loic*	*(a)*
	Tá soc eile ar an muic	*(a)*
	Sin, ná feacamar fós ...	*(b)*
Bríde:	*A Shéamuisín bhig*	*(a)*
	De bhia is de dhigh	*(a)*
	Do fuairis go leor!	*(b)*

I have pointed up the rhymes and I translate below:

Séamus: Woman from Glenlick
              There's a snout on that pig
              We didn't see yet ...

Bríde: My small Shamusheen
              Enough drink and feed
              Is all you will get!

This constant use of rhyme in everyday speech, whether extempore or quoted, undoubtedly affected my personal taste in verse from a very early stage. Rhyming has always seemed to me a natural form of expression, and as long as I can remember I have practised it. Besides, in our family, whether English- or Irish-speaking, versification was taken for granted. My father had been a very promising young poet; my Uncle Paddy wrote English poetry in his youth, but, as he grew older, turned to Irish only and wrote in Irish only, with ever increasing mastery in verse and prose.

Whenever we were not at school we attended my uncle's nine o'clock Mass, that was nine o'clock 'old time' (ie, winter time), of course – country people were still resistant to 'summer time'; cows didn't understand it. Neighbours set their clocks when they saw the priest's car leave the *cill* for the chapel. For a long time there were only two cars in the parish, ours and that of the retired schoolmaster's son, Tom, who was also a skilled amateur mechanic. The 'old' schoolmaster (*an seana-mháistir*), Seán Ó Dálaigh, was the famous 'Common Noun' (his pen-name) who conducted seminars in spoken Irish with all the visiting D. Litts of his time, 'na propers' as he called them; or, as you might say, 'Binchy, Bergin and Best', to quote Myles na gCopaleen, 'Who rose in their night-shifts/To write for the *Zeitschrift.*'

During our earliest years there were two houses beside the chapel on the townland of Baile an Teampaill (the Townland of the Graveyard), that of the King of the Island's daughter, Cáit a' Rí, Synge's 'little hostess' on the Blaskets, and that of my uncle's close friend, Pádraig 'ac Síthigh (Patrick Sheehy). We were welcome in both for the inevitable drink of water (*deoch 'on uisce*) after Mass, always a safe passport for intrusion. The 'Princess' was still a great beauty and was married to a very handsome man. Her husband's parents lived with them and they had no children.

Their then house could have been a model for the vernacular architecture exhibit in a modern folk museum: thatch-roofed, single-storey, white-washed, spotlessly clean and in perfect repair. You stepped straight into the roomy kitchen, where the second door, closed against the weather, stood opposite you across the flagged floor; against the prevailingly shel-tered gable was the chimney breast, with a loft built around it at the level where rafter met wall and, below this, the great open hearth with the crane and the pot-hooks and the fan bellows. If you stood in the ingle and looked up you could see the sky through the chimney opening. There was a table under the window and against one wall a dresser crowded with many-coloured delph. In all these houses, the chairs would be *súgán* (rope)-seated, fashioned with varying degrees of skill. There would be a wooden settle, brightly painted and adorned with a little chintz curtain to hide the pots and pans under it. Hanging conspicuously on the wall would be a picture of the Sacred Heart with the little red lamp lighting before it, or of Our Lady with a blue lamp. All the houses in the parish, ex-cept ours and two other slightly 'grand' dwellings (which were two-storey), followed this pattern, differing only in the degrees of affluence or poverty they displayed. They clung to their sheltered sites, backing into or at right angles to the hill, as if organically part of it; they were enormously pleasing to the eye, and when inclement weather blew in from the sea, to step into the shelter of one of their kitchens through the door 'away from the storm' (*ná luíonn aon tsíon air*) was to experience the true luxury of warmth. Not all were white; some were pastel-washed, yellow or pink, and some had blue-black felt roofing rather than thatch. Most townlands had their own well, some households had hand-pumps. There was no electricity. On the *cill* we had paraffin lamps and candles; the beautiful Aladdin lamp in the parlour (*párlús*) gave the most lovely mellow light from under its alabaster cream ceramic shade.

The 'Princess' (Cáit a' Rí) was a demanding housewife. Her father-in-law, Mickey Casey, complained to my uncle, "*Beir' agus 'tabhair', Athair, an dá fhocal a mharaíonn an duine.*' ('Fetch' and 'carry', Father, two words to kill a man.) In contrast to Cáit's quiet home, the Sheehy house had a 'floor-full' (*lán an urláir*) of exceptionally handsome young people, some already fully grown and emigrated to the States, as was the norm then, when I knew the family. It was in this house that I first realised that the unclothed female body could be beautiful: it took me thirty seconds and I have never tried to tell it until now. I might have been eight or nine that morning when I dashed into the empty kitchen and glimpsed, through the partly-open door up to the 'room', the younger of the two Sheehy daughters, back from America on holiday, stretching as she took off her nightdress. She did not see me, and I backed out quickly. She had seemed to me both translucent and glowing, and it took my breath away. It does still.

Our friendship with the family presented us children with a taxing problem, which indeed we encountered in most company in the parish. Almost every adult male in Dunquin had a nickname and was always referred to by it, but we were never allowed to address anyone by their nickname, or use it in the presence of their kin. It would have been the worst possible manners. Pádraig 'ac Síthigh, the head of the household, was known as 'Piddy' because of his sallow skin, and we had always to remember to say 'Pádraig'. Many, many years later when that family had moved to the new, inland 'Gaeltacht' of County Meath, we, with my Uncle Paddy, visited them and found the old man missing the glory of the landscape of his Kerry home and his skills in the way of life he had left behind. Hanging in the brand new landlocked cowshed were his fisherman's nets; he had brought them with him. '*Ní fhéadfainn iad 'fhagaint im'dhiaidh, Athair*,' he said. (I could not leave them after me, Father.)

⋙ ⋙ ⋙

My Uncle Paddy's Mass was profoundly devotional – it was said, of course, with his back to the congregation and in Latin; it was also economical and elegant, said quite rapidly and with absolute clarity. He had a remarkably beautiful speaking voice and he delivered the timeless Latin Liturgy with no hint of rhetoric or affectation. The little chapel – about a mile from our house across the parish – was almost entirely bare, whitewashed, with plain glass, narrow pointed windows and only two 'pews': 'old' Master Daly's and the Princess's. Some few plain, backless benches of different makes and sizes, belonging to other families, were aligned lengthways against the walls, and the battered wooden confessional stood on the gospel side, just inside the wide open, pointed double doors. The sanctuary, with its red hanging lamp, was railed off from the rest, and the entire interior of the little building was filled with the light and colour of the weather outdoors and with an extraordinary quiet and peace: a truly numinous place. Today there is a beautiful stone plaque on one of the outside walls in my uncle's memory. It bears four lines of verse by the great woman poet of our parish, Cáit Ní Ghaoithin (An Bhab, Bean an Fheiritéirigh), Mrs Kate Ferriter, which capture the spirit of those mornings:

Glóire an teampaill	The glory of the temple
Ag achairt go cráifeach	piously interceding
I Laidean 'si nGaoluinn –	in Latin and Irish –
A mhacalla go brách ann!	his echo [is] there forever!

That Mass was an integral part of our lives, and I still remember, with an almost sacramental reverence, my uncle bringing home the cloths that covered the chalice and the paten and giving them their first washing, and pouring the water out on the grass, before they were laundered by Bríde. I remember, however, one occasion when the reverence wore thin. I must have been about ten. My uncle had driven into Dingle – another world – to do the weekly shopping, and we, that is, me, Biddín, Séamus and the innocent Barbara – whom we always led into mischief – decided to climb the bookshelves in the living room to find out what was on the top shelf. There we found a box of Communion breads, which we promptly ate. We were then, of course, overcome by guilt and fear and we all rushed down to the end of our lane to sit on the ditch and wait for Pábú – we never called him anything else – to come home. When his car reached us we flung ourselves off the ditch and into the car on top of him – all four of us – to beg him to absolve us and save us from certain damnation. He laughed a lot, but explained carefully that what we had done, though disobedient, was not sacriligious, and we were totally reassured. Another time, when we had killed a pet baby rabbit, given to us by the fishermen, with our excessive affection, Pábú was confronted with another theological test. When it became clear that our rabbit would not recover, my brother went straight in to Pábú where he was at work at the sitting-room table, '*A Phábú,*' he asked, '*an dteánn coiníní ar neamh?*' (Do rabbits go to heaven?) My uncle was taken off guard for once. '*Nach bhfuil 'fhios agat ná téann?*', he replied (Don't you know they don't?), whereupon Séamus burst into uncontrollable weeping and declared that he didn't want to go to heaven either if the rabbit couldn't go. My uncle regrouped. Perhaps, he said, if all us children went down to the chapel at once and prayed very hard, for a very long time, God might make an exception. This Jesuitical consolation worked; by the time we got home for tea we were sure that our prayers had been heard. Séamus was always tender-hearted about animals. When we were told the story of the near-sacrifice of Isaac, his sympathies were all with the ram.

❧   ❧   ❧

My uncle's clerk, Mártan Ó hUalacháin (Martin Houlihan), was a small, wiry man, some years older than himself, a subsistence farmer and fisherman of exceptional energy and endurance. He thought nothing of coming straight to the altar to serve Mass after a long night's fishing, or of going on from there to save a day's hay. Like Páid 'ac Síthigh, he was a member of the circle of close personal friends that formed around my uncle and frequented our house every evening. He was extremely witty and, as a result, not altogether popular. From the beginning our house was a great gathering place for the neighbours: various curious and gossipy old ladies, on various pretexts, dropped in during the day to chat with Bríde and to admire the white skin and plump condition of the Dublin children; when school was closed, a constant stream of youngsters of all ages made themselves at home with us, appropriated our wax crayons and depleted our ration of 'wholesome' boiled sweets; and in the evening the men, whose company was my uncle's delight, congregated around the fire in the kitchen. These would not, for the most part, be recognised storytellers, or *seanachaithe* (antiquarians), but men of their host's age group, men in their prime, responsible fathers of families, good companions and superb conversationalists, as good companions had to be in those days before radio when people made their own entertainment, and when the terror of any small, isolated community was the bore.

One of my Uncle Paddy's best poems describes those evenings. It is the lament he wrote on the death of his best beloved among the company,

Peats Mhichíl Connor (Paddy Connor), *trócaire air!* – my little sister called him Percival! – and it is a thing of such perfection that I hesitate to make a botch of it by translating. It is a long poem, fifty-two lines celebrating male friendship and the society in which it flourished, in powerful, unaffected Irish, all at once direct and subtle and wedded expertly to the marvellous, long, flexible line of our contemporary Irish song metres, which echo the rich cadences of Gaelic speech. Indeed, the orchestration of those evenings was by no means the least of my Uncle Paddy's achievements. There was always a text, some book by An Seabhac (Pádraig Ó Siochfhradha), or Tomás 'ac Criomhtháin's *The Islandman,* when it appeared, or, for many hilarious evenings, Father Dineen's wonderful *Foclóir Gaedhilge agus Béarla – An Irish–English Dictionary.* An irreverent friend of mine, Martin Sheridan, God rest him, parodied that Dictionary's famously evocative entries as follows: 'In what other Dictionary could you find a single word for a small, one-legged tailor who was bitten in the balls by a goose on his way to Mass on Easter Sunday?' In other homes in the area it would have been the *Kerryman* newspaper. The readings would be short, just enough to prime the pump, to set the ball rolling, and then, as you have heard, the general discourse would flower. If my uncle were engaged on a translation, say of Plutarch's *Lives,* he would read that, and the company would subject his version to searching and salutary linguistic criticism, driving home their points with quotation and anecdote, while we children sat quiet as mice under the kitchen table, drinking it all in – anything rather than be sent to bed. I can remember that the life of Marc Antony was the great favourite from Plutarch; it had everything: politics, passion, tragedy and war at sea. As Master Daly, the 'old' schoolmaster, whose learning was not marred by any shallow sophistication, once said, when describing the peak of Gaelic felicity – in Irish, of course – '*Dá dtárlófá-sa, Athair, agus Cleopatra mhná, ag feis nó ag* political meeting *ar an* Riviera …' (If you, Father, and a Cleopatra of a woman were to find yourselves at a *feis,* or at a political meeting on the Riviera …) The company sat, prolonging their second bottle of stout well into the summer dusk – two bottles per man, per evening, and whiskey at Christmastime – and their imaginations ranged from the Atlantic to the Isles of Greece, from Puck Fair at Killorglin, where one of them had recently bought a horse, to the ancient world and the siege of Troy.

PART II: CULTURAL CONTROVERSY

Speaking of my uncle's translations brings me to the kind of cultural climate he envisaged for the future of Irish. He set out his credo in the short-lived Irish-language literary review, *Humanitas*. It was, quite simply and brilliantly, to recreate 'the Greek miracle' in the Ireland of the first half of the twentieth century, through the medium of the Irish language. Those of you reading this who may think of the cultural life of Ireland in the 1920s and 1930s as narrow and barren, and blinkered by religiosity, may be interested in Paddy Browne's exposition – in his article in the first issue of the review, in March 1930 – of the distinction between the biblical and the Hellenic, which incorporates his understanding of the 'Greek miracle'. This time, I will translate:

'Let us take the Bible: it contains superb accounts of God and of man's life in accordance with God … They deal with the supernatural … with the miraculous, so that the wonders worked by God are more important [in those accounts] than is the human person … The authors insist on the divinely inspired quality of their discourse. The form of their writings is of far less importance to them than is the content, and they are certainly in no way engaged in giving lessons in form … They were a shy people, who kept their writings and their arcana to themselves.

Think now … of Homer. He also frequently treats of the supernatural, but who would equate his matter with the spirituality of the Bible? Homer cares nothing for spirituality as the Bible understands it: he cares nothing for Truth itself. His attention is rather on the liveliness of the events, the beauty of the narration, the exact description of the heroes and their ladies. The lessons he teaches are those of form and of taste … [Later Greek authors extended their scope.] They taught the arts, etiquette, philosophy, but always after a secular fashion, with that research and demonstration a human being derives from his own secular mental resources alone. Together with the desire to examine and to publish human truth, most of them retained the same yearning for beauty and pursuit of form …

[The early Fathers of the Church] retained many of these traits and strove to adorn Divine Truth with them … but the Middle Ages cared more for the depth of learning and for authority of truth than for literary form. [In the fifteenth and sixteenth centuries, however, the old books resurfaced and intoxicated Europe.] The old qualities were reawakened from their hundreds of years of sleep: human knowledge, human beauty, human form, the human personality. Only too human, it might more properly be said. However that may be, the Renaissance discovered all these and wondered at their comeliness and youth after their long and lonely coma. [The Renaissance had a name for the phenomenon] they called it *Humanismus*. This was the great achievement of the Greek intellect ... that they created it [Humanism] from out their very selves.

The rest of us went wanting till we learned it from the Greeks.'

That is an Irish Catholic priest *writing of the element he found wanting in the Irish society of his day*, and of his determination to make good that absence, at least as far as the Irish language was concerned, even if he had to do it single-handed. His thesis was that the Renaissance had passed Ireland and the Irish language by. Among the other contributors to *Humanitas* were Seosamh Ó Grianna, Donn Piatt, Carol O'Daly, Louis Roche, Liam Gogan, *Torna*, and Daniel Corkery, of whom, sadly, more later.

Brendan Behan, in an uncharacteristically unchivalrous polemical squib, dismissed the rank and file of the Irish-language movement as he encountered it in the 1940s as:

Pioneers páistiúla, pollta, piteánta,
Maighdeana malla, maola, marfánta,
Gach duine acu críochnaithe, cúramach
cráifeach ...

which I translate:

Puerile pioneers, punctured and pansified,
Virgins, slow-witted, insipid, more dead than alive,
All of them done for, care-ridden
and pious ...

John Betjeman wrote a gentler version during his time in Ireland, in the war years:

Along the Dingle peninsula, the Dublin people go,
Some of them speaking the Gaelic and speaking it terrible slow,
Some of them wearing the philibeg and some of them wearing
the shawl,
But Con Curran's daughter, Elisabeth, is the most Gaelic of all!

The Currans were a Dublin family and were friends of James Joyce and self-consciously cultured. All this above *is* funny, and people who remember the 1930s and 1940s will recognise in it a certain accuracy – as far as it goes. It is, however, by no means the whole truth. The ethos of the circle and its values were unequivocally middle-class, but it had the strengths as well as the weaknesses of its caste. As the lady replied to Swinburne in GK Chesterton's glorious parody, 'If you think that virtue is languor, just try it and see.' These people were honourable, industrious, widely read and highly cultivated. It would be easy to base a Chekhovian comedy on the tea parties given by the two unmarried MacSwiney sisters, Mary and Annie, whom we have met briefly in Dublin already, at their house on the townland of Graigue, near Ballyferriter, where the refreshments were, in fact, limited to tea with home-made sponge cake and jams, and where songs were sung in French and German and conversation maintained in – perhaps somewhat stilted – Irish. What it is important to remember, however, is that the accomplishments displayed, linguistic and musical, although ladylike, were genuine, and that an essential ingredient in those idyllic summer evenings – always, in retrospect, bathed in the golden, westering sunlight – was a passionate commitment to Ireland and to Irish: to Irish as the prime catalyst in the creation of a truly 'European' Irish culture.

Perhaps Henry James's New England is a better analogue than Chekhov: New England, all plain living and high thinking. What is certain is that the part played by unmarried ladies, in the years between the two world wars, in ensuring that Irish education through the medium of Irish would not degenerate into chauvinism or provincialism – in the style of DP Moran in *The Leader*, determinedly middlebrow and insular – should not be underestimated. It is owing to the enterprise and generosity of three outstanding religious: Mother Eucharia in Loreto Hall, Saint Stephen's Green, Mother Clement in the Dominican Convent, Eccles Street, and Madame Saint-Étienne in the Drishane Convent in Millstreet, in Cork, that my Uncle Paddy's life's work – his translations of the classical theatre of Europe and the ancient world – did not sink, unperformed, without trace. I wonder how many of us are left who remember the miraculous performance, in Eccles Street, of the young Neasa Ní Shéaghdha (later Mrs Neasa Doran and a formidable Gaelic scholar), as Antigone. Neasa was in time to be the inspiration of the Scottish Highland poet Somhairle McLean, and her hard, virginal, blonde beauty, together with the music of her Munster Irish speech, made her seem the reincarnation of all the indomitable intransigence of the Greek heroine. The elemental confrontation between piety and expedience burned on the stage. It is, of course, a wonderful play for a girls' school to perform, you might say the apotheosis of female adolescent revolt. Other translations of my uncle's which were performed in convent schools were Racine's *Athalie* and Corneille's *Polyeucte*. This type of production, again, was particularly appropriate to *Athalie*, which Racine had written expressly for performance by Madame de Maintenon's academy for young ladies, attached to the court of Louis XIV. I know from personal experience that in the minds of the schoolgirl performers in these pieces, the idea of world theatre, like the music Mendelssohn wrote for the choruses in *Athalie*, became forever inextricably linked with the cause of the Irish language. For us, proficiency in Irish was the gateway to the wider life of the mind. The idea that the study of the language might be stultifying, or claustrophobic was entirely, and unaffectedly, alien to us.

There was, of course, an element of élitism in this, but I am in no kind of doubt but that it is better for young people to conceive of themselves as an élite rather than as victims. It is Saint-Simon, the memorialist of the court of Louis XIV, who is the author of the lapidary phrase, '*Hostile á Racine par gout*': an enemy of Racine on grounds of taste. He seems to have used it descriptively, without pejorative intent, but for my Uncle Paddy that phrase was a touchstone: people whom it fitted were people whose company he did not seek. I never heard him use it of Daniel Corkery, the popular professor of English at University College, Cork, and something of a rival guru, indeed, I never heard him speak of Corkery at all, except to express his affection for Corkery's seminal book, *The Hidden Ireland,* and to recommend it to me as a 'great book', *sár-leabhar.* In light of the events I would now like to analyse, this is a measure of the fair-mindedness and generosity of the man, since there is no doubt in my mind but that Corkery's part in the *Humanitas* controversy led to the untimely demise of that idealistic venture and greatly circumscribed the influence of the movement.

Corkery's reply, in the second issue of the magazine, to my uncle's initial article dismissed the Renaissance as 'an old exploded thing' (*seana-rud séite*) and deplored its effects on English and French literature, urging writers in modern Irish to concentrate on the native production, the classical *dán díreach* (linear composition) and the eighteenth century to the exclusion of all other models. The tone of Corkery's polemic is boorish in the extreme, reminiscent again of that complacent insularity of DP Moran in *The Leader,* which, for my Uncle Paddy, exemplified all his fears for the soul of Ireland. I do not think there was any personal animosity involved, but this was the *animus* of literary politics beyond a doubt. What strikes the modern reader most forcibly is that the 'mindset' of Paddy's antagonist, to use a modern term, is exclusively English; this is not native wrong-headedness, it is the thinking of Eliot and Leavis. Unfortunately, while the great world-language of English can tolerate, and even profit from, any amount of idiosyncrasy and eccentricity, Corkery's nativist ideas coalesced with the know-nothing Philistinism then, as now, so powerful a force in our island in both languages, and provided the adherents of that force with an intellectual camouflage that absolved them, among other things, from the necessity of actually learning any Irish. In the face of such a thoroughgoing attack from such an unimpeachably respectable source, the Free State government of the day, strapped as always for cash and hostile to an ethos they saw as tainted with republican subversion, withdrew its subsidy from *Humanitas,* and the modest little venture, after only four issues, folded. Perhaps it will be easier for the audience to grasp the import of the blow if they consider it in the light of what was happening at the time to the school of Irish writing in English, which produced the work of Tom McGreevy, Denis Devlin and Brian Coffey – all three 'republicans' and, though slightly younger men, close friends and admirers, one might almost say followers, of Paddy Browne. Tom was his constant guest and correspondent; Denis on his deathbed asked for 'Father Paddy'. It could be that his rehabilitation has yet to follow theirs.

It is now realised, of course, that Corkery's perception of Irish literature, for all its acuity, power and charm, was almost entirely imaginative, and that his command of the language was surprisingly weak. His literary utterances 'in the medium' were ghosted. In the *Humanitas* articles he maintained that 'the new Lessing' (the 'father' of modern German literature), 'the Gaelic Shakespeare', the saviour of the Irish language in whose coming, it emerges, we must make an act of faith, would 'have to leave the English-speaking world behind and go into the Gaeltacht, and stay there reading the literature of Irish and doing all his business through Irish, whether mental or material.' Corkery must have known that this was an uncannily accurate description of the lifestyle his antagonist had pursued over the previous fourteen years, but he chose to imply that, without a miracle, such an existence was impossible. In these circumstances, he implied, men of goodwill were justified in contemplating the impossibility of action and in waiting passively for 'the fire from heaven to fall', while at the same time maintaining a barrage of rousing and truculent, but conveniently vague nativist sloganeering, so as to produce a comforting sense of activity. You will note that it had to be Shakespeare – in the original Irish, of course – or nothing: counsels of perfection are often very close to counsels of despair. Puritans make virtue impossible; Corkery was doing this for Irish as a European language.

In the meantime, with characteristic lack of hype, Paddy Browne had rendered an unrebuttable defence even before the second phase of the controversy had ensued. Corkery's first article was followed, in the next issue, by two verse translations in Irish, by Paddy, from medieval French, versions of two famous *ballades* by Villon, versions that almost appear to have been originally conceived in Irish, so masterly is their strength and truth. The translator had been accused of condemning the Middle Ages: this was his reply. In an utterly natural manner, the verse form echoes the movement of the original, with the added grace of unforced, occasional internal vowel-rhyme unerringly used for emphasis. Not for nothing was the poet reared on Tom Moore and the great Gaelic songs of the Decies. He was always a superb metrist (it is sad that this is no longer a fashionable accomplishment).

After the demise of *Humanitas*, my Uncle Paddy's commitment continued unchanged, and so did our golden childhood and adolescence; indeed, the isolation of Ireland during the Second World War prolonged the idyll for us into our early twenties, but the climate had subtly changed. What had been a group enterprise became a solitary undertaking for my uncle. There were, of course, many factors involved; one of the more sinister of these appears already in an article – again in *Humanitas* – by Carol O'Daly, on youth movements in German universities. The writer speaks, with apparent detachment, of the aim of these movements to 'cleanse' – an ill-omened word – academia of the Jewish dominance: 'a cloud no bigger than a man's hand.' Shades of Lessing!

Irish Irelanders became troubled in their allegiance; German culture was an ambiguous brew. The Classics and European languages were already becoming old hat, so that when, at the end of the war, Paddy Browne, his translation of Homer's *Odyssey* completed, sought a publisher, even Sáirséal and Dill, the firm that almost by itself had dragged Irish writing into the twentieth century, turned him down. 'Who,' they said, 'would read it?' Thirty years after the translator's death, the work has, by an extraordinary series of coincidences, at last been published. Who, I wonder, has read it, apart from those to whom review copies were sent, and how many even of those? It will be gathered from the tone of that last question that, in my own case, a certain despondency with regard to the prospects of Irish has replaced the almost unpardonable complacency, not to say arrogance, of my earlier years. I ask myself, where did the great intellectual ferment of the 1920s and 1930s fail? It may be, as my uncle himself, in one of his poems, said of the not dissimilar Jansenist experiment of Port Royal, that it was 'too noble for this world and was shipwrecked' (*Ba ró-mhaorga leis an saol é agus briseadh é*). I was once asked by Séamus Mac Annaidh (the Ulster novelist) how I saw my role in the Irish literary movement. I told him, 'I am your informed public.'

ᏟᎦ ᏟᎦ ᏟᎦ

At this stage I may be forgiven for, very briefly, rounding off the presentation of the humanist case in the regrettable controversy by adducing the arguments that Paddy Browne was both too proud and too innocent of the force of public perception to put forward himself. The reader must realise that these events took place in an atmosphere of cruel post-Civil War bitterness. The absurdity of the accusation levelled against poor Paddy – that he belittled native Irish literary achievement – should, one would have thought, have been manifest. No one was more at home in modern Irish, classical and vernacular, than my uncle, no one cherished a deeper appreciation of its beauties. He had read everything available in print and could quote effortlessly from the *dán díreach*, or from Ó Rahilly and Ó Bruadair, he had edited the works of Pearse and he transmitted his love and knowledge (in the way ideal for the genre, that is, by word of mouth) to an enraptured audience of the young. If ever a man had earned his indentures as an insightful scholar and a constructive critic, it was he, and yet he could be, and was, presented as the xenophile advocate of an outmoded and sterile discipline. It was a charge he was by temperament unfitted to counter otherwise than by ignoring it. The ultimate outcome was the copper-fastening of the Irish-language movement within the all-pervasive sphere of influence of English, and of a levelling 'political correctness', where it became a prey to the alternative dangers of provincialism and impotent hostility to the foreign, which have dogged it ever since. Not all that different, indeed, from any doomed Third World minority language at the present day.

PART III: 'A CLOUD NO BIGGER THAN A MAN'S HAND'

As children we were vaguely aware, instinctively rather than explicitly, of this controversy, as of others even more destructive in tendency. It occurs to me now that perhaps our parents – apart altogether from being happy to have some time without us, to be alone together to get to know each other again after their enforced separation – were content to have us, to some extent, at a remove from contemporary conflicts, external as well as internal, in a society that seemed timelessly settled and enduring, serene and mannerly, and in a dignified symbiosis with nature by sea and land. This did not mean, of course, that terrible things could not happen in

Dunquin and surrounding districts, as elsewhere. My Uncle Paddy's great friend, Paddy Connor, for whom he wrote the great lament I tried to describe earlier, died horribly of a ruptured appendix, a strong farmer in his prime. An unwed girl who got pregnant could disappear overnight without trace, never spoken of again. A woman returned from America to a made match, and her first baby was said to be black – it was never seen again either after the night of its birth. Old enmities between parishes could erupt in bloodshed. There was a whole generation of adults who were brought up by grandparents, since their mothers had died in childbirth, or their fathers had drowned at sea – sometimes both. This last accounted, to some extent, for the richness of the local speech: it mirrored an ancient world where the extended family, Edmund Burke's 'little platoon', was the significant unit. One old man remembered hearing, when a boy, from his grandfather, who had been a boy when the news came, of the death of the great, eighteenth-century poet, Eoghan Rua; only one life separated poet and narrator.

Stories of violence were relished, as were, of course, ghost stories. One of the best of these I heard by our fireside from a brother of Peg Sayers, who was never the goody-goody she made herself out to be in her book, but a thoroughly Rabelaisian old lady with a sure sense of the market for 'harmless' biographies. Like his sister, Peaid Sayers was a noted storyteller. One night he was coming home over the mountain, down towards the graveyard. He had a fair amount of drink on him and he was waving a whiskey bottle, three-quarters full, in one hand. He crossed the stile into the graveyard and, all at once, there were all the dead people thrusting their heads up out of the clay and beseeching him, '*Th'om sciabus, a Pheats, th'om sciabus.*' (Give us a scoop, Peats, give us a scoop.). '"Hook your own ground," arsa mise leo,' said Peats – this phrase in English – 'and over the other wall with me and across the stream to put water between us, and I left them there.' (Ghosts can't cross running water.) Eat your heart out, Máirtín Ó Cadhain! My Uncle Paddy always maintained that the Irish countryman carried three distinct concepts of death in his mind simultaneously, without discomfort: one, that, like the beasts of the field, we died and went rotten; two, that we died and went to heaven; three, that the dead remained live and malevolent down underneath the ground, waiting to get at the living, as in the story above. Uncle Paddy also held that only children and old people had a natural belief in God; a man in his prime made an act of will to believe.

Ꮖ Ꮖ Ꮖ

In or about the summer of 1932 an event occurred that brought the outside world bodily into our Dunquin lives. The daughter of Terence MacSwiney, Máire Óg, was being brought up in Germany by her ravishingly attractive, if somewhat feckless mother and her mother's lover. Máire will correct me if I have any of these facts wrong; I write as I remember, or as I heard from adult conversations at the time. The child – she was twelve – with remarkable courage and maturity, wrote from her German youth camp to her aunts, Mary and Annie MacSwiney, the ladies who gave those idyllic tea parties, asking them to come to Germany and bring her back to Ireland with them. She did not like being boarded out. She told them at what point on the road she would wait for them to pick her up. The intrepid ladies did not hesitate. Taking with them Mrs Professor Stockley, a German friend, as an interpreter, they followed their niece's instructions and, with the help of the Irish Legation in Germany, brought Máire back to Ireland. Enough was known of conditions in Germany immediately before Hitler, even then, for the aunts never to have doubted the propriety of their action. They were then inspired, I use the word advisedly, to send her – she was about two years older than me – to stay with us in Tigh na Cille to get acclimatised to Irish life and Irish children. The visit was a providential success. My uncle spoke German and we sang student songs in German in the evenings. She was an undemanding child and so were we undemanding children, and we welcomed her unquestioningly as someone out of a girls' adventure story. We envied her her smart, navy-blue shorts; we were only allowed wear skirts. '*Muireann i mbríste*' (Miriam in britches) was culturally anathema in the countryside then, like 'the whistling woman' and 'the crowing hen'. Indeed, woman-poets were not welcomed either; it was said that if the 'gift' (*bua na filíochta*) descended to the daughter of a poet, it died out in that family. I know Máire Óg was happy with us for those weeks of summer, and felt safe in our calm, unregimented environment. She became the light of her aunts' declining years and never regretted her tremendous decision. Later, sadly, when the rift between the Fianna Fáil government and the IRA grew more acute, the friendship between the MacSwiney house and ours, separated by barely a couple of miles of road, waned. The ladies could not bear to bathe in Cuaisín, where we bathed, lest the water be polluted by the presence of my poor father. We were philosophical about this, and I think Máire Óg was too.

She was one of many of the children of close friends and old comrades who stayed with us from time to time; living in an Irish-speaking home never seemed to present any problems. Erskine Childers' grandson, Erskine III, was one of these, as were the Cullen children, whose father was our architect and who were our next-door neighbours and near siblings in Dublin, when we lived in Herbert Park. If they couldn't say something in Irish, they said nothing, but they didn't seem to mind. There was always so much to do and no one was ever bored.

As children, we loved visitors to the *cill*. For one thing they brought sweets and books and crayons. Some 'could be jumped on', as my step-children used to say later, and some knew stories, poems, or songs. Adults were allowed speak English. Among them I remember James Stephens, the poet, from whom I wheedled a four-colour propelling pencil, a tool of his journalist's trade; the painter Séan O'Sullivan who, speaking of his knowledge of Irish, said, 'Disappointed perfectionist *isea mise*'; dearest to me of all, my lifelong friend, Dr Letitia Fairfield. Dr Lettie was a sister of Rebecca West – Britain's 'best-paid journalist' – and a cousin of the Dennys of Tralee, a family 'planted' in Elizabethan times, later the 'bacon people'. She had been 'doing' her maternity cases at the Rotunda Hospital in Dublin shortly after 1918 when she met my mother and my Uncle Paddy while she was taking a break in Ballingeary, and they were too. Afterwards she borrowed a party-dress from my mother to go to a Sinn Féin *céilí* in Dublin. Years later my mother received a phone-call: 'Are you, by any chance, the Margaret Browne in whose dress I went to a *céilí* in the Mansion House?' The affectionate association was renewed and, ever afterwards, Dr Fairfield was, to our family, an ever-present source of help in time of trouble.

There were many other distinguished visitors down the years, during and after the Second World War. When Kruger Kavanagh, the famous inn-keeper, opened his famous bed-and-breakfast below the bridge, where three townlands met, fully licensed and with 'all mod cons', he liked to say to his guests, as he pointed out our house on its hill, 'There lives Father Paddy Browne, *Sagart na Cille*, entertaining the crowned heads of Europe with only an earth closet and one cold water tap from a rain cistern'! Kruger had come back from the United States with the onset of the Depression in the 1930s, shrewdly calculating that at least in Dunquin he would eat and that, in the throes of an economy in transition from subsistence to cash, as much of rural Ireland still was, there would be rich pickings for an entrepreneurial brain. His mother, old 'Knack' Kavanagh's wife, Máire Sheosaimh, had kept a *shebeen* (illicit drinking shop), so innkeeping was in the blood. The wives and mothers of the parish were against the licence, and many people dated the beginning of the parish's decline as a community from its granting. Before then you had to walk five miles for a drink if Máire couldn't oblige. Others prefer to date that decline from the filming of *Ryan's Daughter* very much later (1970): 'Walk the walk; talk the talk; kiss the girl; take the cash and vamoose!' Before the licence was granted a *Whisky Galore* situation – as in Compton MacKenzie's novel – ensued. The poet Paddy Kavanagh was staying in Kruger's for Christmas, and not only escaped at night through a window without paying but also wrote up his stay in the *Irish Press*, describing the islandmen calling in for their barrels and bottles of Christmas drink. The Gardaí were interested, but Kruger still got his licence and visitors continued to come.

ೞ   ೞ   ೞ

Sad news also filtered through from the Continent; Paris fell and we learnt of the suicide of Marie Sjoestedt-Jonval, Máire Francach, the beautiful and *chic* young French-Jewish linguist whose brilliant description of the Irish of Corca Dhuibhne we all cherish. Máire's chief informant and, we believed, lover, was Seán Óg Kavanagh, Kruger's brother. He was nicknamed 'An Clóca' (the cloak – the Gaelic *brat*) and Seán a' Chóta – *cóta* here meant 'petticoat' – because in the days of the 'Dingle Republic', in the 1920s, Seán wore the kilt. For many years Seán taught Irish in High School in Dublin, and was 'K' in Father Dineen's *Dictionary*; he had by now retired, and was living in his brother's house and working on his own enormous, but untrustworthy, dialect dictionary, as yet unpublished. From the day he heard of his Máire's death, Seán attended daily Mass for her soul and gave up both smoking and drinking.

Up at the *cill* we sang no more German songs and read no more Heine; the tragedy of that most Jewish and most German of poets was too near the bone. At least one party of germanophiles, led by Helmut Klissman, a very handsome and plausible young Nazi from Dublin, was turned away from our door. Sometime before then a pretty German woman scholar, working (significantly?) on the river names of Ireland and staying in the nearest townland to us, unexpectedly disappeared home to Osnabrück. The only other German-speakers I remember staying with us were the Austrian Jewish physicist Erwin Schroedinger and his wife. Quite recently I was shocked to be approached from Australia by Schroedinger's biographer to know if Schroedinger had ever made a pass at Barbara, my pre-teen sister. I believe she figures in the scientist's diary! None of us would have recognised it if he did make a pass; he certainly wrote a poem for her, in rather poor English, to the effect that she should clean her nails, and he taught her a chess problem. The same biographer asked after the only child of friends of ours at that time, whom he maintained was Schroedinger's. I happen to know for a fact that a child, conceived earlier than my friends' only daughter and who might have been Schroedinger's, if there is any basis at all to this story, died in its mother's womb and nearly killed her. She was staying with us in Dunquin when the haemorrhage set in; for some reason this index was ignored and the baby remained in place and rotted.

ങ   ങ   ങ

Notable 'allied' friends of my parents were John and Penelope Betjeman; they were even closer friends of Paddy Browne's and stayed with him, along with their children, Paul and Candida, in the years when we were growing away from Dunquin. So also did Fred Hoyle, the 'Big Bang' Fred Hoyle, the world-renowned astronomer, with his family. On one occasion they, with my uncle, were visiting an Anglican church where the names of all the previous incumbents of the living were listed on the panelling, with only three spaces left, and Fred's little daughter asked my uncle what would happen when all the spaces were filled. 'Then,' said my uncle, 'comes the end of the world.' 'Father Paddy,' said the child, 'don't be silly.' A chip off the old block!

The poet and art historian, finally director of the National Gallery, Tom McGreevy stayed with us often, as did the historian Mark Curtis of Trinity and Professor Roger Chauviré of UCD. Professor Curtis used to attend my uncle's Mass in the mornings, bringing with him my uncle's *Beatha Íosa Críost* (Life of Christ); 'I suppose, Father,' said 'old' Master Daly, 'that that is the *Book of Common Prayer* he is carrying?' The religious divide was a delicate topic in Dunquin, where many families had 'taken the soup' in hard times and whose children were often well into their teens when they were baptised. Relations between Catholics and Protestants were humane and good-humoured, but the schism was real. One old gentleman applying for a pension was outraged to be told by a young curate that, according to the baptismal records, he had at least ten more years to go. He reached for his stick and rose from his chair saying, in tones of the utmost reproach of age to youthful impertinence, '*Fan bog, a dhuine, fan bog, go bhfagha mé an triú cos!*' (Easy, easy, my friend, till I find the third leg!)

A similar rebuke was made to Professor Chauviré. We had all gone to look at the Iron Age beehive village clinging to the steep hill of Fahan, above the corniche road around Slea Head. A shallow stream there runs right across the surface of the road rather than under it; I believe the technical term for it is a water-splash. Here the custodian of the site, a scholarly old native speaker of Irish and our housekeeper's uncle, was explaining, in his careful, grammatical English, the function of the stream as a millrace, while Chauviré, with a discourtesy by no means typical of him, continued to talk in French to my uncle. We moved on to a gap in the drystone walling, which was blocked temporarily with large stones to prevent cattle straying. The old gentleman calmly removed the stones to let us through, bowed slightly to Chauviré and said, '*Passez, Monsieur, passez.*' His name was Seán Ó Cíobháin and he had been Parson Goodman's 'boy' when that famous collector of folk music was stripped of his living by Lord Ventry for not allowing the 'soup' (evangelical Protestant missionary activity in the nineteenth century) to take place in his parish of Dingle. The parson then set up house with his sister, Mary, and lived largely on the charity of his Catholic neighbours after that. Miss Mary had taught Seán the French language in the long winter evenings. It will be noted that even the most indigent parson in those days had a serving-boy, as would also have been the case with an indigent Catholic priest.

Parson Goodman's collection of pipe tunes – he was himself a notable piper – are now in Trinity College, where, in JM Synge's time, another Goodman brother was Professor of Irish; Synge recalls him as 'a snuffly old cleric', if my memory serves me. Among the pipe tunes is a slow air described as Pierce Ferriter's 'Lament', or 'Caoineadh'. This brings me to perhaps the most striking of my Dunquin memories. One Christmastime, when I was about nine or ten, my uncle officiated at a funeral where the corpse was keened.

Let me digress for a moment to recall the wonder of Christmas in Dunquin: weather so mild that primroses flowered in the ditches, houses all spick and span, and filled with a sense of anticipation, with a lick of paint here and a new flowered flounce on the settle there; we decorated the windows with sea sand and shells and shiny Christmas cards from America – the next parish! We stood a tall, red candle in a decorated jam jar in each window, and we waited for dark on Christmas Eve. Suddenly the whole valley sprung myriad points of light and out on the island lights, never seen at other times of the year, shone out in answer as we ran from window to window lighting our own candles. It was glorious and, while we knew it was not likely that the Holy Family would choose our house that night – we had not been good enough – we still left everything ready for them and hay for the donkey, just in case. All that, however, was behind us on the day of the funeral.

Waking and keening were still the norm in the parish when I was small, although they were strongly disapproved of by the local clergy, but not by my uncle. The bereaved was a very striking-looking old woman called Cáit Mhór (Cáit Ní Shéaghdha). She was widowed and had lost many children. This now was one of her remaining two grown sons, Dinny (Dennis, not to be confused with his brother Danny, who survived his mother). Myself and Biddín were there with my uncle, who wore the traditional white funeral scarf, the *sadhpras*, from the word 'Cyprus', the supposed origin of the linen; it was the 'makings' of a bed sheet and was the priest's fee. When the coffin left the church the women closed in behind it, led by the dead boy's mother. She threw off her *cafairín* (head-shawl), let loose her straggly grey hair, tore open the breast of her blouse and raised the keen. A younger woman behind her, a sister-in-law of Kruger's and Seán a' Chóta's, did the same; she had a beautiful, bounteous bosom. Others followed, keening, but remaining more decorously covered. I was spellbound, and so absorbed by the indescribable wailing that I did not, alas!, retain any of the words exactly other than the *ochón*. The burden of the chant was reproach, alternating with praise of the dead young man. He was addressed by name over and over again, 'O Dinny, Dinny, Dinny ...' and reproached for deserting his mother.' This was the only time I heard actual extemporized keening, as distinct from hearing 'Caoineadh na Maighdine' sung (the Virgin's Lament), or reading 'Caoineadh Airt Uí Laoghaire' (Lament for Arthur O'Leary). It is fitting that it should close my memories of my Irish-speaking self for now.

CHAPTER IV

A Lady's Child

Part i: *Ecumenism*

Part ii: *Virtue Rewarded*

Part iii: *Widening Horizons*

PART I: ECUMENISM

Our Dublin lives differed from our Kerry lives to an almost schizophrenic degree – I do not use the expression lightly. In Dublin, Séamus and I went for walks with Mary, our nurse-girl, all around Donnybrook and environs, one on each side of Barbara, the new baby in her pram, wearing identical tailored tweed coats and grey felt gaiters buttoned up to the knee with buttonhooks – like Christopher Robin. We would never have called Mary 'Nanny': that was British! Our great treat was to go by the Poor Clare Convent on Simmonscourt Road, where we were intrigued by the presence of the nuns behind the grille in the chapel, and devoured the *Messenger of the Sacred Heart* and other devotional booklets left on the benches there for the public. I fell in love with the statue of Saint Anthony of Padua and took his name in Confirmation – Anthony, not Antonia. Often we saw one of the many Dublin 'characters', such as poor old 'Forty-coats', the beggarman – a pear-shaped accumulation of layers of unidentifiable clothing held together by a rope belt and topped by a mass of curly dark hair and beard, under the drawn-down brim of a battered hat. He came regularly to the Convent gate for his alms of bread and tea, and sometimes coincided with us. Other sights I remember from that time, which have since disappeared, are the knife-grinder with his cry and his cart and wheel, the barrel-organ player with his monkey in a little velvet jacket and cap, the lamplighter, romantic at dusk with his long pole to switch on the gas lamps, horse-drawn barges on the canal and, above all, the great Guinness dray horses striking sparks from the cobbles with their metalled hooves.

Money was still tight: my father's quasi-clandestine political activities precluded his earning much and the upkeep of his consultant's office was a constant drain. I remember a lot of laughter as the talented Lydia, with my mother and Mary assisting, 'turned' my mother's winter coat on the dining-room table, and equipped it with a fur collar cannibalised from an even older garment.

 C3   C3   C3

At school, Alexandra, where we paid no fees, we were, probably because of my mother's instant friendship with Dr Isabella Mulvaney, the school pets. As a headmistress, Dr Mulvaney ran a very tight ship – no political emblems; not even a poppy, let alone an Easter Lily. To Séamus and myself, she was simply a wonderful visitor whom we met off the bus when she came to tea; we had now moved out to what was still the village of Rathfarnham. I do not know if this next has any particular social significance, but we always lived in rented houses until my parents were at least in their seventies, and moved around quite a lot when they were young. Dr Mulvaney, in return for the tea, brought us more than once to the Zoo, where, since she was on the Board, we were taken behind the cages to see the lion cubs and the sick monkeys. On one occasion she brought us home in a taxi, on Séamus' insistence and to my mother's intense mortification. It was related of Dr Mulvaney that on being asked, by a proud father, whether she preferred little boys or little girls, she replied, 'Personally, I prefer orphans'! When she retired in 1932 the old generation of teachers faded away; my mother left, without regrets, to lecture in Irish at UCD. One of my mother's former colleagues, meeting her for coffee in Mitchell's – the fashionable Grafton Street Café (now McDonald's, I think) – recounted sadly, 'It's all twinsets and pearls now, Dear, I'm afraid.' Mitchell's was also the scene of a major social gaffe of mine: I rushed in to meet my mother, who was entertaining a nondescript elderly lady to coffee and strawberry ice cream (made with real strawberries!). 'Máire,' said my mother, in a calm-down-and-remember -your-manners voice, 'You remember Miss X, don't you?' Quick as a flash came the reply, 'Why, Mammy? Is she dead?' Mitchell's seemed to bring out a child's capacity to embarrass. Our neighbour, Mabel FitzGerald, and her son, my close friend and contemporary, Fergus, were leaving there on one occasion, and Fergus lingered a moment at the table behind his mother, then rushed after her calling out in his clear treble, 'Mother, Mother, you left threepence under the plate!' The thripenny bit was that useful piece of silver which, in those days, constituted the minimum ladylike tip! It was also significant that the little FitzGeralds called their mammy 'Mother'.

I started school at Alexandra at the age of four. I was perfectly content at school; the lessons I was good at, I loved passionately; those I wasn't, like handwriting, tables and music, I ignored. We were taught French from the age of six, and no Irish till after the age of ten; both providentially for me. It meant that I was never subjected to terrible 'school' Irish; as you will see below, I left when I was ten.

We exercised a patronising tolerance towards our Protestant fellow-pupils (much as we did towards the children of Free-Staters when we met them at parties) – they couldn't help it; it was not their fault. We were enjoined to be particularly nice to them because of this. Little Catholics, like little Jews and little atheists (such as our Marlborough Road neighbours, Pegeen and Kopen Synge), were excluded from morning prayers – it would now be called assembly – and clustered together at one end of a corridor under the remote supervision of Mr Cummins, the school porter, and very much did as we pleased. We couldn't believe our luck! Almost all this non-conforming group were Jewish; later it would include the Chief Rabbi's sons, the Herzog boys, but I would be a big girl by then. I fell in love with a beautiful little Jewish girl, Sybil Orgel, but this was a speechless and distant adoration. My real best friend was Stella Tyrell, daughter of a Trinity professor and, like me, a precocious but unstreetwise child. Streetwise par excellence, *avant la lettre*, was Phyllis Ryan, the actress-to-be, and something of a control freak. With her best friend, Marjorie Popham (tall, long-legged and with a straight, fair bob – how do I remember?), she tried to institute a reign of terror when we were all in 'Transition' (the top class in primary school before first year intermediate) by leaving notes in red ink, bearing a hieroglyph of a ghost in a wizard's hat, in people's desks and schoolbags. The notes prophesied various unpleasant things and were signed, 'The Scarlet Phantom'. I was mildly intrigued by this, but not frightened, it was all rather tame stuff to someone reared on *real* ghost stories in Dunquin. The school, however, took it seriously, and I became involved.

This happened when it was realised that, on one day a week, fifteen minutes of my time went unaccounted for. I had hit on the brilliant stratagem of leaving my piano lesson (thirty minutes) and, instead of presenting myself at my handwriting class (forty-five minutes, and actually then in progress) for the remaining quarter of an hour, hiding behind the coats in the cloakroom. This lacuna was now investigated in the context of the Phantom. My transparent lack of interest in and ignorance of the origins and identity of the phenomenon saved me, nor do I think that the mystery of the lost fifteen minutes was ever actually solved in all the more lurid confusion of the investigation. The Phantom's creators assumed I had given them away; I hadn't. I didn't know who they were until they set out, not very effectively, to be revenged, not only on me but on the totally innocent Stella, by not speaking to us. I retaliated by informing them that I had told my mother how horrid they were and that, in consequence, I was being taken away and sent to a much nicer school. I hadn't, in fact, told my mother anything – although, like other members of staff, she must have known something of the Phantom affair – but I knew I was being taken away at the end of the year to go to a Catholic school and be Confirmed. This ruse was surprisingly effective, probably because my tormentors were already in trouble enough, and because my mother was a formidable presence who taught the bigger girls and was regarded by our own junior teachers with something like awe. Stella and myself were left alone after that.

I remember interesting forms of counter-snobbery associated with being in, but not of, a Protestant milieu. We looked down on stamp collecting as a pointless Protestant activity, and our parents would not allow us join any scouting associations – Brownies, Girl Guides, or what have you – although we would, secretly, have loved to. They were condemned as 'militaristic'; to be fair, we didn't join the Fianna (Countess Markievicz's republican scouts) either. No one taught us the more recent republican songs, not even 'Legion of the Rearguard', which is so specifically Fianna Fáil. There was a distinct intention to shelter us from contemporary strife, and certainly no intention to prolong it. We, however, seemed to pick these rousing anthems up off air. I had an insatiable thirst for ballads and relished their deadpan wit and often savage rhymes and phrases:

> *'God save the southern part of Ireland,*
> *Three-quarters of a nation once again ...'*

– a savagely ironic street ditty, or, from the popular ballad,

> *'They were shot in pairs, coming up the stairs,*
> *By Seán Treacy and Dan Breen ...'*

or, from a somewhat different quarter,

'After the war is over
What will the sojers do?
They'll be coming home
With a leg-and-a-half
And the Shinners, they'll have two ...'

– a 1918 ex-British Army complaint.

One jingle, a 'counting-out' rhyme that we picked up in Dunquin, went back to the Boer War. As we had it, it was slightly rude nonsense and went like this:

'Á-ké, Bá-ké, Oo-nun, Ká-Ké
Calico, Paper, Lady, Stink.'

'Lady' being understood as a euphemism for menstruation. I have since worked out that the original English, totally misunderstood by us schoolchildren and adapted as above, must have been:

'Acky(?), baccy, Union, Khaki,
Calico, paper, Ladysmith.'

Tobacco for the troops, calico for bandages and paper collecting for cash were all part of that 'war effort'; Ladysmith as in 'relief of'. Could 'Acky' have been signallers' slang, short for Ack-emma (AM)?

୯ଓ   ୯ଓ   ୯ଓ

So at ten years old I transferred to the Loreto day school, Beaufort, in Rathfarnham, a separate entity from the neighbouring Loreto Abbey boarding school. This was very convenient as our back garden – again! – gave onto the convent grounds. The outskirts of Rathfarnham village had not been built up in those days and the country roads and fields stretched away to the hills, past Saint Enda's boys' school and past the Priory, where Robert Emmet's Sarah Curran had lived and her sister was buried. Our daily walks with Mary, which continued, became country rambles, with cowslips and blackberries and bluebells to pick in season; we had, of course, May altars to decorate.

Twelve Wilbrook Road was a new house: all white paint and sunny windows. The poet Yeats lived up the road from us and his romantic figure, silver suit and silver hair, often walked by our gate; later my father would refer to him as 'that old Fascist' – it will be remembered that the poet was a Blueshirt, Ireland's version of Fascism. I seem to remember that we always had something to celebrate. One such occasion was the appearance of the new *Irish Press*. It was infinitely more child-friendly than the 'Indo' (*Irish Independent*), with a cartoon strip about leprechauns (which, incidentally, for the first several days didn't change at all). Above all, it was *our* paper, not unionist, not Free-Stater. My mother still worked very hard; I remember, before we set out with Mary for our walks, being taken in to kiss her as she sat correcting mounds of Intermediate exam scripts on the living-/dining-room table. She would give us a penny apiece, which bought four toffees each, and we would promise to be good so that she wouldn't have to worry about us. The family hierarchy, as it had always been and long remained, was parents, maids, children, and we respected it absolutely.

I had been content at Alexandra; I was deliriously happy at Beaufort and made friends who have lasted to this day. Less admirably, I learnt to tell lies. In Alexandra, one told very few; in Beaufort it became a commonplace habit for me – everyone did it and it avoided unpleasantness. I had, consciously, to break myself of the habit of lying in later life, as I came to realise how it impoverished the quality of life not to be able to trust anybody, or to take anything on trust. In comparison with Beaufort, Alexandra, though amiable, was cold. I think it must have been that, to the nuns, whatever faults they may have had, we were their whole life. Even unjust reproaches reinforced our sense of importance. We had many excellent teachers, of whom two were seriously outstanding.

Shortly after I started attending Beaufort, our class was 'streamed': six or seven of us were picked to do 'Honours' Irish and History and Geography through Irish. We became 'Sister Bríd's class'; we still talk together, when we meet, of our good fortune. Sister Bríd was a sister of Paddy Henchy, the National Librarian, and of Séamus Henchy, one-time apprentice Celtic scholar with me in the Dublin Institute for Advanced Studies, subsequently Judge Séamus Henchy. She had taught, as a laywoman, at the Loreto Irish Language School in Falcarragh, County Donegal, and her grasp of Donegal Irish was phenomenal. By temperament she was entirely fitted to control a class of very bright teenagers and her enthusiasm for the Irish language and its literature did the rest. Notably, she took us through Séamus Ó Grianna's wonderfully ironic short stories and through the romantic realism of his early novels, at a level closer to that of a university lectureship than that of an 'Inter. Cert.' class. She tidied up our grammar and spelling relentlessly and demanded absolute attention throughout her teaching periods. We responded with sustained effort and unrestrained admiration.

Mother Elizabeth was an older woman and more reserved. She taught English, French, Maths and Latin – again, it now seems to me, to university standard. She also taught me German, which I was obliged by my family to take – it would enhance job prospects – on a one-to-one basis. I don't think I realised how fond of her I was until, in my last year at school, I had to choose a favourite nun to 'sew my Child of Mary ribbon', as was the custom. I then found that she was the one I loved most – 'love' is the appropriate word. 'My dear,' she said, 'I am deeply touched. I do not sew very well, but I will make a special effort.' I gathered that such requests did not often come her way. In or about this time a friend of our family asked her if I would do well 'academically'. 'She may not,' Mother Elizabeth said, 'she's not competitive.'

I was too absorbed in class and too indifferent at games – though I liked them – to be competitive. I was extraordinarily happy in my relationship with my 'best' friend, a radiantly pretty young woman with a rare distinction of mind, even then at the age of twelve. Our affection for each other was effortless, totally unintrospective, undemanding and enduring. Her name was Margaret, which I had always thought the loveliest of names, and, insofar as I thought about it at all, it seemed to me that this was as it should be. We still love each other, *mutatis mutandis*. I was a year younger than the rest of the class and the older girls looked after me, so that my chronic absentmindedness got me into less muddles than it might have, although I do remember praying that the end of the world would come before Maths class as I had, once again, left my geometry set at home. Perhaps because it was a day school, and therefore in no way claustrophobic, I do not remember much, if any, schoolgirl cattiness. There was a fair amount of mischief though, and I seem to remember that two embryo actresses, Kathleen Ryan and Joan Plunkett, were taken away and sent to boarding school 'because they were interested in boys'. The attendance mirrored post-Civil-War Ireland. In the junior school, which took little boys, including our Séamus, there were a son of Paddy Broy's, the Garda Commissioner, and a son of the Free State officer responsible for the horror of Ballyseedy. I always knew this – I did not consciously eavesdrop, but I heard things, especially if people, mistakenly, spoke French in the presence of us children to keep us in the dark. I did not, however, gossip among the pals about such things – it would either have meant nothing to them, or too much. Children of politicians, of those, at least, whose politics are their livelihood, develop instincts for discretion.

PART II: VIRTUE REWARDED

In glorious 1932, as it turned out, one could throw discretion to the winds. Fianna Fáil was the new government; my father was Minister for Finance, under Mr de Valera as Prime Minister. Years of hard work were rewarded, years of discouragement wiped out, and Divine Providence had decreed that this should happen in time for the Eucharistic Congress in June. The Soldiers of Destiny would play host to the Papal Legate and the Christian world, rather than having to leave it once more to the 'brains and property of the country' to represent the Irish people. We glowed with pride. Our family's palpable triumphalism filled the air, but I still feel that, in the circumstances of the time, it was restrained. Indeed, it amounted to only a very minor current in the great tide of religious enthusiasm that swept the country.

I have been asked why I have said that, after the experience of those days, the 1979 visit of the present Holy Father seemed to me anticlimactic. The answer is surely that in 1932 the Christian peoples of the Earth, from all over the world, gathered in Ireland not to welcome any individual, however august, but to honour Christ in the Blessed Sacrament. From all over Ireland orderly crowds of people thronged into Dublin. The weather was superb. The Dublin tenements were dressed with bunting and adorned with little shrines, till they put the more respectable quarters, for all their expenditure on fresh paint and banners, to shame.

> *'The houses seemed to reel and sway,*
> *And the rooftops flamed, such flags they had.'*

We had two flags on our house: the national flag and the papal standard. The wife of the Labour Party senator, who was our neighbour and whose children were at school with us, remarked sniffily to my mother that she hoped that 'Deevalaera and them ones' wouldn't disgrace us; we were not yet 'respectable', but our joy remained unalloyed. I remember those regrettable words clearly; I had the middle-class child's ear for 'bad grammar'. Not that class was a subject much canvassed among us; our myths were pastoral and egalitarian. We were never allowed to call anyone or anything 'common', and when I once tried to tell the story of the film *Michael Strogoff* at our evening meal one Saturday, my mother became frighteningly angry when I used the word 'peasant'. '*Never* let me hear you say that word again!' 'Countryman', 'countrywoman', and 'country people' were the correct terms. We did not say 'tramp', or 'beggar' either, but 'poor person'. In any event, no begrudgery could spoil the Congress for us.

I was taken – Séamus and Barbara were judged too young – by my mother and father to see the Papal Legate, Cardinal Lorenzo Lauri, and his suite arrive by sea. I had a very smart red-and-white-striped cotton dress and a wide-brimmed, red-and-white-flecked straw hat, white cardigan, socks and gloves, and black patent leather shoes; I liked myself very much. At Dún Laoghaire everything shone and sparkled; Raoul Dufy could have done justice to the scene. My father left us to join the official Rolls Royces at the head of the procession, behind the Cardinal's mounted escort of our new, ceremonial Blue Hussars. My mother and I, in the everyday State car – not nearly as nice as our own beautiful green V8 – were driven home, and, almost immediately afterwards, Séamus and I were handed over to my Uncle Moss and packed off to stay with his house-keeper in Athy, County Kildare, to make room for all our Northern rela-tives who were coming to stay with my parents for the duration of the ceremonies; Barbara was so small she didn't count. Something like this happened in every house in the city: people slept on the floor and in the bathtubs, but no one complained. Whatever else I know of the Congress is hearsay, from which I will merely record the exceptional success of the singing by the women's choir at one of the Masses in the Phoenix Park. I do this because there was, at the time, a strong residual prejudice against female participation in the Liturgy. My Uncle Paddy used to relate that on that day, the women sang like angels; never before or since had he heard anything to equal it.

All this time my father considered himself debarred by the Catholic Church from the sacraments for his part in the Civil War. The rights and wrongs of this position were, are and will continue to be subject to debate in moral theology. In our house we had no doubts on the matter: if the Church came up against Daddy's individual conscience, the Church was in error. I gather that is very much the teaching of the 'new' Catechism today. I haven't checked. Perhaps the weasel word 'informed' is still in-serted before 'conscience'? That would not have fazed us – we had three uncles priests.

Ↄ   Ↄ   Ↄ

If I wanted to refresh my memory on the details of my early political education, I would go straight to the pages of that wonderful, humorous journal of the time, the *Dublin Opinion*. Having the jokes explained to us as children kept us abreast of current events. Adults taught us to see the funny side of serious things: the withholding of the Land Annuities; the Economic War; the Coal/Cattle Pact; the Guinness threat to leave Dublin; the introduction of the 'Dole' (celebrated with bonfires in Dunquin); the Transport Strike, during which I learnt a new meaning for the word 'scab'; the Irish Sweep; the ESB – we knew the orthodox line on these (see my father's view below) and on many other issues, without necessarily having any very deep understanding of what was involved. We knew that Ministers for Finance were not generally popular – we had one in the house – and, around about Budget day my sister and I hoped that no one would recognise us on buses, while comments flew. My father was financially conservative, but he boasted that no government project, in his time as minister, was ever shelved for want of funds.

The realities of the Economic War and the Slaughter of the Calves (when cattle exports to the UK were suspended) were brought home to us when we stayed briefly on the farm in Tipperary where the indomitable Ma Joe of Chapter I had settled. Her husband, Pat Arrigan, was a staunch Fianna Fáil supporter. He also reared greyhounds for my Uncle Moss, who bred winners under the alias of WW Twyford. During our stay, a very promising dog fell ill. Pat and our cousins were up all night with the animal, but it died. In the morning, an exhausted Pat came into the kitchen and sat down by the fire in deep discouragement, 'Christ,' he said, 'it wouldn't be a bloody cow!' It was alright for grown-ups to swear.

The euphoria of the Eucharistic Congress couldn't last forever; here, I let my father describe Fianna Fáil's first years in office, as his views were relayed by Michael McInerney in a series of interviews in *The Irish Times* in 1974:

'The Civil War verdict [in favour of the Treaty] was rapidly being reversed by means of the political party, and, in less than five years, at the 1932 election, de Valera was in Government, but without an overall majority. He still had to depend on Labour support to secure power. Already, however, he began the abolition of the Oath [of Fidelity to the British Crown], the retention of the annual £5m. to Britain for Land Annuity payment, a retention which provoked British counter-measures and thus started the famous Economic War.

But the new course of the politics of Parliamentary-Democracy reached its full flood only with the historic election of 1933, which gave de Valera complete power with an overall Dáil majority. In that historic election, Mr MacEntee can claim a most important role.

That 1933 General election was the greatest sensation of a decade, and the most unexpected. De Valera had been in Government only eight or nine months, relying on Labour's vote in the Dáil. His Dáil measures were causing wide controversy while the Economic War caused grave distress and loss to farmers and there were many urgent social problems. It was no time for another general election. Mr MacEntee, by then Minister for Finance, however was facing a revolt from Labour Deputies about a cost-of-living measure and refused to compromise. Mr Norton, Labour leader, was also Secretary of the Post Office Workers, and was threatening that unless a cut in pay, on a fall in cost of living, were withdrawn, Labour would not support the Government. [Perhaps it was in anticipation of this that our Labour Party neighbour was in such bad form at the time of the Congress.] MacEntee was the catalyst in the sense that Dev. was already thinking about it. He also was preparing his next Budget in a tough economic situation. He decided to raise the matter with Mr de Valera and, through Gerry Boland, Dev's secretary, suggested that the only solution was to call a new general election. To his surprise, Dev. promptly agreed, called a Cabinet meeting and announced the election soon after.

Mr Cosgrave and his colleagues were jubilant that Dev. had made such a bloomer as calling the election at such a favourable time for them, and at such a "suicidal" time for the Government. So certain of victory was Cumann na nGael [the new name for the party of the pro-Treaty heirs] that Mr Cosgrave actually began selecting a Cabinet. Even some of Mr de Valera's Ministers were dubious, but Mr de Valera and Mr MacEntee were somehow certain of victory. They were right. The result gave Dev his greatest victory ever, with 77 seats, an overall majority, 691,800 votes or more than 50% of poll, and a jump of 130,000 in total votes over the previous March, or almost double the June 1927 total.

The political way now certainly had reversed the Civil War verdict. Within another four years the Treaty had been completely dismantled, a Republican Constitution adopted and a new Treaty with Britain [signed] securing the evacuation of the [Treaty] Ports – in 1938. Mr MacEntee was proud. No wonder.

The new strength of the Government, however, brought its own right-wing reaction. De Valera, by dismissing General Eoin O'Duffy – a former pre-Truce Deputy Chief of Staff I.R.A. – from his post as Police Commissioner, gave the rising Blueshirt Movement a dynamic leader who effected a massive growth in its ranks and militancy. Mr MacEntee admits today that he and Dev saw a real threat in it to their power, "and also to democracy". Fascism had succeeded on the Continent, they thought, and there was a danger it could succeed here. [Mr MacEntee describes it thus:] "We saw O'Duffy as a real danger to Parliament and State. We also saw it as a dangerous political plot by former Free State forces to overthrow the new Government. Some former Cumann na nGael Deputies were Blueshirts and we saw an attempt at a *coup d'état*.'"

Shirts of various colours were the prevailing political wear in Europe: brown in Germany, black in Mussolini's Italy. Our right-wing enthusiasts chose blue. It must have been about this time that, on a summer afternoon, all three of us – Barbara had been born in April 1928 – were dressed in our very best and bundled into the State car, which we now took for granted – two in front with the driver – to accompany our parents to call on the Chief of Staff, Major-General Brennan, in his pleasant official residence in the Phoenix Park. We played with the Brennan children – more Barbara's age than mine – my mother took tea indoors with Mrs Brennan, and my father and the General were closeted together in the General's study for what seemed hours. Even at the time, I thought it was an oddly artificial afternoon; I am now virtually certain that we children were 'cover', a 'front' for serious discussions relating to the Army Comrades' Association (ACA), ancestor to the Blueshirts, and the ACA's efforts in 1932–34 to subvert the (Free State) Army, and bring about the *coup* to which my father refers. At that time, ministers had Army rather than police drivers – could that have been the reason for the charade? No special intimacy with the Brennans resulted from our visit; indeed it would have been difficult for that to happen, given the Department of Finance's strong discouragement at that time of fraternisation between elected politicians and permanent servants of the State. My father and the Secretary of his Department, Jimmy McElligott, liked and respected each other – they had been 'out' together in 1916 – but never met outside the office.

McInerney's interview with my father continues:

'The subtle and direct use of State power, however, with some help from militant Labour men and Trade Unionists, ended the rise of the Blueshirts after only a year. Their fall was helped by a split between the Fine Gael Party and the Blueshirts [Cosgrave and O'Duffy fell out] and a split within the Blueshirts themselves. At the same time, de Valera turned round on his former allies, the I.R.A., and by the use of the Public Safety measures [anti-'Irregular' legislation by the previous government], revived to deal with the

Blueshirts, began a tough discipline against them, which did not ease off until the Constitution was passed in 1937. By that time, however, the great bulk of the Old I.R.A. and Republican Ireland had been won over to the new methods of politics. MacEntee rejects the I.R.A. claim that they helped to defeat the Blueshirts. "In fact there was no alliance, once Fianna Fáil was founded, between Fianna Fáil and the I.R.A. remnants. They were a menace to the constitutional revolution he [de Valera] had worked out.'"

It must have been at this point that a series of people, whose names had been household words, dropped out of our circle of acquaintance: Jack Dowling, Andy Cooney and Sheila Humphreys, 'to name but three' – all old friends and all active in the 'new' IRA. This was much easier for my Draconian father than for my intensely sociable mother. One evening she was waiting, appropriately dressed for a formal occasion, for my father to join her in the Gresham Hotel. She was approached by an old comrade, much the worse for wear, and she knew that he was the last person my father would want to see when he arrived. 'Margaret,' said the former friend effusively, 'you're looking great. What brings you here?' 'Seán and I,' she answered repressively, 'are going to the dinner dance given by the Revenue Commissioners.' He got the message. 'Frolicsome bloody crowd!' he exclaimed sadly and drifted away.

McInerney again:

'Later de Valera, MacEntee and their colleagues in Government were to be faced with Ireland's first generation which had been educated by an Ireland utterly, exclusively and completely in control of its own educational system. Admittedly the 'writ' of those first Irish Government Ministers for Education was considerably influenced by the Roman Catholic Church and dependent on the Church and its Orders in control of the schools and colleges, but these men and women [religious and lay] also were Irish.

Every previous generation of pupils had been educated in an Ireland totally under British occupation and rule. Yet the 'New I.R.A.' of 1938 were far more passionately addicted to the gun and the bomb than the youth of earlier years [I recollect that these are my father's *ipsissima verba*]. Perhaps it was that the 1938 I.R.A. lacked the *moral* [my italics] authority which a whole people had given to the Republican Movement through elections to the Parliament and Government in 1918–21 [and they had to fall back on force].'

Perhaps I should also add my father's assessment of the poverty of Ireland at this time, also published in this interview, to offset my own, perhaps too persistently rose-coloured recollection:

'It is impossible for people today to appreciate the Ireland of 1922–32. Though there were about 200,000 unemployed when we took office, there was no unemployment assistance. There was massive emigration and a grave housing problem. The health services were almost non–existent. There was serious poverty in rural areas.'

These statements remind me how I took for granted then and witnessed every day: children going barefoot winter and summer; entire families living in one room; households who saw fresh meat only twice a year, at Christmas and Easter, and much, much more. Even among well-to-do children the death rate from TB, meningitis, diphtheria, polio and rheumatic fever was high.

PART III: WIDENING HORIZONS

Every child should have a fairy godmother, mine was Dr Lettie (Letitia Fairfield), of whom you will have read in the Dunquin chapter. She was Assistant Chief Medical Officer of the Old London County Council, a convert to Catholicism and a founder member of the Sword of the Spirit, the English organisation of Catholic lawyers. She had Denny connections on her father's side (and hence with my hero, Pierce Ferriter) and an uncle had been the engineer in charge of constructing Dingle harbour. That uncle was also involved in the infamous 'Jameson Raid' in Cecil Rhodes' South Africa – with 'all civilised men south of the Zambesi.' Dr Lettie's stories could have doubled for 'English History as told to the Children'. She introduced us to Rudyard Kipling and to the *Children's Encyclopaedia*, having first ascertained that our parents had no objection. Now, in 1934, she contacted them to know if I might accompany her and her fifteen-year-old niece, Alison Macleod, to the Mozart Festival in

Above: My father's family. *Back row, left to right:*
Jimmy, Grandfather, May, John (Seán), Grandmother;
Front row, right to left: Charlie (baby), Meg and Eddie.
(Joe was not yet born.)
Right: My paternal grandfather, James MacEntee.

Above: My maternal grandfather, Maurice Browne.

Right: My maternal grandmother, Kate Browne, with Uncle David.

Below: My mother as a schoolgirl, age fourteen, at the Dominican Convent on Eccles Street. Margaret Browne is the tallest girl in the second row.

Right: My mother graduating from
UCD in 1913.
Below: My mother with her brother, Paddy,
riding through the Gap of Dunloe,
in County Kerry.

Left: My father as a young man.
Below: My parents in their youth.

Opposite page:
Top: On the step of Tigh na Cille, in Dunquin: at the back stand my Uncle Paddy and Bríde, sitting down at their feet are (*left to right*) Biddín, Séamus, Peaitsín (Biddín's brother), me and Barbara.
Below left: My mother and myself.
Below right: A solemn portrait of me and my Uncle Paddy.

Right: Annie and Mary MacSwiney with their young niece and our friend, Máire Óg, daughter of Terence MacSwiney.

Below: My father (*far left*), as chief engineer, was released from Gormanstown Prison Camp to supervise the completion of a project in Wexford, thanks to the efforts of Mayor Corish.

Top: My mother (*far right*), with Séamus on her knee, and me (*far left*) visiting our Northern cousins.

Above: Me, Séamus and Barbara with the Brennan children, on the day my father was holding informal discussions with Major-General Brennan.

Left: Age ten outside our house in Rathfarnham, at Wilbrook Road.

Left: On a trip to London Zoo, Séamus, 'in remission', is thrilled to be allowed to hold some of the inhabitants of the snake house.

Right: My passport photo for my trip to Austria and Germany with Dr Lettie, complete with the plaits the German border officials so approved of.

Salzburg, Austria. Many years later she confided in me that she decided to give us this undreamt-of treat in order to defeat a deep depression consequent on an unhappy love affair. She was that kind of gallant lady. She never married.

There was, of course, no air travel. Boat and train were marvellous adventures. I had never been out of Ireland and had assumed that all cities were built in squares of red-brick, like Dublin. London was a revelation at the very beginning of our journey – Dr Lettie had a flat at Gray's Inn – and excitement went up and up after that. This was before the *Anschluss*; Austria was still an independent country, and Prime Minister Dollfuss had just been murdered. We travelled across Germany by train, breaking our journey at Munich and at Heidelberg. From the train journey I remember most vividly the gangs of shirtless and, to my eyes, impossibly beautiful, sunburnt and blonde young men, the conscript *Arbeitsdeinstmänner* (workforce), engaged in repairing the track. At one station-halt we saw a doorway over which there was a notice saying, '*Eingang und Ausgang Verboten*' (entry and exit forbidden)! German border officials approved my two long, thick plaits. I myself was enormously pleased with my red mercerised cotton sports shirt and my belted, navy, first-ever shorts, with which I had been kitted out in London.

We visited the Bavarian countryside, walked in the woods and picked wild strawberries. I, of course, had never before seen a wooded landscape; it was like a fairy tale. Even more so was the extravagant Wagnerian castle of the mad King of Bavaria, Ludwig, straight out of Walt Disney (forgive the anachronism), with swans on the lake and a portrait of Lola Montez. The politics I was absorbing, from all sources, went like this: socialism, good; communism, perhaps dangerous, but not as bad as National Socialism; we must hope that good Germans, of whom, as we were experiencing, there were many, would soon come to power again and, in the meantime, we must not annoy the existing authorities – perhaps it was not their fault and perhaps they would come to know better. My mother had told me, before I left, that if anyone said, '*Heil, Hitler!*' to me, I was to say, '*Dia's Muire dhuit!*' to them. Nobody made an issue of it. Officials who used the salute perfunctorily didn't seem to expect an answer.

Heidelberg was like walking straight into the world of the light opera, *The Student Prince, Lilac Time*. The weather was flawless, we ate in restaurants in the shadow of the *schloss* (castle) and on the banks of the Rhine and listened to romantic open-air concerts. I was a healthily greedy child and I loved German food, notably venison and wild boar, which were heroic foods such as Cúchulainn, or King Arthur might have feasted on.

Until we crossed the border into Austria, we did not realise we had been under any strain. It was only when, suddenly, there were no swastikas anywhere that we breathed a sigh of relief; '*Grüss Gott*' was such a friendly greeting! Dr Fairfield probably knew, but her two charges did not, that Austrian Nazism was just as virulent as the German kind. Blessedly it was not superficially in evidence – at least at first – and the sunny, Tyrolean temperament tangibly was. Alison was a very adult fifteen to my twelve and, on the whole, we communicated with each other through Dr Lettie, rather than directly. We accepted each other very readily, however, for what we were, and relations were smooth. Alison has since told me that they marvelled that my English was so literary and so free from schoolgirl slang. I, for my part, found some of Alison's English unintelligible, but I did not feel the need to remark on it. She grew up to become a convinced Stalinist and was very happily married to a similarly convinced and very sweet-natured husband. In a jewel of a book, wonderfully direct and humorous, entitled *The Death of Uncle Joe*, she describes her and her husband's very gradual disillusionment, but also their good times together. For many years we believed her to have been the dramatic critic of the *Financial Times* – such strange associations were common in Fleet Street, but we were wrong.

The musical-comedy aspect of our tour intensified. We stayed at the original *White Horse Inn*, high in the Austrian Alps, in Sankt Wolfgang, on the shore of the Wolfgangsee, in a village of fretwork houses, painted white and stencilled in rainbow-coloured floral patterns. Villagers wore Tyrolean costumes with everyday ease and at night, after dinner, the crew of the lake steamer, the postman and the grocer, all came into the hotel and gave folk-dancing displays: lots of *lederhosen*, shaving-brush hat cockades, 'battering' and thigh-slapping. On an island in the lake, at some distance, was a chillingly gloomy *schloss*, just right for a robber baron. The impression was not a false one; it was the headquarters of the local Nazi *gauleiter* (district head); we hoped he was not in residence. We took lake trips to the salt mines – miles of shining white underground corridors, and lakes in which a flat-bottomed boat could barely sink; it is from these mines that the Salzkammergut takes its name. We visited the little village of Halstadt, crouched under a cliff so high that the sun only shines there half the year, which is why those important prehistoric villagers, who once lived there, worshipped the returning cranes, who, in the spring, carried back the sun-disc in their beaks. We went to Bad-Ischel, the summer palace of the last Austro-Hungarian Emperor and the beautiful Empress Elizabeth. It was all very *gemütlich* and bourgeois, with, in one of the bow windows of the salon, a little stage on which the imperial children performed plays for their parents. Dr Fairfield asked the caretaker what had happened to one particular little princess. He replied, 'Oh, she married a communist; one does not speak of her now.'

One afternoon there were no excursions, and my companions were reading or resting. I set out alone to buy a film for my camera – another first. The village of Sankt Wolfgang observed the siesta, and I wandered idly through the empty streets, until I was brought up short in front of a display-case outside the offices of *Der Stuermer*, the Nazi newspaper. I could not take my eyes off it. My feet seemed stuck to the pavement, a drumming started in my head and I could feel my heart thump. The case was full of obscene cartoons, the sort of thing I could never previously have imagined, let alone seen. All the protagonists were shown with dehumanised Semitic features; some were dressed as Catholic priests and nuns, and I think it was this that alerted me to the nature of the whole. I was a very innocent child and came from an innocent culture, but I knew this was evil, although evil was not a concept I had ever considered before. I was aware of casual, social anti-Semitism in Dublin; I had heard 'Jewessy' used as a synonym for vulgar; my Uncle Paddy had had trouble convincing us that Hilaire Belloc's cautionary tale about the little Jewish girl was *not* funny, although the others were – now I knew he had been right. I realised that wicked Germans, and wicked Austrians, too, could be very wicked indeed – I was too young to realise that this could be true of wicked human beings in general – and I was very, very frightened, and a dark shadow seemed to fall on our lovely holiday. I think I went straight back to the hotel, but there is a blank in my memory about that. Contrary to my usual practice of keeping disturbing insights to myself, I spoke about this at length at dinner, and since I was only too anxious to be reassured, I succeeded in putting it behind me. Not all Germans and Austrians were like that.

Any remaining uneasiness was dissipated by Salzburg. I was mildly dyspraxic and had difficulty writing and playing the piano – my mother despaired of my musical ear – but I could, in fact, hear music; my problem was reproducing it. All three of us went to hear the *Magic Flute*, but Dr Lettie could only get two seats for *The Marriage of Figaro* and, nobly, gave them both to us. To begin one's experience of opera with two instances of perfection was an indescribable privilege, and indescribable it has to remain. We had enough German to follow the words and, as for me, every note registered. Some day I must look up the names of the singers, the conductor, the producer; at the time they seemed almost irrelevant to the heavenly, organic reality of the whole. In more sombre mode, we heard an organ recital of the 'Requiem' in the Cathedral and attended an open-air performance of the medieval morality play 'Everyman' in the town square. Not so long ago, my daughter Margaret, who is very musical, went on a school trip to Salzburg; when she got home I asked, 'Did you hear a lot of Mozart?' 'None at all,' she replied cheerfully. 'It was all the Trapp [no Von] family and *The Sound of Music*.' We indulged that side of our tastes as well and were provided with ridiculously pretty *dirndls* (folk costumes), complete with tight bodices, silver buttons, full velvet-banded skirts, puff-sleeved blouses, flowered aprons, neckerchiefs – the works; mine had a brilliant emerald green bodice – I can see it still.

ଔ   ଔ   ଔ

That foreign holiday provided me for many years with a touchstone for judging happenings abroad, as and when they swam into my ken. It is noteworthy how many of them are linked in my mind with snatches of song: Italy's invasion of Abyssinia gives, 'Will you come to Abyssinia, will you come?/Bring your own ammunition and your gun …'; the abdication of Edward VIII and the sleight of hand that took the Crown out of our Constitution recall little English children singing, 'Hark the herald angels sing/Mrs Simpson's pinched our King!' Of course, in those days people sang and whistled a lot more than they do now; from tram conductors and van men you might hear anything from Handel to 'Love thee dearest …'

(By now we had a gramophone and my parents, on the Tom Sawyer principle, recruited us as a willing source of labour to wind the motor and change the records.) At the UN I once had an Ethiopian friend, Judith Imru, whose father had been jailed for the duration of the Second World War by the Italians. She told me, 'In some ways we welcomed the Italians; we are a sad people and the Italians are cheerful. We used to creep up to their houses at night and crouch, just beyond the lamplight, to listen to them sing.' As for Mrs Simpson, she did us invaluable service as schoolgirls: 'Have you heard the latest, Mother,' we would ask distractable nuns, 'about the Prince of Wales and Mrs Simpson?' 'No,' would come the answer, 'and you're all going to fail your Leaving … tell us about it!' Nuns were not allowed to read the newspapers, and a scandal like that was good for at least twenty minutes of class time. You must not gather a wrong impression from this – we were dauntingly intellectual young people. After all, the convent's star pupil, Darina Laracy, who not only came first in all worldly subjects but also secured the Bishop's Medal for Christian Doctrine, grew up to marry Ignacio Silone, the controversial Italian left-wing novelist, and take her place in the history of European literature, not to mention politics. As for me, on the politics of the Spanish Civil War, Dr Fairfield's indoctrination bore fruit, and I prayed that Mr de Valera would hold firm and not recognise the Franco insurgents; to an extent my prayers were answered. The touchstone worked.

 beta   beta   beta

In 1934 or thereabouts we moved house once again, back into what is now Dublin 4, from Rathfarnham to 12 Herbert Park. Here our next-door neighbours were also our family's closest friends; their father was Tom Cullen, the architect, who had conceived what to us was the most perfect house in the world: Tigh na Cille. We were so identified with that house in Dunquin that, locally, we took our names from it: Sagart na Cille, Máirín na Cille, Gramaisc na Cille ('rabble, mob, low people, children', according to Dineen's Dictionary). In Dublin the children of the two households became like siblings. Those of us who survive remain like that to this day. Séamus went to Blackrock, a 'real' boys' school, and he and I tended to grow apart, although he was still only such a little boy – ten years old – yet we were very fond of each other always, while Barbara and I grew ever closer in spite of six years difference in age. With Aideen and Mary Pat Cullen next door, we made a foursome who were always comfortable together and yet made few demands on each other. We even seemed to share our parents: Mr Cullen took us riding; my father's State car took us all to and from school in Rathfarnham. It never occurred to us that that last might be improper, nor, I am sure, did it ever occur to him. Our symbiotic relationship was to become even more mutually supportive in the following years as, in both families, serious health troubles resulted in crippling anxieties.

Little Fergus Cullen, Séamus' contemporary and friend, died of meningitis; I can remember clearly how the finality of death hammered to force its way into my understanding, was repulsed by denial and, quite speedily, suppressed. Then the Cullens' eldest girl, Aideen, twelve days older than me, was diagnosed as coeliac and became a constant invalid, a thin, pale, waif-like creature whom, during her many dangerous bouts of the illness, I saw my father carry in his arms as if she were some almost weightless and unimaginably precious piece of china. Around Christmas 1936, it became our turn to rely on the Cullen family for support and comfort. I leave it to my father at this point, writing to my Uncle Eddie, a medical doctor, to tell the story of how this came about.

1ˢᵗ March, 1937.
Dr. E. F. MacEntee,
89 King Street,
Belfast.

Dear Eddie,

I think I told you that some time before Christmas Séamus seemed to be developing some nasal trouble, and immediately after Christmas we brought him to a Nose Specialist here, Dr. P. Roddy, who is attached to the Royal Victoria Eye and Ear Hospital, Adelaide Road. At the first examination he said that the matter was a simple one and would be easily dealt with by a slight operation. When, however, he was going to operate, on examining the growth more closely he thought it was an unusual one and instead of proceeding to remove it took a specimen for microscopic examination. Even taking this specimen seemed to occasion a great deal of haemorrhage and Séamus seemed to be very white and shaken for two or three days afterwards. According to Dr. Roddy the report on the specimen was that the growth was a fibroma so vascular as to be almost angiemo [*recte* angioma]. He told us that this was most unusual in a boy of his age and that he would prefer not to do anything in regard to it for the present as its removal by the knife would occasion great haemorrhage, that Séamus had bled a lot when he was taking the specimen and that he would prefer to wait until he was built up again. That would be about the middle of January. He saw Séamus again last week and said that a fibroma of this sort was practically unknown among his colleagues in the Hospital; that Dr. Graham, who was acknowledged to be the leading man here in Dublin, could recollect only having had two cases of it, and that as there had been so little experience of it here it would be advisable to bring Séamus to London, and in this connection he recommended that he should be brought to a man named McKenzie who was formerly attached to Guy's Hospital, which I understand is a specialised hospital for the treatment of such cases.

Dr. Hayes has discussed the case with Roddy at great length and he feels that this is the proper thing to do in the circumstances. He has suggested to Roddy, however, that he ought to discuss the matter with Harry McAuley and I think that Roddy will do this.

When Dr. Roddy mentioned that Séamus should go to London, Margaret suggested that she might write to Dr Fairfield, who is on the medical staff of the London County Council and who apparently is in charge of the Children's Medical Service, which she did late on Friday night. This morning Dr. Fairfield was on the telephone to Margaret and the gist of the conversation seemed to be (for the connection was very bad and it was scarcely possible to hear) –

1.   That McKenzie was dead.
2.   That a fibroma in the case of a child of 12 was a most unusual occurrence.
3.   That there should not be any delay in the matter and that Séamus should go to London immediately.
4.   Were we perfectly certain that the diagnosis was correct.

Dr. Fairfield's question about the correctness of the diagnosis is the one that has been put to us by a number of medical friends to whom we have mentioned the matter. They all find it very difficult to believe that it could be a fibroma and some of them have even suggested that maybe the microscopic examination was mistaken. As against this, however, we have the fact that when the specimen was removed there was quite a lot of haemorrhage.

Needless to say the whole thing is very worrying. When we first brought Séamus to Roddy we were inclined to be reassured and not to worry too much about it as we thought that if Roddy decided not to operate the trouble could be dealt with simply and safely by diathermic treatment. We are beginning to feel very anxious and to think that the matter is much more serious than we have been told. Dick Hayes, for instance, told us that until Séamus has had treatment he would not allow him to play games or do anything where he would have the risk of a nose injury. We were discussing the matter yesterday with a Doctor who is married to a cousin of Margaret and who is apparently a very good man, and he seemed to take a grave view of the thing also, provided that the diagnosis was correct. Dr. Fairfield seems to be of the same opinion. Apparently the growth is a benign one but that there is likely to be a great difficulty and possibly danger in removing it, and that if unattended to and injured it may result in very serious haemorrhage.

For my own information I would be very grateful if you would let me know what really is the truth in the matter, as of course if it were serious I should cross immediately to London with Séamus, though it would be most inconvenient to do so just at this time, whereas if we could afford to wait a week or two longer it would be more convenient for me to get away, about St. Patrick's Day. You might consult some of your colleagues in Belfast about the whole case, in strict confidence of course, because I would not like that Dr. Roddy should hear that I have been making enquiries from you. We are satisfied, indeed, that he is exceedingly anxious and abundantly careful about the whole business.

I trust that Ethel and yourself and family are well.

With best wishes to all,

From Christmas 1936 until the 1940s, poor Séamus' life was a series of hospitalisations, long convalescences in London, blood transfusions, surgical operations and radium and deep x-ray treatments, from which he emerged with a cleft palate, which necessitated his permanently wearing an opturator. In his late teens, the growth, a fibro-angioma, which was, alas, malignant after all, was finally extirpated. He was not allowed to play games, or, most of the time, even attend school. My Uncle Paddy coached him, and, in due course, he got a very respectable Matric. In the beginning, he was so distressed and frightened at the onset of a haemorrhage that he would lock himself in the bathroom, or hide under the stairs to escape detection, and all his friends had to be recruited to raise the alarm at the slightest show of blood. He became an almost permanent guest in the home of John Dulanty, the Irish High Commissioner in London, and came to regard the Dulantys as his second family. Dulanty was an old Irish Party man and the trusted agent of successive governments. My mother and father spent as much time with Séamus in London as was humanly possible, and I can remember feeling somewhat bereft at home.

Inevitably, meanwhile, in spite of all the kindness he received in London, Séamus was often lonely. The radium made him depressed and irritable, but he made heroic efforts to keep cheerful. Some warm-hearted adult gave him a pet white rat, and when Dr Constance Wood of the Radium Therapy Research Unit in London was lecturing to her students on his case – a very, very rare one – he gently laid the white rat on the back of her neck. Dr Wood's reaction was gratifyingly feminine, and the students had a ball. On another occasion, when the faithful Dr Fairfield was taking him out for the day and was checking the theatre page of *The Times* to find something suitable, he suggested wistfully, 'Perhaps we could go to something *un*suitable for a change?' Sometimes, in the early stages of the war, when he crossed to London – by boat, of course – a doctor had to travel with him, and once he did haemorrhage during the crossing. When the war continued it was no longer possible to go to London to Surgeon Mollison at Guy's Hospital and Dr Wood at the Radium Unit, but by then the Dublin doctors and surgeons who had initially advised London were sufficiently familiar, from following Séamus' case at a distance, with the treatment required by his desperately rare condition to pursue it in Ireland. At that point, Séamus' life returned to something approaching normal.

CHAPTER V

The Emergency

PART I:
AOIBHINN BEATHA AN SCOLÁIRE
(THE SCHOLAR'S LIFE IS PLEASANT)

My Leaving Certificate results, in 1938, proved better than expected by the grown-ups – I myself knew I had walked it – and I was unceremoniously pitchforked into adulthood overnight. Initially it was a very pleasant experience. My parents came down to Dunquin with my grades in a celebratory mood and took me back with them to Dublin to work for an Entrance Scholarship to UCD. Working at Irish with my mother was an unalloyed joy; our reactions mirrored and complemented each other. We laughed at the same things, were moved by the same things, and happily compared usages together. Her 'Bible' was 'Father Peter' (an t-Athair Peadar Ó Laoghaire), the last great classical writer of Munster speech, mine was *An tOileánach* (The Islandman), the classic of my own contemporary Kerry dialect. It was reassuring to know that the anglicisation of my name, Máire, was Maura – because a slender 'r' in classical Modern Irish became broad in South Tipperary – rather than 'je' (as in French pronunciation) in the Decies, which gave 'Maw-je', or 'y', as in Ulster, which gave 'Moya': I could not have borne to be called either of the last two, but I was worried that 'Maura' sounded so English. It was more like doing the crossword in the *New Statesman*, as Barbara and I used to do with Mammy for fun on Saturdays, than studying for an exam. In the evening all three of us, Father, Mother and Daughter – Séamus and Barbara were still in Dunquin – might go out to dinner, a truly novel experience for me – at home we had tea at six – or to the cinema, or the theatre. My father loved both.

I think my parents were particularly carefree that autumn, after a grim period (which my father later described as 'six years rule in which the State had been threatened, both externally and internally, almost every month – the Blueshirts, the IRA, economic sanctions from Britain and the worst Anglo-Irish relations ever') had ended in the triumph of the Anglo-Irish Treaty of 1938 and the takeover, by Ireland, of the ports ceded to Britain by the earlier Treaty. Mind you, it seemed to us that our house in

Dublin was mostly a fairly stressful place to live, but that year things were halcyon. Séamus, now thirteen, was in remission – we had a photograph of him taken at the takeover of Spike Island, a lovely little fellow with a fringe down to his eyebrows, standing proudly by his father's side. The General Election of 1937 was successfully over and the 'New' Constitution had passed and replaced the Free State Constitution of 1922. If I remember rightly, it did not pass all that overwhelmingly, and I don't remember much popular enthusiasm.

In our own house the passage of the 1937 Constitution was not without its storms. When my mother and father disagreed, they disagreed vigorously, not to say violently – doors slammed, voices raised, blows threatened, the lot. This grieved us children, as would any serious row between close friends or siblings, but I do not think it made us feel particularly insecure. In spite of Mrs Simpson, divorce was inconceivable for people like us, and we knew rows would blow over. We often fought 'rings round' ourselves and yet we knew we loved each other. For my mother, the divisive issue was the article which sought to ensure that married women should not be compelled by economic circumstances to work outside the home. She saw this as compelling them back into the home, or at least as the thin end of that wedge. It seemed to me an excellent provision – I could have done with more of my mother's company – but I had the sense not to say so.

My generation did not feel we had to fight for women's rights; we regarded them as established. It did not occur to us that our freedoms were in any way limited, except by the facts of life, which we regarded as unjust, but irreversible – like not being supposed to be able to bowl overarm. In the same way, as is noted earlier in the McInerney interview, we felt, not without some regret, that we would not be called upon to die for Ireland. I wrote two early poems on that theme – one in Irish and one in English – which reflect, to the best of my knowledge, the rather muted condition of our contemporary mindset. The Irish one is also interesting in that it is not easy to translate. Its warp is the quietist message, and the highly idiomatic and metaphorical language of the medium, with its harmonising vowel sounds, weaves through the whole to pull it together in a way I find I cannot at all convey in English. However, a prose translation at least allows the reader to judge it in the context of the prevailing mood among the young when it was written, sometime in the 1930s. I was never entirely happy with it and did not finally publish it until the 1960s, when I took it out again and dusted it off for the 1966 commemoration of 1916; I titled it 'Birth Defect':

> *'Those who established the rule and worked out the duty, which have*
> *left us, the heirs to the will, tasting insipid, those are the*
> *reason why everything now is flat, other than a tense stance*
> *on a knife-edge of slate, between two fires.*
>
> *The man beneath the middle of the blanket, how would such compre-*
> *hend how the cold affects the brethren at the edges?*
> *What threat can we hold over the man at the centre of the chess-*
> *board? We are a thrust that was stunted at the edge of play.*
>
> *Our habitat and holding is on the confines of civilisation; what*
> *would produce life there, other than principle? Do not reproach us, a*
> *fasting people. Such was our only [fundamental] law; our guilt was*
> *to accept it.'*

Pretty depressive stuff, I'm afraid. Indeed, I now think that the mildly depressive mood swings to which I have always been subject manifested themselves, at that time, as a kind of low-grade contentment, while up-swings presented as sudden intense awarenesses of the possibility of happiness. My English effort was much more facile and addressed to my childhood friend and close contemporary, Fergus FitzGerald (Garret's next older brother), by now a fellow student at UCD and something of a poet himself; I titled it simply, 'For Fergus'. Bear with me if I quote it here; it is the voice of the young woman I was then:

> *Friend, when we die, it shall be in our beds*
> *And, having found no purchase worth the price,*
> *We'll part from life perforce and grudgingly,*
> *For us no trumpets and no sacrifice.*
>
> *Not in this generation, not again,*
> *Inexorable in the riven way,*

The challenge of the single final choice
Making our fathers heroes for a day.

No, we shall see our children grow in peace
Under the tyranny of common hours,
Forget the hopeless loves of the Dark Rose,
And tend the saner and more grateful flowers …

For we have turned our hands to honest trade,
To the dull virtues and necessities,
It is not easy for us, being bred
To barren poetry for centuries.

Somewhat more upbeat this time.

I think these little poems – fairly contemporaneous – mirror and illustrate the differences between my Irish-speaking and my English-speaking selves.

In any event, my mother's loyalty, to my father primarily rather than to the party – overcame her feminist principles on the question of the Constitution. She did not change her mind, but she voted for it as the lesser of two evils, and the run-up to my Entrance Scholarship examination for UCD was, domestically, a very happy time, and the outcome of the exam itself justified our optimism. My father put it like this in a letter to my Uncle David in Rome:

'Máire did particularly well at the Entrance Scholarship examination. She got 2nd place in aggregate marks for all groups, with 1st in Irish, 1st in English, 2nd in German and 5th in French. She was beaten for 1st place by a boy two years older than herself who not merely did the First Arts course last year but actually sat for the First Arts examination, on the understanding, however, that he would not be given the exam so as not to deter him from sitting for the Entrance Scholarship – a most extraordinary procedure.'

The 'boy' was Thomas Desmond Williams, the noted historian, with whom I was always very friendly subsequently, although I never had any illusions as to the lengths he – or more properly his backers in the Fine Gael university establishment – would go to further his academic career.

By tacit agreement we never competed against each other again. There was no point in trying to kick the politicisation of university life. We were the children of the Civil War.

I cannot resist recounting my triumph in the Irish oral examination. Michael O'Brien, a gentle freethinking scholar, who, they said, 'used up all his energy not going to Mass', was the examiner. We chatted happily in Irish about Dunquin and *An tOiléanach*. He asked me did I find any of the usages in the book strange. After my fireside evenings in Tigh na Cille, I was a world expert on this. I explained to him, artlessly, that while the word *ionbhaidh* (opportunity), pronounced '*ionúig*' in Munster, existed in Dunquin Irish, it could not be used, as the editor of Tomás 'ac Criomhtháin's book, Pádraig Ó Siocfhradha (pen name, An Seabhac), had made the author use it, in an impossible phrase, '*b'shin ionbhaidh agamsa ê*', purporting to mean, 'that was my opportunity'. What Tomás had written in the original manuscript of his book, which is preserved in the National Library, was, '*b'shin nú agamsa ê*', '*nú*' representing his pronunciation of '*nó*' ('or'), and the whole meaning 'not otherwise was it with me', a phrase on the model of the unchivalrous, '*bean nó muc!*' (a woman is not otherwise than a pig). In the sixty-four years since that time, I have tried to get this theory recognised – it was published once in *Feasta* – and there is no harm in trying once again. But Glory be to God! no need anymore. As I check this transcript, I have before me the masterly new edition of *An tOiléanach* by Seán Ó Coileáin (Talbot Press, 2002), with an electrifying statement in this context: '*Glactar le míniú Mháire Mhac an tSaoi* (Máire MacEntee's explanation is accepted) ---- *Feasta, Deireadh Fomhair*, 1998.' *Go raibh maith agat ó chroí, a Sheáin.*

಼ ಼ ಼

I went to UCD, in Earlsfort Terrace then – the Belfield campus did not exist and the college was not divorced, as it has now become, from the life of the city of Dublin and the traditions of the old 'Royal'. I wore my schoolgirl's coat, open, as was the custom then for us new university students, to show beyond doubt that the dress underneath was not a school uniform. Across the road from us was my first school, Alexandra, not for many years yet to move to Milltown; UCD male students warned each other that 'those little Protestant girls would eat you!' Two of my classmates from Beaufort – my dear Margaret and another close friend, Norah – joined me in First Arts. We cushioned each other against transitional shock and adapted with glee to our new freedom. This companionship was invaluable to me for, at home, Séamus had had a frightening relapse, which occurred at a Hallowe'en party in our house, attended by, among others, the little girl who grew up to be Rosaleen Lenihan. He was again in London for prolonged treatment, and a climate of parental absences and worry had re-established itself among us.

Our 'troika' did all the things first-year students do. We went to hops; I found them disappointing after Dunquin, where all the boys could dance: sets, waltzes, polkas, you name it, and where we cycled miles to dances in kitchens, or in the now-encroaching, clerically-approved 'halls' that were fast replacing the crossroads as dance venues, and where no one was self-conscious about dancing well. We attended meetings of all the college societies; I was arrogant enough to dismiss the L&H – now technically unisex – as 'young men playing at being grown-up'. I think that, that year, 'young' Tom O'Higgins, who would become Chief Justice O'Higgins in his later years, was in the Chair. Out of a sense of duty I persevered with the Irish-language societies, but, like my mother, I was not really a joiner.

Academically, I think I may have puzzled my professors: I valued lectures purely for their entertainment value – Roger Chauviré (French), Michael Hayes and Colm Ó Lochlainn (both Modern Irish), I remember with gratitude. Old Irish I did not affront till my second year, of which more later. I detested tutorials, being strongly convinced that staff were paid to teach us and not to 'involve us' in discussion – time enough to express my opinion when exams came around and not 'boil cabbage twice'. I had a serviceable academic brain trapped in the persona of a very young and emotionally immature, not to say reclusive, female. The brain was entirely fulfilled, and the persona did not know any better. It was only the persona my teachers saw until it came to written exams. This continued to be the case for many years to come.

I liked the company of boys, but felt I dared not indulge in too much of it for fear of outstaying my welcome. I loved dancing and danced well – too well to be tolerant. My mother said, 'Those that dance well don't marry, and those that marry don't dance well.' My father was the exception and, in those serious times, his love of jazz 'gave scandal', both among friends and political opponents alike. He had taught us to 'follow', and he did not approve of girls knowing the steps – it spoiled them as partners; my mother had more sense and saw to it that we had the necessary elementary lessons. I would have liked a boyfriend, but did not know how to go about getting one. I thought I was irremediably plain and was afraid I might be destined to be a nun – already, as Celtic Studies increasingly absorbed and fascinated me, I was beginning to fear further that I might 'grow up' to be like Miss Knott of Trinity, a distinguished Celticist and spinster – an even worse fate. I had, besides, fallen obsessively in love with an unattainable object, and all my fantasy life revolved around him.

It had been what the French call a *coup de foudre* (bolt of lightning). I was sitting, one evening, on the end of the kitchen table in Dunquin, kicking my heels, after the neighbours had gathered; chairs were at a premium. He came and stood in the doorway, and my awareness of his presence hit me like a stone under the heart. I knew that I would love him forever and that my love was hopeless. I had never seen him before, but I knew who he was. He was a Protestant and he was married. He chatted for a while with the company, but he was not asked to join us. He had a reputation as a rake. Shortly afterwards he left. I know that more than one of my contemporaries carried, like me, lifelong torches for impossible lovers; it went with the territory in women's lives of the 1920s and 1930s, and ran, as it were, parallel with real life. That great and gifted lady, later a close family friend, the actress Bríd Lynch was one such. Among our elders, intense, emotional, *platonic* friendships between the sexes, or, indeed, between friends of the same sex, were a recognised social norm. Some of my Uncle Paddy's found their way into my own dramatic lyrics, notably 'Caoineadh' (Lament) and 'Do Shíle'. I dramatised what I intuited were his feelings. I was fortunate in having the exquisite traditional love songs in eighteenth-century Irish and the classical love poetry of the Irish *amour courtois*, to teach me how to turn heartache – my own and that of others – to some account. Perhaps I should mention here that intense love poetry is characteristic of a chaste society.

ଓ   ଓ   ଓ

My first college year (1938–39) ended; Séamus was again out of danger; I had again done well in my exams. My mother and father, as a reward, took me with them on a coach tour of Normandy and Brittany, before leaving me to spend the rest of the summer with a French family in La Baule, a fashionable Channel coastal resort. Nothing is ever as perfect second time round; it was not quite the threesome of the autumn before. I had become very much 'Daddy's girl', as happens with teenage daughters, and I sensed that this wounded my mother and so tried to offset it as best I could. Nubile daughters cannot help reminding their mothers that those mothers themselves are no longer young. Nevertheless, it was a glorious holiday, bathed, in hindsight, in the irrecoverable glow of the eve of approaching war.

The family I stayed with (recommended by Chauviré) was called Rozay, and my facile affections embraced them all unquestioningly. The parents were quite elderly; Madame was thin and quiet, but gracious and unintimidating; Monsieur was a teacher (*professeur*) at a Lycée, who took pupils during the holidays and tutored them as required. They had one child, their son, Georges, aged eighteen and wonderfully supportive of them. The pupils were Jacques Gaumont, a scion of the famous movie family, and an odd little fellow called Jean, who was nicknamed Le Colonel – I think because he wore blazers with gilt buttons and was always spick and span, and held himself very straight because he was small for his age (fifteen?). Georges was very much our mentor and he reproached me early on for showing a marked preference for Jacques – dark, tall and leggy, with eyebrows that met over his nose: Georges was so right! Actually, we were fairly decent young people and behaved very nicely towards each other. So exemplary was our conduct, and so good were our manners, that it came as something of a shock to me to be invited on a midnight excursion to chop down one of the municipal pines on the hill behind the houses, with a view to constructing a raft for the private use of our circle of acquaintance. Incredibly, at least to me, Georges was the ringleader; as might be expected, he conducted the adventure with maximum order and efficiency. Within twenty-four hours the craft was ready to launch and I was proclaimed her godmother (*la marraine*). I was disconcerted; I had never before been chosen for such a distinction. From that out, my identity among our 'set' – families who had been coming to La

Baule on well-behaved, bourgeois holidays for generations, in no way tourists – was assured. Little girls would come up to me and confidingly take my hand, saying things like, *'Elle est belle, ta filleule'* (your god-daughter is beautiful). I was profoundly touched and pleased. I did not take lessons with Monsieur Rozay, but I was expected to give an account of myself at meals. When I told them I was reading *Le Centaure de Dieu*, an absorbing bodice-ripper by La Varende – I can't remember that he had a first name, but he was France's answer to Georgette Heyer – it was decided, not without relief, that I could not possibly understand it. They were wrong; it was a wonderful read for a seventeen-year-old, full of colourful, nineteenth-century provincial French atmosphere and dialogue. I would recommend it to all Leaving Cert. students, linguists especially, if second-hand copies could still be picked up.

The Soviet–German pact (1939) became a fact, and Low's famous cartoon of the two dictators, Hitler and Stalin, bowing to each other across the map of Eastern Europe went on the wires around the world: 'The tyrant of the Kremlin, is it not?' 'The bloody assassin of the workers, I presume?' General mobilisation was ordered in France, and word came to me from home to go straight to Paris, where I would be met off the train by someone from the Irish Legation – as it was then, before we got above ourselves and went in for embassies. The young men of our *bande* were incandescent with anticipation of war to come and we said goodbye in a blaze of sentimental exaltation. We did not concern ourselves with what the adults might have felt. I never saw any of them again. Georges was called up and, when, under General Pétain, he was demobbed, volunteered to go and work in Germany, so as to free a married French prisoner of war, in accordance with the Vichy policy, after France's defeat. I tried to contact him in 1945–46, but he did not want to be contacted; I can only speculate as to his reasons. He was back from Germany and married himself by then.

Paris was in an uproar, worse than the worst traffic snarls that Dublin today could produce, and much noisier – although all the taxis had disappeared from the streets. This last was the legacy of the Battle of the Marne in 1914, when the taxis ferried troops to the front, and since when the taxi-drivers of Paris were always the first to be called to the colours. I was put on a train to the coast with Mr Paddy Little, the Minister, at the time, for

(I think) Posts and Telegraphs, and his family: Mrs Little and her daughters, by her first marriage, Iona and Caitríona McLeod. Mrs Little was inclined – not so surprisingly – to be hysterical, but her girls and myself were able to calm her, and the journey went smoothly. I was at home in nine Leeson Park – another house move – to hear the announcement on the radio that Britain was at war.

PART II:
NEUTRALITY AND DIPLOMACY

I took part recently in a television documentary about John Betjeman, in the course of which the presenter informed me that John, in a wartime minute to the British High Commissioner in Ireland, Sir John Maffey – Betjeman was his Press Officer – described my father as 'the most anti-British of the lot'. I find this difficult to believe. If it is true, John was extraordinarily bad at his job, or else he was pulling his Chief's leg. I quote again from the McInerney interview:

> 'He [Mr MacEntee] also adds the fascinating information that he himself at that time was pro-American, pro-British and anti-Nazi. "In fact, if I had thought, at that time, that we could carry a united people within the State I would have favoured Ireland entering the War. But it was not practicable and we could not have afforded the manpower. I thought that our whole future depended on the overthrow of the totalitarian régime in Germany."'

Irish opinion at that point was divided. The IRA was pro-German: 'England's difficulty is Ireland's opportunity'. Many ordinary Irish people, without a full understanding of what was going on, were sentimentally on Germany's side. Many more – especially among the middle classes – were consciously Fascist and pro-Nazi. People did know about Nazi anti-Semitism, but, to do them justice, not for some time about the full horrors of the concentration camps.

It was widely known at the time that my father and Gerry Boland –

perhaps also Seán Moylan? – were the 'pro-Ally' members of the Cabinet. Paradoxically, many of the self-considered upper-class stratum – well-to-do, Catholic, professional people, doctors and lawyers and big landowners, those who were still, at that time, often known as 'West British' – were 'pro-German', if not openly 'pro-Nazi'. My father and mother had been asked to entertain for the government – the new house lent itself to such occasions – and I remember Julian Huxley coming to dinner and reporting in the *New Statesman* afterwards that he had been seated beside 'a vitriolic, Fascist blonde', who poured poisonous Nazi propaganda into his ear throughout the meal. She was actually a very pretty lady, with whom my father was, I think, slightly smitten. Perhaps my father thought it no harm that Dr Huxley should know the difficulties that our government's policy of neutrality was facing. My mother was outraged that the confidentiality of her hospitality had been breached; 'Dr Huxley should have recognised that the lady was there solely for decorative purposes,' she held.

ଔ ଔ ଔ

My mother had always brought out the best in any of the houses we had lived in, Leeson Park was her triumph. The large, airy reception rooms (from which, across the grounds of the Carmelite Convent in Ranelagh – where one of her closest Northern friends from the Boycott Office days was an enclosed nun – you could see the Dublin Mountains), showed off to perfection the beautiful period furniture that over the years she had collected and restored. Those were the times when, in an outhouse, or a dairy attached to a 'Big House', or in the parlour of some old-fashioned presbytery, or farmhouse, the contents of which were being auctioned, you could find Sheraton, or Chippendale pieces going for a song. The curtains, carpets and upholstery, were Dún Emer, designed by the Yeats sisters, Lily and Lolly, in blues, purples and greens, specifically for Mammy; the pictures on the walls were by AE, Paul Henry and Humbert Craig, with one small but jewel-like Jack B Yeats, *The Shan-van-voght*. When she gave dinner parties, the glass was old Waterford – not matching, of course – and the silver, Irish Georgian – not matching either – all acquired piece by piece from the most unlikely places at bargain prices, all – alas! – sold advantageously after my father's death; my much-travelled generation had not the lifestyle to maintain the home she created.

One thing she did not have when we first moved into Leeson Park was a complete dinner service. We ate every day off the remains of the first dinner service ever manufactured in Belleek; it was destined originally for the Vice-Regal Lodge and Viscount Monck and it bore a crested M: I do not know the details of how it ended up for auction. Almost all the plates were oven-cracked, but they had wonderfully bright blue rims picked out in gold – I enjoy looking at the last two pieces from what was left of them to this day. A proper dinner service, however, we did not have, so that when, on the afternoon of Christmas Eve 1937, cardboard box after cardboard box bearing the trademark of the new Arklow Pottery arrived in our hall, excitement rose in a crescendo. Under my mother's delighted supervision, all of us, maids and children, set to unpacking; we thought how wonderful of Daddy to have realised what, more than anything, my mother wanted for Christmas: a dinner service! It was a rich cream colour, with vivid almond-green borders and discreet gilding; it was too good to be true. My father arrived back from his office – early for him – and went straight to the telephone. He came back into the hall and said, 'Put everything back into the boxes, they will be called for and taken away.' And so, on Christmas Eve, they were. They were not a present *from* my father, but a present *for* my father from the newly-opened factory! I am not sure now whether he had already made the transfer from Finance to Industry and Commerce, what is certain is that, either way, he could not have accepted. It was not, of course, the end of the world, and a similar service, correctly purchased, turned up in due course. It was, however, interesting symbolically. My father could not even appear to be influenced in his decisions by gifts.

All the parties my parents gave for Foreign Affairs – mostly during the war – were catered by old Mr Tinkler, the father of Ria Mooney, the celebrated actress, or by his son, young Mr Tinkler. Unless it turned out at the last minute that there were going to be thirteen at table – that socially significant superstition – we, the children, did not sit down to eat with the company; we ate afterwards in the kitchen, which was much more fun. We were made to dress smartly, and were produced in the double drawing room, before dinner, to help pass canapés and what have you, and to be civil to the guests. My father chose and looked after the wine. Sometimes one or other of us might join the ladies after the meal; they at that period rose from the table when dessert was over and left the gentlemen to their wine. One such evening I noticed that Lady Maffey, of whom I was fond – she was the wife of Sir John, the British representative – was sitting alone and looking indefinably sad. I knelt on the floor beside her and asked, ingenuously, was it the war? 'Oh, my dear,' she said to me, 'you are so kind, I am afraid it is.' She went on to tell me that she had had three nephews, called – improbably – Tom, Dick and Harry; they had received news, that morning, that the last surviving brother had been killed, as his two other brothers had also been, earlier in the war. 'Do not, please,' she went on, 'tell your parents until after we leave. We must not spoil their party.'

The parties were, of course, intensely political – all diplomatic parties are, or should be. My father liked and respected Sir John and gave him credit for helping to convince the British that neutral Ireland would resist invasion from any quarter and would not become a hostile 'back door' to Britain. Pivotal in all of this was, of course, John Dulanty, our High Commissioner in London, whose kindness to Séamus our family could never forget. It may have helped Dulanty's credibility in his relations with Churchill that the latter remembered his help in delivering the Irish vote in London to the Liberals, when Churchill was a member of that party. David Gray, the United States ambassador, was a more complex proposition; he was a sophisticated American journalist, without a drop of Irish-American blood in his veins, and he was married to an aunt of Mrs Roosevelt's. He was not a career diplomat, nor did he feel any need to wrap the American message in diplomatic language. This was probably eufunctional; with David Gray, you knew exactly where America stood. His wife was a splendid, feisty, elderly American lady, who became a close friend of my mother's. They played poker together. When she left Ireland she made a gift to our Barbara, who was a special favourite of hers, of a double string of graded crystal beads. Barbara considered that they were 'ageing' and, therefore, more suitable to someone already past her first youth – like me! I have them still.

Our closest wartime foreign friends were undoubtedly John and Penelope Betjeman; so close indeed were they that they shared our Uncle Paddy with us. John was wonderful company, and Penelope impressed, by the patent sincerity of her likes and dislikes – the more so as she liked us. In an odd reversal of roles, we regarded John as perfectly normal – poets were like that – and Penelope as exotic, with her Indian Army and High Tory connections, her beautiful white Arab gelding and her unexpectedly practical skills, such as in procuring and milking goats to ensure TB-free milk for her children. Their bohemian lifestyle in the dilapidated 'great house' they rented near the Phoenix Park was refreshing; people sat on the floor and ate curry. My father had to remain always near Dublin, because of the 'Emergency', and our family took a house in Brittas Bay, barely considered a resort at all in the 1930s and 1940s, for his holidays. The Betjemans stayed with us there, and John wrote us a lovely thank-you letter in come-all-ye verse, which ended:

'May they live serenely,
And neat and cleanly,
And may grass grow greenly
On their fine front lawn'.

In a moment of lunacy after my father's death, I let it go for auction in the misguided hope that it would provoke useful publicity for the sale and thus benefit the Estate financially; I was the sole executor. I know it remains in existence somewhere, but where? I have been asked if John influenced my writing, did I show him my poems, etc, etc? The answer is no and no. He belonged in another world; besides, all my own family wrote verse – it was no big deal. John's absurdities were treasured, as when he declared that what endeared the Anglican Communion to him was 'the real absence'. Meanwhile, Penelope took me in hand. I could ride, competently if not elegantly, and was hoping soon to hunt. We went together on a horseback tour of the Wicklow hills: Chapelizod to Blessington, Blessington to Glendalough, Glendalough to Glenmalure, Glenmalure to Roundwood, Roundwood to Powerscourt, and then home. We stayed with people as diverse as Seán T O'Kelly and Phyllis (our then President and his wife) at Roundwood, and the Kemysses (a very Anglo-Irish, old Ascendancy family) at Glenmalure. Mrs Kemyss belonged to that stratum of female society at the time that wore its hat at breakfast; there was a rule of thumb governing headwear: the lower the longer for a male, and the higher the longer for a female. I slept badly in Glenmalure; I was troubled by ghosts: Fiach MacHugh's foster-mother drinking his blood from his severed head in Elizabeth's time, and the like. I think Penelope wanted to socialise me and to ensure that I knew the facts of life. English friends tended to think that Barbara and I were being brought up like boys and to worry about us. If this was so in Penelope's case – and I think it was – she would have had the sense not to mention it to my mother and to do good by stealth. Possibly she thought also that I might prove a useful source of gossip for John. Except for my gathering that it was useful to sleep with one's fiancé before marrying him, 'just in case', nothing very much came of this holiday, but my enjoyment of it was total and uncomplicated. Penelope, with superhuman generosity, allowed me to ride the Arab, while she rode a handsome Connemara pony. A sack of potatoes would have acquired grace riding that Arab horse, an infinitely loving and love-able animal!

My brother and I relished the social whirl of Brittas – my parents con-tinued to entertain officially a great deal – but we slipped away to Dun-quin as soon and as often as we decently could. Séamus was now an advanced medical student and Dunquin was an ideal place to study; hav-ing to work implied no criticism there of anyone else, interfered with no one's holiday.

ʒ   ʒ   ʒ

The New IRA was active and resented government repression. We now had guards on the house twenty-four hours a day – my mother said the male presence made it easy to keep maids – and an escort car followed my father's car everywhere. The rest of us, including my mother, rode bicycles. My mother's stately progress to and from her lectures, bolt upright on the saddle of her sturdy machine, was a sight to see. She also, on occasion, rode down to Brittas, about forty miles distant – quite a feat.

In the ground-floor room (semi-basement) at 9 Leeson Park, which had hitherto been our 'children's den', my mother installed an open hearth on which a great deal of the family cooking was done, in pot-ovens, using turf as fuel to save power and to comply with the energy restrictions then in force. This room now became our family living room, and the first-floor rooms, so spacious and colourful, were only opened and warmed for parties. Blackout blinds were not needed; we had shutters that we closed behind the Dún Emer curtains. The radio controlled our lives: we had to be absolutely silent during the news – BBC, or Irish from Athlone – when my father was listening. There were compensations, however. We three became fans of 'Itma' – 'It's That Man Again' – the precursor of 'The Goon Show'; 'Itma' irritated my mother. She missed the days before the blackout, when people dropped in for tea, or sherry of an evening; neither she nor my father ever tolerated stout in the house, but lager was acceptable in summer. My father brought his files home, and the only place in the house warm enough to work in was the den, now renamed the breakfast room, although nobody ate breakfast there. My parents had theirs in bed, we ours in the kitchen; we children all drank milk, which stretched the tea ration. In time the edge went off this austerity, and, although our family meals were still always served downstairs, our parents now had a fire lit in the 'back' (and smaller) drawing room and sat there: a vast improvement.

The war became a constant in our lives. The young men we knew left their university studies and joined the Irish Army full-time, where most of them were quickly commissioned as Second Lieutenants. This meant that, when in uniform, they were not allowed to carry parcels; that function was discharged for them by their girlfriends. I became an Air Raid Warden, responsible for distribution of gas-masks, inspecting blackouts, learning the importance of emergency communications, wearing uniform, all of which I loved, and I also enjoyed the wide circle of acquaintance all this entailed. I cannot remember at any stage dwelling deeply on the realities of death and pain – not, at any rate, until after the fall of Paris. At that time it was the poems of Louis Aragon, clandestinely published and smuggled out of France, that, when they reached Ireland, alerted me to the complexities and heartbreak of defeat, so that it became the serious object of my life one day to return to France, pursue my love affair with French culture and in some way make amends, as it were, for having been powerless in that country's time of crisis.

ೞ   ೞ   ೞ

Realities our household could not ignore were the continuing activities of the IRA. I will let my father speak for me again here, through *The Irish*

Times interviews with Michael McInerney, in order to put younger readers in the picture. How my father saw it was always how we saw it:

'Anglo-Irish relations had never been better than with the Chamberlain Government in the years before the outbreak of war. "But," says Mr MacEntee, "then, tragically, came the complete reverse of winning public opinion, the 'New I.R.A.' (*sic*) bombing campaign of British cities driving away all the sympathy and the support so laboriously won – blown to the winds."

The Irish Government's triumph was damned [*sic*; for damped?], by the 'declaration of war' by the I.R.A. on English cities, opening, *as a consequence, a new Civil War in Ireland between the Government and the I.R.A.* [my italics]. Too soon also, only a year or so later, came that greater Second World War which threatened the very life of a nation and of its citizens. It was a war in which Ireland had to defend its neutrality on many fronts, external and internal. The Second World War involved Ireland in more crises than ever before in its history and they were crises which too often verged on catastrophe.

The I.R.A. activities during the War had been dangerous to national security and had meant the diversion of State forces desperately needed for national defence. They also compelled the Government to take the most serious penal measures against them. "It was a most trying period," Mr MacEntee says. Some I.R.A. activists were men like Paddy McGrath and Tony D'Arcy, old comrades of Cabinet Ministers in the 1919–22 period. "We gave them every chance but they left us with no alternative but the ultimate penalty."

The most difficult Cabinet discussion concerned Tomás MacCurtain, a son of the martyred Cork Lord Mayor in 1921 and a member of a family well-known to Cabinet Ministers.

Thomas (*sic*) MacCurtain had been arrested after a Civic Guard had been shot dead in Cork. He had been tried and sentenced to death and the Government heard an appeal for his reprieve. "We realised the issue was to 'govern or abdicate', but there was a war on also." De Valera warned, in the Dáil, that more lives could be lost by clemency. Finally, MacCurtain was reprieved, but the discussion went on for a very long time indeed. Another difficult case was that of Paddy McGrath, an old comrade. He had been arrested, but after a hunger strike was released. He was back in I.R.A. activity almost at once and a year later was held after a gun-fight in which two detectives were killed, two wounded and a young I.R.A. volunteer also wounded. McGrath, with another man [Tommy Harte], was sentenced to death, the first sentence of the Military Court. The Cabinet discussion on appeal against the sentence was also tense and prolonged but finally they all agreed with the decision – no reprieve.'

೫   ೫   ೫

By this time (1941), I had, in default of other candidates, become auditor of a small literary society, which met in the afternoon and held its proceedings in Irish: An Cumann Liteartha. As a result of my mother's shameless social blackmail, I was able to produce visiting speakers like Seán Ó Faoláin and Myles na gCopaleen, both of whom drew crowds. (Myles was under double pressure since he was my father's private secretary.) Consequently, the society was enjoying something of a vogue.

At our first meeting after the trial, sentence and execution, in the autumn of 1940, of the IRA men McGrath and Harte (a third man, Hunt, was reprieved), we drew a less welcome crowd, and I was faced, at the opening of Private Business, with a call for a three minutes' silence to protest against the executions. I was moving towards the private, ethical position that all deliberate taking of life was morally wrong, but I was not about to add to the difficulties of the grim decision my father had felt obliged to take. All such executions were Cabinet decisions and unanimous. Instinct – or was it inspiration? – took over: I suspended the meeting, remarking that the attendance were now free to behave as they pleased without involving the society. Almost everybody stood in silence, while the Chair (me) remained sitting. The protestors were a mixed crowd – rather like a 'No' vote in a Nice referendum. Many were genuine sympathisers with the IRA, or genuine advocates of the abolition of the death penalty. Some were Fine Gael opposition supporters – such as 'young' Tom O'Higgins, so called because there was also his father, 'old' Tom O'Higgins, a formidable FG personality, brother of the murdered Kevin O'Higgins – anxious to embarrass the government and without scruples as to how, and still others, quite a few, merely wanted to see how a woman auditor would handle the situation. I gave them ample time to savour the ensuing confusion; then I recalled the meeting to order. There must have been a record of this in the Society's minutes, but God only knows where they are now.

CB   CB   CB

Like almost every other undergraduate Arts student in their final year at UCD, I had a crowd-scene role in the drama of the Stephen Hayes affair. The unfortunate man – you could not but be sorry for him – who had hitherto thought himself Chief-of-Staff of the IRA, had been dislodged, without notice, in a *coup* by the Belfast members of that body, and held 'before trial' in a cottage in the Dublin Mountains belonging to one of our lecturers in English, Roger McHugh. Roger had actually been invigilating our degree exams when he was called out of the hall and arrested by the Garda Síochána. Stephen had been moved by then to another 'safe house' in Dublin, from which he had escaped, more dead than alive, to give himself up to the Gardaí in the Rathmines station. Roger was subsequently released, presumably because it was believed that his cottage had been used without his knowledge, or leave. I had no sympathy with his predicament; as far as I was concerned he was an armchair IRA man and deserved all he got. Worse, he ran what was, to my mind, a particularly intrusive, experimental tutorial, which I loathed but had to attend, and was, for my Puritan tastes, far too pally with his students. He wasn't paid to be hail-fellow-well-met and popular; he was paid to teach.

The closest the killings – there were a good few on both sides, but I don't remember much public disquiet – came to me personally was in September 1942 when Detective Sergeant Dennis O'Brien was murdered. He was shot at his own gate, within 500 yards of our old home on Wilbrook Road, Rathfarnham, and one of our former neighbours witnessed the escape of the suspected killers, although she was subsequently unable to identify them. He was a particularly zealous police officer and, as such, was targeted. I remember my father taking myself and Séamus to call on Dennis O'Brien's brother, Larry, to condole with him, in his office in the GPO – he was Permanent Secretary of the Department of Posts and Telegraphs. As children we knew him quite well, because we had watched various Saint Patrick's Day processions from the front windows of his Department.

PART III: CAREER CHOICES

The Travelling Studentship Award was the most prestigious of the National University awards. It was a horrible competition; competitors were relatively few, drawn from all the university colleges, and only the first place counted. In the nature of things, all the competitors tended to be friends, or at least acquaintances with common interests. In 1942 I won it; I had never worked so hard in my life before and was never capable of working so hard again. Here was my dream ticket to Paris – there was a flourishing school of Celtic Studies at the Institut des Hautes Études en Sorbonne. I could not, of course, take up the studentship in Paris while the war still raged. My teachers tried to persuade me to choose the University of Edinburgh instead, but I remained firm. I was then, most generously, offered a junior research scholar's post at the new Dublin Institute for Advanced Studies. This was like an apprenticeship; the Institute was never a teaching institution, having been founded by Mr de Valera to encourage research. It comprised two schools: Physics and Celtic Studies. My father also had plans for my immediate future; he suggested that I study for the Bar at King's Inns. A suggestion from him was, of course, an order. The outcome was that I accepted the Institute's offer *and* took time off to attend the law lectures.

What I really wanted to be at that time was an actress, not in films – I was too highbrow for that – but on the stage. It came about that in my second year at college, myself and Maria Luisa Ontiveros, the Spanish Minister Plenipotentiary's elder daughter, had become friends. She was a spirited young woman, in the way that only women frustrated by a totally anti-feminist régime, as Spain's was under Franco, can be. Together we applied for admission to the Abbey School of Acting. I had acted already with the UCD Dramatic Society, sharing the stage with Michael Clarke and Danny O'Herlihy (both later well-known in the world of film), in a production of the Elizabethan dramatist Decker's 'Shoemaker's Holiday'; I had loved it and got a good 'notice', with one reservation, ie, that I should pay more attention to the 'virtue of repose'. Now, with Maria Luisa, I was called to an audition before Lennox Robinson. Lennox was something of a legend in our house. When he was being

159

ushered into my father's office, along with WB Yeats, to discuss the Abbey's finances, he was heard to enquire in an aggrieved tone, 'Who is this Minister anyway, that we are going to see?' Another time, my parents had taken his house in Dalkey so that my father could remain near his office while on holiday, and so that our two invalids, Séamus and our little next-door-neighbour Aideen, could be safe there within easy reach of urgent medical care. Lennox forgot that he had let his house. My mother heard the doorbell about midnight and went to answer it. Lennox stood wavering in the pouring rain outside, struggling to reorient himself. Then, in a burst of inspiration, he vouchsafed, 'I've come to count the spoo-oo-oons,' and oscillated past her, to collapse on the living-room sofa. In the morning he was gone. Now, he looked at me over his glasses and seemed as vague about my identity as he had been about my father's. I think – no, I know – I acquitted myself very well, but neither myself nor Maria Luisa were accepted by the school. I have no doubt, whatever – although I never asked him – but that the 'Minister', my father, not hers, had made it quite clear in advance, to the Abbey authorities, that he had *no* intention of 'putting his daughter on the stage'. I did not mind all that much, for my interest in Celtic languages and literature was very real; I could have done without the Law, though.

The Benchers of King's Inns made no concessions to the existence of female students. That meant that there were absolutely no lavatory facilities for us in the building on Henrietta Street. The nearest were in the Gresham Hotel, quite some distance away on O'Connell Street; admittedly, there were only two women students. Henrietta Street was a slum; bare-bottomed children played in the mud of the gutters and added colourfully to my vocabulary. In my memory it is always raining as I push my bicycle across Dublin, from Merrion Square, to attend two hours' lectures four afternoons a week; four afternoons of numbing boredom, enlivened only by the ebullient personalities of my fellow students, notably Ja-ja Wachuku, subsequently Foreign Minister of Nigeria. The one woman lecturer disliked women students only slightly less than she disliked blacks, and she *loathed* blacks. Ja-ja used to observe wistfully, 'In my country, we would eat that woman.' Fortunately, a very few nights cramming on black coffee were enough to get you through the exams in those days, and I was duly called to the Bar, along with several contemporaries who subsequently made legal or academic names for themselves, such as Tom Finlay (until recently Chief Justice), Peter O'Malley (Judge Advocate General), Patrick Meenan (of UCD) and Tony Hederman (also to become a judge). I never practised, but the qualification came in handy when I applied to join External (now Foreign) Affairs.

Ↄ   Ↄ   Ↄ

Working in the Institute for Advanced Studies was like being paid for doing something I enjoyed, and doing it in optimum circumstances. I gave most of my earnings to my mother; I could always ask for some back if I needed it, and I knew that we always lived well beyond our means and that, although our credit was good, overdrafts were always a threat. My relationship with the Institute's professors was peculiar, much as it had been earlier at UCD, in particular with Professor Bergin, who had once dedicated poetry to my mother. All these learned men tended to assure me that they welcomed seeing the children of their contemporaries surfacing in the world of Celtic Studies, but could not disguise from me that, in spite of my good results on paper, they found me an unknown quantity to deal with. I realised fully that we were often at cross purposes, but could not think how to remedy this; some of it undoubtedly had roots in Civil War hostilities, but a major part of the difficulty was, I think, that I had always known Irish, never had to learn it, any more than I had had to learn English. Rather few 'native' speakers of Irish at that time ended up in Celtic Studies – they chose professions with more immediate likelihood of financial returns. I was neither one thing nor the other. I loved the Old Irish poems and sagas, but never felt the need to master Old Irish – it was a course requisite – as a separate language, while my instinct made it easy for me to arrive at what I regarded as sufficient comprehension by guesswork and reference to notes and vocabulary, and I could get by without what was regarded as a 'thorough foundation'. Very early on in Professor Bergin's class at UCD, he wrote on the blackboard, *In t-ech gel* (the white steed, in Old Irish.). 'Now,' he said, 'I want you all to decline that phrase for me, I have given you three of the forms, so you can only make twenty-seven mistakes.' I promptly wrote down, *In t-each geal* (substituting two Modern Irish forms). 'Here,' said Professor Bergin, standing behind me, 'is a young woman who is capable of making twenty-nine mistakes!' When I was just a little girl, and Bergin had sat with Dan Binchy, the great Old Irish jurist, and my Uncle Paddy and the 'Common Noun' on the clifftop near the *caladh* (landing-place) in Dunquin, or on the strand at Com Dhíneoil (Cumeenole), discussing the finer points of language, I had been encouraged to look for sweets in his pockets. Now I appreciated his wit, but felt a bit bruised by it. Similarly, I admired enormously Professor TF O'Rahilly, the Director of the Celtic Studies School at the Institute, on whose masterly collections of medieval Irish poetry, *Dánta Grá* (Love Poems) and *Measgra Dánta* (Various Poems), I had cut my teeth as a student of Irish literature, at sixteen. Nevertheless, I did not always catch his drift when he would ask me did I understand this or that Irish phrase, or would I use it. I used to feel like the 'Princess' in Dunquin when my mother asked her did she 'have' such and such a saying. 'No,' she would answer, 'but I will now.' I could not imagine why he needed to ask. In spite of these misunderstandings, I profited a great deal from my training in the Institute and, in spite of sometimes feeling 'out of step', I was very happy working there. My older contemporaries there, the senior scholars, all of whom became authoritative Celticists in their turn, except for Séamus Henchy, who moved over to the study of Law and became a judge, were all good companions. The three I knew best, Brian Ó Cuív, Seán MacAirt and Séamus Carney, are no longer amongst us, God rest their souls! They were all very kind to me.

ɔ3   ɔ3   ɔ3

The Irish-language monthly, *Comhar*, produced by the inter-university students' organisation, *An Comhchaidreamh*, was founded in the 1940s by Seán Ó hÉigeartaigh of Trinity College and Tomás de Bháldraithe of UCD, among others. It is strange that when I think now of those contemporaries, who became lifelong friends of mine, it is as young men that I remember them – so many of them are now dead, God rest them! The paper was often put together – a literal scissors-and-paste job – in our house, in the 'breakfast' room, now taken over again by our generation. I had published occasional poems in various college magazines, and whenever the jigsaw defied assembly, Seán would say, 'Have you anything, about two inches long, that would go in there? Or maybe Barbara would draw us a picture?' Séamus was our truly talented painter, but all of us could draw; Barbara, however, was the easiest bullied. That was how most of my poems first came to be published. Perhaps this is the point where I should say something about how I came to write them.

The poems were always the result of intense pressure of emotion, although they did not always reflect this directly, and although sometimes the emotion was triggered by a vicarious experience. A phrase – in words, or sometimes one of music, to which words would adhere – would present itself in my head and that phrase would establish the parameters of the entire lyric, whether personal, or dramatic. The whole, no matter what length, would evolve organically as a setting, in sound as well as in sense, from that seminal phrase, which, for me, would always encapsulate the original circumstances of the emotion, almost like an electronic diary – I never kept the ordinary kind. Usually the poems wrote themselves; I rarely edited. I had internalised so many poetic forms by the time I reached my teens that choice of form was automatic, and was always dictated automatically by the original key phrase, so that form could not help but enhance sense – that, at least, was my conviction, and is still. Sometimes there would be one element, often a single word, that would not come right, and I would reluctantly put in a stopgap, which I would always know was a weak link. Equally, I always knew the right link was inherent in the whole, and hoped that, sooner or later, I would hear it click: I have rarely been disappointed and, when I have, I cringe if I have to contemplate the faulty line, even if no one else spots it.

At this stage I wrote verse in both English and Irish – the choice always depended on the initial impulse. It was only years later, in Spain, that I realised – under the influence of Federico Garcia Lorca – that in my Irish I commanded a much richer and more authoritative medium than in my Dublin, middle-class English, but this *eureka* belongs with my Spanish adventures. My father liked my English poems and had them typed up, but mostly my poetry, in either language, was taken for granted. In my parents' generation all educated people wrote verse. Hardly anyone saw it as a livelihood.

ଓ   ଓ   ଓ

Came 1945, and it was clear that the war would soon end in an Allied victory. I spent all those summer holidays working in the Institute, most often alone. I had two tasks to finish: one, to complete the notes and vocabulary of the two medieval texts I was editing for the Institute, and two, to complete my minor thesis on Pierce Ferriter – a re-reading of his poems, with notes and emendations, which, in conjunction with my Studentship results, would get me my MA from UCD. I dealt with both: I handed the notes and vocabulary, in manuscript, to the Registrar of the Institute, and my mother typed up my thesis expertly, so that I could submit it to the examiners. Scholars in those days did not type; manuscripts were supposed to be so clear that they went straight to the printers, thus eliminating the danger of errors infiltrating them in the process of their being copied by a typist. That, at least, was the ideal. My mother had needed to type in the Boycott Office; I cannot type to this day. With all my responsibilities discharged, I felt immeasurably liberated. 'Fair stood the wind for France!'

CHAPTER VI

Francophilia and Foreign Affairs

PART I: POST-LIBERATION PARIS

Four Irish girls assembled, in October 1945, in the bed-sitting-room belonging to one of them, myself, on the third floor of the Foyer Universitaire des Jeunes Filles on the Boulevard Saint-Michel, in the heart of the Paris Latin Quarter, opposite the Luxembourg Gardens. Paris was a strange, empty city: there were virtually no motor-cars on the streets and few buses. The glorious architecture took on a remote, museum-like coldness; the Continental weather, too, was unseasonably cold. We all wore tweed slacks, which were not yet normal wear for young women at home in Ireland, and heavy sweaters. Technically, the building was heated, but not so as you'd notice, and it was hard to keep warm. We were debating whether we would go downstairs to the dining room and face the truly horrible food there, or break into the reserves of food that our parents had been allowed to buy for us from the Irish Red Cross: lovely, lovely tinned butter and tinned ham, and, best of all, tinned *real* coffee and powdered milk. We had only been there a few days and already we were always hungry. Food was plentiful in Normandy and Brittany, but the railway lines had all been cut during the Allied advance on Paris and few civilian goods-trains were running as yet. Those that were, were often derailed and their contents would arrive in Paris on the black market. We had been warned that things might well get worse and, besides, we had realised that our Red Cross rations and the cigarettes we had also been advised to bring – although none of us smoked except the eldest – were *currency;* in stringently-rationed Paris, barter flourished. So our rations were precious and not to be consumed with abandon. As the very first foreign students into Paris after the Liberation, we had many introductions to French families, and we had been briefed that no present could be more acceptable than Irish butter, or Galtee cheese – '*cette merveilleuse crême de Gruyère*' (that marvellous Gruyère cream).

If we chose instead to go down to the restaurant, it would be warmer, but it would also be damp and steamy. A thousand students, male and fe-male, ate there every day, as well as the two hundred or so *pensionaires* (boarders) of the Foyer. The hungry queues stretched for hundreds of yards along the pavement outside, but we were allowed to *couper* (cut) *la queue* at the bottom of our stairs. Inside it was self-service and we collected our sadly-battered, literally, not literary, 'cheap, tin trays' and cutlery as we went in. First came watery vegetable soup, in rough metal bowls utterly disagreeable to the touch, then a tin plate of runny *green* mashed potatoes made, we were assured, with lard (*saindoux*) – wheel-grease more likely, grumbled the clientele – followed by the only edible item, piteously small individual cartons of yoghurt. Every so often there was a *supplément*, labelled '*Don de l'Armée Américaine*' (gift of the American Army), which would consist of not very generous chunks of spam, or some similar meat product – one chunk per head. Americans were not all that popular in Paris; I don't think this largesse helped. The menu never varied, and the restaurant was always crowded. On the first day you felt it could be worse; the soup and potatoes were hot and there was salt. On the second your enthusiasm waned. By the third you shovelled it in like fuel and got out as quickly as you could. Yet even in that grim ambience, I saw young lovers sharing one bowl of that ghastly soup with two spoons!

I wrote a piece for Frank Gallagher, the editor of the *Irish Press*, that December, which may convey a more immediate impression of conditions than I can give now. It was in the Christmas edition; I can't remember was I paid for it?

'Last week, the cold closed in on Paris like a vice. For three days we lived in a world of ice and iron – five degrees centigrade below freezing-point.

In the Luxembourg Gardens, deserted except for the odd, hurrying figure taking a short cut by the long, tree-bordered alleys, the fountains were frozen white columns.

The hands of the woman who sold you your newspaper were black with the cold. You were astonished to realise that the central heating still functioned as it had a few days before, so little perceptible effect had it on the atmosphere indoors.

It became a rare and wonderful luxury to buy a bag of roasted chestnuts at the street corner and carry them home cupped in your hands – a little glowing centre of warmth and comfort.

Everywhere you saw furs and ski-trousers and snow-boots: all kinds and descriptions of extraordinary combinations of garments. Those who achieved the most truly bear-like exteriors were the most to be envied, and you marvelled at the elegance of a Parisienne even in innumerable layers of shapeless garments.

A few grudging flakes of snow fell; and then on the third night it rained.

Rain is important in Paris. The electricity situation becomes more and more difficult as a result of these last months' exceptional drought, coupled with the widespread dislocation of plant.

Further and more serious cuts are expected, for Paris must not only cope with the needs of the city but must also supplement the supply to the provinces where the shortage is acute.

Candles are unobtainable. In the churches, an ingenious slot-device with small electric lamps which burn for half a minute or so on the insertion of a small coin has replaced them.

It does not seem likely that even this modernised form of the traditionalised devotion will be possible much longer. The cumulative effect of several unheralded blackouts daily on the nerves and spirits of anyone to whose work light is essential has to be experienced to be realised.

The streets are, on the whole, well-lighted and they need to be. Reports of robbery with violence are a commonplace; robbery carried out with a bare-faced audacity that takes your breath away.

American uniforms are often worn by the assailants, but whether or not these are a disguise cannot be said.'

You might expect all of us girls to be downcast in such circumstances and surroundings – not a bit of it. We had all longed to come here and we rose to the challenge in high spirits. We had known of each other before we arrived. We all had scholarships; I had my delayed, two-year Travelling Studentship. We had not, however, all met till now and we proved miraculously compatible. Kathleen, the eldest, was not just a student, she was a *disciple* of James Joyce, an irreverent, laughter-loving girl whose unabashed moods added constant drama to our lives. Kay was a Trinity graduate, working on a·thesis on François Mauriac, very pretty and not herself unlike a *'jenne-fille rangée'* (steady young lady) in a French novel; she had been to school in French-speaking Switzerland and her French was impeccable. Sheila was the youngest, very gentle, but with a clear mind and great strength of character, lovely eyes, lovely teeth and lovely hair, totally devoid of affectation and hoping to qualify as an archivist. I was studying Celtic Languages at the Institut des Hautes Études. We all had fur coats, something none of us had ever thought to have, but our parents had been persuaded that these were a strict necessity in the face of the Continental winter. In effect, almost all the French women students wore dyed sheepskin coats over colourful checked cotton skirts, which disguised the shabby woollens underneath. Their legs were often bare, in spite of the weather, and camouflaged with stocking make-up, and their footwear consisted of extraordinarily high and elaborate wooden clogs, like pattens. Their hair was crimped into a mass of Medusa-like curls. They fingered our un-glamorous 'economy-cut' tweeds with longing: '*C'est de la vraie laine,*' (real wool) they murmured wistfully. Nevertheless, such was the authority of Parisian fashion sense that we all surreptitiously tried to tweak our insular appearance into line with it, one way or another.

The Foyer had originally been an American private enterprise foundation; it was now State-subsidised. The *Directrice* was an American lady, who had spent almost all her adult life in Paris without acquiring more than a smattering of drolly incorrect French. At our inaugural get-together, over hot chocolate (ersatz) in the Library – a long, elegant, book-lined gallery made to look welcoming, in spite of the cold, with subdued lighting and warmly coloured Oriental-type rugs – Miss Watson, that was her name, delighted all of us during her pep-talk by reminding us how lucky we were to be so comfortably housed, and saying, '*Il ne faut jamais oublier que vous êtes dans une maison publique.*' (You must never forget that you are in a 'public' house.) *Maison publique* was the polite French for a brothel; she meant State-financed. She was nevertheless an admirable old root, tough and liberal. She had been interned during the German occupation and her close friend was Sylvia Beach, Joyce's publisher, whom the French girls in the Foyer called, totally without malice, purely as a matter of realising foreign phonemes, Miss 'Bitch'. She attended many of the monthly, hot-chocolate *soirées*, which were quasi-compulsory for us.

The *pensionaires* were fifty percent French and fifty percent foreign and, under its veneer of American east coast, plain living and high thinking, the Foyer was a microcosm of the chaotic realities of post-war Europe. Two girls committed suicide, one girl gave birth and another aborted, girls smuggled men into their rooms and, most sensational of all, one girl got engaged to a GI and flaunted nylon stockings and lacy nylon underwear up and down our deprived corridor. This was post-war sex as we had never imagined it in Ireland. We heard stories – oral history – of atrocities committed by retreating Wehrmacht troops, notably by Polish regiments who 'had nothing to lose': a pregnant woman cut in two in a saw-mill – and the baby – for example. Outside a tiny restaurant, next-door to the Foyer, hung a crêpe-scarved photograph of the proprietor and *chef cuisinier,* who had been shot outside his own door by a Nazi sniper stationed in the tower of the Church of Saint Jacques du Haut Pas, just around the corner from us, where we went to Mass. One of our closest French friends was at the time recovering in Ireland from a nervous break-down consequent on her having pointed out to the Free French forces where the fire that killed the restaurateur was coming from. Every night in her dreams she saw the man turn over and over in the air as he fell from that church tower – dead.This was what she had intended would happen, but she couldn't exorcise a sense of guilt. All along the Boulevard Saint-Michel we saw the chipped masonry left by exchanges of fire between the retreating occupiers and the Free French troops.

In contrast to the weather, the welcome was extraordinarily warm. *Entre étudiants* (among students) friendships developed rapidly and I discovered this amazing fact: French people – men and women – *liked* women; not desired, lusted after, or coveted women, *liked.* The grocer, the baker, the university doorman, all called you '*ma petite dame*' (my little lady) and were glad to see you. Camaraderie between men and women students was easy and absolute; romance was oddly secon-dary. Nationalities fraternised easily, we met North African Jews, *pieds noirs* (Algerian French), the sons of Arab *Caïds* – who were vague as to the number of their father's wives or their own sisters, but knew exactly how many brothers they had and their ages. Eastern Europeans – the Iron Curtain had not yet come down – and, of course, every variety of the ar-ticulate, self-assured young of the French *bourgeoisie.* In our Foyer, there was one ashen-faced, desperately thin girl, probably French and Jewish, who kept herself strictly to herself: she was a former concentration-camp inmate. We never knew her story, but, miraculously, with the coming of spring, she was seen chatting across her bicycle with a young man and be-gan a discreet use of lipstick; shortly afterwards she disappeared from our lives. In this favourable social climate, I, now twenty-three, at last acquired a boyfriend, a gentle, clever, intensely musical Dutchman, not, I now think, particularly interested in women, but we kissed dutifully and I considered myself engaged. It was a comforting feeling, but I don't think either of us had any intention of pushing things beyond that. It was a useful social convention, nothing more. It died a natural death when I went back to Ireland.

The Irish students were enormously impressed by the very real official concern for the welfare of students in Paris. It struck us as part of a universal resolve to make up to the young for the humiliations and privations of the war years. Some of its manifestations were less agreeable than others: the blood-testing for sexually transmitted diseases, for example, which all students – foreign, or otherwise – had to undergo. Like lost souls we wandered along the dim, cold corridors of French officialdom, carrying horrid little grey glass vials with corks stuck in them and sharpened quills stuck in the corks, until we reached the appropriate dingy location, where the quills were unceremoniously jabbed into the vein behind the elbow of the bearer so that the blood dripped down into the vials, and the testee set off queasily again to find the forbidding laboratory in which it would be tested. No point in our protesting that we were *virgines intactae*, even if we had had the *nous* to think of such a thing. On the other hand, the wonderful array of student privileges, including free theatre and concert tickets, took our breath away.

That first winter we saw Racine's *Phèdre* at the Comédie Française, utterly transformed from a language textbook into the living poetry and drama of intense passion that the play really is, with exquisite young people of both sexes in the leading roles. We saw Louis Jouvet in *L'École des Femmes*; we saw Mozart at the Opera and *Pelléas and Mélisande* by Debussy; in the commercial theatre we saw Camus' *Caligula*, and as Kay and I walked through the snowy night back to the Foyer, we were filled with a kind of existential excitement and courage with which to address our own petty problems after imagining those of Ancient Rome. We saw *L'Aiglon* by Victor Hugo, *The Love of Three Oranges* by, I forget whom, and innumerable other contemporary pieces, too many to list. Here is how I reported back to Frank Gallagher at the *Irish Press*:

'Meanwhile the intellectual life of Paris seems as vivid and as vigorous as ever. Theatres, concerts and lectures draw crowded audiences. The book-market is flooded with new publications, regrettably so in many cases, for poems and novels of indifferent merit find publishers while the standard classics are out of print and textbooks of all kinds unobtainable.

In this connection, it is interesting to recall an interview with Mme. Desvignes, one of the moving spirits of the 'Éditions de Minuit' [who had spoken to the students of the Foyer].

That is an organisation which, by the exercise of considerable courage and ingenuity, produced and published, throughout the occupation, not merely the simple editions by which the works of Aragon, Vercors [author of the then 'cult' novella, *Le Silence de la Mer (The Silence of the Sea)*] and many others became known in France and abroad, but, with glorious audacity, *de luxe* editions, which are priceless.

The inner workings of this unique publishing company, where the author never knew the editor, nor the editor the printer, nor the printer the binder, nor the binder the distributor, are as fascinating as an adventure story.

One can well understand how Mme. Desvignes looks back with regret on those days, which in retrospect seem a magnificent and successful practical joke, to which danger was only an added spice.'

Perhaps most interestingly of all, we saw Laurence Olivier's 'King Lear'. I remember being unable to suspend disbelief in the glamorous Goneril and Regan – they spoke with such impeccably well-bred English accents, like some of the teachers in Alexandra. Accents also provided a moment of comedy at one point in the gallery, where the free seats were. Our section was so far to the left that we could not see the side of the stage facing us unless we stood up, which, regrettably, some of us did. The rows behind began to shout angrily, '*Assis! Assis!* (Sit down!) In front of us sat a very large, very placid, black American NCO. He turned his head towards the shouters and announced peaceably but clearly, in his warm Southern drawl, 'Well, Ma'am, if you kyean see you is sure lucky, because ah kaan see at all!' He, of course, had heard 'ah see'. French officialdom tended to become ratty when English-speaking Irish people and English-speaking Americans couldn't understand each other, but it happened quite often. There were Americans billeted all over Paris, and their lack of concern for irreplaceable objects, like chairs, or glasses, was widely resented.

೧ଃ   ೧ଃ   ೧ଃ

Another endless source of gratitude was the family hospitality we received from our French friends, especially among those academics with whom we came in contact. You must remember here that an evening meal for seven or eight people, with a roast of veal, say, for the main dish, could easily exhaust a family's entire meat ration for the month. Just at the point where the roast was about to be carved, the accomplished French conversation would always flag and, in spite of themselves, all eyes would fix on the slicing and distribution. After such an evening, the invited student would not feel hungry for days.

The most memorable of many such evenings was when Sheila and I were invited by Sam Beckett and his wife – I never knew her name, we called her Madame – to share a wonderful stew in the comfortable, cheerful kitchen of their Paris flat. Sam, as most readers will know, had been active in the French Resistance (*le Maquis*) and, after the war, had volunteered to join the staff of the Irish Red Cross hospital at Saint Lô, as an interpreter and driver. That was how we had come to meet him. On our first arrival in Paris he had driven us all over the strange, almost deserted city in the Red Cross car in his free time, to orient us. Now he and his brilliant wife fed us magnificently, courtesy of the Red Cross they insisted, on fresh food from Normandy – not a tin in sight. A little know-all among our student acquaintance had briefed us with a lot of nonsense about the Beckett *ménage* before we went there. Sam, she said, had married beneath him, an illiterate peasant woman, while he was in the *Maquis*. I only hope Sheila and I were not too crushingly nice to the warmly welcoming and distinguished lady who actually greeted us, and who, it transpired, was a professor of philosophy. Pray that our natural good manners helped us to avoid giving offence. We knew Sam was a writer; I had tried to read *Molloy* when my father had brought it home, but I had got stuck. We had no idea how celebrated the author would become, and we took his kindness for granted. Hopefully, he found us restful; I'm afraid our minds were mostly on the beautiful food.

೧ଃ   ೧ଃ   ೧ଃ

Another unforgettable evening deserves a full account. We had only just arrived in Paris and were still struggling with the endless formalities required to legitimise our residence, inscribe ourselves as university students and arrange to have our scholarship cheques cashed, when the *Direction* (administration) at the Foyer advised us of a historically significant debate due to take place in the Great Amphitheatre of the Sorbonne, with the scientist Jolliot-Curie, the son-in-law of the great Marie Curie, on the panel, to discuss the question, then vexed and pressing, of sharing atomic information with the Soviet Union. Such advice was, of course, an order, and we all four set out; admission for students was, as usual, free. We had yet to realise, at this stage, that a dangerous current of indiscipline underran the life around us, a kind of distorted individualism, a deliberate, adventurous irresponsibility – the climate of Cocteau's *La Folle de Chaillot* (The Madwoman of Chaillot) – which made a Parisian crowd at all times incalculable and dangerous, whether it was a theatre queue, or a queue at the grocer's, or a rush-hour queue in the Métro. I described it for Frank Gallagher as follows:

> 'This unsettled condition of society accounts, of course, for the crowds of policemen you meet everywhere who, to tell the truth, seem to have little enough to do and less inclination to do it.
>
> Parisian wit flourishes at their expense, the favourite theory being that, as their business is to restore order, they must first ensure disorder.
>
> Like all police everywhere, they are popularly supposed to be incapable of turning up anywhere until everything is all over. I know myself that a riot can be well under way before they interfere.'

We girls had already experienced the *monôme*, when hundreds of students ran in single file through Paris to draw attention to their affairs. You hear them before you see them, as they chant '*Formez le monôme*' (join the run), at the top of their voices. They could cause a great deal of disruption, we were told, but this first time when we heard them and saw them there was no traffic to disrupt and they were celebrating, not protesting: they were welcoming General de Gaulle to the Latin Quarter. Now, in the great courtyard outside the Sorbonne amphitheatre, the dangerous, queuing crowd was the expectant and impatient audience, waiting, demanding to be admitted. The amphitheatre was already full, so was the courtyard. We were in the courtyard.

At first people were witty and good-humoured and might have dispersed, grumbling ineffectually, had the police not decided, for reasons best known to themselves, to throw a cordon around them and, with admirable detachment, hold them there for at least two hours. Was this an example of the French theory on policework, as set out for the *Irish Press*, above? During those two hours women screamed and fainted and were passed out over the heads of the gathering, which had become a furious, unthinking mob, trapped and swaying to and fro in the November night. My friends and I were forced apart and lost sight of each other. Then I felt my arm – the one holding my handbag – being twisted up behind my shoulder-blades until I released my grip, while I realised despairingly that my money, my passport – I had a diplomatic one – and all my academic documentation were in that bag. In the two years I lived in Paris, it was the last time I ever carried a handbag.

I became determined to make my way to the steps of the amphitheatre, where I could see the police presence, so that I could report the loss. I knew that the passport was marketable and that, if it went missing, I was in trouble. While I struggled forward, I became aware that a tall man behind me had stretched his arms each side of my shoulders and was holding off some of the pressure of the crowd. 'Let's get you home, Mademoiselle,' he said in fluent French, but with an American accent. 'Surely you are not all that interested in the atomic bomb?' 'My passport has been stolen,' I replied, 'I must report it to the police.' 'That is another matter,' he said. 'We will get there together. What passport is it?' 'An Irish one,' I said and added stupidly, 'a diplomatic passport.' Someone near us overheard and thought it funny, '*Faîtes attention!*' he cried, '*Il y a des diplomates qui s'écrasent!*' (take care, there are diplomats being crushed!) We finally reached the police, and my companion produced a press card, introducing himself as Sasha Gombergh of the wartime Allied radio station, the Voice of America in North Africa. We made our report, which was taken quite seriously but without optimism, and the man who called himself Sasha said, this time in English, 'You are a student, you must be hungry.' My voice must have been tense with sincerity when I replied, 'I am always hungry here.' He laughed. 'Come with me then, till I file my story at the Bourse (the Paris Stock Exchange, where there was an all-night post office), and I will feed you.' I should, of course, have thanked him and refused politely, instead I accepted at once. I liked him and, after our common experience, trapped in that surging crowd, I felt I knew him. There was a car, with driver, parked beyond the cordon and the driver was moderately glad to see him, having been unable to reach his charge through the crowd. He drove us first to the telegraph office at the Bourse and then to what I was told was a restaurant, although it was completely dark outside. On the way, Sasha asked me how Irish people felt about black people. I replied that we did not have very many of them. 'Do you object to eating with them?' I was horrified, 'Of course not!' 'Good, because we are meeting my fiancée, who is Martiniquaise.'

The blank door opened on a space of light and heat, a typical French café interior, fairly crowded, with tables and a bar, and, at one end, a small platform-stage for musicians. A beautiful, coffee-coloured young woman got up from one of the tables and embraced my companion, reproaching him with being late. She did not seem particularly happy to see me, but she was polite. There was no menu, but there was wine already on the table, and, almost at once, three platefuls of braised ham were set before us, accompanied by bread and the vegetables from the braise. The food smelled delicious, and it was. Meanwhile, Sasha was telling us about the Irishmen he had known in the International Brigade in Spain, when a young man, dressed in a perfectly plain shirt and slacks of some rich, expensive-looking chocolate-brown material, stepped onto the stage. 'This,' said Sasha to me, 'you must not miss. He is going places.' While the musicians tuned their fiddles, he and his fiancée argued as to whether the singer we were about to hear, was a *chansonnier* (stand-up comic), or a *chanteur de charme* (charm singer). Whichever he was, he commanded absolute attention. He sang a sad little ballad called '*Ce monsieur-là*', about the despair of a very ordinary little man whose wife, '*qui cuisinait bien*' (who cooked well), was unfaithful to him. He lifted it high above the commonplace, into a realm of desperate, inarticulate grief. He followed with the ballad of a broken-down prizefighter, 'Battling Joe', penniless in his old age, while '*son manager*' wallowed in wealth. The enthusiasm of the diners was deafening, but he gave no further encores. 'Do not forget his name,' enjoined Sasha. 'It is Yves Montand.' I have not forgotten it.

Kindly and responsibly the couple left me back to the Foyer just before the door closed definitively at midnight. There I found my three friends – to whom I had not given a single thought until now – desperately telephoning neighbourhood hospitals and police stations, hoping and dreading to get news of me. It says a lot for their goodness of heart that they were so overjoyed to see me safe that they barely considered reproaching me. I think also that my story was so fantastic that they hardly took it in and, in their recovery from shock, consigned it as rapidly as might be to oblivion. A day or two later, Sasha rang – there was an extension on each floor of the Foyer and whoever answered the telephone called out the name of the person sought. It was quite thrilling to get a message this way. When I spoke to Sasha, however, I pleaded – God, forgive me! – intense pressure of work and, while thanking him with genuine warmth for all his kindness, told him that I wouldn't be going out in the evenings again for some time to come. This was not, I'm afraid, prudence, or even prudishness, but a kind of indigestion of adventure, a need to allow all these new impressions to settle before risking any more, not exactly cowardice, more an avoidance of excess. In any event, that was the end of that particular 'airport novel' encounter.

You will be glad to hear that my old passport was cancelled and that I got a new one without too much trouble. A little crystal watch to wear on a chain around the neck – a parting present from my parents – was also in the lost bag, which was not recovered.

That year (1945), La Fête des Morts (Feast of the Dead) and its eve, in November, were celebrated with extreme pomp and solemnity. Again on the invitation of Frank Gallagher, I wrote about it in the *Irish Press*. I quote what I wrote below, hoping once more to recapture the immediacy of the occasion:

'My own first inkling of the continued existence of a France not wholly obsessed with and bounded by the innumerable inconveniences and difficulties of mere day-to-day existence came on the evening of the tenth of November, when I stood at a street corner in a silent, waiting crowd and saw above the leafless trees the great dome of the Invalides floodlit against the night sky.

It was very cold. The monotonous repeated peals of distant cannon-fire marking the minutes intensified the atmosphere of waiting. Around me the people were silent.

Then away at the far end of the boulevard the darkness began to glow with a strange, soft light, the flame of hundreds of torches carried by mounted soldiery.

From three of the great gates of Paris, three solemn processions were converging on the Invalides – fifteen bodies, three of the dead of the Resistance, three executed deportees, nine soldiers dead in battle, to lie in state there under armed guard awaiting the great ceremony of the morning at the tomb of the Unknown Soldier.

The procession we watched for bore the bodies of those dead soldiers. I shall never forget the strangeness and simplicity of the whole, nor the beauty and the sheer excitement of it.

First rode the Spahi cavalry, magnificent in the rich cream and scarlet of their uniform, dark and immobile [turbanned] faces, great flowing cloaks and the torchlight, reflected, burning back from cartridge-belt and sword-hilt and the trappings of the horses; then the nine gun-carriages draped with the tricolour, and again by torch-light, the superb Republican Guard, the élite of the French Army, high boots, burnished helmets and long plumes.

The great drums roll, the bells of the churches toll for them, for those fifteen corpses there, at the gates of the chapel.

We cannot see the tribune from here, where the notabilities are gathered, but we hear the roll-call. Then 'The Last Post' sounds, the gates are opened, one by one the coffins are carried within, the guard is mounted and the crowd disperses. All in silence, many in tears.

Since then I have seen the Parisian crowds transported by enthusiasm, when next morning, for example, in the Champs Elysées they cheered and shouted for General de Gaulle, a slim deprecatory figure, upright in an open car, but I will remember their silence of the night before when they received their dead.'

ৎ৪ ৎ৪ ৎ৪

In the nature of things, this marvellously varied and colourfully satisfying life could not go on forever. Sometime about May 1946 an impressive parcelled cube arrived by post for me at the Foyer. I took it up to my small student's room, where I now felt peculiarly at home, with my books on their shelves, my Dufy print on the wall and my Foxford rug on the bed. I had no idea what the parcel might contain and, when I opened it, I was even slightly disappointed to see that it was only the two Arthurian texts I had edited for the Institute of Advanced Studies, now in book form. I had always thought the stories insipid and artificial and barely of interest, even linguistically, but I had grappled with them conscientiously, and there was my name on the cover. I fought to summon up a glow of pride and began to leaf through one of the booklets. I still find difficulty in articulating what happened then. If you have read this far you may remember that before I left Dublin I had handed my vocabulary and notes to the Registrar of the Institute. If I had got any particular satisfaction from my work on the text at all, it was in the compilation of that vocabulary, where I felt I had worked myself into the mind of a reader who might have genuine difficulties with early Modern Irish, or indeed with Irish in general, but who knew enough to attempt these stories for whatever reason, and that I had sensitively ironed those difficulties out for just such a person. I could not believe the printed note that I now read at the end of my introduction, signed by the Director of the Institute, my revered, almost beloved Professor TF O'Rahilly, to the effect that the student editing this text had left the Institute without notice and without supplying either a vocabulary or notes. I was, of course, in shock, but I knew exactly what had happened: our Registrar at the Institute had a drink problem and he had lost the scripts I had given him and then denied that he ever received them, or, at least, not volunteered the information. I could not understand, however, how no one had contacted me before this; I could readily have supplied the material again – indeed in my new, French-triggered self-confidence I would have enjoyed doing it. The thought of everyone who mattered to me taking their cue from this awful judgement, not only of my ability but of my character, gutted me completely. From that moment on I was hatching a nervous breakdown. I had just turned twenty-four.

In the meantime, I decided to make the best of it, which involved downplaying the entire incident to a level amounting, in fact, to denial. I kept one copy on the shelf with my other books relating to Irish, thinking obscurely that I should preserve it for the record. I inscribed another in French for the Library of the Foyer, conscious that the edition of an Irish text in Irish was unlikely ever to be read by anyone there, and feeling I might as well derive some kudos from the presentation. The remaining copies I trashed. It never occurred to me to contact anyone in Ireland about the allegation. I mentioned that I had received the books to Professor Vendryès, my post-graduate Director at the Institut des Hautes Êtudes, explaining how I regretted the circumstances, since I could not offer him a copy. He had been very kind and welcoming to myself and Sheila when we arrived, and his seminars in Old Irish were a joy. I discovered that he was already cognisant of the affair and indignant on my behalf, though I am not sure he believed that the Registrar could have lost my scripts, favouring rather some other explanation that, of necessity, involved inefficiency on my part, if not worse. He was, however, extraordinarily kind and suggested then and there that for my doctorate I should make a study of the poems attributed to St Colm Cille, primarily as a literary phenomenon rather than as purely linguistic material, since he had come to the conclusion that my bent lay in that direction and was considerable. I was enchanted and, at his suggestion, wrote to Miss Eleanor Knott, Professor of Old Irish in Trinity College, Dublin – she whose footsteps I had feared I was destined to follow into scholarly old maidenhood and who was working on the texts of some of the poems in question – to enquire whether she would have any objection to my considering them in a purely literary context. I should have known better, but I hoped against hope. Quite promptly, I got a reply: Miss Knott did not see it as part of her functions to advise students of the National University. After that awful publication, why should she put herself out?

I now know that the affair of the Arthurian texts had made quite a stir in the Irish newspapers, with many younger scholars taking up my defence in letters to the editor, even without their realising the full facts. I don't imagine the Institute replied. To this day, I don't think anybody alive except me knows the full story, and of those who ultimately came to know much of it at the time, such as my parents, the conclusion was that digging it all up again and adding to the Registrar's increasing head of trouble would not be worthwhile, especially as I seemed to have got over it. In a mistaken attempt to protect me they had kept the newspaper reports from me in Paris, not realising that the Institute itself would blow the gaff by sending the books to me in Paris and probably, if the whole truth were told, thinking – like Professor Vendryès – it only too likely that some omission of mine was at the bottom of my misfortunes.

I did get over it, but not until after a summer of extreme wretchedness – both in Paris and on holiday in Dublin – together with a total loss of will-power, during which I was obsessed with the conviction that all my surroundings were dirty and drove everybody mad scrubbing all the white paintwork in our house at home. When the time came for me to go back to Paris for the second year of my Studentship and I was tidying my hand-bag the night before, I took my air-ticket and threw it – God only knows why, and without quite realising what I was doing – in the fire. Next morning at the airport, when my father asked me for it, intending to speed up my check-in, the delayed realisation swept over me, and I told him, 'I threw it in the fire.' I think that was the turning point in my recovery. In any event, everyone was helpful, a new ticket was issued and I got safely off. Back in Paris, I took the advice a Dublin psychiatrist had given me: 'Take one day at a time; do only what you want to do; don't force yourself and you will find that you will get back your energy and get better.' He was right, but in the context of a career in Celtic Studies, nothing could undo the consequences of that unearned condemnation.

☙ ☙ ☙

My second year in Paris was a great deal more humdrum than the first. One of the highlights of it was a visit by Anne Yeats – we had never met before, but Tom McGreevy, her Uncle Jack's great friend, gave her my address. She showed me a drawing of a girl asleep on a wrought-iron bench in the Luxembourg Gardens, and I bought it for five pounds. Alas! I never had it in my possession: it went back to Dublin to be framed and got mislaid. It was called *The Unexpected Sleeper*, and was the essence of student Paris. Later, Anne drew something similar for the cover of my first book of poems, *Margadh na Saoire* (The Hiring Fair), published in 1956.

Barbara, six years younger than me, came to live *au pair* with a French family in a solid, Proustian apartment near the Chambre des Députés. She was intrigued by the notices affixed at regular intervals to the railings around that august building: '*Défense de pisser*' (pissing forbidden). She speculated that when the male population of Paris were displeased with their legislators, they came *en masse* to urinate against the building in protest. Little Una Tierney, daughter of Michael, the president of UCD, came to stay with me in the Foyer and enchanted everyone at one of our compulsory social evenings in the lamp-lit Library with her exquisite singing of traditional Irish songs; her grandfather on her mother's side was Eoin MacNeill, the great revolutionary historian, he of the Countermanding Order. His granddaughter sang like a bird:

'O, I will climb a high, high tree,
and rob a wild bird's nest,
and it's back I'll bring whatever I do find
to the arms that I love best,'
she said,
'To the arms that I love best.'

Generations of subversive students had a folk image of their own of her father as Christy in *The Playboy of the Western World*, or, worse still, as Lyncheachán, Christy's supposed original in real life. There was a scandalous rumour that Michael's western youth had been like that. It is an interesting phenomenon from the Dublin of the 1940s.

My especially dear Mary Pat Cullen, my favourite from 'the family next door', a smashing-looking, merry little blonde, also spent time with us and enlivened our, by now staider and more responsible, routines with her adventures, which included spending a night in a police station (for no offence at all but as a place of refuge – the French police had their uses after all), and vaulting the ticket-barrier at the Gare du Nord to catch a departing train, successfully. Of course, she fell in love with a Frenchman, but that's another story. In the spring my mother came to Paris, stayed with us briefly there and then took myself and Barbara to Rome to visit my Uncle David, whom she had not seen since before the war.

ଓ   ଓ   ଓ

I remember that Easter in Rome as high comedy in glorious weather. We stayed in the pleasant informality of the MacDonald household. Denis MacDonald was Counsellor at the Embassy to the Quirinal (the Italian Government). The Ambassador was Michael MacWhite, whose son, Eoin, and I would shortly become colleagues in the Department of External

Affairs. However, there was another Embassy in Rome – every Catholic country has an Embassy to the Holy See, and some non-Catholic others have also; the norm would be one embassy accredited to the Holy See, and one to the Quirinal. Joe Walshe, our Ambassador to the Vatican, was no friend to informality. I remember his suggesting to myself and Barbara that we should call my Dominican uncle 'Uncle David' in public, rather than plain 'David' as we had always done. But that was only the beginning of it. Joe Walshe had been Permanent Secretary of the Department of External Affairs, as it was then, since its very early days, under Mr de Valera. He was a bachelor, an ostentatiously devout Catholic and something of a papal snob. He was also from Tipperary, and my mother and he were mutually well aware of each other's backgrounds, which were, both of them, perhaps not altogether as exalted as Joe would have liked people to assume. He was, I think, relieved that, on account of a long-standing friendship with the Sheehans, the family of Denis MacDonald's marvellously elegant and witty wife, Una, we chose to stay with her and her husband at the secular embassy, in their airy, slightly untidy, tiled-floored Italian quarters, rather than in the celibate grandeur of Joe's embassy. He was not, nevertheless, on for allowing the secular world to monopolise us. As was proper, he orchestrated our audience with Pius XII. My Uncle David was at this time Master of the Sacred Palace, a title going back to Torquemada and the Spanish Inquisition and borne, in succession, by all the Pope's Dominican theological advisors. In the family we said he was the Pope's confessor; David was certainly the Pope's close and devoted personal friend.

During her stopover in Paris, my mother, Barbara and I had been taken by some French friends, reluctantly on their part, to see the Folies Bergères – 'too beautiful for original sin' was Barbara's verdict. One of the too-beautiful ladies had appeared clad only in generously patterned black lace, and my mother had affected to be seized with horror lest she had forgotten the 'slip' of her black lace dress 'to see the Pope in'. No such frivolity was allowed to impinge on this occasion. All three of us were dressed in black from head to toe: high collars, long sleeves, no jewellery, black mantillas – the utmost *protocolaire* correctness. The Pope, whom, for many reasons, some personal, I later came to dislike profoundly, was totally charming, warm, affable, smiling and effortlessly dignified. Joe Walshe, as Ambassador, droned on and on about our three clerical uncles, the piety of our parents, Ireland's tradition of the Faith … 'We are,' he concluded in this context, 'expecting great things of these two young women.' The Pope turned graciously towards Barbara and myself, smiled and – I swear it – sketched a wink. 'Somehow,' he said in his gentle Italian-English, 'I do not think so.' If Barbara and I had been called upon in that moment to go out on the piazza and be shot for him, we would have gone rejoicing!

Joe's embassy was an exceptionally beautiful Roman villa, set high on the Janiculum Hill, just beside the Church of Saint Peter 'in Montorio', where Hugh O'Neill, first Earl of Tyrone, is buried – yes, one of the two enigmatic and tragic earls of the 'Flight'. It enjoys a magnificent view over the city and it has a swimming pool. Stories cluster around that pool and the threat to Joe's modesty it presented – since Joe's occupation of the Villa Spada, no woman had swum in it – but myself and Barbara did not know anything of this background. It was now mischievously suggested that he should invite Barbara and me to swim there. The joke actually fell rather flat, in spite of provoking a great deal of glee among Joe's unfriends in anticipation. He did invite us, and we did swim, end of story. It was otherwise with a clerical dinner-party that he gave, at which my mother, Barbara and I were the only women guests. Joe was riding one of his hobby-horses, ill-advisedly endeavoring to persuade my mother to go to Confession so that she could 'participate fully' in the Holy Week ceremonies. My mother's religion was extremely private – she would have considered it bad taste to have it otherwise – but Joe did not know when to stop. Earlier he had taken her out on the balcony to look at the lights of Rome and press his case; now, at the dinner-table, he continued his efforts: 'Come now, Margaret, I know a marvellous confessor who hears confessions in French.' 'Joe,' replied my mother, in audible tones of complete finality, 'leave me alone. I do not know the French for what we did on the balcony.' The clerical company was convulsed with laughter and the subject was dropped.

It was during that Roman holiday that our Barbara first met her future husband, the cinematically blonde and handsome Frank Biggar, a Secretary at the Embassy to the Quirinal and, as it turned out, soon to be a colleague of mine in Dublin, so that the element of romance completed the 'comic-opera' atmosphere.

PART II:
PERMANENT AND PENSIONABLE

Back in Ireland, I had one first, and last, shot at an academic post: Professor of Modern Irish, I think, at Queen's College in Belfast. Since I had not even commenced my doctorate, let alone completed it, it was not likely at all that I should get it, but it was thought advisable that I should 'keep my hat in the ring', with a view to possible junior posts, which might be in the gift of some university authority, without a formal application. I had a bouquet of quite exceptionally glowing testimonials from Monsieur Vendryès and from my undergraduate teachers, but there remained a cavernous gap where my Institute years were concerned. I knew all along that nothing would come of this application, and I could not see myself repeating the process indefinitely. Meanwhile, the Department of External Affairs, as it was still, advertised a special civil service exam to recruit cadets. I entered for it, and was successful – the first woman administrative officer to be recruited to the Department by competitive examination. Two dear friends, Eoin MacWhite and Róisín O'Doherty, came in on the same exam: Eoin came first, I was second and Róisín was called later; once again, my life lay in pleasant places.

ೞ   ೞ   ೞ

I was not a particularly good civil servant – I was lazy and numerical accuracy was a problem for me, dates and such – but I got by and was contented. The Department was a small place then and it was easy for likeminded colleagues to get together. There was a distinct aura of literary aspiration about our immediate superiors, some published, some aspirant, people like the poet Denis Devlin, or Tommy Woods, or my Conor – though he was, of course, by no means my Conor then. We were all still very young and managed to get a great deal of fun out of each other's company. Indeed, at one time the place became such a minefield of practical jokes that one was afraid to pick up the telephone. Conor and Eoin MacWhite, in particular, were dangerously accomplished mimics. I once answered a phone-call where the query was so absurd and the foreign accent so bizarre that I took it for granted that it was one or other of those two colleagues of mine and told the speaker, pretty sharply, to come off it. It turned out to be some totally innocent, newly arrived *attaché* – Argentine, I think – whose English was so providentially bad that he did not understand how untoward his first reception had been, but persevered until I realised he was genuine. Our Minister then was the Taoiseach, Mr de Valera, who did not occupy his office in Iveagh House, so that there was a certain sense of saturnalia about his absence. On the other hand, it meant that we were never in any doubt as to what government policy was on any issue, and we did in fact work very hard and were proud of being so close to the springs of power – at least, I was. You were flung in at the deep end as a cadet and learnt by experience; I will always be grateful to Art Boland, my senior in the Consular Section, who marked my card for me and saw that I avoided the worst pitfalls, and who came of a long line of Kerry poets and schoolteachers, God rest him and them!

Cઢ   Cઢ   Cઢ

Many older people too were very good to me at that time, among them the French Ambassador, Count Ostrorog, who was on friendly terms with my Uncle Paddy. I was barely a week or two in the Service when he invited me to lunch. I arrived at the Embassy residence, somewhat nervously, to find that, except for a young French male companion, I was the only other person at table. Oddly enough, I immediately felt at ease and the lunch was actually great fun. I had been missing the French combination of manners and informality, and I was also very good, at that time, at not formulating to myself suspicions I did not want confirmed. I chattered away happily about the wonders of the Department's filing system, which, so far, was about the only aspect of my new profession that impressed me – the only one with which I had had any comprehensible contact so far. '*Ah, mademoiselle*,' said Count Ostrorog, '*vous voilà prise par l'ivresse administrative!*' (... captivated by the intoxication of administration). He then gave me some sincere and practical advice: 'A good diplomatist never lies. You anticipate the occasion for falsehood, and you avoid it.' I have never forgotten these words – sometimes the formula works.

Some time later, I was again invited informally, this time to dinner. Again the young man, as at the lunch-party, was co-host, but there was another guest, a very distinguished lady, the Princess Bibesco – a Roumanian title, I think – who was a much admired literary figure in France at that time. After dinner, I sat at her feet on the floor and listened, enchanted, as she spoke about her friendship with Marcel Proust, and the evening flew. I was often invited again, but to official functions only, never again as part of the Ambassador's 'family'. The warmth of those two early experiences, however, had done much to endear my new way of life to me. It never crossed my mind that I might not have been as entertaining to my hosts as I was entertained by them; I had a lot to learn.

In 1948 the government changed; the first Coalition (Fine Gael, Labour and Clann na Poblachta, Seán MacBride's new party) took over and we had a new minister in Mr Seán MacBride, a resident minister, one might say, and Róisín O'Doherty and myself – dyed-in-the-wool Fianna Fáil supporters – went around in a not unpleasurable state of moral indignation as the Department became galvanised into new and multifarious activity. Mr MacBride was always extremely nice to me personally and, indeed, to all our family, when occasion offered, but my father disliked and distrusted both him and his mother, Madame Maud Gonne, unmitigatedly, believing them, and all their circle, to have been 'double agents' during the Second World War and to have accepted *both British and German money* to destabilise the de Valera government. My mother, who read each book of WB Yeats' poetry as it appeared, as if it were a *roman à clef*, took a more romantic view. She liked to recount how, when I was about four years old and she was walking with me in Saint Stephen's Green, we met Maud Gonne, draped in her unchanging widow's weeds for the husband she had divorced in 1905, poor Seán MacBride Senior, who was executed in 1916. My mother and Maud had one safe topic in common – Alexandra, where my mother taught and where Iseult Gonne, Maud's daughter, had been to school. While they chatted, my mother was thinking, 'Poor Maud, the great beauty is over,' but, as they parted, the four-year-old, me, piped up, 'Mammy, who is that *beautiful* lady?' I remember the day vividly, and the query, and she *was* beautiful.

Be that as it may, it was felt – entirely properly – that a nice safe post abroad, where I wouldn't get in the Minister's hair, would be a good idea for me, as indeed, in many ways, it proved to be. I had tended to be rather arrogantly outspoken about our new Minister's political prospects, saying, to one very senior Ambassador, that MacBride might, on precedent, do very well, 'having a whiff of the exotic and of gunpowder about him, and some doubt as to his paternity.' I was rather proud of the formulation; I now think it was merely silly and offensive all round. In any event I was sent briefly to Paris and then posted, for the next two years (1949–51), to Madrid.

PART III :
LA MALHERIDA ESPAÑA
(SORELY WOUNDED SPAIN)

Franco's Spain was 'something else again': a lethal combination of the baroque and the absurd. It was not a happy place for educated and therefore, by definition, for middle-class Spanish women, to whom all participation in public life was denied. If their 'old-fashioned', ie, pre-Franco, liberal parents insisted that they receive a university education, *women could qualify for the professions, but not practice.* They could not be alone with a young man unless they were engaged to him. It was in this hot-house, harem-like circle I had, of necessity, to find my friends. Frustration had made these women bitter and their undoubted talents were debased to the level of malicious and pornographic gossip. It was hallucinating to sit and listen to these marvellously corseted, couture-clad and hair-dressed ladies, who sipped their *japonesas* (fresh orange juice spiked with brandy) while being witty on such subjects as bestiality, or the sale of little half-caste Cuban boys by the masters who were also their fathers. Younger women, who were yet old enough to remember the great days of the Instituto Escuela, that seminal, liberal, cradle-to-the-grave secondary school founded under the Republic, might fantasise over lost ideals, but unless they were prepared to go into exile, they had little hope of ever living by them.

One of those few who refused to despair was my friend, Fernanda, part of the dispossessed liberal social circle which the Legation had inherited from the Republic, of which more later. Her father had been Chief of Police in Madrid during the Civil War – not that he was at all a person of the left, far from it, but that his loyalty was to the government, legally constituted. After the war he had escaped across the frontier to France with his wife and small son, and thence to Latin America. Fernanda, then in her teens, could not bear to leave Spain and had chosen to stay behind. Under constant surveillance by the authorities from then on, young as she was she learnt to keep out of trouble and to avail herself discreetly of such opportunities as existed for women, qualifying as a doctor and specialising in endocrinology. She was now employed, illegally, as his personal locum, by none other than Franco's son-in-law, and she calculated that, as she had made herself indispensable to him, she was reasonably safe. Nonetheless, she was actively seeking a university post abroad – though it broke her heart to do so – since she could see no prospect at all of any career under the present régime, and since it seemed to all of us that the present régime would go on forever.

Fernanda's friendship was of immense value to me. For two years she drilled me remorselessly in Spanish language, literature and politics – a one-woman department of Spanish studies; helped me cope with the occasional fugitive Irish governess fleeing the unwanted attentions of a titled employer; nursed me when I went down with jaundice and might have died. Given that we were living in a kind of Kate O'Brien novel, it is not surprising that there was a lesbian element to this devotion, it certainly surprised no one in Spain. I have been asked to be more precise about this relationship. Fernanda was a lesbian, I was not. Abnormally delayed adolescent that I was, I could still have been somewhat bisexual. I honestly don't know. Fernanda hoped that I would resign from the Service and emigrate with her to Chile; I procrastinated, knowing that I was too self-centred ever to take such a risk, but reluctant to break off a relationship from which I derived such strength and comfort. My recall to Ireland after two years settled the matter. I stopped opening her letters. I wish I could have behaved with more generosity, but the commitment just wasn't there.

CR   CR   CR

With that out of the way, let me have a shot at describing some of the other factors that contributed to the atmosphere of barely controlled hysteria that prevailed during my two-year posting. The memory of the terrible Civil War hung over everything like a dark, heavy cloud. People were still in jail for participation on the Republican side, indeed, were still being executed by firing squad for such participation. Among the mountains of the Sierra outside Madrid, in a huge stone quarry, work was in progress on the Vallón de los Caidos (Valley of the Fallen), an immense monument to the Francoist war dead. It was being built in the grimmest conditions by hundreds of Republican prisoners, who might as well have been nameless for any public reference ever made to their plight. Since the Second World War, the victorious Allies had withdrawn their Heads of Mission from Spain, and the American, British, French and Italian(!) embassies were being run by quite junior *chargés d'affaires*, under express instructions to make themselves as obnoxious as possible to the Spanish government. They obeyed with gusto: the British *chargé*, for example, was reported to have shot the tyres from under a vehicle that was blocking the gate of the embassy, and I myself was present at a dinner-party in the Portuguese Embassy – our next-door neighbours on the Castellana, 'embassy row' – when the US *chargé*, a lean, rangy, white-hat cowboy type, flung himself physically and literally, full-length, across the dining-table and proceeded to throttle the Spanish Minister for Trade, Señor Suantés, popularly believed to be a member of Opus Dei. I forget what they disagreed about. BEA (British European Airlines) was reputed to keep a seat free on all of its planes out of Madrid until the very last minute, to facilitate the escape – clandestine, or otherwise – of any British subject who got into trouble with the Spanish authorities.

Our own mission – still a Legation, not an Embassy *yet* – was a haven of common sense and good nature by comparison, under the firm but benevolent rule of our Head of Chancery, Miss Maisie Donnelly. Maisie had spent all her adult life in Spain and had been Private Secretary to the legendary Irish minister, Leopold Kerney, who had secured the transfer to Germany of Frank Ryan of the International Brigade, thereby saving his life, after the Spanish Civil War. She had served under Kerney right through that war and had inherited both his pre-war circle of wealthy, liberal – though now, of necessity, discreetly so – friends, and his encyclopaedic knowledge of Spanish politics. To listen to her Spanish on the telephone was a lesson both in language and diplomacy, and I can still hear her many half-joking exchanges, in more popular vein, with our doorman and messenger, Mariano. She accused Mariano of over-tipping delivery boys, post-office messengers and the like to enhance his personal prestige. '*Qué esplendido eres, Mariano*,' she would exclaim, as she totted up his accounts, '*con el dinero del Gobierno Irlandés!*' (How splendid, ostentatious, etc, you are with the Irish government's money!) She was a wonderfully warm and totally uncensorious friend to me, and an invaluable guide through the complexities of my new environment.

ߒ   ߒ   ߒ

Our recently arrived Minister was Leo T McCauley, a shrewd North-of-Irelander and a distinguished Latin scholar. This last meant that the Spanish language, especially Spanish officialese, gave him not a moment's trouble, so that when he presented his credentials to the Chief-of-State, General Franco, his classically-turned phrases excited genuine admiration. A Minister's presentation of credentials was relatively low-key as compared to an ambassadorial one, but as the status of the Legation was shortly to be raised to that of Embassy, and as the consequent second presentation of credentials was to be attended with a pomp and ceremony that I hope later to describe in detail, I will skip that morning's events and go directly to the dinner hosted for us that evening by the Foreign Minister, Señor Martín Artajo, in the Ministry of Foreign Affairs.

The Ministry was housed in a dark and brooding fourteenth-century 'palace' in the old quarter of Madrid, then almost a slum. The walls were of massive grey stone, the ceilings low and the passages only dimly lit. The actual banquet room was a large hall, warm and colourful, with a fire in a huge fireplace at one end, surrounded by seating, cushions and wall-hangings galore. At the other end, up a shallow flight of steps, was the formally-laid dining table. I think I remember that the main course was suckling pig and was delicious; the wines were Spanish. When the time came for the ladies to leave the table, we went and sat around the fire. There, from time to time, one of the gentlemen from the 'high' table would come down to visit us, making a polite circle of our chairs and returning to his place above. One of these was the very personable Spanish Ambassador to the Argentine, who was home on leave. His English was perfect and, as often with Spanish grandees, all of whom had Irish Catholic governesses, he spoke with a slight Irish accent. 'When I was a young man,' he said to me, 'my little sisters had an Irish governess. Her name was Kate O'Brien.' He could not have realised how interesting this remark was to me, firstly because I was an addicted admirer of Kate O'Brien's writing, and secondly and more immediately because I knew, from my mother, that my Chief, the minister, Leo, had been engaged to Kate when she was a young woman, before she left Ireland to go, as a governess, to Spain. Here, under one roof then, were the two prototypes of the main male characters in the novel, *Mary Lavelle* – the Irish fiancé and the Spanish lover! It was the kind of coincidence my mother relished, and I could hardly wait to write home and tell her.

ᘓ   ᘓ   ᘓ

In those days I liked a hint of danger, so I loved bullfights. The first one I saw was with my Minister and Mrs McCauley, who felt they had to see at least one and were not looking forward to it. It was a gala occasion: the great matador Dominguin, the reigning champion of the bullring, was to fight, and Franco was to attend. We arrived early and had only been seated a short time when the crowd began to shout and clap and rise to their feet. We assumed the 'Chief-of-State' had arrived and rose too, but the Royal Box remained empty, and gradually the ovation subsided. Leo enquired of someone beside us what it was all about, and was informed that it was to welcome '... *los que han gana'o de los Irlandeses en Dublin*' (those who beat the Irish in Dublin); it was the Spanish soccer team! The *Caudillo's* (Franco's) arrival was a much less spontaneous affair, accompanied by the playing of the National Anthem, some stiff-armed Falangist saluting and an orderly standing to attention. By the actual bullfighting, I was carried away; I can still taste the flavour of my

Above: I loved riding as a young woman. I am pictured here on the right.

Left: My sister Barbara was a great beauty in her prime. This is her in happier times, as a young woman.

Right: Séamus' wedding in 1951. I am standing on the far left, next to the bridesmaid, then Uncle Paddy, Séamus' new wife, Jean, Séamus, Uncle David, my mother and Uncle Moss, next to him is Jean's aunt who brought her up, then Barbara's father-in-law and finally my father.

Left: Mary Pat Cullen, our next-door neighbour and great friend, on the day of her marriage to Peter O'Malley, a fellow graduate from my days at King's Inns who went on to become His Honour, Judge Peter O'Malley.

Below: My mother and her three brothers: . Paddy, on her right, and David and Moss, on her left.

Above: My father takes his place in the first Fianna Fáil government, in 1932, the year of the Eucharistic Congress. He is second from the right in the front row, seated to the left of de Valera.

Right: Attending the King's Inns was a novel experience, which brought me into contact with such memorable characters as Ja-ja Wachuku, sitting on the steps in front of me.

Above: Standing, the only woman, amidst my male colleagues after our call to the Irish Bar. To my left is Tom Finlay, subsequently Chief Justice Finlay, and to my right is Peter O'Malley.

Right: At the age of twenty-three, I travelled to Paris to study at the Institut des Hautes Êtudes. My friends and I are standing on the roof of the Foyer in this picture: I am standing on the far right; Mary Pat Cullen is seated in the front row, middle; to Mary Pat's right is Kitty, the Joyce Scholar; and Sheila is standing behind Kitty. The other girls are French friends.

Left: Wearing the fur coat seen as a 'necessity' for Parisian winters, I am standing with Dr Shanley of the Red Cross. Behind us is the Red Cross car in which Sam Beckett chauffeured me and Sheila around the sights of Paris, when we first arrived.

Below: After returning from Paris in 1947, but prior to taking up my post at the Department of External Affairs, I enjoyed a brief holiday in America, where this picture was taken, in Washington.

Above: The fashions of the day were irresistible to a young woman with a love of fine fabrics and money in her purse: here I am attending a friend's wedding, which took place on Barbara's birthday, 24 April, in Madrid, in 1950.

Left: As a young member of the Department of External Affairs, I travelled to many places in Europe. This photograph was taken in Strasbourg.

Below: The ceremonial procession of carriages bearing me and Ambassador Leo McAuley to his presentation of credentials to General Franco.

Above: As the sole member of staff of the Irish Ambassador, I am presented, in my beautiful *correctissima* couture outfit, in the baroque surroundings of the Palacio del Oriente, to General Franco and various Spanish dignitaries.
Right: Representing Ireland in the Third Committee at the UN in New York, I am pictured here with the representative for the Netherlands, Father Beaufort, and one of Mrs Afnan's Iraqi assistants.

Above: My handsome father and the very pretty Mrs Seán Lemass make for a striking picture.
Left: My father and mother returning home from Barbara and Frank Biggar's wedding ceremony.

excitement in my mouth when I think of it, but describe it I cannot, except to say that the air of that borderland between life and death is heady stuff. I was taken aback to learn that my Spanish friends, liberals to a woman, disapproved of bullfighting and called it 'the shame of Spain'. It made me question my own attitude and finally, slowly and reluctantly, 'for conscience' sake', I ceased to be an *aficionada* (addict) and stopped going. In all I saw three bullfights; I never lost my taste for them. Now when I think of Spain and remember how the Spaniards drove, or how pedestrians crossed the road, dodging cars, playing the bull comes vividly to mind. Once when I was seriously ill with a dangerous hepatitis, my little maid, Cion, who was helping a male nurse (*practicante*) give me a horrible injection, dropped everything and rushed to the window crying, '*Que choque mas bonito!*' (What a pretty crash!) My flat was on the seventh floor of a building on Claudio Quello, overlooking a star-shaped road junction, and Cion's life was constantly enlivened by the traffic accidents below our windows, which could not only be seen but were also gratifyingly audible. In my experience, Spaniards loved violence and were indifferent to pain, their own or that of others.

℃ ℃ ℃

I have, of course, gentler memories. They are associated with what was often regarded as the downside of the post: the long, hot, dry Madrid summer. A feature of this was the *jornada intensiva* (intensive working day). Places of business opened at six in the morning – fresh and cool – and closed somewhere between noon and two o'clock, depending on various pressures. After that the day was your own. Added to this, the entire government and the Heads of Mission of the Diplomatic Corps moved north to San Sebastian on the French border, away from the heat, leaving a wonderfully relaxed atmosphere behind them. Nothing much happened during the long, hot hours of the afternoon, but as night fell the city came to life again. Evening meals were rarely eaten before eleven o'clock, and then in the open air. The lights were like jewels in the warm dusk and the *verbenas* (little local fairs) opened to fanfares of music, both popular and traditional. I learnt that Castillian intellectuals despised the *cante jondo* (*sean-nós* singing) of the gypsies of Andalucia, which I adored, but that, nevertheless, one heard it everywhere. The works of Federico Garcia Lorca, so redolent of the south, were utterly and absolutely banned; you had to travel to Portugal to buy them, where, since 'practically no one could read', I was told, the censorship was much laxer. In spite of this, songs from his *Romancero Gitano* (Gypsy Songbook) were to be heard, without attribution, in every café and in the popular theatre.

The problem for an unattached girl was to find an escort. My friendship with Fernanda was on another and less frivolous level; we read the Spanish classics together. In any event, Fernanda – constantly shadowed by the police – couldn't afford to make herself conspicuous outside her own immediate circle. One evening, myself and my old friend from her Dublin days, Maria Luisa Ontiveros, took a taxi, with Maria's sister Marita, to the Plaza Mayor, a wonderful old square in the heart of the old city, where we sat and chatted at a table outside a *bodega* (inn) and drank *japonesas* under the night sky. We were perhaps slightly disappointed that the excursion passed off without incident, but on the way home the taxi-driver provided a gem to cherish. We were arguing as to who should pay, partly in English, partly in Spanish, and the driver assumed that we were short of money. With a wonderful show of *hidalguia* (nobility, generosity), he intervened, '*Si no hay, señoritas, es igual*' (If it isn't there, ladies, it doesn't matter). This gesture sums up for me the fundamental pride and generosity of the common people of Spain – very different from the caution and exclusiveness of the establishment.

Maria Luisa and Marita had a brother, Luis, who was in training for the Spanish Airforce, in an establishment just up the road from our offices on the Castellana. Among Luis' fellow cadets was the future King of Spain, the Infante Juan Carlos; I never met him, though I must often have seen him come and go. Luis spread himself as thin as possible to oblige his sisters and me, but the truth was that Spanish young men were not disposed to take out girls they couldn't sleep with, unless those were the girls they were going to marry. Still, with the company of the Irish colony in Madrid – some of them extremely well connected, such as the wife and sister-in-law of Enrique Loewe, the already internationally famous leather-goods merchant – and a constant trickle of holiday-makers from Ireland, I managed to have a very good time indeed. Towards the end of my stay my father came from Strasbourg, where he was attending the Council of Europe, to see me and bought me a second-hand car, so that I was able to visit other Spanish cities: Barcelona, where government notices were everywhere enjoining the speaking of Castilian only, and where everyone spoke only Catalan; Burgos, with its great, fortified cathedral; Toledo; Seville; Cordoba; Segovia; and, of course, Philip II's great palace at the Escorial in the cool Sierra beyond Madrid. I was certainly the only woman driving a car in Madrid, perhaps in all Spain. Whenever I stopped for petrol, the pump attendant invariably asked, '*Donde está el señor de este coché?*' (Where is the gentleman of this car?) I would answer, '*El señor de este coché soy yo*' (The gentleman of this car is me).

❧ ❧ ❧

Mrs McCauley's health was not good, and this meant that I sometimes found myself *chargé d'affaires* in a corps where all the important European countries were represented by (somewhat indisciplined) *chargés d'affaires*. The Spanish Foreign Office, for its part, was reluctant to admit that I existed at all, even as Secretary to the Legation, and efforts to get my name on the official list for invitations elicited the reply, '*Si la Legación no tiene personal diplomatico, la señorita puede venir*' (If the Legation has no diplomatic staff, the young lady can come). I was, if possible, even less welcome as *chargé(e)*, and I soon had this fact vividly made clear to me.

Commercial relations between the two countries were conducted, somewhat cumbrously, under a Trade Agreement in force since 1947. The Agreement covered the export of seed potatoes to Spain yearly, in quantities and at a price to be settled each year before the thirtieth of June.In May 1949 correspondence was exchanged between our Minister and the head of the Political Economy section of the Spanish Foreign Ministry, Mariano de Yturralde, settling the quantity for the year at 10,000 tonnes and the price at £16.50 per tonne, an entirely routine transaction. In the Spain I knew, however, things rarely proceeded routinely; agreed prices for Irish exports had been circumvented, to Spain's benefit, in the past, notably in the case of horses, not, it was generally assumed, without recourse to the bribing of Spanish officialdom. This was the situation when, being now *chargé*, I sent the following request for instructions to Iveagh House:

CONFIDENTIAL AIRMAIL
Madrid, 6th October, 1949.
15/16
An Rúnaí,
Roínn Gnóthai Eachtracha.

I have the honour to report that representatives of the four Spanish firms forming the Association of Authorised Seed-potato Importers (namely, Parinço S.L., Improver, Agrupatata and AEP) to-day called to the Legation. They stated that they had had access to official correspondence between the [Spanish] Ministry of Agriculture and the [Spanish] Ministry of Industry & Commerce in which the former agree to accept the price of £16. 5. 0 per ton f.o.b. [free on board] for potatoes imported from Ireland, with the reserve that there be no lower offer at the time of granting the licences. I have seen the original letter in which the above condition appears. It [the condition] does not of course figure at all in the acceptance of the Irish offer made officially to the Legation on the 9th of June last.

I should be grateful for an indication of the action which I should take. It is difficult to proceed officially as the information had only reached us through a breach of confidence in one of the Ministries concerned.

The importers consider they have grave grounds for uneasiness, as they understand that the Ministry has received a tender from the [Spanish] firm Agricola (see our correspondence re import of Irish horses) to import seed-potatoes from Ireland at £15 per ton. For some reason the importers [known to us] are of the opinion that these potatoes will be imported from the Six Counties, but that the Spanish authorities will affect to believe that the licences are being granted for imports from the Twenty-six Counties, and that in granting such they are fulfilling the terms of their agreement with us. Stated coldly this idea seems extravagant and I have not sufficient experience to judge what weight I should attach to the theory. I should be very glad of advice.

Chargé d'Affaires a.i.

I got my instructions back in double quick time, by telegram:

Telegram No. 55 received from the Dept. in ord. Code
on the 14th October, 1949, at 10 a.m.

55 Your telegram 69 you should make immediate demarche at ministry
of foreign affairs and deliver note stating you have learned ministry of
commerce is departing from price arrangements communicated yturralde's
letter june 9th and is seeking tenders at a lower price. That price arrangement
was made in due accordance with terms trade agreement september 3rd 1947
which it is assumed spanish authorities will continue to honour that agreed
price of £16.5.0 per ton is official price and that no lower tender would
be valid or capable of execution and that action of ministry of commerce
may cause dislocation and delay in arranging shipment planned to begin
about october 31st if import licence issued and necessary credits opened
in time. Add that it must be clearly understood potatoes of 6 counties origin
are not covered by trade agreement. For own information irish potatoe
(*sic*) marketing association had received telegrams of october 11th from
agricola saying import licences would be granted on basis tender and asking
for quotations but association has not quoted any price to them in reply stop
origin £15 quotation unknown here but may be from six counties some of
our shipments are normally made from londonderry but they are donegal
potatoes

[Signed] ESTERO

I acted accordingly and delivered my *Note Verbale*, in those terms, that
very day to the Permanent Secretary of the Ministry of Foreign Affairs, the
Conde (Count) de Casa Real. The formalities went off without incident,
but the very next day the storm broke. I was summoned again to that
gloomy, historic building, and that evening, somewhere in the bowels
thereof, I was confronted by a furious Señor Yturralde. He spoke in English, on which he prided himself; I did not object. I was not asked to sit
down. What did I mean? There had been no Exchange of Notes under the
Agreement for the current year. 'Perhaps not,' I answered, 'but there had
been an exchange of letters referring back to the original Exchange of
Notes bringing the Agreement into force.' 'Can you show me those letters?'
asked Yturralde, unmollified. I handed over copies of our Minister's and
of his own. 'These are not the originals,' he said. I replied that the originals

were – I'm afraid I said 'safe' – on our files. 'Bah!' he rejoined, 'these are still not Notes.' 'No,' I agreed, 'they are the word of a Spanish gentleman.' Whereupon Señor Yturralde came out from behind his desk, took me by the shoulders, forced me back against the stone wall and hit my head off it. At that very moment every light in the *Palacio* went out: such blackouts were commonplace at the time in impoverished and isolated Spain. In pitch darkness, I found my way out past Yturralde, along the passages and out onto the square again, actually feeling quite elated and convinced that had I shown him his original letter, he would have torn it in bits. As it was, the licences were issued in due course, as agreed therein, and the flap was over. I was promoted shortly afterwards, from third to second secretary, so I must have pleased somebody.

ᑳ   ᑳ   ᑳ

My next *démarche* as *chargé* was almost as dramatic and even more comical. The third of December is the feast day of Saint Francis Xavier and was also the name-day of Generalissimo Francisco Franco. There was to be a *Te Deum* in the Cathedral of San Francisco el Grande, followed by a ceremonial call by the Diplomatic Corps on the Head of State in the Royal Palace. The invitation was a command and, although the Foreign Ministry would shed no tears if I didn't turn up, Maisie and I decided to treat it as such. The first problem was to ensure an escort for me so that I would not be turned away at the door of the Cathedral. The Italian *chargé* was well known for his indifference to women, so we felt safe from scandal in appealing to his chivalry to take me under his wing for the morning. With a rather grudging grace he consented and, in due course, I was ushered into the chair marked *Irlanda* on the gospel side of the altar in the cathedral, a few rows from the front, in the seating reserved for the Diplomatic Corps. Behind me, as I took my place, I glimpsed two bemedalled old generals and was aware of their stunned silence. Then came the unmistakeable, gruff, military voice at my back, '*Es una chica!*' (It's a girl!) Another, similar voice replied, equally crossly, '*Hay error!*' (There's some mistake!) and the stage was set for the day's ceremony.

At the Palacio del Oriente, the Royal Palace, the diplomats were herded into an anteroom to the throne room: Latin American ambassadors, Allied *chargés* – all men, of course – and me. Franco circulated with his aides and was perfectly pleasant to everyone, including me, before passing through to the throne room, where we were expected to follow. Then the fun began. The French *chargé d'affaires*, a former naval officer, tall, young and handsome in his gala uniform, addressed his colleagues, '*Chers amis*, for once that we have a young lady amongst us, let us show her proper respect; I will not take precedence over *Mademoiselle*.' There was an outcry from the Latin ambassadors, 'We mean no disrespect to *Mademoiselle*, but …' The Frenchman milked his opportunity to embarrass his hosts, as per instructions, to the last drop. Agitated Franco aides returned from the throne room like sheepdogs to chivvy us in, then, with everything at breaking point, their tormentor relented. Bowing to the ambassadors, he waved them through the communicating doors, '*Passez Excellences*,' next, '*Passez Messieurs les Chargés*' – another wave and bow – then, last of all, 'At least France knows how to treat a lady,' and he took my arm and ushered me formally into the throne room before him.

The throne room was a long, Versailles-type gallery, all mirrors and windows. The throne, on a dais, stood halfway down its length, and *beside* the empty throne, to its left, stood Franco, his marshal's baton on his hip, as if posing for a portrait. The Diplomatic Corps was ranged along the windowed wall opposite him, like flunkeys. My Frenchman did not approve: 'Are we servants? Are we wall-hangings?' he fulminated, deliberately and purposely audibly. On either side of Franco were grouped the dignitaries of his Cabinet and of the Falange, among those last Pilar Primo de Rivera, the sister of the martyred founder, José Antonio. She and I were the only women present throughout.

Then began the long defile past of representatives of all that was esteemed great and good in Spanish society, all parading along the gallery to pay their respects to the Head of State – Civil Service, Local Government, Police, Army, Navy, you name it. It took two hours. When the survivors of the 'Blue Division', who had fought for Hitler on the Russian front, went by, they were under the terrible leadership of Millán Astray, the Civil War General who had coined the watch-word, 'Long live death!' ('*Viva la muerte!*'), a small, hunched, sinister, wooden-puppet of a man, crippled by his war wounds, held together as if by wires and blazing with medals, a black patch over one eye and the Iron Cross on a ribbon at his throat. My

French neighbour took his cue to explode, audibly again, '*Cochons! Salauds!*' and less printable expressions. I enjoy it in retrospect; I didn't at the time.

When I finally got back to the office, I kicked off my shoes, threw away my 'witty' French hat, which really didn't impress in Spain where women of all classes went hatless, and collapsed at my desk in weak laughter, with my head on my arms, while I tried to think out my report home on the day …

 C03   C03   C03

The next manifestation of the Spanish love for almost operatic display was our Minister's second presentation of credentials, this time as Ambassador. The ceremony was set for one o'clock on 5 October 1950, to take place in the very antechamber to the throne room in the Palacio del Oriente, where I had already had my baptism of fire. Promptly at twelve noon two Cinderella-type coaches, all gilding and plate glass, one drawn by four horses and one by two, drew up before the gates of the now Irish Embassy. They attracted quite a crowd. They were escorted by footmen in cocked hats and by troops of Franco's Moorish cavalry, mounted on horses with gilded hooves. The horsemen wore pale blue cloaks and their helmets were wrapped in matching blue turbans. The procession proceeded at a walking pace and took an hour to cross Madrid. The Ambassador was in the four-horse coach. I travelled in the two-horse coach behind, with a young man from the Foreign Office. I doubt if we exchanged a single word. At the Palace the ceremony was relatively simple. Leo presented his letters of credence – strictly formal – to General Franco, and spoke his beautiful Spanish. He then introduced his staff: me.I bowed with self-conscious grace – somewhere between an inclination and a curtsy – and the *Caudillo* shook my hand graciously and said something polite. He was a rather small man, plump and amiable. Of all the Madrid establishment, he was the only one who was ever remotely civil to me. Perhaps he will get a night out on an iceberg for it.

I must tell you that my dress was a triumph. I was tired of my Parisian black silk, 'new-look' Dior-type suit, which had seen me through so many previous, formal 'dos'. This time I went to Victoria, the foremost Madrid *couturière*, who later figured internationally as one of the greats. She said, 'Do not worry. I dressed all the women ministers under the republic. You will be *correctissima* (most correct), but very feminine.' She was as good as her word, and that dress, shortened or not and otherwise altered or not, as might be needed, did yeoman service for me for all occasions for the rest of my career in the Foreign Service. To meet Spanish protocol, it had to be high-necked, long-sleeved, floor-length and black; I could, if I wished, wear a hat rather than a mantilla; I wished; this time a discreet, Spanish-style hat. Male cadets in the Department got dress-allowances to cover formal wear; on the basis of that dress, I got the same allowance for our young women. I hope it is still the case that they get it.

PART IV: THE REALITIES OF LIFE

The two years I spent in Spain were momentous ones in the life of my sister, Barbara. Barbara was that indefinable phenomenon, a 'beauty'. Rooms lit up when she came into them; heads turned when she passed in the street. It is not an easy role to live up to; all other aspects of her personality tended to be subordinated to the impact made by her appearance. She was very bright, of strong character, very witty, very sweet-tempered, very pious and, from her schooldays on, she was good at all ball-games, with swift reactions and an unerring eye. Such was the fashion in looks at the time – plucked eyebrows, dark lipstick and Lauren Bacall hairstyles – that she was always taken for older than her age. Just before her twenty-first birthday she became engaged to Frank Biggar, a senior colleague of mine, whom we had met in optimum circumstances in Rome, on that famous, post-war Easter holiday. They were ideally happy, but fortune was not kind to them. Shortly after the birthday celebrations, Barbara was stricken with a sudden, violent, delusional mental illness, then described as schizophrenic, but later manifesting rather the symptoms of manic-depression. It is impossible to describe how deeply this affected my poor mother. People said that when they met her, they always knew at once how Barbara's health was, 'from Margaret's expression'. Within a year Barbara had recovered, but she had been through such a terrible ordeal that her natural confidence in life was irreparably affected and, indeed, not without reason. From then onwards, unpredictable circumstances could always trigger a return of the original condition. My parents were anxious that the engagement be broken off – she was twenty-one and Frank was eleven years older – but neither Frank nor Barbara would hear of it, and in 1951 they were married by my Uncle Paddy in a storybook wedding in University Church on Saint Stephen's Green. I was a bridesmaid – one of four. Séamus, by now, had qualified as a doctor and, influenced no doubt by Barbara's illness, had chosen to specialise in psychiatry. I had come back from Spain, and it seemed as if the hopes and happiness of the entire older family centered on the newly-married couple. We rejoiced in their new lives together, but always with an undertone of anxiety. Those early days and the birth and babyhood of the first grandchild, a boy, John David (Eóin Dáibhí), I remember as being a peculiarly halcyon interlude. When someone asked my mother did she miss Barbara, 'now that she was gone?', meaning 'left home', my mother replied joyfully, 'I would, if she had.' My little poem about a toddler's first shoe was written at that time for John David. It was beautifully translated by the late Breandán Ó hEithir and I give it here:

The First Shoe
Translated by Breandán Ó hEithir

We put the shoe on him the first time this morning,
minute, stitched-together, a little jewel of leather,
a miracle of shoemaking, in the first choice of fashion,
on the flowerlike foot never before in bondage,
the first shoe ever on that small honey-sweet foot.

Little treasure, heart of the house, here you go tramping,
strike the new sole like this on the ground stoutly,
hold up the precious head pluckily, determined,
a man-baby you are in your walk and your bearing,
the height of my knee, and so soon to leave me!

You have a long road to travel before you,
and tying your shoe is only the first tying.

ᘓ   ᘓ   ᘓ

I now gravitated naturally back into the editorial circle of *Comhar* and into Dublin's Irish-speaking world where it was possible, at that time, to go for days sometimes without needing to talk English. This became even more so when I was seconded from the Department of External Affairs, where I held down the post of Secretary to the Department's Cultural Relations Committee, to assist Tomás de Bháldraithe over at the Department of Education in the compilation of his new English-Irish Dictionary. One of my brilliant fellow workers for the Cultural Relations people before I left was Niall Tóibín, who had been brought into the Department by Seán MacBride, a circumstance which, sadly, militated – to my lasting regret – against my getting to know him at all well in my brief stint as Secretary to the Committee. I have two memories from that time: one uniquely pleasing and one farcical. One concerns the sculptor Oisín Kelly, who described himself in his CV for the Venice Biennale as: 'member of the Select Vestry, no back teeth.' He was suffering under the ministrations of a dentist at the time. His exhibit was a wonderful, life-size, granite baby, so warmly rounded and huggable that the grey stone seemed to melt into soft life before your eyes. The other arose from a visiting exhibition of Scandinavian painting, in which there figured a canvas of a female nude, featuring pubic hair. It is difficult now to believe quite how shocking this was in Dublin then, but readers will have to take it on trust. Tactlessly, I steeled myself to back the woman curator of the exhibition, against my Committee, in her decision to hang this picture prominently. I thought it very ugly, but if that was how the Scandinavians chose to portray themselves … Fortunately, the curator had more sense, and on being approached by a senior member of the Committee – I think it was Mrs le Brocquy – agreed to hide the offending figure away in a dark corner. Only a very immature diplomat would have dreamt of doing otherwise in those days.

ᘓ   ᘓ   ᘓ

Working on the Dictionary was – as working in the Institute had been – being paid for pursuing a hobby. We had a team of highly literate native-speakers, representing all the dialects. These included the cynical and immensely authoritative 'Máire', pen name of Seámus Ó Grianna; the gifted young Cork story-writer Donncha Ó Céileachair; and Siobhán Ní Shúileabháin from Corca Dhuibhne, who went on to make a name for herself for her Irish prose – recently she has published poetry. We got on amazingly well with each other, and learnt a lot from each other, and I cannot remember so much as a single hostile word exchanged between us in the three years I spent there; the incredible sometimes happens.

During this time I occasionally did duty for the editor of *Comhar*. This was the admirably principled but somewhat rigid Ulster poet and novelist, Séamus Ó Néill. Séamus distrusted Munster writers and felt they were always engaged in efforts to defeat his Northern orthodoxy of language with some degenerate Southern sleight-of-hand. To counteract this tendency of his, I always, when I took over from him, went straight to the wastepaper-basket to see if any of his discards should be rescued; just once I was remarkably lucky. I found in the basket a half-sheet of crumpled letter-paper scrawled with some handwritten lines in ink. It was a treasure trove – Brendan Behan's amazing little lyric on the deserted Blaskets. I tidied up the spelling a little, but did not interfere with the affecting, slight clumsiness of the whole, which proclaimed its learner's spontaneity, and it was published in our next issue. For this and for other occasional help, Brendan became fond of me, and often referred to me in his column in the *Irish Press* and elsewhere in highly complimentary terms. Unfortunately, the achievements which gave rise to the compliments were often totally fictitious, as for example: 'Máire MacEntee, with whose magnificent translation of 'The West's Awake' you are all familiar ...' Dear Brendan.

ভ   ভ   ভ

It was inevitable, given the circles I was moving in at that time, that sooner or later I should find myself in association with the object of my adolescent obsession, this time as a woman of thirty rather than a schoolgirl of sixteen. He was separated from his wife, and we became lovers. As many people know, or knew, my '*Ceathrúintí Mháire Ní Ógáin*' (Quatrains of Mary Hogan) charts the course of the affair. He was a distinguished Celtic scholar and wonderfully entertaining company. For three years I did not look ahead, or ask for more, and I felt myself totally at ease and happy. Many people at that time knew his identity – most of them are dead now – including my parents who were considerately kept up to date – by the police! He had left-wing and IRA associations. I wish now I could have spared them the hurt I caused them, but I was insensible to everything except the extraordinary culmination of those years of longing. As was the convention of the time, I denied stolidly that there was any impropriety in the association, and they affected to believe me. I took the occasion to leave home and set up in a flat of my own. I continued to divide much of my time between my parents' house in Leeson Park and my brother-in-law's house in Mount Merrion, where Barbara's two babies were being looked after by a trained children's nurse, whom I paid, while their poor young mother was desperately and pathetically ill in a mental hospital in Scotland, having broken down once more after the birth of the second. This way of life still left me ample time for love-making and conviviality. My expectations in that line were modest. My lover, for his part, was fond of me and enjoyed picking my brains to increase his already considerable competence in the Irish of Corca Dhuibhne, but I by no means meant everything to him, as he did to me. His wife and he had divorced in England, but he had no thought of marrying me. I tried not to mind – my hands were full at the time with the care of my two small nephews; Séamus had insisted that their mother's disappearance had left them particularly vulnerable, and that they must never be left to cry uncomforted. All this time there was another young woman in my lover's life – had always been – whom it would suit him to marry, and whom, I came reluctantly to realise, he eventually would marry, if I were out of the way. It was an unhappiness I learnt to live with, but by the winter of 1956 I was very near breaking point.

I give here one of the lyrics I wrote around about then; it exemplifies how my versifying could act as a safety-valve. The translation is by Aidan Hayes and it is the only convincing version, in truly modern English, of any of my love poems that I have ever read – not excluding my own trans-lations, which are 'keys', or 'cribs' rather than realisations of an original poem in a new language.

For Your Sake
Translated by Aidan Hayes

For your sake I kept love dark
But here I declare an end.
Enough of this dance.
I've had my fill of the slave's part.

I'm giving it up. I've decided.
I count the price that's been paid:
My night on night of lost sleep,
The urgent servility, the wasting sobs.

My heart-stab, my laugh-stopper,
If you have some shame remember
Pain and plague and torment —
My fate without luck, without grace.

How should I charge you with
Eclipsing the sun by your absence,
With each dreary day under servitude's shelter?
A fool's payment for a counterfeit freedom.

Hard being beside you,
Worse being without you:
My intimacy with you was
A bad bargain either way.

ଔ ଔ ଔ

I had other reasons for anxiety – perhaps they distracted me from my more immediate trouble. My father had undergone a series of operations for suspected cancer in or about the time that my sister's illness was in crisis. As we know he lived to be ninety-four, but during this time and for some time to come he was exhausted and enfeebled and in need of special care. He had 'made his peace', as they say, with the Church and, paradoxically, seemed to us to have become much less compulsively devout. By 1955 his recovery was complete, and he and my mother had arranged to go for a long and restful holiday in Portugal to undo the wear and tear of the last few years, when a further family crisis arose.

My Uncle David had, in that year, been appointed Master General of the Dominicans. My Conor (as he was not yet) happened to be in Rome at the time as the guest of Denis Devlin, then our Ambassador to the Quirinal, and he told me the following story. He and Denis were lunching in the refectory of the Angelicum – the Dominican university where my Uncle David had been Rector and was still a professor – when the news of the appointment was announced. Two French-Canadian clerics were discussing what they had heard. '*Qu'est qu'il est au juste, ce père Browne?*' said one, '*C'est un Anglais?*' (What is he exactly, this Father Browne? An Englishman?) '*Ah non,*' replied the other, '*c'est pire* (it is worse). *C'est un Irlandais.*' '*Mon Dieu!*' exclaimed the first, '*Ils sont partout!*' (They are everywhere!) Now we were told that my uncle was gravely ill, and was coming home. It was out of the question to cancel my parents' holiday; they had been through too much. On the other hand, the doctors warned that David was dangerously weak and seemed to have lost the will to live. They recommended that his family surround him with love and care; that left Moss and Paddy and me – Séamus, still unmarried, was now an intern at the Maudesley Hospital in London, and chiefly preoccupied with ensuring a proper régime for Barbara and her two little boys. His advice was invaluable, but not always, as I have hinted earlier, easy to follow as a practical proposition. As a result of this conjuncture of demands, I became the almost constant companion, throughout his convalescence, of the great and simple man my uncle was. His doctors told us he was like a man who had been exposed on an ice floe. He was refusing to eat or drink, the roof of his mouth was a mass of ulcers, and he was reduced to skin and bone. His clothes hung pathetically on his big Tipperaryman's frame; he had no energy left to help himself. He was carried off the plane from Rome on a stretcher, straight to hospital.

As he was nursed back to health, my dutiful affection for my almost unknown relative warmed to a fiercely protective love, and I managed to piece together the circumstances of his frightening decline. My Uncle David had been a member of Pius XII's intimate circle, and his loving devotion to the then Holy Father was the mainspring of his life. The

Dominican conclave to choose a new Master-General of the Order was deadlocked, as was usual, between conservatives and liberals. David was despatched by the Pope to report progress. The conclave assumed that he came as a compromise candidate of the Pope's choosing; nothing could have been further from the truth. When, carried along by events and totally mystified, David found himself elected Master-General, Pius XII was furious and never spoke to him again. Hearts do break, and David's did at that juncture. Further, the office thrust upon him was not an easy one, involving, as it did, the suppression of the Dominican 'worker' priests – those priests, especially in France, who went to work in the factories to be close to their flock, and whom the Vatican saw as creating 'an occasion for scandal'. David was a conservative theologian, but the gentlest of men and totally unfitted for this charge. He nearly died of it. I have never been in any doubt but that David wished this record to survive him and, accordingly, I set it down. It was left to Pius' humane successor, John XXIII (1958), to heal the hurt to the extent that was in his power. He elevated his old opponent in theological debate to the Cardinalate, and ensured him a highly privileged old age in an apartment overlooking Saint Peter's Square, where the astronomer Galileo Galilei had been held by the Holy Office in the seventeenth century! Conor and I, after we were married, sat with him there and watched, on television, the space probe, *Mariner II*, approaching Mars!

 Cϵ   Cϵ   Cϵ

This may be the moment to tell another Vatican story involving the uncles – a less grim one this time. When my Uncle Moss contemplated his book on the Browne family, *The Big Sycamore*, which I referred to in my early chapters, he intended it simply as a memoir. Like the good and serious priest he was, he mentioned his project to the Diocesan authorities. From that moment his problems began. It was intimated to him that the unvarnished, respectful, but humorous account he planned would damage David's Roman career; it might even 'injure my father politically'! Moss was stunned and also deeply hurt, but he rallied and settled for a fictionalised story with the principal names changed. Drumcondra – the Archbishop's chancery – was still having difficulties with this project.

Then Pius XII died and was succeeded by Pope John XXIII. 'Moss,' remarked my Uncle Paddy to my father, 'will have no more trouble. The fashion in family backgrounds at the Vatican has changed.' He was right.

There is another story about the brothers which I cannot resist telling. When David was Master of Novices in San Clemente in Rome, one of his charges, after he was ordained, decided to go on a bicycle tour of Ireland for his well-earned post-ordination holiday. In due course he reached Grangemockler, with its single street and its idlers at the public-house gable. 'Is it here,' asked the romantic young man, 'that the great Father Browne was born?' The reply came in chorus, 'It is indeed, Father, and a better judge of a greyhound you won't find this side of the Shannon.' Moss enjoyed this story; Paddy felt it was overrated.

One more clerical anecdote dates from those days: the story of my Uncle Paddy's second miracle. You will remember that the dead voted in the Roscommon by-election at the start of my narrative. Paddy was now a Monsignor, a fantastically impressive sight in his robes, and had been appointed President of University College, Galway. He was representing the National University at an academic function somewhere in Britain, and beside him at dinner sat a disconsolate, papist Scots laird, whose wife was about to give birth. 'Pray for us, Father,' he said to my uncle. 'The title is entailed, and we have only daughters.' My uncle agreed that he would and mentioned the laird and his lady in his Mass. He thought no more of it until, casually picking up an English newspaper one day, he noticed his dining companion's name; there was now a male heir. The laird's eldest daughter, a medical doctor, had changed her sex and married her housekeeper; she was now the 'Master of X'. My sister was expecting one of her own five babies when this story reached us. '*Beidh mé ag guíochtaint ar do shon,*' (I will be praying for you) said my uncle to her. '*Ná dein, a Phábú, in ainm Dé. Beidh piscín agam!*' (Don't, Pábú, for God's sake. I'll have a kitten!) Whether he prayed or not, she went on to have a lovely boy. And that exhausts my memories of the mid-1950s for now.

CHAPTER VII

United Nations

PART I: TOKEN WOMAN

Ireland, after a long wait, eluded the Soviet veto and, in 1955, became a member of the United Nations. I returned from Education to External Affairs that year, to a catch-all section titled 'International Organisations other than the United Nations' – I can't remember was I a first secretary, or second secretary. It was, in fact, a kind of glorified travel agency for Irish delegations going abroad, and it also provided the secretariat for our Council of Europe representation. This last became of special interest when the Irish government was arraigned before the European Court of Human Rights over the detention without trial of the IRA man Gerry Lawless (1957–61), but that was still in the future when I first arrived back. My most striking memory of the Lawless case, incidentally, is that of travelling back from Strasbourg with Peter Berry, the formidable Secretary of the Department of Justice, and hearing him wax lyrically avuncular over his new Minister for Justice – young, liberal, intelligent and hard-working; his name was Charles J Haughey!

Meanwhile, I was often bored and had to make work for myself, so I took to summarising Government policy on the various issues that pre-sented in various fora, for the benefit of Irish delegates to the Council of Europe and elsewhere who, for one reason or another, did not fancy coping with the voluminous documentation which was always only too available. I got into trouble over this in the case of the delegation of par-liamentarians, deputies and senators bound for the European Parliament in Strasbourg. Declan Costello of Fine Gael affected to believe that my notes were dictating their conduct to the opposition deputies. As I had known Declan as a schoolboy, in a college cap, short trousers and grey knee-socks, when his family were our neighbours in Herbert Park, I found this difficult to take seriously, and, in effect, his colleagues of all parties on the delegation rallied chivalrously to my defence, declaring that they found the notes very useful, so that the storm dissipated as quickly as it had blown up. I had pointed out that, if one wanted to take a stand against government policy, it was useful to know what that policy was.

All in all I found it a pretty dispiriting change after the absorbing interest, human and linguistic – for me at any rate – of the Dictionary (published 1959). Even so, as always in the old External Affairs, life had its enlivening moments.

One of these occurred when our Counsellor, Miss Sheila Murphy, the most ladylike of unmarried, middle-aged female mandarins, and a very pretty one, came agitatedly, in her street clothes, ie, wearing a hat, into the room where my colleague Róisín O'Doherty and I were working. Miss Murphy was a survivor from the old, pre-Treaty civil service, and she tended to treat all her subordinates as if they were difficult and not particularly bright schoolchildren. Just then, she had been coping with an international transport commission, which was about to present its report on Dublin's traffic problems, then, as now, intractable. She more or less told us to be good girls while she was away as she was going to the National Museum to collect the pieces of eighteenth-century Irish silver, which – scandalously, in our estimation, though not, I think, in hers – the government had decided to present to the commissioners. Róisín was quick off the mark: 'Thirty, I presume, Miss Murphy?' she enquired sweetly. 'Not at all, not at all, Dear,' replied Miss Murphy, 'only eleven.'

The other story I treasure was told to me by Fine Gael Senator Sir Thomas Esmonde about his time on the Strasbourg delegation, when MacBride was Minister. In those days the Irish delegation mostly went to Sunday Mass, but rarely received Holy Communion, conscious, as they were, of the fairly worldly fashion in which their evenings were spent in that gastronomically celebrated city. MacBride, however, always made a point of Communicating; he also carried an ostentatious, large, black missal. It all became too much for Senator Esmonde, who happened to be attending the same Mass. 'When I saw that bastard approaching the rails,' he told me, 'I said to myself, "Tommy, you may be no saint, but you're a damn sight better than he is," and up I got and followed him, and I felt great after it!'

CR CR CR

The international organisation that had outsoared the humdrum International Organisations section and had a new section all to itself was the United Nations. Already that section was seen – at least by itself – as the most important section in the Department. The Irish delegation to the eleventh session of the General Assembly of the United Nations in September 1956 was Ireland's first. It was led by the then Minister for External Affairs, Liam Cosgrave and Conor (not yet mine), who had returned from his post as Counsellor of Embassy in Paris to head the new UN section at headquarters in Iveagh House, accompanied the Minister; in New York, Ambassador Freddie Boland, formerly Secretary of the Department at Iveagh House, was our Permanent Representative. It was something of a baptism of fire for Ireland – the year of Suez and Hungary – but, under a Fine Gael-led coalition government, our delegation remained safely, if in no way necessarily disgracefully, in the camp of the United States. Conor, who took to the heady atmosphere of international politics as to his native element, was nevertheless frustrated by the subservient line that his country was content to follow, and also by a degree of duplicity, almost for its own sake, with which that line became attended. He had other reasons for depression nearer home: his marriage of sixteen years to Christine Foster, a beautiful and talented young woman of liberal Northern stock – her mother was a Lynd – had broken up and the strain of maintaining a domestic façade 'for the sake of the children', not to mention his career, was almost intolerable. I had always known Conor and Christine as a couple, slightly. Because, in part, of the Lynd connection, my parents were very fond of her, as was my Uncle Paddy. Now Conor had come back from New York for the Christmas holidays, but by the Thursday after Christmas – I have reason to remember the day – he had come in to town from Howth in search of some distraction.

It so happened that my own Christmas had not been particularly happy either. I had spent the holiday with my parents as a dutiful daughter. We were, all three, desperately missing Barbara's two boys, who, after a year in our care while their mother was so ill, had rejoined their parents, on her recovery, in London, where their father had been posted, something which left us disconcertingly bereaved. I have always loved small children, not sentimentally but with a deep – and I hope clear-sighted – abiding interest, as some people love dogs, or horses. Up to this, minding my two small nephews had, to some extent, masked the emotional waste that my life had become. Now, with Christmas over and the need for a show of seasonal good heart past, I had taken myself into the Department on the pretext of having arrears of work to clear. As I remember my then working habits now, I am pretty sure there were arrears, but I was certainly not engaged in clearing them. I sat at my desk and tried to confront the reality that my all-consuming love affair was over, and that only habit now disguised the fact that it was ending, for me, in rejection. Some lines of GK Chesterton's went round and round in my head: 'Nor stretch the folly of our youth to be the shame of age,' and I felt that I was both very foolish and no longer young. It was at this point that I heard *click, click, click,* an electric snapping of fingers along the corridor outside. This had always been a warning of Conor's approach; he had that habit of shedding surplus energy like static, as he walked briskly and purposefully about some activity, as like as not some mischief. I felt a pang of envy of people who obviously had interesting and entertaining uses for their Christmas leave, and then my door opened, and Conor said something like, 'What exemplary industry! Chuck it and come and have a drink.' It was all as simple as that.

I had always affected to have no time for Conor, in spite of his dazzling intelligence and charm and his meteoric success in his career; he was also slim, black-haired and handsome. Anyone who had found favour with Seán MacBride was discredited in my eyes. It did not matter whether they espoused the Minister's new, IRA-backed republicanism from conviction or self-interest – one was as bad as the other. My mother was not fooled; in her day such a display of hostility by a young woman for a young man was always an index of attraction. We never discussed any of my affairs of the heart as such, but she always knew.

I had indeed proclaimed, during a truth-or-dare party, way back when I first joined the Department, that there were only two men in Ireland I would be bothered marrying, and that both of them were already married. I had to name the two, and one of them was, of course, the object of my continuing adolescent passion. The other, perhaps for purposes of cam-ouflage, to distract the company from the first mentioned name, was Conor. The Spaniards have a proverb that fits the case: *"Toma lo que quieres," dice Dios, "y pagalo."* ('Take what you want,' says God, 'and pay for it.') Now I was absurdly flattered by the present invitation. The Depart-ment was hierarchical, and a counsellor was always a counsellor, and this was not just any counsellor, but the Department's white hope; the govern-ment's policy had been to meet the demands of UN membership by keep-ing 'more of our stronger men' at home. At the very least, going out for a drink beat sitting alone in an empty building working up a suicidal gloom. We went to Davy Byrne's on Duke Street.

We had a wonderful evening talking shop. The dramas of Hungary and Suez were played over at first-hand: it was, as you might say, the view from the corridors of the UN. People familiar with Conor's writings will realise how fascinatingly this differed from the official accounts. For my part, I had an inside track on home affairs to share with him. It was 1956, the year of Seán South's funeral (the IRA man killed in an attack on Brookeborough police station in Northern Ireland), and there was a gen-eral election coming up. I had told Conor that Fianna Fáil expected to be the next government, specifically thanks to the plank in their platform that promised to bring back internment for the IRA. I bet him a good dinner, when he next returned from New York, on this outcome. I hope he laid off his bet, because I won mine, and he paid me a very good dinner in-deed on losing. By the spring of that year we knew we loved each other, and that it was a committed relationship. He brought his two small girls, Kathleen (later called Kate) and Fedelma, in their smart Irish tweed over-coats and their smart French haircuts, to see me (his eldest, his son Dónal, was away at boarding school), and I knew that their happiness, no less than their father's, would preoccupy me for the rest of my life.

Ↄ   Ↄ   Ↄ

In due course the general election took place, and in 1957 we had again a Fianna Fáil government. Our new Minister in External Affairs was Frank Aiken – 'General' Frank Aiken, that was, of the 'Fourth Northern', my father's old IRA division in the 1920s. Aiken's almost symbiotic relationship with Mr de Valera had been cemented in their years out of office. Róisín and I – in our triumphalist Fianna Fáil manner – were delighted. The Department anticipated changes, but not, I am convinced, changes as radical as they got. From the beginning, to general surprise – ministers do not normally take over their predecessor's right-hand man – my Conor established an inside track with Mr Aiken. I quote from Dr Joseph Morrison Skelly's book on *Irish Diplomacy at the United Nations,* which gives an objective, American view of what happened next:

'Conor O'Brien hit his stride at the Twelfth Session [of the General Assembly in 1957]. His intuitive comprehension of Aiken's point of view, his empathy for the Minister's ideas, and his uncanny ability to express them coherently lent even greater importance to his role as the delegation's pre-eminent speech writer. This duty placed O'Brien in close and frequent contact with Aiken. Because the two had such similar outlooks this arrangement suited Aiken. It also meant that O'Brien exerted a greater influence on Ireland's policy. He attended caucus meetings where resolutions were framed, represented Ireland in important Committee meetings, and assumed a more visible role in the Assembly.'

Conor and some of his senior and contemporary departmental colleagues, as also many of the Department's younger members, had hoped for an 'non- committed' role for Ireland at the UN, that is, an autonomous, activist stance in international politics more commonly associated with Scandinavia. As Conor himself put it in his *Memoir* (published in 1998):

'For some of us ... the ideal of what constituted good international behaviour was exemplified at this time by Sweden. Sweden's action in the international field was, as we saw it, independent, disinterested and honourable. The Swedes in international affairs did not spend much time in proclaiming lofty moral principles, but they usually acted as men would do who were in fact animated by such principles. Their voting record was more eloquent than their speeches. It seemed to contain few or no votes against conscience ...
[As it happened,] Mr Aiken required little, if any, advice from us, his juniors and subordinates, on the subject of the virtues of a 'Swedish' position, of

resisting [Great Power] pressure, and so on. The views he had long held were along these lines and, being a man of integrity, he proceeded to put them into practice. In his first intervention [speech in the Assembly] he urged the advantages of a policy of disengagement in Central Europe; in his second, very soon afterwards, he explained why Ireland would vote for a discussion of the question of the representation of China in the United Nations. [China – with backing of the United States – was somewhat absurdly represented at the UN by Taiwan, its offshore anti-communist island, rather than by the government seated in Peking, the capital of mainland, communist China.]

I had told the Minister that if any delegation at the General Assembly wished to be accepted as following an independent line, the test was the annual vote on the question of the representation of China. Because of differences in the positions of Britain and the United States in relation to this matter, the question of the representation of China at the UN had attained a condition of Byzantine complexity. If it came to a straight choice between seating Peking or Taiwan, Britain would have to choose Peking; not because it liked Peking, but because it had to recognise Peking or run the risk of having the Chinese re-occupy Hong Kong, many years before Hong Kong was due, under treaties, to revert to China. The American government understood the British position, but not to the point of agreeing to recognise China [not with a Republican, anti-communist party in office]. So a compromise was worked out. The General Assembly would be allowed to debate the question, each year, but would then vote, not on the substance, but on the question of whether or not to discuss the question which had already been discussed at length: whether Taiwan should continue to be seated as representative of China, or whether a delegation appointed by Peking should take its place.

Now, the position of the United States government on this matter was adopted for internal political reasons, having to do with international 'face' and, in particular [under President Eisenhower], Republican face. No well-informed delegate, among America's allies, was prepared to defend the substance of the position of the United States on this matter. The line was simply that the United States would probably come round on this issue some day, but that, until it did so, western solidarity required support for the Leader of the Free World, however misguided the Leader's position might appear to be on this particular matter.

On a free vote, there would have been a majority in the General Assembly for seating Peking. As it was, the United States (with Britain) could still muster two-thirds for the nonsense of not discussing a proposition which had already been discussed *ad nauseam*. This question was therefore central to the matter which was preoccupying Frank Aiken: how to establish Ireland's position as a genuinely independent country. No country which voted in favour of the Anglo-American 'compromise', aimed at continuing to exclude Peking, would be accepted as representing a genuinely independent position in the Assembly. The minority of countries who voted against the 'compromise' would certainly regard any country which voted for it as not being genuinely independent. But even the countries which voted for the compromise – such as the Latin American countries – knew that their own votes in favour were constrained votes [the product of US 'arm-twisting', see below], and would assume that anyone else who voted 'for' was also operating under constraint.

I explained all this to Aiken; much of it he knew, or at least sensed, already, but I was able to fill in a lot of details, and what I said made sense to him. In the end he simply said: "Very well, we shall vote against the compromise, and in favour of a straight vote on the question of which delegation should represent China in the General Assembly. We had better begin to prepare other relevant delegations for a change in Ireland's voting position on this matter.'"

ᘓ   ᘓ   ᘓ

It is perhaps not entirely surprising, in view of what I have remembered above about my changed feelings for Conor and his for me, that I was a member of the Irish delegation to New York when our Minister cast this crucial vote. Conor was free to pick his own team, and in those days every delegation to the United Nations included at least a 'token' woman. It was a part I had played often and did not resent at all – I saw being a woman, since we had to have at least one, as being an added and providential qualification. This was how it came about that I had direct experience of the lengths, sometimes absurd, to which the US administration of the time was prepared to go to ensure a propaganda victory. We called it 'arm-twisting' and knew those members – 'arm-twisters' – on the US delegation whose sole function it was to corral maverick votes.

On the afternoon of the day that the Minister made public his intention to vote against the US 'shelving' resolution 'not to discuss the representation of China at the UN during the current session', I happened to be in the Delegates' Lounge, a long, comfortable, lightsome room running the length of the Assembly building, furnished with couches and coffee-tables, with a bar at one end. During the session, messages for delegations were announced over the public-address system in the lounge, and I now heard the message, 'A representative of the Delegation of Ireland to the telephone, please', being broadcast repeatedly. I picked up the nearest telephone and found myself in conversation with a Monsignor, one of Cardinal Spellman's secretaries. The Cardinal had been a friend of Senator Joe McCarthy's and was famously opposed to 'the communist peril'. A Monsignor is defined as a 'domestic prelate'; because of my Uncle David's Vatican connections, I knew several such and was not at all overawed by them. This one, however, was, to quote the witty Archbishop Mannix of Australia, 'one of the wild variety.' He demanded angrily, on behalf of the Cardinal, whether it was true that 'Aiken' was going to vote for 'Red China'? I replied that the Minister was voting for the discussion of the question of the representation of China at the United Nations. The Monsignor allowed as how that, in his book, was a vote for Red China. As emolliently as possible – and I was very good at this sort of thing – I repeated my original formula. The Monsignor shifted his ground: was the Irish delegation not shortly holding a diplomatic reception? I agreed that it was. Was the Cardinal not invited? Indeed he was, and the delegation much looked forward to his attendance. 'Well,' said the Monsignor, 'the Cardinal would find it very difficult to attend if it is true that your Minister is going to vote for Red China.' I was genuinely concerned, feeling myself to have assumed the office of hostess. 'Oh dear!' I answered. 'The Delegation will be very disappointed if His Eminence cannot accept our invitation. It appears as if he may have misunderstood our Minister's position.' We had reached a Mexican standoff. 'The Cardinal,' repeated the Monsignor, 'would find it very difficult to attend, etc, etc.' It was clear that the conversation was stuck in a groove. I paid the Cardinal the compliment of taking him seriously and said, in tones of resigned regret, 'His Eminence must do as he thinks right.' The Monsignor was outraged and slammed down the telephone.

What had happened was that the US 'Perm. Rep.', Cabot Lodge, had sent the 'token woman' on their delegation, Irene Dunne, the film-star, who was also a Catholic, to complain to Cardinal Spellman about Mr Aiken's nefarious intentions. The Cardinal had promised 'to raise the devil'. What all concerned had forgotten was that a public man such as Mr Aiken, who had once survived, unscathed, when excommunicated for his politics by the Irish Bishops in 1922, was unlikely to be much influenced in later life by threats from ecclesiastical quarters, more especially foreign ones. In the event, the vote did us very little harm with Irish-Americans. The US government of the day was Republican (under President Eisenhower) and our American ethnic brothers still, at that time, mostly voted Democrat.

ය   ය   ය

The United Nations Assembly provided a wonderful grounding in the realities of international political life. I learnt that if you were anxious to forecast how delegates from the various member countries were going to cast their votes on any given issue, you could get a very plausible result by attributing the lowest possible kind of self-interest consistent with known circumstances to each and predicting that their representatives would vote accordingly. On the other hand, I experienced, in many of my personal contacts, a human warmth and magnanimity that transcended not only cold-blooded political calculation but deep cultural and ideological divisions as well. This was particularly so, in my case, with my neighbour on my right on the Third Committee, the delegate from Iraq. The Third Committee dealt with economic, social and cultural affairs, including, most importantly, human rights, and was considered a particularly appropriate sphere of activity for women. It was, nonetheless, as intensely political as any of the other committees, and it was notable that, if any particularly thorny matter cropped up, many of the seats tended to be taken *ad hoc* by male delegates. For example, Conor replaced me when the Committee discussed 'self-determination'. It would still be normal today for a senior delegate to take over the Irish seat in any UN committee for the discussion of a particular, important issue. I presume that nowadays that senior delegate might well be a woman and take over from a man. I cannot remember that happening in my time.

My Iraqi neighbour was Mrs Bedia Afnan, known to her colleagues as Um Farou (Oom F'roo, phonetically). This was a title of respect; Arab ladies are often addressed as 'Mother of X', their firstborn son. Mrs Afnan had an only child, a daughter, Farou, and, as an affirmation of feminist principles, chose to be called 'Mother of Farou'. She was indeed the matriarch of the Iraqi Foreign Office. Her husband had been Minister-Counsellor at the Iraqi Embassy in London during the Second World War, and was the friend of Churchill and of the oligarch Nuri es Said, virtual ruler of Iraq, under the Hashemite Kingship of Faisal I and his young son. Mrs Afnan's father had been Governor of Bulgaria under the Ottoman Empire, and she had all the self-confidence of a 'service' aristocrat. Politically and ideologically she was a person of the extreme left; personally she was a warm and outgoing elderly lady, not unlike my own mother, both in temperament and appearance. She was widowed and appeared to have inherited her husband's status. She had trained almost all the present members of the Iraqi delegation in their youth and carried great authority. Someone had once said to Nuri, 'Your Mrs Afnan is a communist.' He had replied, 'Nonsense! I knew her father.'

When I took the Irish seat beside her, she greeted me saying, 'I am so glad you have come. It is painful for me to sit everyday beside a Jewish lady and never say "Good Morning".' Before I joined the UN and sat between Iraq and Israel (in alphabetical order), this had been the situation. In the early years of Mrs Afnan's marriage, her best friend in Baghdad was Jewish. After the *Anschluss*, Minister Afnan and his wife, returning from London, had found themselves in Vienna. Mrs Afnan, who looked exactly like a fashionably dressed, American 'Yiddishe Momma', had been arrested and thrown into prison. When her husband finally located her, she refused to come out. 'These people,' she insisted, meaning the Nazis, 'do not like Semites. I am a Semite and I am staying here.' (Arabs are, of course, Semites, just as Jews are, linguistically at all events.) She had to be more or less forcibly removed. The more I knew her, the more I realised how truly this anecdote reflected her character.

When I made my first speech – I think it was on the right of married women to work, *vis-à-vis* the provisions of the Irish Constitution on the family, and that I was defending our government's constitutional position, as I would be obliged to, unless I wanted to resign the Service – Mrs Afnan congratulated me, which was customary between neighbours on such occasions, barring extreme hostility. She said, 'That was a very good speech, but you are wrong, and I will vote against you. You must not mind.' My neighbour on my left, in the Israeli seat, Mrs Shoam Sharon, was also very civil, but a great deal more detached.

Mrs Afnan survived the Kassem *coup* in 1958, when Iraq first moved tentatively away from the West and towards non-aligned status, and when Nuri es Said and the young King Faisal II were murdered. I profited from her wisdom for my remaining years at the UN, until, as Conor's children used to say, 'The bed fell on father' – a quote from Thurber, indicating utter disaster. I remember many instances when her opinion was invaluable. When Sir Abu Bakar Tafewa Balewa, President of the newly independent Nigeria, addressed the General Assembly, I said to Mrs Afnan, 'That was a splendid speech.' I did not add, 'for an African', but it must have echoed in my tone of voice. Mrs Afnan shook her head gloomily and said, 'It was a terrible speech. If Nuri Pasha [Nuri es Said's Ottoman title] had come to this Assembly – but of course the British would never let him – that is the speech he would have made!' Within the year, Abu Bakar had been murdered, in circumstances horribly similar to those surrounding the death of Nuri. Mrs Afnan laboured to make me realise that the highly educated, sophisticated Iraqis I knew and liked, such as the young women on her Third Committee team, were representative of only a very small upper stratum of the heterogeneous population of Iraq, and that there was explosive poverty, alienation and discontent among the other eighty-plus percent. She told me this following story to illustrate the dual legal system: modern statute law in the cities; tribal customary law in the *bled* (countryside). Two Bedouin tribesmen of the desert, armed and wearing *agal and keffiyeh* (head-cloth and band), waited on her in Baghdad, believing her to have inherited her father's inside track with Nuri. It appeared that one of them had killed his wife and wished to make sure that he would be tried by a tribal court. As a tribal court would not regard the killing of an adulterous wife as murder, Mrs Afnan assumed that adultery was involved in this instance. She protested, 'Surely you did not kill the poor woman merely for being unfaithful to you?' 'No, no,' replied the tribesman, 'God forbid, lady, that I should slander the mother of my children. I killed her because she was a shrew'! Whether Mrs Afnan was able to help him further or not, she never said.

The young Hashemite King of Jordan, Hussein, cousin of the young, murdered Iraqi King Faisal II, came in his turn to speak before the General Assembly. I made some innocuous remark to Mrs Afnan about his youth and charm. Her voice broke, 'I cannot look at him,' she said, 'I held his cousin on my knee.' When I last heard of Mrs Afnan, twenty and more years ago, she was in charge of the Iraqi Office in Geneva. I met her once after my marriage, when she came, with her daughter, to see Conor's play, *Murderous Angels* (1968), in Paris. On that occasion we had only time for a short hug, and I have not seen her since; she lives in my affections.

Cʒ   Cʒ   Cʒ

I was not long frequenting the great purpose-built building of the UN on the East River at Forty-Second Street when I became aware of a mean kind of linguistic bullying employed by some of the English-speaking delegations – to be fair to the Americans, these were mostly 'old' (ie, white) Commonwealth countries – to unsettle their 'Third World' colleagues, eg, 'You may *request,* but not *require* the Chair to do something.' It must have been catching, because our Perm. Rep. sometimes tried it on our Minister, with minimal success. Mr Aiken was too old a hand to be patronised. In my Committee, the Third, where we did a lot of drafting of documents and editing of drafts, it was rampant. In the case I remember, the victim was actually the USA. Their draft of an article on the right to life, in the UN Human Rights Declaration, employed the word 'arbitrary'. The UK, seeking covertly to protect their own native institution of 'Orders in Council' – which might indeed be loosely described as arbitrary – without actually mentioning that institution and so drawing attention to its existence, insisted that the word 'arbitrary' was not capable of any meaning in English Law. We (Ireland) were being accused just then of being beastly to the USA over the China vote, and I thought that here was a chance both to be nice to the Americans and to do a bit of linguistic bullying of my own. I got Freddie Boland's permission to go ahead and we made a big production of it. Conor and Paul Keating sat in the advisors' seats behind my chair to give ballast. I demolished – at least as far as the Third Committee of the United Nations was concerned – the absurd British contention. Several non-anglophone delegations, who had been about to vote with the British as being authorities on correct English, changed their minds. The Yugoslav Delegate, a female Professor of Law, told me she had telegraphed her government for 'fresh instructions'. Accordingly, when the time came for the vote to be taken, the American draft carried. As I finished speaking, the British representative, Sir Samuel Hoare (not *the* Sir Samuel), scribbled a note on his pad, tore it off and gave it to his 'runner', who brought it across the floor to me. It read, 'Even the ranks of Tuscany …' The quote is from Macaulay's *Lays of Ancient Rome*, and the line Sir 'Sam' left unfinished is from 'The Ballad of Horatius', who saved Rome from Tuscan attack by demolishing the access bridge into the city, over the River Tiber, under the eyes of the enemy, before leaping into the river and swimming to safety. It goes, 'Even the ranks of Tuscany could scarce forbear to cheer!' It was a good moment.

PART II:
WELCOME BE THE WILL OF GOD

My Uncle Paddy died. His lifelong friend and fellow-student from his Paris days, Monsignor Hayes of Muintir na Tíre, telegraphed his grief, in the words of Kickham's Matt the Thrasher: *Knocknagow is no more!*

Paddy Browne had just turned seventy when, in the early summer of 1960, after he had retired from the presidency of University College, Galway, he suffered a massive heart attack. He died in Saint Vincent's Nursing Home, on Leeson Street, on Whit Sunday, the fifth day of June.

Before the attack he had been in the highest spirits. After a dinner given about then in his honour by Mr de Valera, then President of Ireland, he had confided to his host, whom he counted among his close personal friends, that he was experiencing such euphoria that he felt it must presage some imminent disaster. We now know that this state of mind was a clinical indicator of what was to come. I had met him myself that week and he had asked me, in Irish as always, had I anything to drink in my flat. He said he had just parted from the poet WR Rodgers (known to us as Bertie), whom he was anxious to dissuade from becoming a Catholic, and needed a drink. All I had was gin, which he did not much like, but it broke the tension, and that was what he needed. He always had a healthy distrust of the motives of aspiring converts. He did, however, contact his brother, Moss – now parish priest of Ballymore Eustace, in County Wicklow, at the source of the Liffey – and suggest that he undertake Bertie's instruction, as being more skilled than himself, Paddy, in pastoral matters and less personally involved.

Some days later, when the heart attack struck, Bertie and a BBC crew were with Paddy; they were filming an interview with him on Oliver St John Gogarty who, in *As I Was Going Down Sackville Street*, had characterised my Uncle Paddy as 'the man I loved'. Bertie telephoned me; by the time I got to the little house by the sea at Seapoint, into which Paddy had just moved – at the express request of Mr de Valera, who did not want Paddy to leave Dublin in his retirement and live in Dunquin, as he himself had proposed – the doctor and the heart specialist had been and gone. My poor uncle was propped up on cushions on the floor, where he stayed, in great discomfort, for twenty-four hours or more because it was considered too dangerous to move him. Finally it became clear that he could not be nursed properly as he was and, perhaps also, that the damaged heart was not going to recover. The ambulance arrived and took him to Saint Vincent's, and he seemed happier in a comfortable bed. Then came a series of further attacks, and on the Saturday the doctors told us there was no hope.

I decided to spend the night in his room. His night-nurse strenuously objected, 'You don't want to hear the dreadful things these old priests say when they are dying.' 'Nurse,' I said, utterly shocked and furiously angry, 'when I was a little girl and had a nightmare, he took me into his bed to comfort me; I will not leave him alone now.' She gave way on condition that I remained behind a screen and did not interfere. I had a copy of *Eugene Onegin* in Russian and a small flashlight, and I concentrated as best I might on construing the text to keep awake. As for my interfering, the nurse settled herself in an armchair by the gas fire and slept solidly through the most spectacular thunderstorm I ever remember. 'The heavens themselves show forth the death of princes!' At about two o'clock in the morning, as if my uncle had become aware of some sudden and profound physical change, he cried aloud, in English, 'My God, I'm done for!' The nurse didn't stir, and I came out from behind my screen and went to him. He was now talking rapidly and urgently in Irish, about the passage of time, debts to be paid, trains to catch. I said to him, '*Ná bí buartha, déanfaimid é sin go léir ar maidin.*' (Don't worry, we will do all that in the morning.) He recognised me and was reassured. He smiled his wonderful smile and said, '*Agus ansin raghaimid go dtí an* flat *agat-sa,*' (and then we will go to your flat) and dropped back to sleep. He always enjoyed visits to my flat; they made him feel *gallánt* and unconventional. When he awoke again, at dawn, he did not seem to know me and said angrily, in English, 'You're not bringing them, you know you're not.' I knew he meant my mother and his brothers, and I left at once and drove in my mother's borrowed Mini to Leeson Park to fetch them. As I went upstairs to my parents' bedroom, I was startled to see that the portrait, by Séan O'Sullivan, of my Uncle Paddy as a young priest, which hung on the landing, had snapped its cord and fallen to the ground. We contacted David, who had returned from Rome, at Dominick Street; the storm had brought down telephone wires throughout the country and we could not reach Moss in Ballymore.

When we got back to the nursing home, it was full daylight. My Uncle Paddy seemed comfortable and content, propped up on pillows, while an elderly nun gently fed him sips of water from a teaspoon. My mother sat in the bedside chair at his head. He turned to look at her and knew her, and his whole face lit up with a wonderful, youthful mischief. He spoke clearly and without effort, 'My father says I don't have to go for the cows.' They were his last words. David began to recite the Prayers for the Dying and Paddy, holding my mother's hand, slipped quietly away. It was as if he had walked composedly out of the room. My mother did not at first realise he was dead. Meanwhile, word had reached poor Moss, that most tender-hearted of the brothers. He came posthaste to Dublin, driven by a parishioner, wisely not trusting himself to drive. I met him in the hall of the nursing home, and he knew at once that his brother was dead. Standing under the lofty, Georgian stairwell, filled with cold light, he threw back his lovely, erect head – he had inherited my grandfather's proud carriage – and he howled like a dog, like one of his own beloved greyhounds, 'Oh Paddy, Paddy, Paddy, we slept in the one bed, Paddy, and you would not wait for me.' Later, while saying the funeral Mass, he broke down, and again at the graveside. Moss wept for all of us.

We expected that Paddy would be buried in Dunquin, but Mr de Valera again intervened and begged that he be buried in my father's plot in Glasnevin, head to head with the de Valera family plot, and so it was done, in deference to the lifelong affection between them. None of the three eldest Browne brothers is buried in Grangemockler: Moss lies in his parish graveyard at Ballymore Eustace, and David in the Dominican cloister in Tallaght Priory. Paddy's Requiem Mass was celebrated in the Pro-Cathedral. With uncharacteristic sensitivity, John Charles McQuaid, the Catholic Archbishop of Dublin, stayed away; relations between him and the Browne brothers had always been strained, though formally correct. The great building was packed with mourners. My brother Séamus said to me, 'I used to think it was sad that he had no children; now I know that this whole church is crowded with his children.' I think poor Barbara's health at the time made it advisable that she and Frank not come home from Brussels, where Frank was then posted as Ambassador. At Glasnevin, the younger members of Paddy's staff, from Galway, shouldered his coffin and carried it to the grave. I remember that Frank Forde and Colm Ó hEochaidh (son of the old headmaster of Ring College, the Fear Mór's son, and one day to succeed my uncle as President of UCG) were among them. That evening, Bertie Rodgers 'phoned me; he was inconsolable. 'You don't know,' he sobbed, 'what this means to me.' I could have said, 'Or you to me.' I refrained.

For a long time afterwards all of us were numb. It was some two weeks later that my mother pulled herself together and set out downtown, intending to hear Mass in Clarendon Street and have morning coffee afterwards. As she walked down Grafton Street from the Saint Stephen's Green end, she saw Brendan Behan coming towards her from the opposite direction. She wasn't at all sure that she was in the mood for Brendan, but good manners prevailed, and they greeted each other. 'Margaret,' said Brendan, 'I'm sorry for your trouble and I'll miss the man that's gone, but you won't mind my saying that that was a lovely hat you wore at the funeral. A woman in grief needs a good hat.' My mother didn't mind, in fact she felt better than she had for a long time. Brendan's compliment was like the champagne cocktails that my father made for us all when we came back from Glasnevin, frivolous but effective.

The last time my mother had all her brothers alive around her was at Séamus' wedding (1959) to a lovely and talented Donegal girl of whom we were all very fond, Jean Doherty, soon to become the youngest nursing sister in these islands. Moss married them in the chapel at Ballymore Eustace, and it was a warm, simple, affectionate family wedding, in glorious June weather, without a hint of cloud. Jean told us later that when they were about to register at their hotel that evening, Séamus hissed at her, 'Take off your gloves.' He wanted the receptionist to see the ring. Life went on. *Dé do bheatha, a thoil Dé!*

 Cℜ Cℜ Cℜ

Meanwhile, I had become – like Bríd Lynch, the actress, or Paddy Lynch (no relation), the economist and already almost an elder statesman, together with Val and Sheila Iremonger and Martin and Patsy Sheridan – a well-worn member of the generous and somewhat unconventional Cruise O'Brien circle of friends; Christine's as well as Conor's. Dónal, who was a boarder at the Quaker school in Newtown, Waterford, I knew less well than the little girls. There is a letter that Christine wrote to Conor sometime later, which reads: 'Máire ... has been wonderfully good with the girls, and the relationship between them is a most happy one.' Even today, I cannot read those words without an overwhelming feeling of relief and gratitude.

From the very beginning, Christine and I worked very hard to keep the rearrangement of family ties as untraumatic for the children as possible. Part of this consisted in not at any time pretending that the break-up of Conor's first marriage was not desperately sad for them. We have always built on this fact and have done our utmost to make up to them for that time. We may not have succeeded as well as we would have wished, but they – all three of them – have always remained a great source of happiness, support and fun to me and to us all. I could fill volumes with stories of their courage, wit and charm, but, in the nature of things, it would not be fair to the adults they have become, or to the memory of the youngest, our dear, dead Kate. Perhaps one day one of the grandchildren will do for us what I have tried to do for my grandparents here and complete the picture …

PART III: THE DAY JOB

I now travelled a circuit – Dublin, New York, Strasbourg – and lived out of suitcases. The Council of Europe, in the light of my New York insights, had become much more interesting. I was alive now to *realpolitik*, to politics as skulduggery. Besides, I had discovered that the Secretary of the Department, the supremely amiable Kerryman, Con Cremin, not only read my reports but laughed at my jokes. My immediate superior, our Permanent Representative in Strasbourg, poor Tommy Woods, was ill and dying, so that much of his work fell on me. In his place I attended a meeting on Nuclear Power in Europe. My colleagues were mildly surprised to see me, as we had indicated that, as a government, the subject did not concern us. I had decided, however, that given the cross-border nature of nuclear fallout, it would be no harm to know what they were up to. Their surprise, however, was as nothing to mine when I saw the Belgian nuclear expert who accompanied that delegation; he was a dead-ringer for Professor Tournesol (Calculus in the English version) in the *Tin-tin* books. My brother-in-law was now our ambassador to Brussels, and I could not help thinking how my small nephews would have enjoyed a glimpse of this legendary nursery figure. The Belgian scientist had, in fact, served as the model for Hergé's Professor and was his perfect double: bald head, spectacles, sparse eccentric side-locks, down to every detail of his formal, old-fashioned suiting, bow-tie and diminutive bony frame. I put all this in my report, not thinking anyone would read it, and forgot about it. When I got back to Dublin, Mr Cremin sent for me. I couldn't think why he would and was uneasy. It turned out that his children had also been reared on *Tin-tin* while he was *en poste* in Paris, and he wanted to share his enjoyment of Professor Tournesol's *doppelgänger* (double) with me. He was that kind of man.

Tommy Woods died in hospital in Strasbourg, despite dedicated efforts to save his life. One young doctor said to me, 'It is important that Monsieur Woods lives and continues to write.' Tommy had just published his elegant treatise on John Stuart Mill, and European respect for learning, together with his wit and clubbableness, contributed to the many friendships he had made there. Ladies were particularly fond of him and grieved for him; the Hungarian wife of the British Permanent Representative came every day to see him in hospital, and the wife of the proprietor of the Grand Hotel, where he had lived, brought him little covered dishes, cooked with her own hands, to tempt his appetite. I do not think it ever crossed his mind that he would not recover. When he died, I took over as 'acting' Perm. Rep., but my days in the Department after that were not to continue all that long.

Not that I foresaw, when I attended the 1960 session of the UN General Assembly in New York in September, that this would be my last such posting. Freddie Boland was due to be elected president of that Assembly and I remember thinking that, not unlike my Conor, he was what the ancients described as a 'fortunate man': even his reverses turned to his advantage. He was well able on his own account to garner the votes of the 'Western' bloc of nations, but without the Afro-Asian and non-committed votes, which he owed to the independent 'Aiken line', for which he had little personal enthusiasm, he could not have made the presidency. In the outside world, John FitzGerald Kennedy became President of the United States, and our delegation followed his election eagerly on television – still something of a novelty. The new Chairman of the Soviet Committee of Ministers, Nikita Khrushchev, reported to be, humanly speaking, a considerable improvement on his predecessors, would be attending this session. Of the many anecdotes illustrating his perceived humanity, this – still in the future then – is my favourite. At the time of his fall and exile, it is told that he addressed his opponents saying, 'You have not won. I could go forth tomorrow with a begging-bowl and a staff, to walk the roads of Russia, and, wherever I journeyed, I would be known and welcomed and given food and shelter. Which of you can say the same?' Pope John XXIII reigned in Rome. It seemed then, to my unassailable innocence, as if the world might yet be run by three leaders at least amenable to reason and capable of generosity.

ᄋᔑ   ᄋᔑ   ᄋᔑ

The year before (1959), China had invaded Tibet, and the Irish delegation had demonstrated that it could be useful to a Great Power – in this case the USA – to have a friend among the non-committed. We achieved this by spearheading the condemnation, in the Assembly, of China's use of force. It was, of course, strictly a propaganda exercise – no one was going to fight for Tibet, which was not even a member state of the UN but a former British quasi-protectorate; however, it pleased the Americans and redressed the balance of the 'China vote'. As an introductory course in ethnology, it was invaluable to us. We were joined, in an advisory capacity, by a delegation representing the Dalai Lama, who had made his escape from Lhasa to India, and also, even more usefully, by a former British Agent in Lhasa, Hugh Richardson, who was a learned Tibetan scholar, knew the delegates personally and had frequently done business with them in the past. He volunteered his services to us in protest against British inaction on this issue.

The Tibetan delegation was led by Diallo Thondup, the Dalai Lama's 'Chinese' brother – Tibetans are polyandrous and his father was Chinese. It also included a former Tibetan Minister for Finance, who, when our Minister lectured him on economics, as he tended to do, invariably replied, 'Quite right, Excellency, quite right.' We came to realise that this was a Tibetan euphemism for, 'No! No way! In no set of circumstances!' Another member was the Dalai Lama's youngest brother, who was a student at, I think, Yale. He was movingly anxious to help his brother's cause and undertook all the boring material chores that go with running a diplomatic offensive, such as cyclostyling and distributing documents, franking envelopes, etc, etc. He was very young and charming and engaged to an American girl, who was an Episcopalian. He was also a minor emanation of the Buddha, and there his troubles began. The Episcopalians would not allow him to join their Church unless he ceased to be a minor emanation of the Buddha and this, existentially, he could not do; he *was* a minor emanation of the Buddha, who wanted to become an Episcopalian. We never learnt how the story ended, but when Conor and I got married, his older brother, Diallo, sent us a wonderful Tibetan rug bearing a design of a fierce supernatural being in brilliant, jewel colours of ruby and emerald. When we were in Ghana, a year or so later, and the Chinese Ambassador called on us, he saw it, and he was so taken aback that he almost tripped over it. 'That,' he said, recovering himself, 'is quite good.' Years later it was stolen from a *Chinese* dry-cleaners in New York.

PART IV: INTO AFRICA

Tibet was last year (1959); we had got the Tibetans an international hearing and established their nuisance value. No one could do more. This year (1960) the big dramas would be, unexpectedly, the defence of the Office of the Secretary-General of the UN, held by Dag Hammarskjöld, against Soviet attack, and, all too expectedly, the plunge into anarchy of the newly independent Republic of the Congo, formerly the Belgian Congo, now newly seated in the UN. From its inception in June 1960, the independence of the Congo was planned by the Belgian colonial power as a sham, a *feall ar iontaoibh* (betrayal of the trusting), as Irish puts it: a façade of black rule, behind which white interests – economic, political and religious – would continue, as heretofore, to exercise power and dictate events. My fantasy of the three virtuous rulers did not last long. The world remembers Mr Khrushchev taking off his shoe and hammering the desk in front of him to interrupt the British Prime Minister, Harold

Macmillan, in full rhetorical flight on his 'winds of change' theme. They also think they remember Freddie Boland calling Khrushchev to order so vigorously that his gavel snapped – actually, that last was a separate incident in which Freddie gavelled the Bulgarian representative and broke the gavel. The shoe was the opening salvo of Khrushchev's *Troika* (triumvirate) campaign, the anti-Hammarskjöld onslaught, which he chose to mount in the context of the 'mismanagement' by the UN Secretariat – criminal, he maintained – of the United Nations Operation in the Congo. The Soviet Union had initially supported the operation at the time of its inception when the Utopian illusion, created for foreign consumption by Belgium, shattered irretrievably with the mutiny of the Congolese National Army in July 1960, which, contrary to the proposed metropolitan script, got rid of that Army's Belgian officers. The other Congolese ranks then ran amok. Subsequent Soviet dissatisfaction, we now know, was by no means groundless. At the time, Hammarskjöld's undoubted charisma carried the day.

My own abiding memory of the session is seeing, in January 1961, on the television in the Delegates' Lounge, the arrest of the elected Congolese Prime Minister Patrice Lumumba by his enemies within his own government – already subverted from without by American 'Cold War warriors' reacting against the *direct* Soviet aid requested by Lumumba at that time. These moves aborted Lumumba's escape to his powerbase in Stanleyville and led directly to his subsequent murder, in 1961, by the Minister for the Interior of the revolting province of Katanga, Godefroid Munongo. At no stage during this process did UN personnel intervene to protect the legitimate Prime Minister of the Congo, who had invited them in to restore order after the mutiny and to counterbalance the rapid return of Belgian forces occasioned by the murders of Belgian nationals by the mutineers. Our Minister, as we stood, in the Delegates' Lounge, in the unaccustomed crowd around 'the box', watching the unhappy Premier being brutally bundled down the steps of an aircraft to his death, exclaimed, 'It is like the Descent from the Cross!' More than one viewer familiar with Christian iconography had the same thought. And if the reader is confused by the above recital, we were no less so.

Perhaps a table of events will help:

Congo Chronology

1960

30 June: Congo becomes independent;

4 July: Congolese Army mutinies;

11 July: Province of Katanga, impelled by Belgian and international big business and hoping to retain control of the province's mining resources, declares independence under Moïse Tshombe as president. This would-be state was never internationally recognised, even by Belgium;

12 July: Prime Minister Patrice Lumumba and President Joseph Kasavubu invite the UN to send troops to the Congo to help restore order. Belgium has already sent troops to protect European lives;

14 July: UN accedes to Congo government's request and Belgium troops begin to withdraw;

12 August: Katanga receives UN Secretary-General Dag Hammarskjöld and the first UN troops;

24 August: Soviet troops and transport arrive in Congo independently, to the alarm of the USA and the 'Western Alliance' at the UN. From now on, the USA will use all of its influence to bring down Lumumba, whom they label a communist;

5 September: US pressure splits the government of the Congo and Kasavubu arrests Lumumba;

28 November: Lumumba escapes from captivity in Léopoldville and makes for his powerbase at Stanleyville, in Northern Congo. UN troops are expressly instructed, from New York, not to protect him, or to help him in any way;

2 December: Lumumba rearrested.

1961

17 January: Lumumba handed over, by Kasavubu, to Godefroid Munongo, Katangan Minister for the Interior. UN troops stand by and do not intervene;

13 February: Lumumba's death announced; few, if any, doubt that he was murdered.

After the initial collapse of law and order throughout the Congo, Katanga had seceded from the new Republic so as to protect the mineral wealth of that province for European interests – principally, but not exclusively, Belgian – rather than have it dissipated throughout the considerable area (four times the size of France and relatively poor) that remained loyal to the Central Government in Léopoldville (Kinshasa nowadays, but not yet then). It was to the province of Katanga, which had now declared itself an independent state under its President, Moïse Tshombe, that, under extreme Cold War pressure from the West, Patrice Lumumba's former colleagues in government had deported their overly charismatic, suspectedly communist Prime Minister. Disillusioned with what he saw as the UN's dilatoriness in reintegrating his territory, Lumumba had appealed directly to the Soviet Union for help. It was said of him – by a hostile observer, note – that if, dressed as a waiter and with a tea-tray on his head, he went into any gathering of Congolese politicians, he would come out Prime Minister. Something of this phenomenon can be gathered from Conor's play about him, 'Murderous Angels'. When it was produced in Los Angeles in 1970, Lou Gosset miraculously created the part of Lumumba. We did not know then what is now public knowledge (see Alan James, below): that a factor in the Cold War pressure to bring down Lumumba and keep out the Russians was the British Foreign Office's preferred option – his 'removal from the scene by assassination'. This was accomplished by his transfer, as recorded by the television cameras, into the hands – literally – of his chief political and tribal enemy, the Katangan Minister for the Interior, the very terrible African ally of the European interests behind Katanga's secession, the larger-than-life Godefroid Munongo, who, it is believed, personally stabbed his wretched prisoner to death with a bayonet. During this process, the UN stood by and did not move a muscle to protect or rescue Lumumba.

⋈　⋈　⋈

As the world knows, in March 1961 Mr Hammarskjöld asked the Irish government to release Conor for service with the United Nations. In May, the government reluctantly agreed and Conor left for New York knowing that his ultimate destination would be the Congo, although this fact had not yet been made public. In *To Katanga and Back*, Conor has written a very detailed and highly entertaining account of his mission, calling it, clinically, 'a UN case-history'! He wrote it in our house in Howth, after the events it records, and read it aloud to myself and the girls, Fedelma and Kate, and to their friends in the evenings. Kate's bosom friend, Elizabeth Finn, aged about twelve, went home to her mother saying, 'Dr O'Brien is writing such a *funny* book about the Congo.' Funny indeed, but also enlightening, so that, for background to my own memories of that time, I will refer the reader to Conor's book; they won't be disappointed.

Part of the international reaction to Lumumba's murder, mostly one of horror and anger, especially among the African nations and throughout black America, was Conor's posting to Elisabethville, the capital of the new, would-be state, as the UN's local representative, which, in May 1961, followed his initial short stay in New York. Tshombe's puppet government, in which Munongo was the real power behind the throne, would not have been allowed by its white creators to accept a black representative, and a white man was only acceptable to wider Afro-Asian opinion, now in shock, if his background was impeccably anti-colonial. Conor filled the bill; further, he had amply demonstrated his skills, as orator, negotiator and administrator, since Ireland first joined the UN. It was believed also that Hammarskjöld had read and liked his essay in literary criticism, namely his book on French and Irish Catholic authors, *Maria Cross*. I think this is probably so, although, at the time, Conor dreaded the thought of the subject being brought up in conversation by the Secretary-General, with Scandinavian-type thoroughness and lack of humour. Dag Hammarskjöld's personality was notoriously enigmatic. I saw him often, shook hands with him once, shared his charismatic cult unquestioningly and did not know him at all. Conor knew him better and was puzzled, not without reason, by what he knew. In his *Memoir*, he writes:

'I had … been reading Markings, Hammarskjöld's spiritual diary, in which he sees himself as a persecuted Christ-like figure. [The book] had a weird effect on me. I had a dream in which I thought I had come into possession of a kind of political analogue to the spiritual Markings: a diary in which

Hammarskjöld candidly examined the nature of his political decisions and the reasons for them. The dream was an extremely vivid one and during it I was delighted with the discovery of the political diary. When I woke up and found that there was in reality no such document, my sense of loss was acute. I decided that I myself must fill the gap by writing a play, setting out the interaction between Hammarskjöld's spiritual aspirations and his Machiavellian course in practical political decisions.'

The play became *Murderous Angels*, referred to above, and is the best I can offer readers of these recollections as an introduction to, or explanation of Dag Hammarskjöld.

ભ   ભ   ભ

With the election of John F Kennedy as President of the United States, US policy had swung away from the position of accommodating European economic preoccupations and towards one of wooing the newly independent African states – you might say, one of countering communism by kindness. As before, this policy included respect for former colonial boundaries, a respect universal among the former colonial powers. This, in the context of the Congo, meant that Katanga was ultimately doomed, for all that it was a strictly European creation. This conclusion, however, took several disturbed years to bring about.

Under a sheaf of UN resolutions, whose disparate provisions could contradict each other, and whose deliberate ambiguities invited diverse interpretations, ONUC (acronym for Organisation des Nations Unies au Congo) was both *prohibited from* intervening in any Congolese conflict classified as 'internal' (eg, the fall of Lumumba) and also *authorised to* provide the Congolese government with such military assistance as they might require, including, as a last resort, military measures to prevent civil war, ie, the use of force. It was from the last of these rubrics that Conor's mandate derived. All the relevant documentation is available in the UN archives.

In June, Dónal, just seventeen years old, joined his father in Katanga for part of his holidays. Christine and I thought he looked very young and brave as he crossed the tarmac to his plane at Dublin Airport. We tried to dismiss our anxieties – we thought he might be killed – as irrational; we had not yet come to realise how well-founded such anxieties could prove to be. In early August, Conor came briefly back to Europe to act as a consultant at a Quaker seminar for Foreign Service personnel at Clarens in Switzerland, and the two girls and I joined him and Dónal there. On the twenty-second, he flew back to Katanga from Rome, without giving any inkling to the little group, including Dónal, that saw him off, that UN action in Katanga was about to take an aggressive turn. The holidays were over and 'Poppa' was returning to the day job.

ꞔꞛ   ꞔꞛ   ꞔꞛ

It was now over a year since Moïse Tshombe, styling himself President of Katanga, had proclaimed it an independent state. The aspirant state was essentially a European construct, maintained by a scaffolding of white military and civilian advisors. The military advisors were a formidable bunch. An Irish Army officer said of them, with distaste, 'They *clank* – very disconcerting for a peace-loving soldier in UN service.' He was referring to certain – mostly French and Belgian, but including some Anglophone – mercenary officers of Katanga's paramilitary *Gendarmerie*, who liked to parade, in bars among other places, festooned with weaponry. They were proud of their soubriquet of *affreux* (adj. frightful, pl.). The higher echelons might be less flamboyant, but were even more dangerous: French white-supremacist veterans of the Algerian conflict, for example. Clearly the decommissioning of these gentlemen was a primary necessity if Katanga were ever to rejoin the Central Government of the Congo without civil war. 'President' Tshombe had in fact agreed to this step during a brief period of detention, when he was held by the Central Government, but that agreement had been repudiated on his behalf, after his release and return to Katanga, by his white masters and, more pressingly, by his grim 'minder' and Minister for the Interior, Munongo. I have been asked what 'the people of Katanga' wanted. I imagine that is something we will never know. Those who were believed to want reintegration with the original state were being efficiently silenced in the

Gendarmerie's 'pacification' campaign, a technical term for massacre. In the move to expel foreign 'counsellors' – Belgians, French and Brits – from Katanga, 'by force, if necessary', which the UN was now planning, one of Conor's preoccupations was the saving of Tshombe's life, not only from his Central Government opponents, but from the manipulators of his presidency, white and black. Tshombe was a timid and eminently rational man, living in fear and under constant threat, and Conor had come, in some sense, to like him.

The events that followed in the second half of 1960 in Katanga are recorded in great detail in several publications. (For readers looking for a more 'disinterested' source than Conor's book, I would recommend *Britain and the Congo Crisis* by Alan James, published by Palgrave Macmillan in 1996.) On 2 August the Congo had a new Prime Minister, Cyrile Adoula, duly elected by the Congolese Parliament. On 28 August, UN troops in Katanga (Irish, Indians and Swedes), with the backing of the new, recently constituted, UN-recognised Central Government, occupied strategic points in the provincial capital, Elisabethville, with the aim of formally expelling foreign personnel, 'by force, if necessary'. This operation, code-named *Rumpunch*, was initially regarded by UN headquarters in New York as a great success: a number of the 'wanted' officers were arrested. Hammarskjöld telegraphed his congratulations on 'an exceedingly sensitive operation carried through with skill and courage'. Unfortunately, in the subsequent euphoria, it was decided that further withdrawal of foreign 'counsellors' might be voluntary, which inevitably meant that it did not happen at all in many cases.

Even this modest operation caused consternation in the British Foreign Office (BFO), and the British Press echoed what, to judge from internal documents since released, must have been some very hostile briefing. In particular, the BFO was scandalised at 'O'Brien's pretty *Irish* methods', and at the thought that he might be 'deliberately working for the disintegration of the Katangan government'. Oh my! The British attitude was illogical, not to say two-faced, but that's what it was. I tried to follow events in the Belgian Press, which, although equally hostile – the *Libre Belgique* headed an article, '*La trahison (treason) de M. O'Brien*' – was well-informed and had business readers who needed accurate reports. During the entire Katanga conflict, 1960–64, the price of copper, Katanga's main source of wealth, never fell on the international market, in fact it actually rose, as I wrote to Conor at that time. The Press in Ireland was, predictably, confirmed in its favourable reactions to the UN's performance in Elisabethville by its British colleagues' disapproval. A newspaper placard outside Howth train station proclaimed, 'Tshombe attacks Howth-man!' Conor had graduated once and for all from being a 'runner-in'.

So far there had been no loss of life, but it was clear that *Rumpunch* was unfinished business, and a more ambitious sequel was planned under the combined authority of the Congolese Central Government and ONUC, this time manifestly to prevent civil war on several fronts, and even to deter a possible overt invasion of troops from Roy Welensky's neighbouring Rhodesia; covertly this was taking place already. Welensky was Prime Minister of the British dependency, the Federation of Rhodesia and Nyasaland, and, not surprisingly, strongly pro-Tshombe. Conor was about to find himself engaged in serious fighting, in what the wife of one of his British colleagues at the United Nations, Lady Cohen, actually a close friend, described as 'every man's dream, a small, manageable war in which you don't get killed'. It would not be her compatriots' fault if Conor didn't get killed; they were actively stirring up trouble for him.

Meanwhile, the only voice missing from the concert of support in Ireland for his actions was that of the government. I was constantly telephoned by journalists, who knew or suspected my relationship with Conor, to know if he still enjoyed Aiken's backing. I gave them positive answers, but I was not at all sure of how long that backing would last. So far it had not been made explicit, and the hysteria of the British hate campaign appeared to have infected the views even of our own delegation at the UN. Our new application for membership of the European Economic Community did not help either; as I hope has emerged from my memories so far, Europe was equivocal, to say the least, on the UN operation in the Congo. *Morthor* (Hindi for 'smash'), as the follow-up ONUC operation, launched in early September, was christened, put the tin hat on things.

CR   CR   CR

Morthor was both bloody and abortive. Its intention was to replace President Tshombe's government, after the arrest of that President and his ministers by the UN forces, with a Commissioner appointed by the Central Government. The arrest warrants and Commissioner arrived in Elisabethville from the capital, Léopoldville, but someone had tipped off Tshombe and his Cabinet and they had 'gone for bush' – Tshombe to Rhodesia, ferried there by the British Consul in Elisabethville. From under Welensky's protection, Tshombe could broadcast rousing, inflammatory addresses all over the world. Outside Elisabethville and its immediate environs the previous ONUC enterprise, *Rumpunch*, had been notably successful. The initial use of white, mercenary officers, commanding strictly subordinate black Katangese troops, had been to bring terror to the so-called 'rebellious' (read 'loyal to the Central Government') areas north and west of Elisabethville, between December 1960 and July 1961, under the euphemism of 'pacification'. On his visits to UN garrisons, Conor had overflown tracts of that area and had seen, from low-flying UN aircraft, the advancing jeeps of the Katangan *Gendarmerie* and the waste of burnt-out villages in their wake. At least *Rumpunch* had put paid to that.

As Conor summarises: 'Tshombe still claimed all of Katanga, but had in fact lost and never was to regain authority over all the northern part of the province, which now accepted the authority of the Central Government.' In a sense, the resistance to *Morthor* was covert white supremacy's last stand in Katanga, and Conor's much reprobated statement, of 13 September, that the secession of Katanga was at an end, was closer to the underlying facts of the situation than the propaganda outcry, raised by the publicity agents of the European financial and political interests involved – more particularly the British – made it appear at the time.

The great propaganda set-piece was, of course, the siege of Jadot-ville (3 September), located about fifty kilometres from Elisabethville, where the Irish company sent to protect the white community from un-specified black 'disaffected elements' was promptly besieged, in an 'open camp', by the white-officered Katangan *Gendarmerie* on behalf of the very townspeople the UN had sent the Irish to protect. *Rumpunch* had been successful up to a point in deporting military 'experts', but less so in preventing them coming back. For days the European Press screamed horror stories – all false – of death and casualty among the camp defenders. In fact, they defended themselves against various forms of attack, including bombing by the single, notorious Katangan 'Fouga' jet-fighter, with creditable success, until the municipal authorities cut off the water supply. When the company surrendered, their total casualties amounted to five wounded. The indirect cost of the siege was, however, much greater. Jadotville was used by the Katangan tacticians to draw off more UN troops – Irish and Swedes – from Elisabethville to raise the siege. These troops were ambushed en route at the Lufira Bridge, on the outskirts of Elisabethville, where a pitched battle cost the lives of many brave men. Prominent in the orchestration of the siege was that key figure in Katangan interracial friendship, Godefroid Munongo, whom the UN had hoped to arrest and deliver to the Central Government. He took the surrender of the Jadotville company on 17 September and they became his prisoners and hostages. Munongo was indeed an asset to virtual, free Katanga, a 'real' black, paramount, tribal chief. His people were the Bayeke, and his grandfather, Msiri, had ruled pre-Belgian Katanga. Old Msiri was reputed to eat babies to restore his virility. No need for such therapy was reported of Munongo – as yet; he was quite terrible enough as it was.

ଔ   ଔ   ଔ

Meantime, in Iveagh House in Dublin, an informal caucus had formed of younger officers who had been trained by Conor and who were increasingly distressed, not so much by British and Belgian government and media attacks on Conor, as by the fact that the Irish mission to the UN appeared increasingly to endorse these, even to the point of agreeing, facetiously we must hope, with the British 'preferred option' of assassination. The tone of despatches and telegrams was that Conor's death, no matter how regrettable, would solve many problems. With Mr Aiken absent at the General Assembly in New York and later in the Congo (16–29 September), in pursuit of reliable information, these 'problems' were discussed uninhibitedly by our superiors and, of course, got back to us. The gravamen of the anti-Conor case was that he had acted without instructions in permitting the use of force at all. All of us who had worked with him knew this could not be so; he was a punctiliously correct civil servant and we were proud of him on that account, among others. What we did not know was that throughout the civil service, in its various departments, colleagues and contemporaries of Conor's were equally worried for his safety. This was to be made clear to me some time in or about 10 September.

A distinguished public figure, who was a former senior civil servant and a friend of Conor's, called on me in the Department. I was told he was waiting for me in the Minister's waiting-room – he was that kind of person. I feared vaguely that he might have bad news. He came with a proposal: he could arrange an appointment for me with the Taoiseach, Mr Lemass, and he suggested that I should, in the context of an up-coming general election, tell the Taoiseach that there was general unease in the Service at the lack of explicit support for Conor and that if such support were not forthcoming, I personally intended to resign and to make public my reasons for doing so. Further, I was informing the Taoiseach of my resolution as a matter of courtesy, as it could affect the results of the coming election. I was dumbfounded, but I could see I had no choice. It was felt by the planners of my démarche that my relationship with Conor, insofar as it might be known or guessed at, would make my threat of resignation doubly effective by adding an element of sexual scandal to the brew. They may have been right.

My path was smoothed as promised and, in due course, I found myself sitting opposite the Taoiseach, Mr Seán Lemass, in a quite small, unpretentious office. He heard me patiently and then said, 'Dr Cruise O'Brien is an international civil servant, he does not depend on the Irish government for support.' I can only say that, as once before over the execution of the IRA men in the 1940s when I was a student, I experienced some sort of inspiration. I heard myself give a totally unrehearsed reply, 'I do not know, Taoiseach, how it may be in the corridors of the ILO [International Labour Organisation; Lemass had made his way up through the portfolios of Industry & Commerce & Supplies and was familiar with ILO politics], but at the UN an international civil servant who has lost the support of his home government is a bad risk.' He nodded politely, 'You have a point, Miss MacEntee,' and he stood up to see me out, sending his regards, as he did so, to my father, who was, of course, his Deputy Prime Minister. In his outer office I had an impression of people hugging me as my head swam. As I walked across Saint Stephen's Green back to Iveagh House, the Government Bureau of Information (GBI), jubilant, had already 'phoned one of our group to tell them that they should look next day at the columns of the *Irish Press*. The Bureau allowed as how it was what the 'grass roots had wanted all along'.

On Wednesday, 15 September the *Irish Press* carried, unprecedently, reprinted in full and prominently displayed, a special leader-page article from *The Times* of London, which signalled a departure from the prevailing tune of the British Press. Under the heading, in bold type, 'O'Brien May Save UN Congo Plans', and over the byline *The Times' UN Correspondent*, not otherwise identified, it stressed the importance and the good sense of Dr O'Brien's course of action in Katanga, in the context of Third World reaction. Could there have been a connection? A GBI call perhaps to the UN press corps? Fedelma and Kate were relieved and pleased; they said they had not 'feared for Conor's life, only for his honour'. As for me, I felt that 'desperate ills called for desperate remedies', but I knew that my loyalties had shifted, almost without my realising it, from the public to the private sphere, and that I should think seriously of bringing my service with the Department to an end.

Before leaving for the Congo, Conor had asked me to marry him and I had eagerly said yes. I didn't wear an engagement ring. I didn't have one; Conor doesn't believe in rings. Christine and he had separated legally, and she had moved into her new home. I went to live in *Whitewater*, Conor's battered but comfortable house, an old-fashioned bungalow such as, all around the coast of Ireland, you find retired sea-captains settled in, with a pyramid slate roof and a uniquely wonderful view out over the Bailey lighthouse, east as far as Snowdon and south to beyond Wicklow Head. It has been our home ever since, as it was his before the divorce. Conor was confident that he could make his living writing and teaching, and I was convinced that, in looking after him and his interests, I had at last found the occupation in which I, as an individual, was wanted and needed.

ℭঌ   ℭঌ   ℭঌ

The network of Conor's 'in-service' allies remained in being. The nightmare of the death of Dag Hammarskjöld (17 September 1961) had altered many perspectives. We never doubted for a moment that it was murder. For some terrible hours, we believed that Conor was with the Secretary-General on that doomed plane. You will remember that it was flying Hammarskjöld to Ndola, in Welensky's Northern Rhodesia, to discuss with Tshombe – spirited there from Elisabethville by the British Consul – a ceasefire to end the *Morthor* hostilities. Three days after that plane had crashed, near Ndola, killing all on board (with the exception of the ex-Irish Army UN security man, Private Julien, who was alive when the Rhodesians found the crashed plane, but did not long survive), a provisional such ceasefire was signed. Already, in the shocked confusion resulting from the tragedy, it was easy for pro-Katanga propaganda to scapegoat UN officials 'on the ground', as having provoked the violence that brought about the death of a 'great international apostle of peace'. They were thus enabled to 'exonerate', as they put it, Hammarskjöld and present him as having been unaware of *Morthor*, whereas documentary evidence, not available then, but available in detail since (see Alan James), shows him to have been consulted on the action and to have sanctioned it every step of the way. Finally, almost the entire force of the British-and-Belgian-led attack focussed on Conor.

Conor, at a later stage, summarised the then situation thus: 'The British delegation at the UN was particularly active in this respect and not unduly fastidious about the methods it employed.' At the time we at headquarters were, if anything, more aware than he of the sordid details of these methods, which involved, alas!, what can only be described as the complicity of the Irish Mission to the UN. For a blow-by-blow record of these démarches, with copious quotes, many of which read like the meanderings of a malevolent Bertie Wooster, I recommend Chapter 10 of Alan James's *Britain and the Congo Crisis*, cited above. The chapter is tellingly titled, 'Complaining about the UN Secretariat II: The Irishman'. What worried the 'friends of Conor' in Iveagh House, and beyond, was what we felt to be his dangerous isolation; international telephone exchanges refused calls made to him, mail was uncertain and Elisabethville was out of bounds to unauthorised civilians. The caucus decided that some one of us should try to reach Katanga in person and let him know that support for him in Ireland was a great deal more solid than the international hype over Jadotville might suggest. The obvious one was me: I travelled constantly between Dublin and Strasbourg; I could take my annual leave from the Department and not be missed. And that is exactly what I did, hoping, indeed expecting, that no one would enquire where I took my holiday. It has been stated that I was 'absent without leave'; this is not so. I often stopped over at the embassy in Brussels, on my way to or from Strasbourg, to see Barbara and her family. The children were currently in a state of delighted indignation because someone had painted '*O'Brien au Poteau* [gallows]!' on the embassy gates. This time, however, I went straight to the airport in Brussels from Strasbourg and took a Sabena jet, without any trouble at all, to Léopoldville and thence, on a Cuban plane – anti-Castro, flying charter for the UN – to Elisabethville in Katanga on 1 October. This second plane carried a cargo of dried fish and had only the most rudimentary seating; I was soon to get used to that sort of travel.

PART V: HAPPY ENDING

The climate in Elisabethville is wonderful – air like champagne, days pleasantly warm, nights pleasantly cool. There is an old Irish concept, 'the hero's sleep', where the warrior fights all day, sleeps well at night and rises refreshed to fight again. Life in Katanga seemed to me to follow something of this pattern. The house where Conor and other UN officials stayed, the Villa des Roches (rocks), called by 'other ranks' the Villa des Riches (rich, pl.) – it had a swimming pool – was a rambling, one-storey dwelling, smothered in shade trees and jacarandas in flower and refreshingly dim after the sunlight, as tropical houses should be. No one questioned my presence there, and there was plenty for me to do in an easy mix of domestic and official. Conor once said about me, 'Máire shares my views and interests, only more so ...' and everyone seemed content to leave it at that. Conor's PA, Josie Donzé, an indomitable French lady whose courage under fire had become legendary, regretted, as indeed I did myself, that I could not type – administrative officers didn't in those days. I could, however, help in other ways: I answered the telephone, did some drafting, some housekeeping and a lot of what I thought of as constructive listening. Conor's other house-guest was George Ivan Smith, senior UN official and close friend of Hammarskjöld's, who became a dear friend of ourselves and is now, sadly for us all, dead. In memory of him I would like to quote Conor's description of him, as he was on the day I first met him:

'The 'Ivan' is an Australian remnant of Sullivan and that has always formed a bond. I like Australians generally and this Australian in particular, and his arrival at this time was a ray of light. George was a very old UN hand, who had known Hammarskjöld well and was the principal UN expert in Press Relations. It was in that capacity he had come, I believe, to see that I made no more 'dreadful statements' [to the effect that the secession of Katanga was at an end]. He did this effectively and so nicely that one hardly noticed him doing it. George is tough and wily, with a face like a sunset over a sheep farm; he was a friend of James Stephens, loves poetry both good and bad and recites it with a strange plangency; he has an exuberant sense of humour, both personal and Catholic, and he is apt to break, on suitable occasions, into a solo dance of his own design: a sort of shuffling saraband with both hands clasped over his head.'

George used to say that the only thing that frightened him in Katanga was 'the shellshocked babies with the sub-machine guns on guard-duty round Conor's swimming-pool.' These were teenagers, under eighteen years of age, who had enlisted in the Irish Army on elder brothers' birth certificates; I believe the practice was common in most armies. When Tshombe's jet-fighter flew over they trembled like aspens, and their weapons trembled too. They were awaiting repatriation, and the Villa des Roches was regarded as a benign place for them to recuperate in the interval. It was one of the many instances of the humane quality permeating the codes prevailing in the Irish forces, which I remember from the Congo.

Two responsibilities weighed heavily on ONUC at this time: the Elisabethville refugee camp and the question of local administration in Northern Katanga. The camp at Elisabethville was a vast shantytown, housing as many as 45,000 souls, under the protection of the UN. These were mostly, but not exclusively, members of the Baluba tribe and had fled the persecution of Munongo's mercenary *affreux* and their black rank-and-file. They included, effectively, all the white-collar, black élite of Elisabethville. They were an uncowed people. When their UN protectors tried to bring about a *modus vivendi* between them and the Katangan authorities, the leaders of the refugees addressed those authorities in something like the following terms: 'We, the Baluba, are your masters, have always been your masters and will always be your masters.' Further, they were not averse to conducting guerrilla warfare beyond the frontiers of the camp, when occasion offered, against the said authorities and their white supporters. This obviously made the ceasefire situation an unstable one and caused a permanent headache for UN personnel in charge of the camp. I went most days to the house, located just outside the camp, of the chief UN civilian worker with the refugees, Joost Kuitenbrouwer of the Netherlands, to take Swahili lessons with one of their number, a gentle-mannered young schoolmaster from whom I learnt how to say many useful things, such as, 'Close the door, quickly, quickly, the lion is coming!' and 'The snake is in the swimming pool.' Swahili is a Central African *lingua franca*. I always meant to take it up again.

The other major concern was to establish functioning local administrations, loyal to the Central Government, in North Katanga (Katanga is an area of roughly 482 kilometres by 300 kilometres) – an area now under UN control – preferably before the arrival of the Central Government troops, whose diplomacy might prove a little rough and ready. The capital of North Katanga, Albertville, had been taken in September, with great dash and brio, by ONUC's Sikh troops, under the command of an unforgettable officer, Major Padda – straight out of central casting for the 'Lives of a Bengal Lancer': a tall, bony, middle-aged man, bronze-skinned and hawk-nosed, with a gentle, almost feminine courtesy. With a single armoured car, to which he would refer deprecatingly as, 'my lo-o-onely armoured car', on 17 September he cleared the streets of Albertville of armed white civilians and black *Gendarmerie*. It was now decided to consolidate the restoration of normalcy – already begun by the UN civilian representative on the ground, Mr Jerkovic, a Yugoslav with the authoritative presence of a Roman centurion. To this end, Conor and George Ivan Smith were to proceed to Albertville, bearing the flag of the Central Government for presentation on the spot to Prosper Mwamba Ilunga, leader of the Lumumbist Balubakat party (the party of the Baluba people, as the name indicates) and Provincial President of what was now to be styled the Province of Lualaba, which would comprise a considerable area of Northern and Central Katanga that was hostile to Tshombe and loyal to the Central Government. I was lucky enough to be able to go with them, and I wrote about the events of our journey to Dónal, now reading history in Cambridge, on 14 November. I quote from that letter below:

'My last [letter] predicted that before long the Central Government flag would fly over Albertville – it does so now, as from yesterday. Manono will be the next and that will leave only Kongolo under the Katangan flag in the North Katanga – I beg its pardon – the loyal province of Lualaba ... Everything so far has gone swimmingly, but one false step could mean disaster, not to the ultimate outcome, which is certain, but to the morale of the Balubakat and the credit of the UN. To take up where we left off last time – after we left Kabalo, [Prosper] Mwamba Ilunga, as good as his word, flew to Albertville and did a magnificent job of work, rallying the Balubakat, 75 percent of the population ...'

I interrupt myself here to amplify the mention of Kabalo, a big rail-and-river junction in North Katanga. Kabalo had never fallen to the troops of the Katangan 'pacification'. The UN troops stationed there were Ethiopians, and when a *Gendarmerie* steamer came up the Lualaba river to 'pacify' the local population, they blew it up. (I am in shock now to realise that I did not then know, or care, what loss of life there had been, if any.) The UN troops were under the command of Colonel Alemu, of whom Conor writes, 'I found his disposition was exceptionally sunny, with a slightly mad-cap, "Brigadier Gerard" touch.' He came to meet us, when I (Máire) first met him, standing upright in a UN jeep with a running escort of small boys around it. After he had greeted us, he distributed sweets from his pockets to this retinue and shooed them laughingly away. I wonder is he still to the good in his homeland?

'In Albertville,' my letter goes on, 'it was Mwamba Ilunga's task to persuade the Baluba to abandon hostilities, to trust the UN and the local administration and to work with their Conakat [Tshombe's party] brothers for the good of the community within a united Congo ... The truce has been maintained and there is now in Albertville a joint Balubakat–Conakat administration, loyal to the Central Government, while Albertville itself awaits only the arrival of Sendwe [Jason Sendwe, representative of the Central Government] from Léopoldville to be instituted the provisional capital of Lualaba.'

Sporadic violence could still, of course, break out in Albertville and environs, and indeed had, just recently, resulting in the death of three Baluba. It was necessary to forestall a Balubakat revenge and a new flare-up of feuding. A UN presence attended the funeral and, again, I was lucky enough to be included as I went on to tell Dónal:

'Conor, Jerkovic and George, with myself tagging along and expecting to be sent home any minute, set out for the native township to try to ensure that there would be no hostile demonstrations in revenge for the lynchings. Halfway up the steep mud road to the houses we met a truck coming down loaded with as ragged and anxious-looking a bunch of Africans as I had ever seen. To my astounded amazement, these were the party leaders. Jerkovic was out of the car in a flash, shaking hands, throwing his arms round their shoulders, introducing us. "*Courage, patience, dignité, mes amis, pas de venge-ance.*" You could feel the cloud of grief and panic and hate dissipating as he spoke. They had in fact been coming to look for him to ask for Indian protection for the funeral. The famous Major Padda of the armoured car is whistled up and, standing there on the muddy road, it is arranged. The ragged men with the moth-eaten leopard-skin badges are Monsieur le Président du Cartel, Monsieur le Secrétaire, etc, etc. It is all very friendly and formal and everyone is presented punctiliously to me ... I am reminded of political meetings in Dunquin and Dingle [County Kerry] after the Civil War, with the Blasket Islanders in for the day: same poverty, same strong sense of tradition, same class angle, same language difficulty; someone like Daddy or Ernest Blythe in a city suit explaining that the war is over, no more enmity, etc, etc, and the local party bosses and clan chieftains constituting an uneasy liaison between two worlds ...

'That afternoon we watched the funeral, intolerably pathetic, file on file of ragged people singing Lumumbist songs and giving the Cartel salute ... It was a Catholic service and there were no inflammatory speeches. The Indian officers stood to attention as the truck – the one we had met that morning – trundled past with the bodies, and the relatives, mostly women, crouched over them in the back ...

On Sunday [12 November], Mwamba Ilunga [now Acting District Commissioner] addressed a meeting of several thousand people on his constant theme, work, co-operation, no reprisals, united Congo. As you know he is a superb figure and he wore his leopard-skin *kepi* insignia like a field-marshal. The meeting was enthusiastic and orderly, distinguished among other things by a body of women *militantes* [activists] marching, carrying green branches for all the world like Palm Sunday ... I had been learning a little Swahili and could follow some of Mwamba Ilunga's speech, which was forceful, simple and repetitive ...

Afterwards the crowd dispersed in good order and went straight home to their villages as they had been instructed, and the European community opened their shops again and breathed a sigh of relief.

The flag of the Republic of the Congo had been hoisted over Albertville.'

The relief of the shopkeepers, however, was destined to be short-lived. The first units of the ANC (National Congolese Army) had arrived at the border of the province, engaged, they would have said, 'in a great, patriotic war', but in fact looting and burning much as the mercenary-led *Gendarmerie* had done. Conor's last instruction, given in Katanga before he left for America (16 November), was for the disarming and punishment of offenders.

☙ ☙ ☙

Conor left Elisabethville to attend a meeting of the Security Council in New York, and I stayed on in the Villa des Roches, expecting him back from day to day; Josie (his French PA) and Paddy (his driver, Private Patrick Wall) were there too. George Ivan Smith, who was acting as Conor's deputy, travelled to and fro between Elisabethville and Léopoldville and brought me news of him. The remainder of this account is based on my letter to Conor, written immediately after the events related.

In the afternoon of Tuesday, 28 November, a little after three o'clock, I had just left the Villa des Roches in the UN car for Mr Kuitenbrouwer's house, on the edge of the refugee camp, for my Swahili lesson. Another UN car, piled with luggage, passed us on the road from the airport. I thought it was Conor, and Paddy turned back. It was, in fact, George Ivan Smith and Brian Urquhart – a very senior and influential British member of the UN Secretariat. They brought me a message from Conor for me to go straight to Dublin; it did not occur to me to ask why. There had been strong rumours that Brian was to succeed Conor, and I was uneasy and depressed. I arranged to take the first plane next morning.

I had been invited, that evening, to a cocktail party at the American Consulate in Elisabethville, 'in honour of Senator [a Republican member of the well-heeled 'Katanga Lobby' in the USA] and Mrs Dodd.' I liked the Hoffackers, the Consul and his wife, very much and I had accepted. I thought it might be a slightly sticky occasion and that by going I could be of some help to Mrs Hoffacker, who had arrived in Katanga only a few days before. I felt now that I would rather stay at les Roches and pack for the journey home. George and Brian persuaded me to change my mind and go with them.

It was an exceedingly good party. The drawing rooms of the American Consulate look out on a courtyard shaded with tall trees and while the guests, very elegant and *mondains*, moved about inside under the bright lights, the 'Apostles', a Christian religious sect supportive of the Tshombe régime, came from the President's Palace up the road and gathered in the dark of the courtyard outside to put on a show for the Senator. They danced and sang, swaying and stamping in and out of the shadows, the women wearing their lovely African dress – richly coloured cottons, elaborately draped, and complicated, knotted turbans. Watching them was the Senator's motorcycle escort, in the bravura uniform of Tshombe's guard. As the evening moved on, guests drifted out to the dancing and 'Apostles' began to infiltrate towards the buffet, through the French windows. I should explain that all this was taking place during one of the periodic suspensions of hostilities which occurred frequently between the UN and the Katangan authorities, and which were liable to break down without notice.

Most of the UN people I knew were at the party, as well as everyone else, practically, who played any avowably important part in the life of Elisabethville – and some of the less avowably important, too. Tshombe and several of his Ministers were pointed out to me and I was introduced to Mr Kimba, 'the Minister of Foreign Affairs,' who had great charm. Munongo was also there, wearing his trademark dark glasses.

The UN officers were not in uniform. I imagine that, like myself, they came to the party solely out of affection and respect for Lew Hoffacker and did not want to make things more difficult for him by the risk of provoking 'an incident'. Tshombe had made a murderous speech on the Sunday before, just after the news of the new Security Council resolution, that of 24 November and the toughest yet, had broken, and there was considerable tension in town. (This was the speech in which Tshombe threatened to resist implementation of the resolution using *pangas* – woodcutters' knives – and bows and arrows.) As I was talking to General Raja, the Indian overall commander of the UN force in Katanga, a young Indian officer joined us, looking harassed and said, 'You shouldn't have come, Sir, you're being marked.' Raja was clearly not pleased. I thought the Indians were rather overplaying the military melodrama and put the whole thing out of my mind.

We left early. George had another party for the Senator to attend, a dinner this time, given by the Mobiloil representative in Elisabethville. (In fact, as we found out later, this gentleman had to go to Léopoldville on business and a cousin of his wife's was acting host.) I was going to eat in town with Brian Urquhart and Fitzhugh Greene of the US Information Service (USIS), who was covering the Senator's tour. We all got into a UN car, driven by Paddy Wall, intending to drop George at the party first. I thought a meal out would make a nice change from the veal and spinach which was served up regularly at les Roches.

The Mobiloil house is only a few doors away from the suburban residence of General Muké, Commander of the Katangese forces. Paddy knew this was not a healthy area for UN personnel, but his opinion wasn't asked and he didn't volunteer it. As we turned into the avenue, we saw a military truck parked at the side of the road with some soldiers in it and heard them shout, 'ONU! ONU!' We drew up at the gate of the Mobiloil house a few yards farther on and were immediately surrounded by a sullen, aggressive crowd of Africans in camouflage uniforms, very heavily armed. Someone said they were 'paras'.

They asked for documents. Through the window of the car Paddy handed his UN pass. The man who took it flung it down in the roadway and stamped on it. I heard George Ivan Smith say, 'Easy, Paddy' and saw Paddy visibly control himself. Then he got quietly out of the car, picked up his pass, put it in his pocket and stood still in the middle of the road with the 'paras' all around him.

Meanwhile the Senator's hosts had heard the commotion and three or four gentlemen came out of the house. One of them, a big man, had short reddish hair, almost a crew-cut, and a bow-tie; I had seen him at the American party. They expostulated with the 'paras', who were, it appeared, General Muké's guard. They explained about the dinner-party, that Senator Dodd was 'the friend of Katanga', that even President Tshombe might turn up. The 'paras' were not impressed, but, reasonable according to their lights, they agreed that their NCO would go with us into the house and telephone Minister Kimba for confirmation that we were there in good faith. At first they wanted to hold Paddy as a hostage, but finally gave way on that and let him come with us.

As I remember it, the house had a fairly large hall from which a door led into a very large L-shaped room with French windows. One could not see the entire drawing room from the hall. Perhaps a dozen people were already there, among whom I recognised Mr Dunnett, the British Consul. The Hoffackers and the Senator had not yet arrived. The telephone was on a low table to the left of the hall door; people busied themselves contacting Kimba. George went on into the drawing room as an invited guest, and Fitzhugh Greene – as a good USIS-man alert for copy? – did likewise. Brian stayed with the group at the telephone and sat, I think, on a low chair near the table. Myself and Paddy sat on a bench opposite, feeling a little awkward. The lady of the house came very kindly and offered us drinks, which we refused.

The telephoners contacted Kimba and handed the phone to the 'para' corporal (I think that was his rank) who was actually in conversation with Kimba when the action, so to speak, suddenly speeded up. The hall door burst open and six or eight 'paras' exploded into the room, fantastically overexcited and brandishing lethal weapons, sub-machine-guns (I think), which they seemed to be constantly loading and unloading, as if to make it quite clear that they really had ammunition. Someone tried to explain about Kimba. The first man in screamed, *'Je me fous de Kimba'* (F– Kimba), snatched the 'phone from his fellow-soldier and dashed it to the floor. I think at the same time a similar group had come through the French windows in the drawing room, out of sight of the hall, and gone for George Ivan Smith. We thought later that it was probably Conor they were looking for.

By now Paddy and I were on our feet. I could see Brian Urquhart, his face unrecognisable, covered with blood. In the confusion, I had moments of not being sure even that it was Brian and thought, irrationally, that it might be Fitzhugh Greene, although I knew him to be in the other room. I had not seen the blow, but Paddy had; the 'para' had head-butted Brian on the nose as he rose from his chair. He seemed to stand, swaying, as we moved across to him and then to collapse back again. He was saying firmly and politely, *'Il y a erreur, Messieurs, il y a erreur'* (There's some mistake). I stood in front of him; the telephoners had been dispersed. I have never spoken French in my life with such an urgency of conviction as I did to those 'paras'. I called them *'mes enfants'*; I even touched one boy on the cheek. I said that this was not the way to treat a visitor, that they had hurt the poor gentleman and that soldiers should be ashamed to behave like this. I said, *'Soyez gentils'* – be nice. I had the impression that, under their bluster, they were frightened and disconcerted. I was certain that if I could only keep on talking I could win. They weren't used to breaking into Belgian houses; they *were* used to doing as they were told by French-speaking ladies. They were like children, who, having begun to

Left: Conor as a baby, with his mother.
Below: A rather dashing young Conor presents a speech at the Historical Society in Trinity College, Dublin; he was later awarded the Speaker's Gold Medal by the Society.

Left: *At our wedding party, after our marriage, in 1962, in New York.*
Below: *Conor and I at our wedding party with (left) George Ivan Smith and (right) Ralph Bunche.*

Opposite page:
Top left: *My marriage to Conor brought me two wonderful step-daughters: Kate (left) and Fedelma (right).*
Top right: *Dónal, Conor and Christine's eldest son, with his father.*

Below: Conor at the lectern during the conferral of an honorary degree on WEG Du Bois, the great American academic and black rights activist. Standing next to Du Bois, bearing a scroll and a proud carriage, is our dear friend, Kofi Edzii, university registrar.

Above: Conor and Irish members of the UN's forces in the Congo. The British Press 'wittily' took to calling Conor, 'a stripe-shirted Castro'.

Below: Conor and myself with the Sikh unit at Albertville, in Katanga, in 1961. Jerkovic and Mme. Jerkovic are on Conor's right.

Right: Back home in *Whitewater*, enjoying a chilled glass of wine on a sunny day with my parents.

Below: A marvellous reminder of a marvellous day: Conor, Patrick and I visited President Eamon de Valera and his wife, Sinéad, at Áras an Uachtaráin, just after we had adopted our Patrick.

Above: Conor, Patrick, myself and Margaret.

Left: Patrick celebrated his First Holy Communion wearing a traditional Ghanaian costume, which I had ordered specially from Northern Ghana.

Right: Margaret in her beautiful white dress on her First Holy Communion day, with family and friends.

Below: Patrick was conferred with a degree in History from Trinity College, Dublin. Conor, as Pro-Chancellor, conferred him. His sister Margaret and I were terribly proud of him.

Left: Conor and myself.
Below: On the occasion of my eightieth birthday in 2002, our adorable Milo, along with his father, Patrick, came to celebrate the day with his grandparents.

stone a cat, are unable to stop and yet half hoping to be prevented. Paddy stood beside me and held them off: he put aside the barrels of the sten-guns with his arm as they came at us and they didn't persist. I seemed to be thinking on several different levels simultaneously: 'Perhaps I am only making things worse' – the classical argument against interference, espe-cially by women – but I knew I wasn't; 'Here goes our hope of a quiet di-vorce' – and I knew that that was for sure; 'I don't think I could bear it if they smashed my face with one of those things', and I was so frightened that fear was a new dimension, but I kept on talking. Brian's head had fallen forward against my hip from behind, and the back of my white skirt, all the way down, was covered in blood. I knew absolutely that he would never forgive me. He had been a member of a crack parachute regiment; hiding behind women's skirts was not his thing.

And in the moment I thought that I might have persuaded them, the worst happened. A third wave crashed in, older and somehow darker men, with faces carved in deep wrinkles like gashes, grim, tough and ex-perienced – not at all children. One of them hit me with his open hand very hard across the face. Paddy and I were simply thrown bodily aside. Poor Brian was yanked from his chair and, as he was thrust out the door, George Ivan Smith, heels dug in and fighting every inch, was forced past us from the drawing room, along with another battered figure, through the door and into the garden on a wave of 'paras'. I saw Fitzhugh Greene, volubly protesting but unharmed, swept out with them – and that was strange because in some way I had thought, at intervals, that he was the man behind me.

Someone shut the door and stood against it. A terrible despair, such as I never hope to feel again, flooded over me. I was quite certain I would never see George and Brian alive again. They would be killed in spite of my trying so hard, perhaps because of it, and I was so desperately tired. My friend with the crew-cut said, 'This is your fault. They were trying to protect you.' Indignation flared up in me. I can't remember exactly what I said, but I got my own back. I held out the white skirt of my dress – the front was clean, the back, where Brian's head had rested, heavily stained with blood. I indicated, with some force, that what protecting there had been, had been done by Paddy and me. Mr Dunnett, the British Consul, was standing in the entrance to the drawing room. Paddy was insisting on being allowed to use the 'phone to call UN headquarters. Someone said, 'If your Indian friends get here we'll all be killed.' Someone reported that the 'para' truck had driven off, accompanied by a big car, at high speed. Paddy got Indian HQ on the 'phone and gave the alarm. I spoke to them also. We both had the same impression: the Indians thought it was a joke – in poor taste. It would be hard to blame them, perhaps we were not as coherent as we might have been.

The lady of the house was having hysterics, 'I will not sleep another night here with those savages loose. *Franchement, je préfère l'ONU!'* (Frankly, I prefer the UN). Paddy said, 'It's no good waiting here. I'll try to get to the civilian mess and come back with an armoured car.' He went out over the back-garden wall and did just that – only he didn't wait for the armoured car, but came back almost immediately with a UN civilian driver and a machine-gun in a Volkswagen, having run the whole distance to the civilian mess, where they thought at first he was drunk. Meanwhile the dinner guests were telephoning broadcast: the police – 'they would come if we sent a car'; Muké – 'if the animal could talk any known language.'

A neighbour came in through the garden. He had the strange detachment of people who are no longer shocked by violence. His wife would take the children, it might be safer. All was quiet now outside, he reported, the UN car had been driven off by a white man, *'un blanc'*. A frightened teenager and a sleepy little girl, wrapped in a blanket, were brought downstairs and handed over. *'Proteste pas, mais fous-le-camp, que je te dis,'* (Don't argue, just F– off when I say to) said their Mamma. We sat and looked at each other. There was a telephone call for Mr Dunnett. Rather grudgingly he told us that George and a Belgian banker, the second captive I had seen carried out, were safe in the US Consulate; there was no news of Brian. Mr Dunnett did not say at the time that it was George himself on the 'phone and that he was asking for me – perhaps it did not seem important. The front door opened; it was Paddy and the UN driver. I have never been so glad to see anyone in my life.

The story of George's rescue has been told elsewhere, but I would like to set it down here now as I heard it from him in the small hours of that morning. It is a heart-warming story to tell.

The 'paras' got the three men onto the truck and ordered them to lie down. Brian and the Belgian banker did so and were savagely bludgeoned. Perhaps it was some atavistic stubbornness which made George an enemy to lying down to be beaten, perhaps it was his Australian upbringing, either way, he got his back against the cab of the truck and fought them off with his feet. A glare of headlights and a roar of motorcycle engines and the US Consulate car, with its superb escort of Katangese 'Keystone Cops', swept up behind them. They were arriving for the party! Mrs Dodd was heard to exclaim, 'Why, if it isn't that nice Mr Smith!' and Hoffacker was out of the car, hurling 'paras' left and right and shouting '*Consul Américain!*' – I should add that he was a thin, rather lightly-built young man. He got George Ivan Smith off that truck and went back for the banker. He was going back a third time when the 'paras' realised what had hit them and drove off. Crouched on the floor of the big, luxurious car, the senatorial party with its rescued got the hell out of there. So quickly was it all over that, in the house, we did not know it had happened. All we knew was that an unidentified car had driven away rapidly. I never heard what became of the Katangese escort.

At about four o'clock that morning, Brian was released from Camp Massart – the paratroop camp – where he had been held. The negotiations and operations which led up to this are a matter of record and I will not try to re-tell them. Nor will I attempt any interpretation of the night's happenings. We thought, and think still, that the paras confused 'Brian' and 'O'Brien', and this is likely. I will only add a picture of George Ivan Smith, with his face swollen and holding his cracked ribs together with both hands, directing, advising, restraining, imperturbably at the centre of everything until the very moment he fell asleep, exhausted; and of Brian being brought into Indian HQ and saying wryly, 'A pity it wasn't some other fellow – if they'd killed me what a magnificent *casus belli!*'

When we got back to les Roches, I couldn't sleep. It was about six o'clock in the morning and I sat on the verandah listening to the Gurkha guard going about their breakfast and writing my account of the night for

Conor. Banza, one of the Baluba servants, who arrived on his bicycle imperturbably every morning, came up to me. '*Mademoiselle,*' he said, 'there is a dead Indian on the road near Tshombe's Palace.' Quite cheerfully he went back with the Gurkhas to show them where. When they got there, the body was gone, but there was little doubt that it was a Gurkha driver, who had been missing for some days, and that he had been murdered.

Later that day I flew, in a UN plane, to Léopoldville. The Cuban pilot landed too steeply and snapped the blade of the propellor sharp across. It seemed quite an everyday occurrence to me by this time.

℃   ℃   ℃

My father met me at Dublin Airport; he was furious. I was too tired and battered to argue when he insisted I go back home with him to Leeson Park, where his guards would keep the Press at bay, but I, in my turn, insisted on visiting Foreign Affairs. Was it on our way home from the airport then, or was it later? Even next morning? I cannot be sure, but, in any event, I succeeded in reaching my office, writing my letter of resignation and dropping it in my out-tray, without meeting anyone, except the doorman – for which I was glad because of my bruised face – and without indicating to anyone what I had done. I didn't feel called upon to inform anyone. Looking back now, I realise that I did not fully appreciate how pivotal the surfacing of my Katanga visit was in inducing the outcome that, hitherto, all the bad-mouthing of Conor by his unfriends – mainly British, but with considerable help in the Security Council from Belgium's Foreign Minister, Mr Spaak – had been unable to achieve, namely Conor's resignation. Actually, Mr Spaak's histrionics merely made it impossible for the Afro-Asian members to withdraw their support from Conor, but then came the news of Senator Dodd's party and my role in the events there, and the Katanga Lobby in the USA and elsewhere was presented with leverage in the form of a 'sex scandal' that forced the hand of the Irish government.

Mr Aiken was requested to recall Conor to the Irish Service, which he did. Conor, still in New York, promptly resigned, both from the UN and from External Affairs. It was no part of his plan to go quietly. As he puts it himself: 'One cannot, as a member of the foreign service of a small and friendly country, go round publicly denouncing the British Government. To permit oneself that luxury one has to become a private citizen. This I now determined to do.' He also announced that we were getting married, but that was by the way. Alan James comments:

'[Cruise O'Brien] had to go, and indeed he went. To that extent, Britain was successful. But even if it was a battle won, the war was well on the way to being lost. For, in one of those ironies which help to give history its fascination, the policy with which O'Brien believed himself to have been supplied, but which the UN then disavowed, soon came to receive [the UN's] more or less open endorsement. Against this development Britain fought a spirited rearguard action. But from now on it was downhill almost all the way.'

Forty-two years later, this is the received wisdom on the Katanga chapter of the UN's history. On 15 January 1963, Tshombe submitted to UN force, and I remember reading, with wicked glee, a news item that described the UN Ethiopian troops – Colonel Alemu's people – taking over the great smelter at Kolwezi, which, during the entire period of hostilities, was never extinguished, till then. I was and remain utterly partisan in this context. Back in December 1961, my principal reaction was relief that Conor and I were both alive, and there is now little point in speculating what might have happened had I stayed at home in Dublin. My part, however unintended, in terminating Conor's civil service career does, as I see it now, explain a despairing question of my father's during the time I spent at home with my parents, after my return, under a kind of house arrest. 'Why,' he asked, 'did she have to go to the Congo?' It seems to me now that he may have been thinking primarily of Conor's future. My mother had a ready answer, 'Seán,' she said, 'when I was young and I loved you, I would have followed you to the ends of the Earth.'

Things got much better after that, and when Conor called to see my parents on his return from New York, my mother opened the door to him saying, 'Conor, you led us a terrible dance,' and embraced him; my father opened a bottle of champagne. Conor replied, 'I'll make it up to you, Margaret.' The activities of the British Press had, at first, seemed threatening to all of us. They broke into *Whitewater* and stole papers and photographs; in New York they had stolen and published the separation agreement between Christine and Conor. They waylaid little Kate on her way home from school and published her sturdy denial of any scandal, 'It's all lies!' under the attribution, 'A member of the family stated ...' Now we could afford to laugh at them; they could do us no more harm. I remember my mother having breakfast in bed, surrounded by all the British newspapers that carried the most sensational accounts of our recent adventures. The telephone rang, it was the *Daily Express*. My mother answered. Was Mr MacEntee available to speak to them? 'No.' Had Mr MacEntee seen their front page that morning? 'I cannot say.' Have *you* seen our front page this morning? 'Of course not. I never read the British papers.' She put down the 'phone.

ଔ   ଔ   ଔ

Conor and Christine had originally been married in the registry office in Dublin, which meant that, although they could not legally be divorced in Ireland, their marriage was not recognised by the Catholic Church. This meant that if Conor got a divorce abroad, I could marry him legally in a church in any country that had civil divorce, but Irish law, as distinct from the ecclesiastical authorities, would not recognise our marriage. All that has, of course, changed with the introduction of divorce to Ireland. At the time it was fine by me, although my parents could never quite get over the feeling that we were wronging Christine, of whom they were very fond. They thought that there was something underhand about our 'exploiting the Sacrament', as they saw it. My dear Uncle Moss, on the other hand, was most helpful. He said his one regret was that he had always hoped that at the UN I would meet and marry a black man. His American years had made him a very positive enemy of racism. 'However,' he continued, 'I suppose he's an honorary black man anyway. I only hope he's good enough for you.' So, Conor having obtained a divorce in Mexico, where, contrary to popular belief, there are very stringent conditions as to the welfare of the children of the previous marriage, we were free to marry in New York. On 9 January 1962, Father Donal O'Callaghan, an old friend of

Frank Aiken's, married us in the Carmelite Church on the Lower East Side. It had been a long wait, more especially for our friends Ed and Vicki Solomons, who put us up for all those weeks of bureaucratic delay and bad flying weather, during which no 'Letter of Freedom' arrived for Conor from the diocese of Dublin. I was glad the Liturgy was in English, because Vicki was so thrilled by the Biblical allusions to Rachel and Sarah and Leah that she wept ... so, it was a real wedding.

My mother and father did not attend; perhaps they felt their indulgence had gone far enough. It is, however, true that at the time a transatlantic flight was not lightly undertaken and that they were no longer young. My mother gave me a present of a beautiful, fine oatmeal tweed suit with a silver fur collar in which to be married, and of an exquisite lace-trimmed hat, which cost twice as much as the rest of the outfit put together. I was 'given away' by a young man from the Irish Consulate-General in New York, who had actually been one of my third secretaries in Dublin in the past. We spent our honeymoon in Trinidad with the O'Duffy family, cousins of Conor's whose uncle-by-marriage was Eimar O'Duffy, the playwright. We found that interracial paradise faintly unnerving after our African experiences.

CHAPTER VIII

Wrap Up

Part i: Ghana, 1962–65

Part ii: America, 1965–69

Part iii: Ireland

Part iv: Journalism, books and travel

PART I: GHANA, 1962–65

After I got married I felt, for the first time in my life, real; as if what I was and did mattered. I registered this new feeling, but had no particular reaction to it other than acceptance. For those first spells at *Whitewater*, living out of suitcases and orange boxes, leaving to earn a living wage and returning for holidays, I did all the things that married women on limited incomes do. I mended rather than replaced, washed walls and windows, freshened faded coir matting with 'deck' paint from the marine chandlers in Howth and bought our petrol from stations which were giving away domestic utensils, such as steak knives. No one was going to pay myself and Conor to stay at home. The Department of Foreign Affairs had generously affected to believe that I had resigned on marriage, in the normal way of the time, and offered me my 'lump sum'. At first I felt like telling them where they could shove it – Conor had forfeited his pension rights for good by resigning – but in time I came round, and the money was very handy. We bought a set of cheerful, bright red garden chairs, which solved our acute seating problem. I remember cooking an evening meal for fourteen, with the *Penguin Cookery Book* open in one hand, on a tiny oven that had one hot-plate on top and which came from my flat.

We gave a great wedding party: space was one commodity we were not short of. Conor began work on *To Katanga and Back* and had various speaking engagements which paid. Fedelma and Kate moved easily between the two households – ours and Christine's – and, when my father or mother called and Conor did not answer the telephone, I could hear the disappointment in their voices. After all, he had spent most of his adult life learning to get on with difficult ministers, and my father had always been that; his son-in-law had not lost the skills acquired in the civil service. As well as Conor's children and their friends, we saw a lot of Barbara's boys – their father was still posted abroad and they often stayed with us for school holidays – and of Séamus' daughter, Margaret, my godchild. *Whitewater* has always had an immense attraction for children, with horses and boats and a lighthouse adjacent – today there is also a helipad, for sea rescue, just below the house – and there never was any furniture that had to be respected. We were undemandingly happy and we did not look ahead. When John XXIII – Increase to his glory! as they say in the country when a good priest dies – raised my Uncle David to the cardinalate in March 1962, Conor and I accompanied my parents to Rome for the occasion and thereby caused quite a flutter in the dovecotes of Iveagh House. We had been punctiliously crossed off all the official invitation lists and had to be rapidly restored, at President de Valera's personal insistence. The next instalment of our lives emanated from a totally other and unexpected quarter.

☷   ☷   ☷

As an adolescent I had read Rider Haggard's *She* and John Buchan's *Prester John* with enjoyment, but I had never felt drawn to Africa as I had always felt to France, or Greece. The Congo changed all that. I now saw Africans as people, for better or for worse, whereas before I saw them as black. During the grimmest days in Elisabethville, the President of newly independent Ghana, Kwame Nkrumah, had concerned himself, personally, about Conor's personal safety. We felt sincerely grateful towards him, and when – through his Attorney General, the left-wing, North-of-Ireland-born British politician Geoffrey Bing – he offered Conor the Vice-Chancellorship (academic headship) of the University of Ghana, we were disposed to take the offer seriously; Conor had acquired considerable prestige in the Third World by this time. We did not, however, take it so seriously that Conor would allow himself to be imposed by the government of the new State on an unwilling academic body. Kwame's response was to invite us to come and find out for ourselves whether or not we would be welcome. This we did, and discovered that, since the likely alternative would be the abrasive Mr Bing himself, all shades of politics and pigmentation making up the staff of the University of Ghana at Legon, just outside the capital city, Accra, would prefer Conor. We accepted the invitation, and it was one of the happiest decisions of our lives.

The people of Ghana had a reverence for education comparable to that of the Scots, from whom, indeed, over a hundred years and more, many of them had learnt the rudiments thereof in Mission schools. They felt their university belonged to them; to the people of Ghana. It had been built with the cocoa credits accumulated during the Second World War, and cocoa is a small-farmer's crop. Many such had a stake accordingly in Ghanaian higher education. The new university's courses admitted to the degrees of the University of London, and most Ghanaians were determined its teaching would not be reduced to mere political indoctrination, or to providing 'jobs for the boys'. On this basis, for the three years of his contract, Conor was able to coordinate the very real and, on the part of the Ghanaian academics, very brave opposition to the lethally frivolous and irresponsible piecemeal attrition of academic freedom which, from the basest of political motives, went on both covertly and openly under Kwame. The story of the university's struggle for autonomy has been told in detail many times, and I will not recount it again here, but it must be understood at this point that it formed the constant background to our private lives as long as we remained in Ghana. As dictators go, Kwame could present as benevolent and charming, not wantonly cruel or vindictive, but a dictator he was nonetheless. After an initial honeymoon period, relations between him and the university, of which he was Chancellor, became irretrievably strained, so that for three years, of which we loved every minute and during which we grew to love the country and its people intensely even while some of their ways drove us to distraction, our bags remained metaphorically, and to some extent literally, packed against the ever-present threat of deportation. Kwame was reported as saying, 'That bastard wants me to sack him, and that's why I'm not going to do it.'

Sir Eric Ashby, in his authoritative work on Third World universities, *Universities: British, Indian, African*, summed up Conor's effectiveness as follows:

'The morale of the university was restored in the autumn of 1962 by the appointment of Conor Cruise O'Brien as vice-chancellor. For three years, with masterly skill and extraordinary patience, O'Brien worked to preserve autonomy in the university and to ensure that it served Ghana's needs. From the beginning he affirmed his belief that there was nothing in the university's constitution inimical to autonomy; and at his last address to congregation, when he had finally decided that he could do no more to help the university and would have to resign at the end of his contract, he reiterated this belief. Here is a passage from the address:

"Now the autonomy of this University is, on paper, well established. The report of the 1961 Commission on University Education rests on two main principles: 'that Universities should be able to respond to the immediate and future needs of the community and that they should have the greatest possible autonomy in their organisation, teaching, and research.' The principles of the Commission's report were accepted by the Government and are embodied in the University of Ghana Act.'"

This stance cost Conor considerable vilification in the totally-subservient-to-Kwame local Press. On one occasion Dr Christian Baeta, a Methodist clergyman and formerly Head of the World Council of Churches, who was the warmly admired and respected Head of our School of Religions – the plural is significant – called in the morning at the Vice-Chancellor's Lodge, where we lived, to apologise for a particularly virulent attack which had appeared in the party Press and which coupled me with Conor. The gist of it was that the Vice-Chancellor was clinging disgracefully to his post because his wife would not give up her 'bone-white' Mercedes, or her villa on the hilltop. Dr Baeta was almost in tears, 'I am ashamed of my countrymen,' he said. 'But, Dr Baeta,' I replied, longing to hug him to console him, he looked so crestfallen, 'doesn't everyone know it is the truth? I wouldn't give up this wonderful house and that wonderful car, or my friends here in Legon for anyone.' And at that we both laughed and embraced, and our inspired university 'steward', Yanqui, who, as Chief of Protocol, would have been an ornament to any Foreign Service, brought us freshly-made tea.

I am almost overpowered by nostalgia when I try to describe the Vice-Chancellor's Lodge. The University of Ghana is built on the side of Legon Hill, overlooking the dusty stretches of the Accra plain to the west, which lie between it and the sea. The Lodge stands on the hill crest and there is always a fresh breeze blowing, although we are right on the equator. That last is a point that the architect may have forgotten for the Lodge is built around a Mediterranean-style courtyard, which traps the vertical tropical sun and reverberates the heat throughout the shady, airy living-space, almost cancelling its natural advantages. At least it used to, until I remedied this defect to my own satisfaction, although not, alas!, to universal approval. I had 'Grounds and Gardens' build a rustic wooden pergola in the centre of the courtyard and plant it with flowering vines, which shot up to give us shade. Now, Ghanaians, like the rest of us, hate and dread snakes and regard any vegetation near a dwelling as a refuge for snakes, scorpions and other such menacing forms of life and, therefore, by no means to be encouraged. I once saw a scorpion, horribly magnified against the sky, climb over the brow of the ridge outside our study windows, and once also I chivvied a snake into our laundry room and shut the door on it. Fortunately, all the pergola ever attracted were humming-birds. At a given season of the year it became alive with these tiny, darting, multicoloured, jewel-like creatures, and from the screened balcony outside our bedroom on the second floor you could look down on them from above with endless delight. Another seasonal wonder occurred after the rains in October/November, when the whole inland promontory that was the hill was covered in a glorious mist of wild purple orchids as far as the eye could see. Expatriates brought them into their houses by the arm-full; Ghanaians preferred to leave them in place.

In this marvellous home we had two stewards and a cook, a washer-man and relays of gardeners, a driver for the university's Mercedes – tall, handsome John Amartey – and three little boys, aged between ten and twelve, who were actively discouraged by all our adult staff and who declared their function to be looking after my car, a little red runabout that actually belonged to us rather than to the university. Their real and inestimable value was the company they provided for me. Not that I was home-sick, I was too happy for that, but the boys were a bonus. They came shopping with me and carried my parcels; they came to the beach and on other short excursions with Conor and myself and had a ball; they slept in an empty steward's room in the Lodge at night. (The adult staff did not live in.) The boys belonged to the Ewe (pronounced eh-veh) people, who straddled the border between Ghana (which incorporated an area of the old Gold Coast, formerly British Togoland) and modern

Togo (formerly French), where they were the predominant tribe. Their fathers were university stewards – a highly dignified and proficient body of (naturally) men, almost a caste. It was intimated to me that I was ruining the boys' prospects by giving them ideas above their station in life; Ghanaian society was an endearing combination of Victorian propriety and left-wing political ideals – the *conservative* members of our Ghanaian academic staff read the *New Statesman and* were sternly paternalist. I realised I had to take their strictures seriously.

The little boys were Anani Quashie, Alfonse, *tout simple* (without qualification) and Yaw (similarly). Anani was a kind of genius, a small, thin, attractive child who could read absolutely anything in English, which was the *lingua franca* of the State and the medium of instruction in schools. When the kitchen floor had been washed, newspapers were always laid down to protect the clean tiles and to soak up the moisture. Anani would crawl all over these, reading all of them indiscriminately, from the London *Times* to Nkrumah's party organ, *The Spark*. When I told this to IA Richards, the great British authority on the teaching of English as a second language, who was visiting us, at first he could not believe it. However, when he produced a cookery book and opened it at random for Anani to read, the child, totally unfazed, read on fluently until he was stopped. Professor Richards acknowledged the phenomenon with warm congratulations.

None of this affected the little triumvirate, who remained inseparable. Alfonse sang – rock and roll and The Beatles, and songs like, 'Is it a bird? Is it a plane? No, it's Superman!', 'Rock around the clock', and many more; he was a very handsome boy, tall and well-built. Yaw was a plain little fellow and very affectionate; he couldn't read. I decided I would teach him. I bought what I felt was a very child-friendly first reader and Yaw and I got down to business. The book fell open at the letter M and Yaw recognised the letter; he also knew that it said 'em' and we said 'mm, mm, mm' together for a little while. Then I pointed to the picture, which showed a woman with a baby on her knee and was labelled 'Mother'. 'Muh, muh, muh,' I prompted. Yaw looked at the picture. 'White lady, white baby,' he said. We persevered, but the reading didn't improve, and Yaw, who was having a hard time at school, began to stay away from school altogether.

His two friends asked me to put things right for him, and I went down to Christian Village, hoping to talk to his family. Christian Village was an Ewe village, and the majority of its inhabitants, paradoxically, were pagans – all of this I learnt much later. My memory of the compound where Yaw lived is dark and shady – projecting eaves? – but I do not recall it clearly, for there, immediately in front of me, stood the hefty, blackened trunk of a very ancient tree and it was smeared with chicken entrails and blood: a sacrificial animist shrine. I turned tail and fled. Later, Yaw's father came to see me at the Lodge and assured me that Yaw's troubles at school were over, and my symbiosis with Yaw and Alfonse and Anani slipped back into its original live-and-let-live mode, untainted by any more proactive do-goodery.

ᐅᔑ   ᐅᔑ   ᐅᔑ

The healing common sense and good nature of our Ghanaian environment at Legon was in welcome contrast to our Congo experience. Nevertheless we learnt early that it was not easy to insulate ourselves against the inherent tensions of post-colonial Africa. Ghana is an English-speaking enclave in former French West Africa, and, across the border I have mentioned above, independent, Francophone Togo was presided over by Sylvanus Olympio. This President, who had played a pivotal role in pre-independence politics, was widely loved and respected by the Ewe people on both sides of the border; a close cousin of his was married to our Dr Baeta, whom we have met above, and Olympio followed the same old-fashioned, West African coast, middle-class lifestyle, simple and intensely respectable, as the Baeta family did. He rode a bicycle to his office. After successive waves of occupation, Togo was a pleasant country to visit; the Germans had left its streets lined with tall shade trees, and the French had revolutionised the cooking in its hotels and restaurants. Conor and I are both Francophile in such matters and we liked to take short breaks in Togo. Then came one night, in January 1963, when no one on Legon Hill could sleep for the beating of Ewe drums in Christian Village. In the morning, we learnt that Sylvanus Olympio had been murdered.

Grim as it is to write, there is no doubt but that this was a French-orchestrated assassination – perhaps a settling of old scores from pre-independence by the French Right. Bonuses and pensions were owing from the French government to the demobilised Togolese veterans of the Indo-Chinese and Algerian wars. Instead of paying these directly to the re-patriated ex-soldiers, dangerous men by virtue of their very profession, the French representative in Togo is reported to have said, '*Mes enfants, vous avez bien mérité de la patrie* (Children, you have deserved well of the Fatherland), President Olympio has your money, claim it from him.' President Olympio had no such money and Togo was, as usual, strapped for cash. The President made this clear to the former Togolese mercenaries, before going home as usual on his bicycle. Later that evening the malcontents dragged him from the bed where he slept beside his wife and butchered him in the garden of his modest villa.

A pall of grief and anxiety lay for many days over the Ewe community in Accra. It cannot have been altogether reassuring news for President Nkrumah either, although his relations with Togo were cool. Indeed, an attempt on his own life about that time, when a group of women supporters – dancing under the neem trees outside the Presidential headquarters at Flagstaff House – were cut to pieces by hand-grenades, was popularly interpreted as a forceful French message to him to lay off Ghana's Francophone neighbours. Official Ghanaian opinion preferred to attribute the massacre to an anti-left-wing CIA – it played better to an English-speaking public, they thought. Whichever it was, it did not improve the Ghanaian President's temper, and relations between him and the university were not helped.

Two further, separate attempts on our President's life punctuated our three years in Ghana. The first had dark consequences indeed, the second elements of farce. The first happened just before we arrived, in September 1962, and was an engrossing topic of conversation among all our new acquaintance. It had been Nkrumah's habit, as an aspiring politician, to make forays into remote chiefdoms, there to consolidate his party support. Now that Ghana was, to all intents and purposes, a one-party state (CPP – Convention People's Party), he seems to have wished to make something of a triumphal progress through some of those remoter regions. At a place called Kulungugu, on 2 August 1962, the presidential cavalcade was bombed; Nkrumah was injured and an unspecified number of people killed, or maimed. Exact facts were difficult to come by at the time, and it cannot be said that events have been much clarified since.

The President suspected three of his senior CPP colleagues from pre-independence days: Tawia Adamafio (Tom Adams), his Minister for Presidential Affairs; Ako-Adjei, who had introduced Nkrumah to the ' now in disgrace' (see below) hero of the independence struggle, JB Danquah (as it were, the Ghanaian equivalent of Douglas Hyde); and one Cofie Crabbe, of whom I can only say that he bore an old Gold Coast surname. Kwame had long been aware that some within the party resented his by now awesome personal power. For all that power, however, he was not able to produce sufficient evidence to have these three men convicted, after he had had them arrested, charged and brought before a bench of judges, consisting of the Chief Justice of Ghana, Sir Arku Korsah, and two senior colleagues. It seems that Kwame had not realised that the Ghanaian judiciary was not – yet – as cowed, or as corrupt as he had hoped. He promptly sacked the Chief Justice. This process took until December 1963, by which time myself and Conor were beginning to feel that we had played ourselves in; we still had a lot to learn.

Conor was in Europe at this time on a staff-recruitment drive for the university. When the news broke, he promptly appealed publicly to Nkrumah to reinstate the Chief Justice. No one expected such an appeal to go down well with the addressee. What it actually did was to enable Kwame to 'forget' French–African hostility and old-party-comrade jealousy and to concentrate, in public, on supposed US subversionary threats, involving supposed conspirators at the university, thereby laying our high-minded, objective and totally-sympathetic-to-Third-World-development American staff, in the Department of Law, open to endless vicious attack in the media, on the streets and in the corridors of power.

Meanwhile, sometime in 1964, deep within Christiansborg Castle (a great Danish fortress on the sea coast of Accra, dating back to the slave-trade and to which a scared Kwame ultimately retreated from his old headquarters at Flagstaff House), a second trial of the three political figures, of whose innocence nothing would convince the President, took place in absolute secrecy, before a single judge and a hand-picked jury. They were found guilty in or about February 1965, but we, like almost everybody else in Ghana, had other things to worry about by then.

Here in Accra, in January 1964, the second significant assassination attempt took place. A crazy security man, Constable Ametwee, had fired on Nkrumah in Flagstaff House and had pursued the President into a kitchen, where Kwame had hidden under the table. As it was put in court, 'the President increased the distance between himself and his pursuer.' It was an open-and-shut case and the poor lunatic guard was hanged, but in his desperation he tried to incriminate everyone he could think of, including the sadly vulnerable, transparently virtuous JB Danquah, the great intellectual founding figure of the Ghanaian Independence movement, displaced by Kwame's demagogic populism and still the object of the President's fear and jealousy. Arrested and imprisoned without trial, he subsequently died in jail. Both JB Danquah's death and the sentencing of the Kulungugu Three were announced on the same day.

I would not have inflicted all this detail on my readers had it not, bizarrely, affected me personally. Anyone interested in pursuing these events further should read Professor Ofosu-Appiah's revealing *Life and Times of J.B. Danquah* (Accra, 1974). Shortly before the double announcement above, we received a visit from Geoffrey Bing. Now, Geoffrey gets a universally bad press from friends no less than from enemies, but he was not necessarily 'the worst'. He could be very good company, but he could also be a crashing bore. He had an exaggerated 'welcome for himself', and he drank other men's whiskey while rarely producing his own. Yet he was a loving husband and father, and his adopted, Ghanaian son, Adoutey Bing, was a brilliantly talented and much-loved child. Geoffrey saw himself as genuinely devoted to the interests of Ghana. This evening, his business was with me: would I write to my father asking him to approach Mr de Valera on behalf of the Kulungugu Three, now under sentence of death? Would Mr de Valera write, as President of one newly independent State to another such, and conjure Kwame not to sully the record of emergent Ghana with three political executions? Only one answer was possible for me. I sat down and wrote my letter. In due course, I got a, not surprisingly, grumpy reply from my father; he had – reluctantly

– done as I had asked. What Mr de Valera did, I do not know, but after we left Ghana in 1965, the Kulungugu Three were, in fact, pardoned.

In the face of the death of Danquah, however, these prisoners had become irrelevant. The government did not dare withhold Dr Danquah's body from his family. Nobody doubted but that this elderly, asthmatic gentleman had died of hardship in prison. From all over, politically-conscious Ghana flocked to his funeral. A contingent of younger academics from our threatened university carried his coffin. For Nkrumah it was the writing on the wall, could he but read it. A young Ghanaian journalist, Cameron Duodu – whose physical appearance and mental make-up reminded Conor of another young journalist, his own father, Francis Cruise O'Brien – had been among the mourners, and his account of that extraordinary occasion, where the police state was set at naught, was so vivid, so shot through with genuine pride and grief and yet so chastened by professional cynicism, that we felt as if we had actually been there, almost as part of a documentary film-crew.

Well before this, early in 1964, CPP mischief-makers – or perhaps merely the President's pleasure – had seen to it that the university's Law School was gutted by deportations and, further, that a generous offer which came from a consortium of US medical schools, under the Kennedy administration, to create a University Medical School at Legon was sabotaged: all in aid of Kwame's anti-American propaganda spree. The Head of the Law School, Professor William Harvey, a most distinguished, conscientious and humane American scholar, with both practical and academic expertise in the Law, together with his deputy, Dr Robert Seidman, a former editor of the *Harvard Law Review* and very much a man of the Left by US standards, were both deported. Their offence was declared to be participation in a CIA plot, or plots, to assassinate President Nkrumah. Now, all rational people knew that there was/were no such plot, or plots. The USA and the CIA were perfectly happy with Nkrumah, which, obviously, the people behind the series of grenade attacks and bombings that I have been listing were not. The intended victim of the plots was, however, in denial. All right-thinking Ghanaians loved their President; he could argue, therefore, that any attack on him must have been suborned by a foreign power.

These were the days of the Cold War, and the popular imagination might be expected to be receptive to tales of CIA machinations, more particularly in an ostensibly socialist State. Furthermore, in those days people were not as prone to challenge any government's absolute right to deport non-nationals, even on no stated, or on absurd grounds, as they might be today. The bonus for the State, in the present instance, was the reversion to State patronage of those desirable employments held by foreign nationals at a time when the State was anxious to nativise its professional classes. In the cases of our academic lawyers, their deportation would also silence 'pedantic criticism' of the current spate of 'constitutional reforms', whether in contemplation or already carried out by the President.

The university administration fought hard for its faculty, but it had no chance of winning, and on Saturday, 8 February, the deportations took place. Conor and I drove to the airport in low spirits to say goodbye to our so unjustly wronged friends. We went in my little red car, rather than in the official Mercedes, because we did not want further to compromise the university. To our immense delight we discovered that the university administration was cheerfully compromising itself. The imposing figure of Kofi Edzii, the Registrar and a former District Commissioner, under the British, was very much to the fore, collecting the deportees' passports and air-tickets in order to facilitate their embarkation – there were now five families involved as five academics were being deported – while other Ghanaian faculty members and their wives and families soothed children, embraced spouses and sorted luggage. Poor Professor Harvey, stricken with Dengue fever, together with grave heart and lung complications, was carried on a stretcher. There was no mistaking the supportive nature of the collective leave-taking, nor its openness and dignity. It was a straw in the wind.

CS   CS   CS

I fear that a degree of gloom has descended on my narrative; although what I have written is strictly factual, a general impression of gloom would be misleading. Our material circumstances were about as comfortable as they could be without becoming oppressive. With the university bookshop and the School of African Studies on campus, it was impossible to be bored. All the great contemporary Africanists – linguists, political scientists, anthropologists – came and went, and many highly entertaining dons from other disciplines were also frequent visitors. I think we all felt that we had a significant contribution, great or small, to make to Ghanaian life, and I think we all were sustained by that conviction, although some might consider it an illusion. Dónal and Fedelma and Kate came and stayed with us. Dónal was by now a confirmed Africanist; the girls had reservations. They deprecated the outward signs of respect shown to Conor as a male by elderly Moslem ladies in Northern Ghana, and they were not mollified by an offer of an unspecified number of cows for Fedelma in marriage. Our friend, Bríd Lynch, the Abbey actress and Fedelma's godmother, who came in 1964 to teach a course in Western stage-craft at the School of Music and Drama of the Institute of African Studies, received a similar proposal, which she tactfully turned down. The young man thought she looked as if she might be good at accounts!

Bríd put on a performance of *Mother Courage*, with Maya Angelou in the eponymous part, and the British Council gave us *As You Like It* in the open air, with Judi Dench as Rosalind. You may remember that in the play Mother Courage plucks a chicken on stage. This usually looks like a stuffed parrot, but Bríd gave her stage-manager money to buy a real chicken each night for the purpose. Imagine her feelings when, some nights into the run, the evening's chicken got dizzily to its feet and staggered off the stage. 'Mees Leench,' explained the stage-manager, contrite, 'the cheeken deed not die.' The great glory of the School of Music and Drama was its faculty of traditional Ghanaian music, dance and song, under the world-renowned musicologist Kwabena Nketia. The last time Conor and I were back in Ghana, to celebrate the recent fiftieth birthday of the university, both the solemn ritual music, which accompanied the academic ceremonies, and the glorious cabaret, to which we were entertained that evening, were devised by Professor Nketia and presented by his students. Both were unalloyed triumphs of imagination, talent and piety. I remembered as if it were yesterday how, when I attended classes in African languages and culture at the Institute long, long ago, I used to hear the music students rehearsing and envy them.

We were able to travel extensively, more or less on business always. On at least one occasion we covered 1,126 kilometres in one day over unpaved, red, laterite roads. Frequently we drove ourselves, but on one epic journey, which we made at Christmas 1965 and of which I have just turned up the account I wrote home to my parents, Amartey, the university driver, came with us. Here is my letter:

Telegrams & Cables : UNIVERSITY, LEGON.   Telephone : ACCRA 77631 Ext. 617

from The Vice-Chancellor

Mrs. MacEntee
9 Leeson Park
Dublin.
January 29, 1965.

Dearest Mammy and Daddy,

... Let me try to tell you now about our Nigerian trip, which was a splendid success from beginning to end. Bríd came with us, and the University driver Amartey, so we had plenty of company, and three people to spell each other at the wheel [Bríd didn't drive]. We went first along the coast through Togo and Dahomey – very beautiful and picturesque stretches of beach and palms and wonderful French food in French hotels. The last proved rapidly to have one major disadvantage and we discovered on our second day that we had already spent half our total estimate for the entire fortnight. The C.F.A. [French African Confederation] franc is lethal. Fortunately we crossed the Nigerian border on Christmas Day and the cost of living returned to more nearly normal. In Dahomey we visited the palace of the great and blood-stained kings of Dahomey at Abomey. It is rather strange and desolate, and has been turned into a museum, although women of the royal family still come twice a week to lament the dead kings and leave little dishes of food and bottles of Dubonnet for them. We tried to cross into Nigeria from there by bush road, which led us deep into the forest, getting more and more bush

279

at every mile, and finally brought us to the banks of a broad river where, on the far side, there still remained standing two arches of a three-arch bridge. We asked a local gentleman whether it was possible to cross, and he replied, '*Non, pont fatigué*,' which I think should get the understatement prize for 1964. As a result of this we were not able to cross the border that night, Christmas Eve, but in compensation we saw Christmas Eve in a West African border village, and it was quite unforgettable: drums and Christmas carols, and bands of children parading about the streets, and the highest of good humour everywhere. We had to drive 30 miles back to the nearest hotel and set out again next morning, after a very un-Christmas-like Mass, with all the African children in new cotton dresses and little straw hats – the influence of the French millinery trade no doubt. Christmas itself we passed very quietly in a flat we had been lent at Lagos and also Stephen's Day. The highlight for me was several dry Martinis at a fashionable hotel, as this is a drink which, for one reason or another, is almost impossible to get in Ghana. We were also entertained to Harp lager by Kevin Rush [the Irish ambassador] and his wife, who were terribly pleased to see us and very disappointed that we could not stay longer.

For the remainder of our time in Nigeria we rather cleverly managed to move from University to University, which considerably lessened the problems, financial and otherwise, of accommodation. We were, of course, there for all the excitement of the [general] election and collected a great deal of most illuminating information: for example, the estimated death toll in the riots in Tivland, where there is an endemic state of revolt against the Northern domination, is 3000; source, the Catholic Bishop of Tivland via Fr. O'Carroll, Department of Political Science, Ibadan. We passed one very tense army road-block on the borders of the Tiv country, and saw one burnt-out village. But for the actual day of the election we were in the Eastern Region, where, of course, in response to Zik's [Governor General Azikwe's] boycott no election at all took place, and there seemed to be a fairly impressive solidarity [amongst Ibos]. Bríd had a nightmare in which she dreamed she was being shoved down a well by the Tivs. This is what they do to tax collectors.

The best part of the journey came after this, as we moved north. First we traversed the Jos plateau, very high, with temperate climate – Conor says, a special dispensation of providence to enable the Europeans to mine in comfort and take away all the metals – like Katanga, it is a mining area. The indigenous people not engaged in mining live in beautiful houses with high hedges of cactus round them and wear no clothes at all except leaves. This seems to make the urban Europeans even more clothes-conscious than most, and on New Year's Eve we were put out of the smart hotel because Conor was in his shirt sleeves, although wearing a beautiful silk tie and gold cuff-links! However, we got a very satisfactory dinner in more congenial and multi-racial company at the Government Rest House.

North of Jos again is like the *Arabian Nights*: rolling, well-irrigated and richly cultivated plains, beautiful and distinctively castellated houses, built of mud and white-washed, with strong Arab influence reminiscent of Spain, splendid mounted aristocrats in flowing robes with outriders, and camel trains plodding towards the Sahara. One had heard, of course, about the re-actionary and oppressive Moslem régime in the North, but one had dis-counted the wealth and orderliness of the region. An actual visit makes a useful corrective.

Camel trains soon became a commonplace, and on the borders between Nigeria and Niger we stumbled by accident on an immense horse and camel market at a place called Jiddia, which is one of the starting points for trans-Saharan caravans. It is right on the edge of the desert, dusty and parched, and the wind hot and full of sand, but oddly exhilarating, and there, standing in the middle of the market-place in navy blue robes, with veiled faces, armed to their invisible teeth, knives, silver-mounted cartridge belts and all, stood a party of veiled Touaregs, which is like out of technicolour films. The women are even more splendid and, although technically Moslem, go un-veiled, and wear silver coins in their hair.

These are only one of the fantastically decorative peoples that we saw in the next few days as we made our way over the ghastly roads of this incredi-bly poor country [Niger]. In the capital, Niamey, there is a combined pleas-ure garden, zoo and ethnological museum which is fantastically popular with the local population, and there you can see the extraordinary spectacle of a Hausa or Fulani woman, superbly dressed, looking into a glass case at a rep-lica of herself not any more superb. You could have switched them and no-body would have noticed the difference. It was the nicest museum we ever saw, full of children admiring the animals and old men sitting in the shade of the trees listening to piped indigenous music.

Any account that I can try to give you of all this must seem terribly lame. I could talk about it to you for weeks. Since we have come back, Bríd, Conor and myself, we have all been a little dazed with nostalgia for the desert, more particularly as the Institute of Education crisis crawls on [just one more university crisis!]. The visit from Maeve and Howard [friends of Christine's] was a tonic, but an exacting one, and showing them as much of Ghana as possible in six days got our feet back on the ground again. They have now departed, carrying a grip of gifts which they will be sharing out in due course.

Academically, in the Institute of African Studies this term is a whirlwind. Half the great names in anthropology and linguistics are here as visiting professors, and I am kept so busy trotting from seminar to seminar that I don't get anything done on my thesis [I was working for a diploma at the Institute], which is supposed to be in by the 19th of April, ha ha! I am concocting a plan to get the exam part of the degree, which I now feel I will do, and to be referred on the thesis, which I can finish in Howth, or Sussex, or North Western (U.S.A.), or East Africa, or any of the other places where we are likely to be at the end of our term here. I had a note from Dorothy Cole [the architect Michael Scott's secretary] saying she was sending on the *Miserere* proofs [these were proofs of my Uncle Paddy's last collection of poems], but so far nothing has arrived. To some extent I am relieved, as I do not know how I could fit them in just at present. Of course, when they do come I will do so.

Lots and lots of love,
Máire.

I cannot resist adding two more vignettes of the Sahel (sub-Saharan belt). Driving through one of the great mud-built towns we saw this sad *tableau vivant*: a little girl, who looked about eleven but was probably thirteen, weighed down with gold and jewels and cocooned in many-coloured veils, stood on a street-corner, surrounded by a crowd of other little girls in skimpy cotton frocks, mopping and mowing and dancing around her in celebration. The little girl was a bride on her way to her wedding, and she was crying. The other sight was more exhilarating: parked at Jiddia, among the camel trains, was a great trans-Saharan truck – Timbuktu to Tamanrasset! – wheels over ten feet high. The owner-driver, an elegant Frenchman in spotless safari clothes and protected by windbreaks from flying sand, was dining at a natty picnic table beside his mobile home, served by his black mistress dressed in dazzling traditional colour, and seated before a steaming casserole and a bottle of (presumably French) wine. As all we could get to eat or drink were couscous and warm soda-water – as prescribed by Moslem law – we were livid with envy! I can resurrect the feeling still.

ۍ   ۍ   ۍ

I am sure readers at this point have been impressed by the length and detail of my dutiful letters home from Ghana. These virtues were made possible by the good offices of Ilse Yardley, Conor's personal assistant, to whom I dictated them. Before Ilse came, with her architect husband Maurice, to Ghana, she had been secretary to the founding editors of *History Today*. Before that again and before the Second World War, she had come as a little girl on a *kindertransport* train of Jewish child refugees from Vienna to live with an uncle and aunt in London. She was a young woman of great poise, intelligence and charm, and she coped with magical efficiency and tact with Conor's literary and personal correspondence, as well as with an output of letters to the President which amounted to a collection of political essays. Conor's deputy, the Professor of Classics, Alex Kwapong, who would succeed him as vice-chancellor, used to say to us – to myself and Ilse – 'Let him write them, but try not to let him send them!' He didn't expect us to try too hard. Both he and Ilse remain valued friends to this day.

ۍ   ۍ   ۍ

At the end of that academic year we left Ghana, and, on 24 February 1966, I wrote the following amazing information to my parents from New York:

'I predicted the Ghanaian *coup* to an audience of ambassadors and such like last night [in New York]. With all his faults, I hope no physical harm comes to poor Kwame for whom I cherish a *faible* – still less would I want his nice wife and his lovely children hurt. Please God, it will be a typically civilised Ghanaian *coup* with a minimum of bloodshed. It means among other things that Conor may now be invited back to Ghana – not as V.C. of course – but perhaps to give the Aggrey–Frazer–Guggisberg lectures, or on some other such ceremonial jaunt. Boy, would I love it! I left a little of my heart in that country, in spite of everything.'

What had happened was that we had been invited to dinner by an Africanist colleague of Conor's at New York University, and the consensus around the table was that Kwame was secure in office for the foreseeable future. I could not rid myself of the memory of the sombre faces of our young men on Legon campus after JB Danquah's funeral, and I burst out, 'Don't be absurd. A *coup* could be taking place there at this minute!' And, of course, it was.

I had fallen in love, when we were in Ghana, with Kwame's little boy, who was four years old. I met him when I called on his lonely-and-rather-to-be-pitied Egyptian mother; we observed these courtesies scrupulously in Ghana. The little fellow had an English nanny and he was not at all shy. He said to me, teasing me as little boys, so charmingly, can, 'You have green eyes. People with green eyes are very wicked.' My instinct that he and his mother would not be harmed proved – thank God – correct.

The military behind the well-planned *coup* chose the moment to strike when Kwame was absent in Hanoi, expressly so as to avoid bloodshed. The 'foreign woman and her children' were brought out of Flagstaff House by the besiegers under a flag of truce and put on the next plane to Egypt. Kwame's tribe were the Nzimas, from the Ivory Coast border, and his bodyguard was made up of Russian-officered Nzima tribesmen. When the attack came, they knew they had no hope; it is said they fought to the last man.

I was also right in anticipating our return to Ghana. We were invited back that year for the post-*coup* conferring of degrees. We stayed in the Lodge, as of old, the new Vice-Chancellor, Alex Kwapong, our old, much-loved friend and one of the great Ghanaian patriots and personalities of the age, not yet having taken up residence there. So it was that we met the famous Colonel Kotoka, the animating spirit of the *coup*. Kotoka, like Alex's lovely wife, Evelyn, was an Ewe and a family friend of the Kwapongs. We all of us, the Registrar, Kofi Edzii, the historian, Adu Boahen, and other allies of the struggle for academic freedom, gathered in the lovely, airy main room of the Lodge, and the Colonel, now a General,

young, animated and handsome, and totally without affectation, told us
his story:

> 'As you all know, we had been talking *coup* for months. I used to keep notes
> of our ideas in a little notebook that I kept in the breast-pocket of my tunic
> and changed into a fresh tunic pocket every day, when the worn tunic went
> to the laundry. The notes were in code, but it was not a very good code.
> Then one morning I picked up yesterday's tunic to make the change, and the
> notebook wasn't there. I said, "Kotoka, it's you or him now," and I marched
> my battalion from Kumasi to Flagstaff House.'

Someone asked, 'Were you sure they would follow you?' The reply
was deprecatory, 'You don't get to be a Colonel without knowing that sort
of thing.'

Poor, brilliant, idealistic General Kotoka, he was shot dead somewhere along the airport road not long afterwards, and much of the promise of those days died with him. 'You don't get to be a General' without
provoking murderous envy and hatred. I wrote a lament for him in Irish. It
is called 'The Blue Soldier' – '*An Saighdiuir Gorm*'. *Gorm* (blue) is the correct Irish for the pigmentation we call, in English, 'black'. The term goes
back to the Middle Ages and to the indigo-dyed clothes of the veiled
Touaregs we met earlier; the dye rubs off on their skin.

PART II: AMERICA, 1965–69

You will have gathered that during our stay in Ghana we were more than
a little preoccupied with the subject of presidential assassinations. Of
course, by far the most significant assassination of those years was that of
President John FitzGerald Kennedy of the United States. In his *Memoir*,
Conor describes how we, in Ghana, heard the news:

> [One of our evening parties] 'was interrupted by the arrival of a large number
> of [uninvited] students, rushing through the large dark area of 'bush' outside
> into the lighted circle around the Lodge. They were already in a state of great

distress, verging on panic. The news they brought was of the assassination that day of President Kennedy. They clearly all thought of Kennedy as a friend of Africa's and that he had been murdered for that reason, by American racists. Some feared that, in the confusion, racists might come to power in America, with horrible consequences for Africa, and themselves personally. Others feared that Kennedy might have been murdered by a black, and that white racists might come to power in the United States in the general revulsion against the deed. But it was clear that all the students tremendously admired Kennedy, had indeed loved him from a distance, and that they felt an acute sense of loss at his passing in such a terrible manner.

After my own experiences with the Kennedy administration over Katanga, I could not feel quite the same way as the students did, but I couldn't help being moved by the sincerity and intensity – and somehow the purity – of what they felt.'

Now in the library and seminar room of the Schweitzer Chair of Humanities, recently created at New York University by the legislature of the State of New York and to which Conor had just been appointed, Conor and I sat and contemplated the fourteen volumes of the Warren Report on that murderous event, which Conor had been asked to review for the *New Statesman*. I do not know how many people can claim to have read that report through, with the annexes, from cover to cover, but we are two of that number, and, whatever one may think of the report's conclusions, what is certain is that they are not, in fact, supported by the evidence adduced. The realities of power politics are the same the world over. Conor had chosen 'Literature and Politics' as the overall theme for his courses – the university discreetly changed it in their prospectus to 'Literature and History'; 'politics' in America was a dirty word! The founders of the Chair had intended that the programme should be interdisciplinary and that it should attract distinguished, foreign, visiting scholars to lecture at NYU. The Warren Report could be considered 'required reading'.

As so often before, our lives lay in pleasant places. NYU is an urban university; much like UCD was when I was a girl. The charm of its campus consists in its having no campus. Its various buildings converge – not without some town–gown resentments – on one of New York's best-loved public open spaces, Washington Square (much as UCD might have done on Saint Stephen's Green had our planners had more vision). Emily Kies Folpe, an architectural authority on New York, writes about the Square in these terms:

'In his novel *Washington Square*, written more than one hundred and twenty years ago, Henry James described the Square of his childhood as having a "riper, richer, more honorable look" than other parts of the city – "the look of having had something of a social history." His words are quoted in nearly every related book or guide, because they capture a lingering quality of the place. Washington Square remains a palimpsest; the past has never been fully erased. Although much has changed since James's youth, still embedded in the earth of the park and in the brick and stone of the buildings around it are clues that yield a remarkably full picture of the past. By examining this cityscape, we gain a greater appreciation for a neighborhood's legacy and a deeper understanding of our urban and national heritage.'

Where Fifth Avenue debouches into the Square, on the site of four old brownstone houses – that once sheltered a fashionable academy for young ladies, where Jenny Jerome, Winston Churchill's mother, went to school – stands a multistorey, Art Nouveau building that dates from 1927 and is something of an architectural show-piece itself: One Fifth Avenue. When we were married, it was an apartment-hotel, and it was there that we spent the first night of our honeymoon. I still remember the bliss of ringing room service for *two* large breakfasts. Now, it had been acquired by NYU and one of its floors had been purpose-converted into the lightsome quarters of the Schweitzer Program. Between One Fifth Avenue and the rear of the 'Greek Revival' brownstones of Washington Square North runs what was once a service road for stabling and is now a cobbled alley between two rows of compact townhouses – Washington Square Mews, an address to die for. We lived at number three Washington Square Mews. It is now part of NYU's School of Irish Studies. At the risk of emphasising my age and outlook, I must stress that Washington Square in the late 1960s, when the 'hippy' phenomenon could still be regarded as benign, had not yet been overrun by the drugs culture of the

1970s. My one-year-old, Patrick, used to play there, and in my memory it still corresponds to Ms Kies Folpe's perhaps idealised picture of what, on a good day, it should be like now:

'Washington Square at the beginning of the twenty-first century is thriving. Its pathways are full of pedestrians, its playgrounds are brimming with children, and its benches are well occupied. Clusters of young people sit on the low concrete rim encircling the central plaza; dozens more lounge around the fountain basin. In the chess area, players hunch over their games, fingers poised on timers. Mounted police pass by, the clip-clop of their horses evoking an earlier century in the park. Rarely does noise from surrounding streets intrude.'

I must comment, however, that the hoof-beats of the New York Mounted Police evoke in me a wholly different set of reminiscences – which brings me to the Vietnam War. NYU was not one of the flash-points of American student protest in the 1960s, but a sizeable majority of its student population was Jewish, and the Jewish community in the United States was the backbone of the protest against the country waging 'an unjust and imperialist war', as they were also the backbone of the Civil Rights protests against racist discrimination. This was a climate in which Conor was at home. He takes up the story in his *Memoir*.

'Towards the end of my first year at NYU I was approached by a group of my students with a political proposition. These students were all Jewish and also all very bright. They knew that I had written and spoken against the war in Vietnam around the theme of 'Counter-Revolutionary Imperialism'. But now they wanted me to join with them in breaking the law, to register the seriousness of the issue and of our concern with it. They did not propose any violent action, or any flamboyant gesture, such as the burning of the American flag, as practised at that time by the extreme left of the anti-war movement. What they did propose was a sit-in outside the Induction Centre in Manhattan in order to obstruct the progress of recruitment for the war. We would no doubt be arrested and charged with a breach of the peace. We might be jailed for a short time. Whatever happened would signal a stiffening of the resistance, by moderates, to the continuance of the Vietnam War.'

It was a highly respectable protest, led by none other than Dr Spock, the great American guru of child-rearing; it took place in December 1965. While Dr Spock was ceremonially arrested in front of the Centre for the benefit of the television cameras and the massed ranks of 'New York's Finest', numbering about 3,000 policemen, the NYU contingent, comprising staff and students, sat down in the roadway at the rear of the building, completely blocking all traffic. We were acutely aware of the presence – about a block further downtown than we were, I have the impression – of a sizeable contingent of mounted cops, and when they began to move towards us, a wave of unease swept the demonstrators. I had had a fair amount to do with horses in my youth and I had been assured that a horse will never step on a body on the ground if the animal can at all avoid it. I shouted at the top of my lungs, hoping to God I was right, 'Sit tight! Don't move! The horses won't walk on you!' No more they did; they picked their way amongst us, and the mounted manoeuvre failed anti-climatically. It was now the turn of the cops on the ground, and they proved much more dangerous. The accepted drill for demonstrators at the time was to go limp when manhandled by the police; it proved a mistake. Conor was kicked expertly in the kidneys and carted off, in considerable pain, to Bellevue Hospital. Meanwhile the women who had been arrested – of whom I was one – were lodged in a large, dark, basement 'holding-pen' under one of the city's courthouses. We were driven there in 'Paddy Wagons'! In one corner of the room stood a white lavatory bowl with no seat. The women immediately organised a rota to stand around the bowl facing outwards and spreading out their arms in their opened winter overcoats, so as to form a screen for the privacy of those who needed to use this facility. Middle-class New York people had already become very 'demo-wise' by 1965.

We were all subsequently released on bail, and I will let Conor finish, as he began, the story:

'These proceedings attracted considerable publicity at the time, of which we could not complain, since attracting attention was a large part of the exercise. The kick – for the results of which I was treated at Bellevue Hospital – was part of the news. I received a telegram from my friend Wilton Dillon [an official of the Smithsonian Institute in Washington]: "I see you were kicked by a cop. What was his ethnicity?"

The cop's ethnicity, just as Wilton had surmised, was the same as my own.

I spent several hours in jail and was then brought to trial in the local district court. The presiding judge was black, which I felt to be a point in my favour. There was no major difference between the physical events as described by the police and as described by me, except that the police neither corroborated nor disputed my story about being kicked. The judge then asked me whether I wished to say anything before he passed sentence.

I said I was charged with a breach of the peace. But I had not gone to the Induction Centre to breach the peace. I had gone there to protest a breach of the peace being carried out by the government of the United States in Vietnam …

At this point the judge interrupted me. "Dr O'Brien," he said, "I was about to dismiss the case against you, but I might change my mind if you don't stop talking."

I stopped talking right there, and the case was duly dismissed.

My arrest and injury had been reported in the press, and Mayor Lindsay of New York [a Republican mayor] wrote me a letter of sympathy and good wishes about the injury. I thought it was very decent of him in the circumstances.'

One of Conor's biographers states that Conor took part in the epic anti-Vietnam War march on Washington in the following year, when students from all over the United States scaled the walls of the Pentagon Building with grappling irons. This is not so. Conor's academic workload, which was very heavy, did not permit him to be there on that occasion. I, however, was there. I travelled with a trainload of supportive Jewish parents, and marvelled with them at the elegance and daring of the young men who swung like spiders against the cliff-like face of that sinister, symbolic structure. All the fathers in our party carried hefty bank-rolls of ready cash with which to bail out their sons once the spectacle was over. So different had my own experience been from that of these young people that when I heard one young female demonstrator lamenting, in near-panic, that she 'had forgotten her pills', I hadn't the slightest idea what she was talking about …

❧   ❧   ❧

During our first year in New York, the seventeen-year-old Kate lived with us – technically. Conor and I were old-fashioned parents; formulae like 'teenage crisis' meant nothing to us, and even when we were told that Kate was anorexic, it meant very little. Fortunately, however, we were able to realise that she was unhappy, and that the break-up of Conor's first marriage had contributed in large part to this. Our feelings of responsibility caused us to resolve, consciously and conscientiously, to let her do exactly what she wanted, or thought she wanted, where this was at all possible, while at the same time providing her with a permanent safety net, as unobtrusively as possible. How this method would have worked if Providence had not taken a hand I dare not speculate, but Providence did and put in our way the ideal mentor for Kate, and a very dear younger friend-to-be for ourselves, in the person of Deirdre Levinson, a colleague of Conor's from the English Department at NYU. Kate went to live with Deirdre in a beautifully unstructured but totally safe existence, and a major cause of worry evaporated for us. Kate was a very pretty and exceptionally talented child, and when I went shopping with her, I used to feel as if I were accompanying the young Maud Gonne …

❧   ❧   ❧

There is a saying among international civil servants that you cannot qualify as a UN expert on post-colonial Africa unless you have at least *flown* over at least *one* African country, *by day*. There was a touch of this about our knowledge of Nigeria; the Nigerians we knew were educated Nigerians, and they were almost exclusively Ibos – Zik's (Governor General Azikwe's) people. We had read the splendid novels of Chinua Achebe, an Ibo; our invaluable steward in Ghana, Yanqui, was an Ibo; the Vice-Chancellor of Nigeria's oldest university at Ibadan, Kenneth Dike, was an Ibo. The Ibos felt themselves to be 'the Jews of Africa': brighter than anybody else and resented on that account. When the Ibos, in 1967, took their oil-rich home territory of Biafra out of Nigeria and declared independence, our sympathies were with them, and not with the Central

Government. Contrariwise, those of our old Katanga enemies, Britain and Belgium, were on the opposing side. Coincidentally, most Irish people were for Biafra, like us. A sizeable number of the Ibos were Christians and had been evangelised by the Irish Holy Ghost Missionary Fathers. Indeed, the example of Ireland's 1916 Rising had become part of the mythology of Ibo independence. Conor became active in the Ibo cause, mainly as a propagandist, and flew twice to Biafra during the ensuing civil war. As we now know, Biafra was defeated, but it is probable that the international publicity generated worldwide by friends of the Ibo people may have averted the more terrible consequences of that defeat. It certainly added to Conor's African expertise, but it was a sad time, redeemed for me only by an actual meeting with Chinua Achebe, who, briefly, represented his people in the States.

೧ ೧ ೧

If meeting celebrities had been my aim in life, I could not have chosen a better place to pursue it than on the fringes of the NYU Schweitzer Program. People like John Arden, the playwright, and John Caute, historian and novelist, were capital colleagues and companions. John Arden's Edinburgh Festival play, 'Armstrong's Last Goodnight', was said to have been inspired by Conor's adventures in Katanga. It contained the line, spoken with a heavy Scots accent, 'I deem it unwise that your leman [mistress] should accompany you on a diplomatic mission' – or words to that effect. Arden's ideas of anti-war protest ran to street, or at least barn theatre, and his students loved them. I wrote a poem for one of his displays and called it 'Hatred', I think it is probably a good poem because John was not altogether happy with it. It is equivocal. I read it first in the original Irish aloud to the audience, for the sound's sake, and then translated:

What hatred requires is long vigil and long suffering,
What hatred requires is the blindness and nonrecognition of
patience,
What hatred requires is a steady finger on the catch of the rifle

And do not fire till you see the whites of their eyes, like the whites of eggs, in your sights!

***

In the day when hatred flowers, there will be fighting on street trenches,
And broken glass will be spread before police horses, galloping –
But in the meantime, hatred is a good dressing for a garden
On a sand-bank between two tides, where our women and children are living.

Other names I remember with affection are those of David Erdman, a specialist on William Blake; Jonathan Mirsky, the sinologist; the British Marxist historian EP Thompson; Cal (Robert) Lowell, that wonderful poet; Professor Eugene McCarthy, the presidential candidate who saved the honour of the US Democratic Party; and the lovely Melina Mercouri, film-star and Greek Cabinet Minister for the Arts. There are many, many more and many others, technically not so famous, who became close friends.

Among these, surprisingly because I had admired him, I do not include George Steiner. I found him an intellectual bully and suspected that in debate he played fast and loose with verifiable facts. To crown all, he supported the US government over the Vietnam War. It was he who suggested, with hostile intent, in an article in the *New York Review of Books*, that protestors should withhold their income tax from the US government if they were sincere. 'George,' I said to him, after one of his seminars, also with hostile intent, 'that was a felon-setting article.' He had a 'coniption' fit; 'What does she mean by it?' he kept asking Conor. I think myself he was mainly angry because he had to admit that he was not familiar with the good old eighteenth-century word, 'felon-setting'. We, of course, with many others, had now, once it was put up to us, to refuse to pay our taxes. It is not true that, as is sometimes stated, we broke the law and refused to file returns. We filed them – I know, it was me that made them out! The university then stopped our tax out of Conor's salary, so that our gesture was basically only symbolic.

Our closest and dearest American friends were Tom and Jean Flanagan. Tom will be known to Irish readers as the author of the trilogy of novels that begins with *The Year of the French.* He was the only Irish-American I have ever known whose mindset was that of a native-born Irishman. He was brought up by his grandmother, who was born in Ireland – that must account for it. His knowledge of Ireland, its history and literature, was encyclopaedic, and his understanding of Ireland was fault-less. His wife Jean, a tall, beautiful woman whose forebears had come from Scotland, could and often did contribute a useful independent point of view to the long, happy sessions of wonderful talk that ensued when-ever Tom and Conor met. Jean and Tom had two daughters, Ellen and Kate, who in their teens were, at their own request, received into the Catholic Church during the sabbatical year they spent with their parents in Ireland. I was their godmother. Their father and mother are now gone to their reward. Dear Ellen, dear Kate, should you read this, you should know that not a day passes that Conor and I do not miss them. Even closer friends of the Flanagans than we, were Seamus and Marie Heaney; it was a charmed circle.

ᑕᔆ   ᑕᔆ   ᑕᔆ

In 1965, while we were still in Ghana, Dónal had married, in California, a beautiful American girl, Rita Abel. The Abels were Sephardim and came originally from Spain. Rita, like Dónal, was an Africanist; her main field in that context was communications. The young couple stayed with us in the Mews and filled our house with life again, after Kate's departure to study in London for her A-levels. I now had three adult stepchildren, and I think this is the point where I should sketch in their subsequent lives.

Rita is an intensely life-loving person, and over the years her multifari-ous energies have engaged her in forays into many fascinating pursuits, from politics to restaurant proprietorship. Throughout it all she has re-mained faithful to her original academic insights and ideals and has been deeply concerned with their practical application. Her recent publication, *Trust: releasing the energy to succeed* (John Wiley and Sons Ltd, 2001), epitomises the creative experience of a lifetime. Her family, us, were enor-mously impressed when an entire window of a fashionable London book-shop was recently devoted to a display of this work, presided over by a photograph of its photogenic author. She and Dónal have one beautiful, petite, blonde daughter, Sarah, the eldest of Conor's grandchildren and a graphic artist and advertising expert by profession, who is, at the time of writing, happily engaged to marry in the near future. God bless you, Sarah and Jamie! Dónal is recognised as being one of his generation's profoundest and most humane scholars and teachers in the field of African Studies. His area of expertise is Senegal, where his ready command of French is, of course, an asset. He holds a Chair of Political Science at the School of Oriental and African Studies in London. Some years after Conor and I returned to live permanently in Ireland, Dónal was stricken with multiple sclerosis. At who knows what expenditure of emotional and mental strength, he has contrived not to let this misfortune interfere with his profession, or sour his essentially sunny and gregarious nature. It would be difficult to put into words how dearly all the family loves and admires him.

I think, of all my stepchildren, Fedelma has always been my pet. Kate and I struck sparks off each other, often, if not always, in agreement, but the little, dark-haired, neat-limbed, bright-eyed Fedelma made her way straight into my heart. She is the cement that holds our odd, extended family together: she remembers birthdays. She is immensely competent, while never having lost a certain endearing vulnerability – when she was a little girl, she would not read a book unless she was assured in advance that it had a happy ending. Now she is equal to all the demands of life: she can act as research assistant for her father; she is a wonderful cook and also a seamstress, carpenter, stone-mason and interior decorator, lately, most recently, a manager for Oxfam in Dublin. To the great joy of us all, she married her student sweetheart, Nicholas Simms, a pillar of Ireland's semi-state economy and the son of Archbishop George Simms, who was chaplain in Alexandra when my mother taught there. Nicholas' warm affection and steady common sense have sustained us through innumerable crises, and he and Fedelma have two splendid sons, Mark and Laurence. Mark is an endlessly cheerful environmental scientist, and is also soon to be married to a very sweet-natured girl, Eilís, a highly skilled map-maker whom we all like and respect enormously. Laurence is a Secretary of Embassy in Ireland's Foreign Service, who writes very moving, original, minimalist poems. This is one he wrote for his mother, Fedelma:

She sits there,
with a condensation wrapped glass
that numbs,
legs tucked under
in a self-created nook,
and throne,
in benevolent supervision
of warmly-lit talk.
Above,
to one side,
glorying in the connections
that flow and crackle,
revelling in a smile of family.
One so wise knows
that happiness is fragile.
Now she teaches me
that it can be drawn back
from the dark.

When Kate was a little girl, she knew what people were thinking and she had 'perfect pitch'. She sang effortlessly, like a lark. Perhaps the vessel was of too fine clay to go often unscathed to the well. After a troubled, but by no means an unrelievedly unhappy adolescence, she matured into a successful writer and businesswoman and was happily married. Her husband, Joseph Kearney, was, and is, a free spirit, an intensely rational, alternative-lifestyle advocate. He suited Kate, and steadied her. They had a son, Alexander, now a professional art historian. He and Patrick, our adopted son, became very close; Ali in his Moses basket attended rehearsals for Patrick's First Communion. Kate's promise as a writer was well-known, and ever so many of her contemporaries attested to her skills as an editor, when, out of a clear sky, in her fiftieth year, she was hit by a fatal brain haemorrhage; she never recovered consciousness, but died on the morning of 26 March 1998. That was a long way in the future at the time when we lived in New York and contemplated her A-levels, but sooner or later it had to be written, and perhaps 'sooner' is easier. Conor asked me to write a poem for her when she died, and I add it below in translation:

In Loving Memory of Kate

She swung ever between the tides of neap and spring;
Halftide was unknown to her –
The Irish disguises her,
But if I spoke in English,
Heart could not endure.

Her friends weep for the wealth of her ability
And for her generosity;
Her husband mourns his stormy, tender wife,
Her son his mother –
But what of her mother?
And of her father?
Who will read their grief?

The gap in the little brood –
The other nestlings prostrate –
I draw back from that …
I will remember the lovely little girl –
How she laughed!
Before her weight of talent
Descended on her shoulders.

ೞ ೞ ೞ

I think it was in 1967 that I taught a course on 'The Gaelic Background to Anglo-Irish Literature' on the Queens campus of City College, New York. I was fortunate enough to be able to persuade Liam and Máire de Paor to come and teach it with me. They looked after History and Archaeology, and I coped with language. We were, all three, good friends, and I learnt a great deal very pleasurably, but I mention this experience here because it made it necessary for me to read *Finnegans Wake*, which I did from cover to cover. I was disconcerted to find that it read very like a summary of the course we were giving, not like a parody exactly, simply a bleak summary. It brought home to me a great undertow of unarticulated sadness, of which I was barely aware, beneath the glamour and satisfactions of the New York scene. This would be my life for the rest of my days: I would always be a foreigner; my interests would all be at second-hand.

There was, undoubtedly, a physiological element to this malaise. Conor and I had no natural children, and it was unlikely now that we would have any. I had conceived in Ghana, but the poor little scrap was extra-uterine and, providentially, I lost it. Now, almost without discussion, we knew we wanted to adopt. I remembered a picture, in a propaganda film, of a Vietnamese orphan admiring the reflection of himself in the back of a spoon, in the intervals of eating his porridge, and how I ached to hold him. It turned out not to be possible for us to adopt a Vietnamese baby in the USA, as we were not American citizens. We then went to our local American Catholic Adoption Agency and, when it became clear that we would like to adopt a black child, we were asked was this on the principle that an ocelot would be a more fashionable pet than a cat. Conor was appalled, and we abandoned that project.

When we were back in Ireland on holiday, in the summer of 1968, we told the story to my Uncle Moss, still parish priest of Ballymore Eustace and supremely happy in that beautiful mountain parish. He said, 'If you want to adopt a black child, there's the most beautiful little Ghanaian you ever saw in Saint Patrick's [Mother and Baby Home] on the Navan Road.' We followed his advice, and the baby was our Patrick. At first the nuns, in their saintly worldliness, did not want us to see him. He was not 'looking his best,' they said; he was three months old and had infantile eczema. They wanted him to make a 'good impression'. Finally they relented, and the moment we saw him, we loved him. Conor said, 'I like him. We'll take him.' From then on, I went everyday to nurse him and give him his bottle, and we bonded like super-glue. He loved to see me coming, and I adored him. We had his passport photographs taken and applied to have him put on my passport. It was then that we ran into difficulties.

A baby 'fostered with a view to adoption' cannot, by law, be taken out of the Irish jurisdiction by the prospective adoptive parents until it is a year old. This measure was introduced to put an end to a veritable trade with the USA in white babies for adoption, which resulted in many trage-dies, including the rejection and return to Ireland of many of the little bun-dles of merchandise. My father – Patrick's first name is Seán – and our staunch and constant friend, Paddy Lynch, applied to have our baby made a ward of court, hoping that the court might then overrule the law in our favour. Entirely properly, the court refused. By this time we had brought Patrick home. I had hesitated – I had always distrusted happiness – but his father said, 'He is expecting us to take him out today.'

Fedelma, who is his godmother, met him at *Whitewater*, and the tele-phone never stopped ringing in congratulation. I remember Fedelma de-terminedly stirring fried onions for supper with Patrick under one arm, while I answered the 'phone. Séamus and Jean and their second little girl, Sarah, came out to see the new cousin. Sarah brought him a string of plas-tic ducks for his carry-cot. At the last moment she was reluctant to surren-der them. 'I'm breaking them in for him,' she said. She and her sister lived in Kent, and had ponies. Patrick was mesmerised and never cried once. He learnt immediately what fathers are for: fathers are for throwing you up to the ceiling. He never forgot it.

We now had to consider our practical options. Conor was a tenured professor in New York and that was our livelihood. NYU behaved with immense generosity and gave him compassionate leave until Patrick should be free to travel. Within a matter of weeks the little clinging, spi-dery baby had blossomed into the sturdiest and most beautiful child, a small, bronze image of a grown man, with broad shoulders and narrow hips, splendid physical coordination and a hunger for life. No day passed when we did not thank in our hearts my dear Uncle Moss, the good nuns, the wonderful paediatrician who had picked him out for us and who, ever afterwards, remained a staunch friend, the late Dr Victoria Coffey, and, of course, God, who alone could understand the profundity of our gratitude and our joy. Dr Lettie Fairfield, whose advice throughout was invaluable – as Assistant Chief Medical Officer under the old London County Council, she knew more about fosterage and adoption than probably anyone else in the world – said to Conor, 'I know you don't believe in God, Conor, but at this conjuncture, you will find Him very useful.' While the passport question was still unsettled, I had rung President de Valera's secretary, hoping he might be able to intervene on our behalf; one does things for one's children one would never dream of doing for oneself. He rang back himself almost at once to tell me gently that that was impossible and he added, 'At my age it doesn't do to put off a pleasure, can you bring the little boy to see myself and Sinéad tomorrow?' Of course we could, and the photographs taken at Áras an Uachtaráin on that joyous day keep it forever fresh in our memories.

Conor was not the man to sit idly in *Whitewater* watching his son grow. He became involved again in Irish politics, rejoining the Irish Labour Party, and the rest is history …

CႽ   CႽ   CႽ

The following winter we were approached by the journalist and historian Neil Acherson to know if we could offer a temporary home to a little German family of refugees, whose plight had been making European headlines. We agreed to. Rudi Dutschke was a student left-wing activist who had been shot through the head during a demonstration (against the State visit of the Shah of Persia, that right-wing symbol) and had miraculously survived. His wife was an American Bible scholar and they had a toddler named Ho – not, as you might think, after Ho Chi Minh, but after Hosea, the prophet of peace. They were gently impressive people. Rudi had had to relearn German, by main force of will, after his recovery, and was now laboriously resurrecting the English he had formerly known well. *Whitewater* had, at that time, two ramshackle, do-it-yourself 'sun-porches', gloriously warm in summer and kept habitable in winter by paraffin-oil heaters. Rudi asked to be given some routine domestic task that he could perform everyday without having to devote too much thought to it. We gave him charge of the paraffin stoves, and they functioned efficiently as never before for the length of his stay. Ho now slept in a grown-up bed, and he and Patrick were both 'dawn-wakers'. Every morning, Ho got up and let down the side of Patrick's cot and they both came into our sparsely furnished bedroom, where the telephone lived on the floor, and settled down to get through to Australia. Sometimes they hit the jackpot and muffled curses were heard from the earpiece. We trained ourselves to ignore them; we needed our sleep.

After we returned to America with our year-old Patrick, the Dutschkes stayed on in *Whitewater* with another young couple, an American grand-nephew of Seán MacDermott's and his girlfriend. I am not sure that relations were particularly harmonious from that on. In any event, the poor Dutschkes were soon free to return to Britain, from where they moved to Denmark, where Rudi's second lease of life ran out and he was found dead in his bathtub. They had lived their lives on strict, Christian principles, and there was no unquestioning welcome for them anywhere. At one stage, prior to Rudi's death, the liberal Mayor of Berlin, Willy Brandt, had wanted to adopt little Ho, but Ho's parents wanted to keep him with them through all their journeyings …

ℜ ℜ ℜ

My mother and father came to the airport to see us off to New York for the academic year 1969–70. My mother was a little tearful over Patrick, whom she called 'the flower of the flock' – unprecedented praise from her. The flight was trying: the baby's ears hurt and his eczema flared up. In Kennedy Airport he looked like a little beetroot with a tearful, screwed-up face. It took us two hours to get him through immigration; we had a medical certificate to say he could not be vaccinated because of his skin condition and immigration made heavy weather over it, but I think their main problem was his pigmentation. In those days, all white-collar airport personnel were white; all sky-caps were black. When all three of us finally got through all the barriers, there was a positive queue of porters competing to take our luggage. The winner smiled at us delightedly: 'That's a soul baby you got there,' he said.

When we arrived at Washington Mews, sad news was waiting for us. My much-beloved cleaning-lady, Amelia Williams – whose surname for a long time I thought was 'Weems' – had died. Amelia had shared all our plans to adopt from the beginning and had constantly rearranged all the furniture 'to have things ready for the baby'. 'Never fuss it about its hair,' she advised, and we never did. We missed her terribly, but her husband Phil, a former 'hoofer' with a courtly manner, came in her stead and Patrick loved him. Those were halcyon days. Patrick, as he always did, acquired a harem of babysitters. Two of them were black students of Conor's: the daughter of the Ethiopian Perm. Rep. at the UN and a quiet, studious American girl. The little Ethiopian was a beauty and 'a bold strap', as my mother would have said. She had a crush on a white barman on the famous Eighth Street, just outside our door. She wanted me to lend her Patrick, so that she could walk up and down outside the premises where the man worked, carrying the baby and a placard to read: If You Would Like A Baby Like This, I Can Give You One! When, after some months, Patrick and I followed Conor back to Ireland, where he had gone to fight a general election, these two young ladies stood on the pavement of the Mews, crying and wringing their hands and wailing, 'Come back, Patrick, come back!' while our airport taxi drove away. The taximan turned to me and said, 'I know it's none of my business, Ma'am, but are you sure you are right to take Patrick away from his Mammy like that?' I replied repressively, '*I* am Patrick's Mammy,' and we continued in silence on our way. I have a more tranquil memory of all four of us – the two black girls, Patrick and self – sitting on the floor in our living room in the Mews watching Goldie Hawn on television; needless to say, Patrick loved her.

While our personal lives in New York that year were tranquil, public life was other. This was the year of the murders of Martin Luther King and Bobby Kennedy. We had become very close friends of Leonard Boudin, the great civil rights lawyer, and of his wife and family. Their Sunday morning breakfast table was a good place to gauge tensions. I remember meeting Jessica Mitford there; her barely grown-up daughter was, as we used to say then, even in liberal circles, 'living in sin' with a 'black Panther'. Jessica told how, in a cocktail-party crush, she was confronted by the kind of racist argument that one still frequently heard at that time, the question: 'Would you want your daughter to marry one of them?' The Holy Ghost descended on her and she was able, with absolute truth, to reply, 'Wouldn't I just!' Myself, I was once told by an 'educationist', at a similar party, that 'urbanised black children', from 'south of the Mason and

Dixon', were ineducable. 'Why,' he said 'they say spigot for faucet.' He did not seem to understand, when I told him that *I* said 'tap' for both. The Boudins had two children, a boy and a girl. The boy was quiet and underestimated; the girl was brilliant, the kind of daughter other parents envy you for having. She worked in her father's office, to his great delight, but already a cloud had begun to form: Kathy's devotion to the civil rights cause became fanatical. Not very long after we went back to Ireland, she joined the protest organisation known as The Weathermen, took part in a bank raid in which a man was shot dead, was arrested and is still in prison. I read the other day that her son, who was born before she was imprisoned, is now a Rhodes scholar, and I thanked God that we had not had to bring up our Patrick in the New York of those years, as that other young man's grandparents had had to do their children.

PART III: IRELAND

It was, of course, out of this world when Conor was elected, in June 1969, for the constituency of Dublin North-East, on the first count. Of course, Mr Haughey had headed the poll, but nevertheless! People often ask me how I felt when Conor abandoned the security of a tenured, American professorship for the uncertainties of Irish electoral politics. The answer is that to me it felt entirely natural; I was conditioned to think that all fathers would, if they could, be politicians, that there was no higher calling and that money was a secondary consideration. How hopelessly dated all that seems now! Similarly, when Conor became Minister for Posts and Telegraphs in the coalition government of 1973, while continuing to be Labour Party spokesman on Northern Ireland, I took it for granted that we would have guards. I remembered my mother, with her impeccable good manners, instructing her grandchildren, all at that time sub-teens, on how to address their grandfather's 'plain-clothes' guards: 'Not Guard Duffy. Not Guard Dolan. *Mister* Duffy. *Mister* Dolan.' Conor's guards became our friends, and we called them by their first names – polite forms of address change with the passage of time – but the principle was the same: they did not take orders from us. I met one of them not so long ago and he said to me, 'Tell us, what became of that rabbit?' Conor had been reading *Watership Down* to Patrick and Margaret when this guard last knew us.

ℙ ℙ ℙ

Even more wonderful than the election victory was the arrival among us of our Margaret, named for her grandmother and, perhaps a little bit, for the 'best friend' of my youth. Like many second babies, she could have chosen her moment at a more convenient time. My mother was seriously ill in hospital; my nephew, Barbara's son, Maurice, who had been living with us, was seriously ill in hospital; I myself was about to go into hospital for a fairly serious gynaecological operation. The telephone rang, it was Saint Patrick's. 'We have a sister for Patrick,' they said. I said to Conor, 'They say they have a sister for Patrick.' 'Tell them,' he replied, 'that we'll come and take her home tomorrow.' Fedelma, by now Mrs Simms, came with us. Conor remained in the parlour with the Reverend Mother while Fedelma and I went to collect Margaret – part-Irish and part-Zambian, born in Ireland. She was warm, glowing and velvety, like a lovely dark rose. When they put her into my arms I felt the shock of an encounter with a formidable intelligence; that impression has never changed. It was as if I had always held her close, and as if she knew she had found her rightful place. We brought her back to the parlour; the Reverend Mother said, 'That child is fostered already.' She was just eight months old. She fluttered her long lashes at her father and he became her devoted slave. When we got home, Mrs Bridie MacCarthy, from the caravan across the road, where she and her young husband lived on their family's land, was waiting for us with her two children and our Patrick. Patrick, unprompted, put his little arms above his head and danced for his sister. I thought, 'Like David before the Ark of the Covenant, only fully clad!'

Bridie MacCarthy was a Wexford girl from Bunclody, married into a 'Hill' family in Howth. Her husband was a fisherman. Once when, in the very early morning, he was out alone in a small boat lifting lobsters, he had seen a fox crawl on its belly down the sloping cliff below the light-house to steal seagulls' eggs from their nests.

CB   CB   CB

Before Margaret came, Patrick and I had spent an autumn in Dunquin. We had gone down in August with Conor for a short break, and it was at the time when the protest over the closing of the Dunquin school was at its height. The organisers came to me and asked would I stay on and teach when they reopened the school in September, until they could employ a professional headmaster. As I had my Leaving Cert., I was qualified to teach children under the age of twelve without any other special training. Conor very generously consented to the plan, and I stayed. The older children were taught by Máire Feiritéar, the daughter-in-law of my dear friend, Bab, and she was a proper teacher. I loved every moment of those months and wrote probably my two best poems as a result: 'Codladh an Ghaiscígh' (The Hero's Sleep), for Patrick, and 'Maireann an tSeana-mhuintir' (The Old Generation Lives On), for all my pupils. We stretched a point and put Patrick's name on the roll, for the record, although he was only two. That school, under the brilliantly gifted headmaster we ultimately found to take over, Mícheál Ó Dúláine, has gone from strength to strength. Dunquin people from all over Ireland send their children back home to school there, to learn that they are 'no mean people', but the custodians of a great memory …

Patrick and Margaret know Irish well, but the world in which I grew up Irish-speaking was not theirs. I hope we gave them access to it, as we did to religion and music – I know they are proud of their mother's poetry, as they are of their father's politics, and this is a great happiness.

CB   CB   CB

These were the years of 'Free Derry', the Defence of Saint Matthew's (in Belfast), civil rights marches, the Arms Trial, internment without trial in the North, Bloody Sunday and the burning of the British Embassy in Merrion Square, Sunningdale, the Ulster Workers' Council strike, the murder of the

British Ambassador, Christopher Ewart Biggs and, of course, the controversy over 'Section 31', which is what most people remember about Conor's time as a hands-on politician. It is clear that the common factor in all these events is the situation in Northern Ireland. The evolution of Conor's views on this topic is entirely in the public domain and he himself has always been prepared to analyse and discuss those views openly. In his *Memoir* he defines the 'unionism' in which his evolving stance on the North involved him:

> 'I didn't feel myself so much to be a Friend of the Union as a friend of the unionist people of Northern Ireland, and a person determined to associate with them in support of their determination not to be pushed in a direction in which they didn't want to go ... [of their right] not to be pushed around or conned ...
>
> I did, however, have some qualms about associating with either of the unionist parties then existing. Both had strong sectarian associations and habits of sectarian rhetoric. I found all that both uncongenial and compromising to the cause of the Union.'

It will be remembered that, for eight years, he held down the spokesmanship of the Labour Party on Northern Ireland and fought off many challenges from IRA sympathisers. Further, by virtue of being the minister responsible to Mr Cosgrave for the Government Bureau of Information, he was also virtually government spokesman on the North during those years. What Conor maintained today, the rank-and-file would espouse tomorrow; the trouble was that his reasoning always ran those twenty-four hours ahead of the consensus. So it was not until 1995 that he found his niche in active Northern politics when, in the summer of that year, as he tells it, 'a formidable non-sectarian unionist, with no Thatcherite baggage, Bob McCartney, asked for my help and got it.'

This was an extraordinarily happy conjuncture not only for Conor but for me. Maureen McCartney and I knew each other as kindred spirits immediately, not least because we were two women of independent mind who were married to two dearly-loved husbands, both of whom could be impatient of wifely criticism. In such a friendship you realise, with delight and surprise, both how much the friends have in common and how little the areas where they differ can affect the positive affections that bind them. Where Bob and Conor are concerned, I think they have no areas of disagreement at all – or none that they will admit to.

Another family friendship of an almost organic kind resulted from Conor's years as spokesman on and for the North. The Head of the Government Bureau of Information when Conor was in government was Muiris MacConghaíl, whose wife was the daughter of that Neasa who, as Antigone, burnt her beauty into an entire generation. They brought up their brilliantly successful family of five Irish-speaking, but with no hostility towards Britain. I don't think Patrick and Margaret ever felt too much put-upon by ancestral loyalties, but insofar as they might have, the young MacConghaíls redressed the balance. If to be good at Irish was to accept membership of an élite, Patrick and Margaret had no qualms about accepting. Máire Mhac Conghaíl has for years now acted as an amateur research assistant for me in this book as in almost everything else I have written in my middle-age. She is about Dónal's age, a trained genealogist, a wonderful cook and a gentle version of her mother's beauty. Muiris is the son of the great painter Maurice MacGonigal; coming down to Earth is not always easy for him.

ા ા ા

Back in 1970 Conor and his friend Jack Dowling (of RTÉ fame) witnessed the 'defence' of Saint Matthew's Church, which I list above. The church stood in a small Catholic enclave on the Newtonards Road; the attackers were from the surrounding Protestant housing estates. They were armed with torn-up paving-stones and torn-down iron railings. Two of them were shot down by IRA marksmen from the church tower before the British Army moved in to defend the building, to the general relief of bystanders. I think that, at the time, almost all southern nationalist opinion reacted to the events in terms of 'we' and 'they': 'we' being the marksmen and 'they' the thugs. Catholics and nationalists could not help feeling smug, and, indeed, did not try very hard not to. Then my father wrote to *The Irish Times*; I quote from memory: 'I see no cause for rejoicing that

Irishmen, once again, are killing other Irishmen on the streets of Belfast.' I vowed that I would never again allow Northern differences to become polarised as 'we' and 'they' in my mind.

This brings me to my own reaction to Conor's unionist position in regard to Northern Ireland. I support him absolutely in it; it is, for him, a matter of conscience. I would not myself have had the courage or the persistence to do the same, nor would I be entirely honest were I to do so. Poets have difficulty shedding the picturesque, and I, who am not only a poet but a pacifist – a form of chickening out – still have difficulty abandoning the luxury of old conflicts. It is Plato's dilemma; poets are troublemakers. In principle I am against the use of force in all circumstances, but I cannot help being glad that a sufficient number of my fellow human beings disagree with me to provide a constant flow of those adventure stories, from Stevenson's *Kidnapped* to Dick Francis, which are my preferred recreational reading. I do most strongly hold that in going the whole way politically to defend the human right of our Northern fellow-Irish, who wish also, or primarily, to think of themselves as British, not to be bullied or conned, Conor has rendered a signal service to both communities on this island. He has shown that a basic belief in the primacy of justice can transcend even the most cherished tribal values ...

CB   CB   CB

In these years also my parents died and my children grew into their teens, fulfilling all the promise of their baby years. My mother died in September 1976; she was progressively weakened by cancer of the bloodstream and slipped quietly away, just as her doctors were contemplating a radical treatment, one they would not have tried normally on someone her age. 'Your mother's quality of life,' they said to us, 'is such that we feel we owe it to her.' She did not wait for it.

The day before she died I brought the children in to the hospital to see her, and it was a very happy visit. As we were leaving, we met the patients' tea-trollies in the corridor. 'I think,' said Patrick, 'that Grandma would want me to eat that toast.' I wish I had let him have it because, of course, he was right ... The next day I brought himself and Margaret into town again, this time on the bus, to do our back-to-school shopping in Easons. As I stood on the pavement outside afterwards, I felt a frightening compulsion pushing and dragging me towards the Mater Hospital; I called up all my reason to fight it down and I took the children home. It was while I stood there in O'Connell Street, indecisive, that my mother died quietly, sitting up in an armchair, having her tea with my father and Barbara. Séamus was out on his motorbike looking for me. This is a lasting regret, which I wrote about in my poem, '*Bás mo Mháthar*', on her death.

All during her time in hospital, every evening, my father drove himself over from Booterstown to see my mother and would sit with her until I came to say goodnight to her at about nine o'clock. Her greeting to me was always, 'You're very early. Does your father have to go now?' They were like lovebirds; he held her hand and called her, 'my lovely girl'. After her death *my* fantastic Margaret, who had taught herself to read and write in nursery school, wrote him this letter:

Dear Granda,

I am sorry I did not go to Grandma's funeral, but I do not like funerals. However I will go to yours.

Love, Margaret

He kept the letter in his pocket-book until it fell to pieces …

છ છ છ

Shortly before that, Barbara's gentle, handsome husband, poor Frank Biggar, died of smoking, of lung cancer. The last time I saw him in hospital he knew there was no hope. He said to me, 'Don't grieve too much. Ours was a good marriage.' Afterwards, more than ever, Barbara and her children became part of our family, most particularly Maurice, her second youngest, who had followed his eldest brother, John, into Foreign Affairs and for whom *Whitewater* has always been, in some sense, home while his parents lived abroad. Maurice was staying with us when Mr

Cosgrave and Mr Corish were forming their coalition government. When the telephone rang that afternoon and Conor got up to answer it, Maurice, anticipating correctly who the call would be from, said, 'Tell them, Uncle Conor, that I will accept a parliamentary secretaryship, if offered.' He was and is very witty and always great company.

ℤ ℤ ℤ

My father lived to the great age of ninety-four, full of years and honours. At that point his kidneys began to fail and he was taken into the Mater Hospital for dialysis. It was tacitly assumed that his stay there would be a long one; they reckoned without my father. When I was visiting him one day, he said to me, 'Tell Dr Alton that, when he comes to see me, he is not just to pop in and pop out. I have something important to discuss with him.' I gave the message to Brian Alton; what my father wanted was to go home 'to die in my own bed among your mother's things.' He got his way and on 12 January 1984, he died. He remained almost fully conscious to the end. Barbara's tall, handsome, second boy, Frank, lent his young strength to the nurses to lift his grandfather and stayed by him day and night.

Almost the last person my father spoke to was Patrick. I was saying goodbye to him one evening before going back to *Whitewater* for supper with Conor and the children. My father asked, rather testily, 'Will you have to cook for them when you get back?' He and my mother, having presided over my expensive education, always somewhat resented my domesticity. I told him, no; Patrick would put a stew in the oven. The next day I took the children with me to see him. He opened his eyes and recognised them. 'Patrick,' he said, 'how was the stew?'

The children adored him. Margaret – who never wept unless it was for some overwhelming reason – cried all night when he died. She had visited him on the day she was confirmed, a tall, graceful thirteen-year-old in an elegant, white, grown-up costume with a broad white hat. 'Margaret,' he said to her, 'you look so pretty. And so holy! I suppose now you will want to be a nun?' 'No, Granda,' she had answered, 'but I might like to be a priest.'

There was 'an army presence', as the officer who contacted me in the matter phrased it, at my father's funeral. We were honoured. On the evening before, when he was taken to the church, the house was 'open'. It poured rain outside and his old comrades, from all stages of his career, who came to pay their respects were glad of their cup of tea – we had been advised by the undertakers that stronger refreshments might be counterproductive. When the time came for the hearse to leave the house, the workers from his old constituency, the South Dublin Townships, lined up along the seafront at Trimleston Avenue, outside the last house he lived in (a final move), under the still relentless downpour, to form a guard of honour. The next day at Glasnevin Cemetery there was another, unofficial honour party waiting, this time made up of medal-wearing War of Independence veterans, some from as far north as Louth, under the command of our near neighbour on the Hill of Howth, one of the last people ever to farm there, the patriarch, 'Pop' O'Rourke.

The formal contribution of the State's forces was, as you would expect, superb. Barbara and I with the grandchildren, and Conor with Garret FitzGerald, now Taoiseach, and his ministerial colleagues walked behind the hearse and its military escort, between files of soldiers presenting arms. Behind us came Mr Haughey and his front bench. Our Séamus, who had set out from Gravesend in Kent, where he lived alone, turned back and never made it. He was too overcome by conflicting emotions to travel.

When we gathered at the graveside, I am told by my father's grandchildren that the Soldiers of Destiny, on the opposite side, looked complacent. As my father was not a serving soldier when he died, we did not have 'The Last Post' played, and I think that Mr Haughey's Fianna Fáil believed he would be buried without any specific acknowledgement of his political and republican past. They were wrong. When he died, I immediately contacted Jack Lynch and asked him if he would honour us by speaking the funeral oration at the grave. He accepted at once, and added a warning, 'Tell no one, not even the undertaker.' As you might expect, Daddy's undertaker was a Fianna Fáil supporter. Now, like the hurler that he was, 'coming out of the sun', the 'real Taoiseach' appeared from nowhere and began to speak. He spoke beautifully, remembering also my mother and my Uncle Paddy, who were buried in the grave where we had laid my father. Again the grandchildren are my source; I am told that Mr Haughey turned beetroot red.

It was especially fitting that the Taoiseach who walked in my father's funeral procession should have been Garret FitzGerald, my mother's godson. Garret was the only politician, other than Conor, that my father asked to see when he was dying. It was to tell him how deeply my father regretted the Civil War, though not that he was ashamed of his part therein, and also how proud my mother had always been of her godson …

Cʒ   Cʒ   Cʒ

Once, at a Labour Party Conference, I said in the corridors, 'Behind every liberated woman is another woman doing the dishes.' I am not sure how liberated I am, but I am vividly conscious of what I owe to the domestic help I have had since I got married. The reader has already met Bridie and Amelia. When Patrick first came to us we had Mrs Reid, a veritable Mother Courage, whose love of Patrick was such that, after we had left for America and when she herself was dying, she made her daughters, Breda and Nuala, promise that they would always look after him for me. Coincidentally, their sister, Patricia, had reared Conor's first family. Then there was Mrs Evelyn O'Riordan, a neighbour with a sparkling personality and many, many talents. After I had been seriously injured in a car accident, she took over my household and ran it for a year. Her children grew up with mine, and one of my most cherished memories is listening to her son Paul, aged about ten, who had the most wonderful boy's singing voice, delivering 'Rhinestone Cowboy' and 'By the Rivers of Babylon' in a concert in our kitchen, which my pair and a troop of their pals had organised.

Today we have Mrs Eileen O'Shea. Eileen is from Howth and is married to a Kerryman – the best of all worlds. Her youth and strength and cheerfulness, her endless capacity for generosity and fun, brighten our house five mornings a week and, much as we value her practical help, it is her company and friendship that keep these two old people going. Our sincerest thanks go to all these ladies, who all in their different ways have made our less-than-predictable Irish lifestyle so amazingly plausible.

PART IV:
JOURNALISM, BOOKS AND TRAVEL

When, in June 1977, Conor lost his seat, his devoted personal assistant, Kitty Quinn, said to me that she could hardly understand how the buses could go on running. This reaction reflected accurately my own sense of shock. It did not take us long, however, to come to see Conor's departure from Irish electoral politics as essentially beneficial to him. He was now free to mine half a lifetime's experience of how the world is run to fuel his chief and abiding vocation, that of a political philosopher, historian and commentator who wrote like an angel. During this period, as Editor-in-Chief of the *Observer* newspaper in London, he initiated his use of the newspaper column as a literary medium and turned it, as one of his admirers has put it, 'into an art form'. In 1980, when Conor was voted Granada TV's Columnist of the Year, the citation read: 'Dr O'Brien has done as much as anyone to restore wit and elegance – yes and irreverence too – to the British press'. Unfortunately for our long-term economic prospects, we could never get the Irish Revenue Commissioners to see his at least one thousand newspaper columns in anything like this favourable light! Not that we didn't try. Just now, after the election disappointment, it so happened that the Editorship-in-Chief kept the wolf from our door very nicely.

All this time our family would not have been viable without Conor's succession of invaluable personal assistants. Before Kitty, who 'minds' us to this day, there was Miss Corringham, who came of a long-established, Dublin, Protestant (Methodist) family. When she came to us she had re-tired from Siberry's, the celebrated tailoring firm, where she had been their accountant. When our finances, or lack of finances, became too complicated, she simply had all incoming cheques endorsed by Conor and paid them into her own bank account so that she could carry on on our behalf until the current crisis was resolved. In 1916 her father and uncle had owned a newsagent's and tobacconist's shop in the basement of Liberty Hall, and her poor uncle, caught in crossfire, had been killed. Her maternal uncle, Mr Codling, had been Conor's first boss in the Irish civil service, in Finance, before Conor transferred to External Affairs. Mr Codling is credited with this rebuke to Conor, delivered in a strong North of England accent, 'It is a mis-taa-ke *almost* anyone might have made.' I was with Miss Corringham in hospital just before she died. The young clergyman from her church in Sutton was with her, and held her in his arms; no son could have been more loving. After her death, I went to the Methodist service of thanksgiving for her life and for long afterwards I felt her loss.

⚃ ⚃ ⚃

As for me, I did not in fact see all that much of London during Conor's time with the *Observer*. Conor commuted to and from home and I stayed on at *Whitewater* with Patrick and Margaret, who now went to the Gaelscoil in Harmonstown, Scoil Neasáin. In November 1978 I was driving them to school along Thormanby Road, towards Sutton, when, somewhere about Somali village, a car coming from the opposite direction seems to have driven, possibly dazzled by the horizontal winter sunlight, straight into the right-hand wing of my little Renault and folded it over on my right leg. I deduce this from what I have been told; I have no independent memory of what happened, only disjointed fragments, such as the voice of the fireman who cut me out of the wreckage. Margaret's account goes, 'You said "Jesus!" Mammy, and I passed out.' The children were cut about the face and head. Patrick still carries the scars, just below the hairline, and also suffered a greenstick fracture of his arm. A 'foreign body' – of which she used to be very proud – lodged under Margaret's jaw, where, thankfully, it is not visible. My femur was shattered in thirty or more pieces and for a long time I was delirious and in intensive care. It was at this point that Evelyn O'Riordan stepped in and took over the management of *Whitewater* and the children, earning our undying gratitude.

My delirium was quite interesting: I thought I was travelling on the Trans-Siberian railway and had to speak French; I also thought that Conor was going to marry a Japanese lady and I was unhappy about it. Poor Conor had been in Japan on *Observer* business when he got news of the accident, and came home at once, almost mad with worry, which the delusions didn't help. Suddenly, on Christmas Eve, I snapped out of them, and we had a wonderful Christmas in the empty ward with Conor and the children, Kate and Fedelma and smoked salmon and champagne and a Christmas Tree! – all the other patients had been sent home. For all of that, I had to stay in hospital till the following April, and the children were miserable. My clever Patrick, one morning, rang the local hackney cab, where we had an account, and came in to visit me on his own; it was wonderful. Another time my surgeon, with his students on his rounds, found both Patrick and Margaret in the bed with their Mammy, one on each side: Patrick wasn't quite ten and she wasn't quite eight. When I got home at last their helpfulness was extraordinary; I was still bedridden for many more months and wheelchair-bound, and no nurse could have been more loving, or more efficient than those two small people. God love and bless!

Getting back to normal was not easy, but, by great good luck, a rather 'grand' day-school near us needed an Irish teacher for the junior classes and the nine-to-five job did the trick. My Patrick said hopefully, 'If you have any trouble, Mammy, I'll put manners on them for you.' I didn't have any trouble, and if any of my old pupils read this I want them to know that teaching them was great, and that I often think of them fondly. I made good friends too among the staff, notably Douglas and Mary Sealy and Madge O'Neill. Douglas Sealy is the nephew of our first President, Dr Douglas Hyde, and his wife Mary is a cousin of Conor's son-in-law, Nicholas Simms. Douglas taught Irish to the senior classes and Mary was the form mistress of one of the junior classes to which I taught Irish. I could not have had kinder or more understanding colleagues, although I suspect that Douglas sometimes deprecated my enthusiasms. Madge is the wife of our learned and genial Presbyterian pastor that was, here in Howth. They are both retired now and are our very near neighbours. Everybody knows Mrs O'Neill and her family. She and I frequently discuss husbands, grandchildren and religion. She has an ear and a helping hand for everyone.

∽ ∽ ∽

There was another happening which, in the spring of 1980, gave my convalescence a great boost. Conor was invited to visit the Soviet Union in his editorial capacity at the *Observer,* and I went with him. It was the Brezhnev era and metropolitan Russia was exactly as you would expect it to be from Western accounts: gloomy, mistrustful, self-absorbed, but superbly centrally-heated and efficiently warmly-clad. The outlying states were another story altogether. In Georgia, the quality of life was sparkling; Tiflis was like a Mediterranean city, with parading crowds of holiday-makers, and cafés and ice-cream parlours shining with cleanliness and colour. In the hotel there, our first evening, there was a huge family party – at least four generations, from high-chairs to ancestors. Waiters went around with trollies (plural) piled with bottles of champagne; Georgia supplied the entire Soviet Union with champagne, but made sure to keep the best for domestic consumption. Enormous Georgian gentlemen would stretch out large hands, fingered like sausages, and seize as many as four bottles at a time.

Russia's war in Afghanistan was in progress and we visited the border state of Tajikistan. At night, from the crest of the mountain range that marks the Afghan border, you can look towards Afghanistan and all will be dark; look backwards to from where you came and you will see a city, blazing with light. The Tajiks are Moslems, and it certainly seemed to us as if the Central Government had achieved a benign symbiosis between the local religious culture and 'enlightenment'. Everywhere the mosques were crowded with men, but the women went unveiled and held positions of considerable status. Persian is the classical language of Tajikistan, and, among the writers and academics who received us with unaffected pleasure, there were many women. The local Moscow representative was flippant and handsome, like any British or Roman proconsul. He took us for a drive towards the border: the mountain villages were like an illustration from a child's geography book; old men sat in the sun outside tea-shops, on iron bedsteads with string stretchers, and smoked their water-pipes; children, goats and donkeys wandered freely; 'I like donkeys,' said the pro-consul expertly avoiding one. It was a scene of frugal peace, interrupted only rarely by the passage of troop-lorries for the front. No one tried to propagandise us about the war. 'The Afghan is his own man,' said the pro-consul.

Our interpreter was a young and entertaining journalist, and on long airplane journeys he told me the plots of popular, Soviet, *avant-garde* movies. One of these was a musical about a mountain airplane pilot who flew essential missions from valley to valley in the Caucases – wonderful scenery for the camera. Sometimes the pilot – a Walter Mitty character – got snowed in. His theme-song still runs in my head:

Dlya Kovoto prosto
Lyotnaya pagoda –
Dlya menya konyets lyubvi …

For whoever other
Simply flying weather –
But for me the end of love …

ᘓ   ᘓ   ᘓ

When Conor was appointed Editor-in-Chief, in 1977, the *Observer* had already been sold to its American owner by the Observer Trust, the successors to the Astor family, in the person of the celebrated and charming, left-of-centre liberal, David Astor. Conor was to give the paper 'tone', which he undoubtedly did, but also to fire-screen the executive editor, Donald Trelford, from the possible foibles of the new millionaire owner. In this he was, initially, fairly successful, and had Robert Anderson (the owner) been someone of the calibre of Frank Aiken, it might have worked for longer, but what Anderson wanted was a courtier rather than an independent counsellor, and the relationship soured. In 1981, Conor 'for family reasons [me] asked to be relieved of his duties …' I was still very lame and tired easily and was profoundly pleased to have him back. It is also true that any other explanation would have hurt the paper and the careers of many of its Board and staff, including Conor himself. He continued as a regular contributor, with the title of Consultant Editor, and had a seat on the Board. Then, in the winter of that year and in a fit of pique, Anderson sold the paper to Tiny Rowland, a powerful Rhodesian businessman with a dubious reputation for ruthlessness. David Astor and likeminded *Observer* Board members, including Conor, fought the sale before the Monopolies Commission, but were defeated. As Conor said afterwards, 'I had testified ... that [Tiny] Rowland was an unsuitable person to own the *Observer*, Rowland ... decided – naturally enough – that I was an unsuitable person to write for the *Observer*.' *Finis*.

Cʒ   Cʒ   Cʒ

How to draw the threads of the years that followed together and achieve a closure? Perhaps I could attempt a tabular form? Thanks to, among other things, brilliant negotiation by Conor's literary agent as also our dear mutual friend, Elaine Greene, it was now entirely possible for Conor to earn his living by writing, and this was further facilitated by many generous offers of research fellowships and visiting professorships at American universities.

1982

Conor conceives the project of a 'short' book on the Middle East, arising out of his journalistic visits to Israel and discussions with the *Observer*'s Middle East correspondents. It grew into a volume of eight hundred pages, *The Siege* (published 1986), 'the best book about Israel written by a goy'. While the book is evolving I go with him to Jerusalem on one occasion. There, we stay in the Mishkenot Sha'ananim, the almshouses built by Sir Moses Montefiori more than one hundred years ago to accommodate pious Jews who wished to die in Jerusalem. In our little dwelling, looking straight across the valley to the Old City, there is separate kitchenware for milk and meat, and I feel guilty that I have not been brought up to keep a Kosher house. Israelis are, I find, very helpful, but their help can be abrasive. I ask the receptionist one day can she tell me where to find a dry-cleaner's. 'What,' she queries, 'do you want a dry-cleaner's for?' I tell her, food has been spilt on my best blouse. 'Show it to me,' she says. Like a fool, I do just that. 'It is not silk,' she pronounces, 'it will wash.' 'I have no iron,' I object. 'I will put a board and an iron in your room,' she offers. I haven't the courage to say, 'I hate ironing and I'm on my holidays.' It is worse than living in France, where, when people are at their most obstructive, they call you, '*Ma pauvre dame*' (my poor lady), with malice.

1984–85

Montgomery Fellowship at Dartmouth College – Ivy League – Hanover, New Hampshire, on the Canadian border. Town and campus are like an eighteenth-century film-set; lily-white (racially). Three enormous, Wagnerian cleaning ladies, white, storm like Valkyries through our grace-and-favour dwelling every morning at seven o'clock, destroying sleep, until I plead to have their services removed. Patrick drops out of Hanover High School, twice, because he can't stomach the way they teach American history! Margaret achieves highest possible grades and loving comments in her end-of-year report, even from the misogynist maths master who puts the girls at the back of his class: 'I shall miss that calm, philosophic presence ...'. I work the wonderful inter-library loan system to get some research done on my own account on the wizard Earl Gerald of Desmond, who fascinated my childhood, and also teach some Irish to a very promising student, Julie Mundt – no Irish connection. Conor continues researching and writing *The Siege*.

1986

Conor commissioned by *Atlantic Monthly* to visit Nicaragua and report on the Sandinista régime; his six-week stay results in the essay, 'God and Man in Nicaragua' (*Atlantic Monthly*, August 1986; reprinted in *Passion and Cunning*, 1988). I am enchanted by Nicaragua, for me it is science fiction *couleur de rose*: a nationalist government that is both left-wing revolutionary and Christian – three priests are Cabinet ministers: Monsignor Miguel d'Escoto, Foreign Affairs; Fathers Ernesto and Fernando Cardenal, two brothers, Culture and Education respectively. Thanks to introductions from Bishop Eamonn Casey of Galway, who knows Central America well, we meet Father César Jérez, the Jesuit Head of the University of Managua, a well-built, handsome man with an urbane conversational ability and a humane smile; he wears the *guayabera*, the Nicaraguan dress-shirt, made of fine cotton with *broderie anglaise* eyelets, cool and comfortable. Make mental note to buy one for Conor and do. Through César – as with my uncles long ago, we are rapidly on first-name terms – we meet the Minister of Education, who presents us with a copy of his brother's poems. It is hallucinating: he could be either Moss, or Paddy – same spare frame, same cultural background, same total social ease, same good manners, same common sense, same lack of affectation. We do not meet Monsignor d'Escoto, the Foreign Minister, but when Conor's article appears, d'Escoto buys copies of the *Atlantic Monthly* by the dozen and has them distributed through all the Nicaraguan diplomatic and consular missions.

It is in Nicaragua, too, that we first meet our firm friend and our indispensable ally on this journey, Ana Carrigan. Ana is half-Colombian, half-Irish, and is a journalist and *cineaste*. We set out together to cross, by car, to the Atlantic coast; Ana's cradle Spanish is an undreamed-of asset, her dashing style of driving a constant threat. We lose our way, run out of petrol in the forest and appeal for help from a tiny village – of charcoal-burners, I think. They direct us to the nearest military camp and give us a handsome boy of about thirteen to be our guide; he tells us his name is Stalin! All the soldiers in the camp are teenagers doing their *servico militar patriotico*, and they fill our tank for us *for free!* They say they realise we are 'friends of Nicaragua'. Then Stalin puts us back on the right road for Bluefields on the coast; he refuses any reward until we tell him that the money is for his education, to buy books, at which point he accepts with dignity and thanks. Bluefields is *en fête*, it is carnival time. Here the people are of Caribbean origin and speak English. One winning little black girl, carrying her ballet-shoes, asks us, 'Is it true that the Queen and the Princesses (*sic*) are up for Reagan?' We reassure her that it is not so; it is all part of the fairy-tale haze through which I cannot help seeing this small, poor, brave country, standing up so gamely to the giant United States, although I know it is only a matter of miles to the north where the *contras* – CIA-officered – are razing villages and murdering young, foreign, Christian, left-wing enthusiasts, including Americans, who have come to teach in schools, work in hospitals, or harvest the coffee.

1986

Conor and Patrick leave for South Africa at the invitation of the University of Cape Town; Fedelma, Kate and Dónal's Rita are distressed that his father is taking 'little Patrick' on such a dangerous journey. Conor is breaking the academic boycott of South Africa urged at that time: he cannot accept a boycott on ideas, since he sees any such as essentially injurious to the liberation of the black majority. Patrick knows how to make himself useful – tickets, money, appointments, bags; it is the making of him. He goes away a charming boy and comes back a serious young man. After I leave them to the airport, I drive back into the centre of town; I am about to get an unexpected insight into the troubles they will run into. I go into a hotel bar, near where I have parked the car, for a sandwich and a glass of red wine, an early lunch before doing my shopping and collecting Margaret from school. At the far end of the lounge there is a bay of tall windows and in it a group of people are having a late-morning coffee. I am hidden from them by a potted palm or whatnot, but I can hear them. Two of them I think I recognise, from their voices, both are active in anti-apartheid circles, and one, a journalist, has clashed frequently with Conor on republican issues. They are gleeful; they have contacted their friends in South Africa and arranged for Conor to get a hot reception there.

I slip out unnoticed, without actually identifying anyone by sight, but by the time I have contacted my menfolk in Cape Town the 'hot reception' has begun and my news is old hat. Conor's lectures are being threatened, and are finally broken up by rioters, some of whom carry placards in set terms supporting the IRA. Far more important than the identity of our enemies on this occasion is the identity of our friends, in particular Professor David Welsh, Head of the Department of Political Studies at the University of Cape Town (subsequently an advisor to the first post-apartheid South African government), and his wife Virginia, a distinguished demographer and one of the first to assess the perils of AIDS on the African continent. The support of people like these turns the attacks by the protestors into a moral victory for Conor. Conor and Patrick, in tandem, write up the trip for the *New Republic*.

1987

Williams College, Williamstown, Western Massachusetts; rural Ivy League again; filmic period surroundings again. Margaret says, 'When you've seen one rural, Ivy League, American university, you've seen the lot. And they're all dumps!' She is an urban child, but Conor and I like it here. I find another bright student to tutor in Irish. Conor lectures at Harvard and writes, *God Land: Reflections on Religion and Nationalism* (Harvard University Press, 1988).

1988–89

University of Pennsylvania, Philadelphia. We arrive with no money except a very large dollar cheque – prize-money my poetry has won from the Éire/Ireland people. The cheque is so large no bank will cash it, and Conor won't be paid till the end of the month! Eventually we find the daughter of an American benefactor, who works in a bank. It is away out in the sticks, which obliges Margaret and me to take a taxi there and the driver has to wait for his money. This time I have teaching duties as well as Conor; I teach my old staple, 'Gaelic Background to Anglo-Irish Literature', and two Irish classes, one advanced, in the Folklore Department. I have enthusiastic students and Julie Mundt, from Dartmouth, joins them. At the end of the year my students, to my complete surprise, present me with a silver Paul Revere bowl.

Philadelphia is not a friendly city, but our next-door neighbour, Jean Haskell, on the lovely little street of 'row-houses' we inhabit, proves a pearl beyond price and a friend for life. A wonderful knee-doctor gives me steroid injections for my arthritic knee (triggered by the accident) and I have a pain-free year. Fedelma and Nicholas bring their boys to see us and we tour the revolutionary war battlefields. Conor researches and writes *The Great Melody* (published 1992), his life of Edmund Burke and my favourite among his books. Patrick and Margaret, both now at university in Ireland, join us for Christmas, bringing smoked salmon and champagne – highly sophisticated! We invite Jean-from-next-door to a Christmas breakfast. We don't have television, but Jean does, and Margaret watches the Olympic games in her house and is heartbroken when Ben Johnson tests positive for drugs.

1991

The Wilson Centre, Washington DC. Living conditions very cramped, a studio-apartment with bathroom and kitchenette; Conor still absorbed in Burke. Patrick is in Washington also; he has got an internship in Bill Clinton's pre-election think-tank. We find him a single-bed *gîte* in the same apartment building as ourselves. He is not able to stay long enough, alas!, to take part in the actual campaign because he has also been offered a *stagiaireship* in Brussels and feels he cannot let down his sponsors. Brussels turns out very much an anti-climax, but Patrick sees a great deal of Eastern Europe. Our building in Washington is refreshing, many of the tenants are middle-class blacks; a little black boy comes up to me in the supermarket and says, 'You know me, Ma'am, I live in your building.' The check-out clerk says, 'I love your accent.' I work in the Library of Congress on the Rinuccini papers, with a view to the Ferriter book. When Patrick and I have lunch in a fashionable restaurant on the banks of the Potomac, we realise that he is taken for my toy-boy!

1993–95

The National Research Centre for the Humanities in North Carolina, probably our pleasantest stay ever in the United States. The Centre is a purpose-built research foundation in the Research Triangle Park, so-called because it is bounded on three sides by university campuses: Duke, Chapel Hill and the University of North Carolina. I am given library privileges and really get to advance the Ferriter book. Conor works on his book on Thomas Jefferson, falling more and more out of love with his subject at each page. Piles and piles of the writings of the 'Founding Fathers' arrive on his desk, some with the pages uncut! The countryside is beautiful, alive in season with dogwood and other flowering trees. The southern citizenry are cordially friendly, that is, once you get over the shock of the pick-up trucks, painted in jewel-bright colours and with several guns in gun-racks on the back! They are driven by long-haired, backwoods types wearing broad, shady hats and boots with pointed toes. People make jokes and love to chat: a liquor-store clerk says to me, 'I caint sell to you, Ma'am, you're too young!' – he makes my day. Racial relations seem good and there is full employment locally, but one rarely sees a mixed couple, or even group. In the Centre a young black married couple become our close friends; she is beautiful and very independently-minded, he is working on a doctoral thesis on black slave-owners – some minefield! The Jefferson book will be called *The Long Affair* (published 1996). Conor's take on Jefferson is not popular; it is regarded by the average American somewhat as rubbishing the Virgin Mary would have been in the Ireland of my youth. Conor has dedicated the book to three little boys, all born in 1993–94, all sons of younger friends of ours who have been particularly helpful and hospitable to us over the years: Paris Young, Jonathan Waters and Conor McDowell. I can only hope it will never be held against them.

1997

This spring semester at Fordham Law School was a spin-off of the Jefferson book. The change of tense signals a kind of closure. Conor was invited by Dean John Feerick to take part in a programme of lectures on the history of the American Constitution with two of the younger members of faculty, Professors Martin Flaherty and Bill Treanor, both obviously fellow tribesmen and both on very short acquaintance turning out to be the kind of Irish-American academic that makes Irish people proud of the connection: independently-minded, right-thinking, liberal and outspoken, above all lively and entertaining company. They brought out the best in Conor and he, I think, in them; they took turns at playing devil's advocate in the Jefferson debate. They both had, and happily still do, two utterly charming wives to match, Christine Loo and Marylyn Treanor. Christine and Marty have now a little girl, Aislinn. We have also met Marylyn's mother and Bill's, both amazing ladies. Bill's mother had read and admired Conor in the *Atlantic Monthly* long before she ever thought she might meet him. No wonder we took to the family; it now includes Liam, aged six, and Catherine, aged four.

The Law School campus stands on what must be the most advantageous site in Manhattan, directly across West Sixty-Second Street from the Lincoln Centre, the headquarters of the New York Metropolitan Opera, the New York City Ballet, the New York Symphony Orchestra and any other number of manifestations of the American performing arts. On the northwestern corner of the campus, at the nearest point to Lincoln Plaza, is a tower block on the twelfth floor of which, looking due east and south, we were lent an apartment. The morning sun rose directly opposite our bedroom windows, over the far end of Columbus – or was it Amsterdam? – Avenue; from our living room you could glimpse the Hudson River beyond the Plaza. RTÉ came to do a film (in Irish) about us and could not believe how scenically we were situated. I need hardly say our stock rose vertically when the camera followed Conor in to his lectures.

A particular happiness was to be living again in the same city as Deirdre Levinson, Kate's rescuing friend and to some degree our surrogate daughter. She is now married to a professional psychologist, Alan Bergson, and they have two children, a little younger than Patrick and Margaret. I have reason to believe that Deirdre is at present coming to grips with her own wartime childhood in an orthodox Jewish household in Britain, so I will not attempt to encapsulate her here – with any luck you will shortly read it from her own hand. Let me just say that when her daughter, Miranda, a tall, graceful girl, as lovely as her name, brought the RTÉ cameras to film at the store-front school she taught in in Harlem, her pupils stole the entire documentary and are still remembered with awe among Irish film-makers. Alan and Deirdre's Malachi is a Cambodian and adopted – as often happens in such cases, he is startlingly like his mother, as Patrick is like Conor; it makes a further bond.

CB　　CB　　CB

While we were still living in North Carolina, I had disturbing news of our Barbara's health. I came home and went across town from Howth to Mount Merrion to visit her. She answered the door, and death looked out of her face – I can think of no other way to convey the change in her. While I was away, she had suffered one of those clinically severe, protracted attacks of depression to which she was subject; that 'dark' strain in the Brownes which has continued on even into the next generation. She had stopped going for those periodic medical checks against cancer, which, for fifteen years, since she had had a mastectomy, had been mandatory for her, and the dormant enemy woke up and took hold. It was only a question of time. She was the sweetest-natured of mortals and always kept something of the girlishness of her prime; I missed her indescribably when she died. When she was dying she slipped back into the habits of her childhood, and the nurses marvelled at the naturalness and beauty of her Irish, uncontaminated by academia and much more pure than mine. At other times, when old friends from her husband's diplomatic career in Europe telephoned and she spoke French to them, the nurses were only slightly less impressed. Her friends from childhood and school were constantly with her: her bridesmaid, Paddy White – they had always been inseparable – and our especial friend-from-next-door, Mary Pat Cullen. I think that perhaps we worked too hard to keep Barbara's spirits up in those last days; she may have thought that we were not sufficiently grieving. When the last moments came, it was our Margaret, who is her goddaughter, who read aloud for us the Prayers for the Dying until the chaplain could get there: 'Though I shall walk through the valley of the shadow of death, yet I shall fear no evil …' Afterwards, the chaplain thanked her gravely for supplying for his absence.

There is a striking memory from the time I stayed with Conor in Jeru-salem while he was researching *The Siege*, which is probably appropriate here. It concerns my religious beliefs. In the building in Jerusalem known as Pilate's House, on one of the massive pillars supporting the cellar roof, a little stick-figure is scratched. It wears a spiky crown and carries a pa-thetic sceptre; it is wrapped in some kind of drapery. There can be no doubt as to what it represents: it is an icon. It may not be Our Lord himself, but it is just another such victim, the 'king' in some Roman soldier's deadly game of dice, two thousand years ago. The husband of a very dear friend – he is a practising psychologist, actually Deirdre's Alan – once asked me, when I told him of how this little graffito affected me, did I really think that the laws of nature were suspended to permit the birth of Christ and the Redemption? I am a Catholic, though not a particularly good one, and the only possible answer, for me, was 'yes'. I do not think that it is probable or demonstrable, but I do believe, and my belief is rational insofar as it corresponds to an emotional conviction which I actually experience, and which is entirely palpable. Long may it continue! Something momentous happened, and the technical terminology of our faith is, of necessity, inadequate to express it, to express the inexpressible. It is, however, the best we can do in our particular circumstances. I am reminded of the first Elizabeth of England's prayer on the Eucharist, which so affected me, when I discovered it, that I translated it into Irish, as an act of faith:

His was the word that spake it,	*An Té do labhair an briathar*
He took the bread and brake it,	*Le linn Dó an t-arán a riaradh,*
And what that word doth make it,	*Fé thuairim na céille 'chiallaigh*
I do believe and take it!	*Glacaim, is géillim sa phroinn seo!*

'In my end is my beginning.' I have not verified the quote. In February 2002 my sister-in-law, Jean, her children and grandchildren brought Séamus' ashes back to Dunquin to scatter them. '*Ní haene anois tú muna leatar do luaithreach i nDún Chaoin,*' (You are nobody now if your ashes are not scattered in Dunquin) said a neighbour, with the saving irony of the Gaeltacht. With age, our Séamus had become reclusive and he lived alone, although he and Jean were not legally separated and were not, in fact, estranged. That, alas!, was not true of his relationship with us. That very warm friendship, which embraced Conor and the children, was a casualty of the Northern 'Troubles'. By pure coincidence his Mass was said on Saint Gobnait's Day and was combined with the celebration of her feast. The schoolchildren sang the hymns in Irish and recited the old prayers and stories. I wrote a poem for him, but it does not gel in translation.

I was the eldest of three siblings; now, I am the last one living. Life has been very good to me. Conor and his children – all of them – have given it meaning. Now, with Patrick's marriage to his lovely and strong-minded Sarah and the birth of their inimitable son, Milo, to whom I dedicate this book, my cup runs over. I am so old now that it is not only Sarah whom I think of as a beloved daughter, but also her mother, Arlene Hogan, Milo's other grandmother. Arlene is an elegant and indomitable widow, who, having reared four daughters after her seriously talented and much-loved architect husband died young, is now completing a doctorate on Early Irish monastic charters. Obviously scholarship will run in that little family, and this proud grandmother concludes her efforts here with a copy of Milo's first school report (aged two-and-a-half!). Milo's full name is Milo (Maolra) Maurice Conor, after both grandfathers, but he goes by Milo.

THE PLAY ROOM
Spring term - March 2003

MILO:

Milo is a delightful boy, and an absolute pleasure to have in our school. His wit and bright sense of humour brightens up all our days. His concentration skills since he has been at our nursery have improved remarkably. Milo responds well to all instructions and tasks given to him even over long periods of time.

Milo has excellent colour recognition and maths skills. Milo can recognise all his colours and most of his numbers.

Milo is very artistic and he enjoys using a variety of materials and expressing himself widely.

Milo has very good manners and gets on extremely well with all his classmates as well as his teachers. We are all so happy to have Milo as apart of our team. His politeness, helpfulness and eagerness to learn are exceptional.

Group Teachers: Miss Cathy
                 Miss Trezza

AOSDÁNA AND FRANCIS STUART

I have been asked specifically to write about my connection with Francis Stuart. I have failed signally in conveying the atmosphere in which my life has been spent if the reader has not by now gathered that the dramas, major and minor, of Irish politics have always been present in my consciousness, as a background to my personal experience. The *odi-et-amo* relationship of my family with Maud Gonne and hers was built into my frame of reference as far back as I can remember, as was the conflict of emotional and cultural loyalties between France and Germany. In the script for this constantly running cinerama, especially, but not only, in the war years, Francis Stuart played a part somewhere between Osric and Rosencrantz and Guildenstern, alternating between the trivial and the dangerous. I can't say I devoted much thought to him; he was just a given. I haven't checked the dates, but it seems fairly certain that we were both in Paris at the time he was held by the French, after the war, for collaboration with the Germans. Understandably, my view and his of the Fascist sniper on the roof of Nôtre Dame would have been diametrically different.

Years went by and Aosdána was established in 1981, with much fan-fare, under the Haughey aegis, and in great part through the efforts of my late, dearly loved, but in this case, I am convinced, ill-advised friend, Eilís Dillon. Eilís and I differed on many points and only loved each other the more for it. I am not a professional writer and never at any stage thought of being a member of the organisation. Gradually, I became aware that many people assumed I was a member, and I was frequently asked to nominate candidates for membership. I did not know that only members could nominate candidates and I always agreed to these requests. As far as I know, all these candidates were accepted and the validity of their nomi-nations was never questioned. Early in 1996 I was approached by some of the younger members, mainly those interested in Irish, to allow my name to go forward as a candidate. I was immensely flattered and agreed; I was elected. Apart from my being horrified at the fact, which I soon discov-ered, that no one in the secretariat was willing, or perhaps competent to conduct business in Irish – in spite of the Celtic Revival terminology in which the organisation clothed its proceedings – my membership did not impinge much on my day-to-day life.

Then, in October 1996, Francis Stuart, already a member, was elected to the office of *Saoi* (sage, n.). This is the highest distinction in Aosdána's gift and is held by people of the calibre of Seamus Heaney and Louis le Brocquy. With what I now recognise as unconscious, but possibly offensive, officiousness, I was outraged on their behalf. I had, of course, myself voted against Mr Stuart's being so honoured, but I now hesitated to protest further, primarily because I felt that, at my age, to cut myself off from a possible future source of funding by overreacting to a majority decision would be an imprudence. Then, gradually, I became aware of the near-despair this appointment was causing among my Jewish acquaintance, and also among Germans who had suffered for their anti-Nazi principles. I had left it late, but I was compelled by a deep inner conviction to make a stand, and so, on Wednesday, 26 November, at Aosdána's annual public meeting, I proposed, in effect, that the organisation should define its abhorrence of the Fascist and racist views expressed throughout his life by Francis Stuart and never repudiated, and should deprive him of his office of *Saoi*. At an extremely rowdy meeting, after a highly convivial lunch for the members, where I was careful to drink only water, my proposal was howled down, in spite of profoundly cogent arguments by, among others, Louis le Brocquy and Ann Madden, who proposed that the fundamental issue of possible conflict between aesthetic and moral values be further discussed – I had left my proposal open to amendment – before any vote be taken. The original proposal was roundly defeated; those sympathetic to my idea abstained, and I voted for my own draft, unamended, in a minority of one. Conor quoted from Napoleon, on the occasion of whose elevation by the Assembly from First Consul to Emperor there had been only one vote against, that of Cambon, the 'architect of the revolution'. The new Emperor commented, '*L'opposition est de choix*' (The opposition is distinguished). I was very proud.

The newspaper piece below, from the *Sunday Independent* of 30 November, is approximately the speech I delivered, from notes, to Aosdána. Such was the clamour from the floor that I doubt if even my friends could follow it. It gives a fair idea of my thinking at the time and since, and I follow it with a notice of Brendan Barrington's book on the wartime broadcasts of Francis Stuart, published in 2000. Had that book been available at the time of Stuart's elevation to *Saoi*, and had the bulk of the membership of Aosdána been aware of its content at the time, we might have had a more seemly debate and, perhaps, a different outcome. The review I wrote of the book, in the *Irish Independent* of 6 January 2001, which I also add, probably exhausts, I think, what I have to say on the matter.

Sunday Independent, 30 November 1996

WHY FRANCIS STUART'S STANCE OUTRAGES ME

Máire Cruise O'Brien, who resigned from Aosdána last week, explains that she cannot approve of honouring an 'unrepentant racist'.

My resolution was a draft merely. It was open to amendment. It was drafted under pressure of time and ill-health. It is perhaps naïf to categorise any utterance of Mr Stuart's as 'opinion'. Statements of opinion are not his line; deniability is. A more elegant formulation, more accurate and economical in the context, might be:

That Aosdána unequivocally dissociates itself from the racist content and brazen sophistry of the remarks attributed to Mr Francis Stuart in the television programme, etc, etc.

The original formulation has, however, clumsy as it may be, the advantage of reflecting accurately the underlying gravamen of this issue, and my deep sense of outrage at the fact that this body has placed itself in the position of being seen to award its highest distinction to someone who unrepentantly chuckles over his role as wartime propagandist for Nazi Germany.

I could wear Mr Stuart as a fellow-member and a pensioner of Aosdána, though with difficulty. I find I cannot live with him as a laureate.

Of the arguments put to me before the meeting, the most important philosophically was the contention that aesthetic judgement should be independent of moral values. That is, of course, a subject entirely appropriate for discussion by this body but, in this instance, not by me.

I do not suffer from this dilemma because I do not think that Mr Stuart is a good writer. He is a fashionable writer, a notorious writer, even, in a historical context, a useful writer. He is not a good one, he does not write well. His weird, artistic voyeurism is psychologically interesting, but his style – once he departs from straightforward narration (which he does at the drop of a hat) – is depressingly Edwardian, dated and baroque, like James Stephens on a bad day, or Wilde without the wit. In the extract from his work in the Field Day Anthology of Irish Writing, the horrible prose blankets the immediacy of the horrors described. Mr Stuart's is the kind of prose that lends itself to the Myles na gCopaleen school of literary analysis: What colour is the moon if it is "the colour of grey-blue decaying flesh"? Answer: grey-blue.

The words complained of here are a good example of what I mean: "The Jew was always the worm that got into the rose and sickened it." An ugly metaphor and an ugly meaning, no matter how it is wrapped in sophistry. It is a metaphor Mr Stuart is fond of; you will find it again on p64 of [*Black List,*] *Section H*: "If there was a Jewish idea, it was surely a contradiction, it was a hidden, unheroic, and critical one, a worm that could get into a lot of fine-looking fruit."

Mr Stuart professes to like Jews; his work tells you why. He has an affection for them because they are pimps, smugglers, even quasi-collaborators; he likes them, as an old-time Southern colonel liked blacks, for their defects. It is a common and not very subtle form of racism.

That is probably enough about the purely literary side.

I would not want you to think that this motion was the result of a superficial or sudden impulse. I am a younger contemporary of Mr Stuart's and his activities were taken very seriously indeed in my family, as endangering the safety of this state, both before, during and after the war.

My father had only one explanation for Mr Stuart's post-war literary success and relative impunity: that he had been a double agent and that this was the pay-off by the Allied establishment.

Paranoid? Possibly. Black humour? To a degree. But my father in his day was well-informed, and his speculation accords very well both with the character of Mr Stuart's anti-hero in Black List, Section H and with what we know of Allied policy about the rehabilitation of Germany in the '50s.

Stuart's publisher was Victor Gollancz, a Jew; a magnanimous Jew, who saw himself single-handedly as the saviour of post-war Germany. He was a Renaissance man, a pillar of the Left; but also an establishment man. We can imagine, as in a spy novel, a lunch: "Poor Stuart – useful to us during the war – practically a son-in-law of Yeats – down on his luck – deserves a boost?"

The rehabilitation of Stuart is a spin-off both of the desire to destabilise Irish neutrality, shared by both combatants during the war, and of post-war Allied geopolitics in the '60s. Victor Gollancz's generosity in this context honours him – but it does not become the government agency of a state that was neutral during the war. What we are doing is not merely forgiving Mr Stuart's past, we are exalting it.

We are an agency for distributing state patronage. We are not arbiters of artistic excellence; that is not something that can be done by democratic process. What we do is copper-fasten and rubber-stamp popularity. This is a perfectly respectable function, provided we don't get starry-eyed about it.

We are not an Olympian body that can transcend the greatest evil of our times in the name of literary values; we are not above conscience; we are not independent of the common good; we need to realise what we have done: we have bestowed the highest honour at our disposal on an unrepentant – indeed gloating – racist.

We must recoil from the full enormity of what we have done. I am not proud of my delay in bringing this matter before you. It is ironic – in that truest sense of that much-abused word – that we have accorded Mr Stuart that very seal of establishment approval which he himself has always maintained was the kiss of death for the artist. He must be laughing like a drain.

Press Release/Review Copy

THE WARTIME BROADCASTS OF FRANCIS STUART 1942–1944

In 1940, shortly after the outbreak of the Second World War, the novelist Francis Stuart (1902–2000) moved from County Wicklow to Berlin, where he had accepted a university lecturing position. Stuart remained in the Third Reich for the duration of the war, and between 1942 and 1944 he made over one hundred broadcasts on German radio to Ireland.

The German sojourn and the broadcasts have been at the heart of the long-running controversy over Stuart, and yet remarkably little is known about them. This book publishes, for the first time, the surviving transcripts of Stuart's broadcasts. While Stuart avoided explicit anti-Semitism and never criticised Russia or communism – and referred to himself as a 'neutral', uninterested in making propaganda – the talks were consistent with the broad thrust of German wartime propaganda to Ireland, and took an often fiercely anti-Allied line. Stuart spoke repeatedly of the importance of a united Ireland, and suggested that a German victory could bring this about. He spoke warmly of his admiration for the German people and for Hitler.

The editor's extensive introduction shows that Stuart's pre-war political interests and commitments were consistent and often passionately held – from a 1924 essay comparing Ireland's struggle against Britain to Austria's against the Jews, to a 1938 letter to *The Irish Times* opposing plans to receive refugees fleeing Hitler – and intimately tied up with his creative work. (Stuart more than once stressed to his listeners the continuity between what he had tried to express in his fiction – for example, the pro-Brownshirt 'sympathies' of a 1933 novel, *Try the Sky* – and the message of his broadcasts.) The introduction also gives an account of Stuart's involvement in collaboration between the IRA and the Germans during the war, and suggests that his achievement as a writer can never be adequately assessed until the nature of the relationship between his novels, his politics and his life is confronted squarely.

Irish Independent, Saturday, 6 June 2001

Stuart and the Nazis

Máire Mhac an tSaoi on a new assessment of the broadcasts made by Francis Stuart from Germany during World War Two.
   The Wartime Broadcasts of Francis Stuart 1942–1944, **edited by Brendan Barrington, Lilliput Press.**

This collection of the wartime broadcasts from Germany of Francis Stuart, edited by Brendan Barrington, is an impressive contribution to the history of the State and of our neutrality during World War Two; it also sheds considerable light on the personality of Francis Stuart.

This last is due not to any intrinsic literary merit in the substance of the broadcasts, which were compelled by the exigencies of German wartime policy towards Irish neutrality to be models of dullness and deniability, but to the masterly introduction by the editor which situates these broadcasts in the life of Francis Stuart. Barrington gives us a brilliantly thorough and fair-minded analysis of Stuart's political beliefs and – more importantly – emotions, from the twenties of the last century on, as expressed in his writings and demonstrated by his actions.

It is impossible, in my opinion, to digest the material adduced here and not come to the conclusion that Stuart's political bent was strongly anti-democratic and, further, that in his admiration for Hitler's Germany, anti-Semitism was always a conscious factor. But then, as a somewhat younger contemporary of Francis Stuart's, I was always convinced of this, and had read quite enough of Francis Stuart to regard him as a novelist of indifferent merit.

I had no objection to his receiving state funding as a charity in a penurious old age from Aosdána, since judgements as to who is or is not a mere hack writer are, of course, subjective. I did object and still do object to his being signally honoured by the state which he never regarded with anything but contempt, and in a manner which could not but appear to endorse both his Fascism and his anti-Semitism, at a time when racism and contempt for democracy pose real dangers to our society.

On the point of contemporaneity, it may be of interest that, in the real-life original of the incident in which the protagonist of Black List, Section H falls asleep at his post and occasions the discovery and punishment of his comrades tunneling out of gaol, the republican engineering squad tunneling to meet them into the gaol was commanded by my father, who was consequently arrested.

Because, of course, it was not in order to discover hints or declarations of anti-Semitism that the Irish defence forces from 1942 to 1944 monitored Stuart's broadcasts from Germany; the issue which concerned them was the provision of aid and comfort to subversive republican elements within the state.

Cautiously worded as the broadcasts are, there can be no doubt but that they created an atmosphere of German interest in Ireland, which greatly encouraged the rank-and-file of the IRA, whatever its leadership may have known, or subsequently discovered, about the realities of the situation. They oxygenated the water for the fish.

Brendan Barrington cautions – rightly – against building too much on the autobiographical elements in Black List, Section H, but it is surely impossible to read that book without forming definite opinions on the psychological proclivities of the author. In particular, his remarkably consistent sado-masochism and his nostalgie de la boue.

In Nazism it is the jackboot that attracts him; in the Irish civil war it is the extra element of brutality in Cogadh na gCarad that he relishes; insofar as he expresses any sympathy for Jews, it is their supposed criminality that appeals. In Redemption his perverse affections are already veering towards the Russian conquerors. I find these books illuminating and disturbing as case-histories. I cannot find in them any edifying element that might excuse the author's deliberate and considered political actions. The concept of 'Stuart the political innocent' is well and truly laid [as in 'ghost unlaid'] by Barrington himself in his editorial essay here.

It is somewhat surprising, among the exhaustive list of sources given by the editor of this book, to find no reference to any official account of the Aosdána meeting of the 26th November 1996, at which I proposed that Francis Stuart should be asked to resign from that body. I know that the meeting was recorded. Before resigning from Aosdána, I asked for and was promised a transcript of the proceedings. When I subsequently requested this in writing it was refused, and I was too weary of the subject to pursue the matter.

Now, however, when tempers should have cooled, is it not extraordinary that the record of a public meeting of a publicly financed body is not available to the taxpayers who finance it? It must, however, explain why Brendan Barrington appears to ignore the magnificent intervention of Louis le Brocquy's on that occasion, in which he addressed the problems of conflict between aesthetic and moral values, with particular reference to the issue of the dehumanisation consequent on racism.

As against this omission on the editor's part I must thank him, among many other benefits, for publicising the merits of my friend, Raymond Patrick Burke's MA thesis, The Representation of Jews and "Jewishness" in the Novels of Francis Stuart, unjustly slighted in the course of controversy as 'a mere MA thesis'. I quote, "Burke's research is impressively vast and his conclusions [are] often compelling." As I have already indicated, I could not say fairer than that myself of Mr Barrington's work on this book.

A CHRONOLOGY OF
THE AUTHOR'S CAREER
AND PUBLICATIONS

MÁIRE CRUISE O'BRIEN

(née Máire MacEntee, in Irish (Gaelic) Máire Mhac an tSaoi, under which name she publishes in that language)

Whitewater, Howth Summit, Dublin 13

Born: Dublin, 4 April 1922.

Educated: Alexandra School, Dublin; Scoil Ghobnait, Dun Chaoin, Co. Chiarraí; Beaufort HS, Rathfarnham; University College, Dublin (Entrance Scholarship in Irish [Gaelic] and Modern Languages; scholarship in each subsequent academic year); and University of Paris (Institut des Hautes Études en Sorbonne).

Primary Degree: BA, Celtic Studies and Modern Languages: First Class Honours, First Place in each of the following individual subjects: Modern Irish (Gaelic), French and English; September 1941.

Travelling Studentship in Irish (Gaelic) and English from the National University of Ireland, 1942.

Studied Law at King's Inns, Dublin, 1941–44; called to the Irish Bar, 1944.

MA Classical Modern Irish, 1945. Thesis on Pierce Ferriter, a seventeenth-century Gaelic poet. She is at present engaged in further research into the historical background of his production, which she hopes will, very shortly, be published by Sáirséal Ó Marcaigh, Dublin.

Scholar, Dublin Institute for Advanced Studies, 1942–45; Publication: *Two Irish Arthurian Romances* (ed.), Dublin 1946.

Studied Celtic Languages at the Institute des Hautes Études en Sorbonne, University of Paris, under Professor Vendryès, 1945–47.

Diplomatic Career:

Entered Dublin Ministry of Foreign Affairs, 1947, as Third Secretary.

Served briefly in Paris, 1949.

Served, Madrid, Second Secretary of Embassy, 1949–51.

Served, Dublin, as Secretary of the Irish Cultural Relations Committee, 1951–52.

Seconded to Ministry of Education to work on compilation of modern English/Irish (Gaelic) Dictionary, 1952–56.

Served International Organisations Desk, Ministry of Foreign Affairs, 1956–61.

Member, Irish Delegation to General Assembly of the United Nations, 1957–60; served as Delegate on the Third Committee (Economic and Social Affairs, notably Human Rights).

Appointed Permanent Representative of Ireland to the Council of Europe in Strasbourg, 1961.

Resigned to marry Dr Conor Cruise O'Brien in 1962 and has since accompanied him during his periods of residence in Africa, London and the United States.

Family: Two part-African and part-Irish adopted children, Patrick and Margaret, now in their thirties.

Teaching: Has taught Irish (Gaelic) at various levels, from elementary to university, for varying periods, in and outside Ireland.

Lecture courses: Attended courses in African Studies, including courses in linguistics, history and sociology, University of Ghana, Legon, Accra, 1963–66.

Instituted and taught courses on 'The Gaelic Background to Anglo-Irish Literature', Queens College, New York, 1969–70, with Dr Liam and Dr Máire de Paor.

Visiting lecturer in the Department of Folklore and Folklife, University of Pennsylvania, 1989.

Writer-in-Residence, University College, Dublin, 1991–92.

Associate Fellow at the National Humanities Centre, Durham, North Carolina, 1995.

Publications include:

Three slim volumes of verse in Irish (Gaelic), to wit *Margadh na Saoire*, 1956, *Codladh an Ghaiscígh*, 1973, *An Galar Dubhach*, 1980 (all published by Sáirséal agus Dill, Dublin).

A selection of translations from Classical Gaelic poetry entitled, *A Heart Full of Thought*, Dublin, 1959.

Articles, short stories, poems and essays and translations in various newspapers and periodicals, including essays of substance on: 'The Female Principle in Irish Poetry', in *The Celtic Consciousness* (ed. Robert O'Driscoll, Canada, 1981); 'The Origins of Poetry: Points of Comparison between Medieval Ireland and Early Greece', in *Studia Hibernica*, No.24, 1984–88 (see Appendix 3, letter from Professor Gregory Nagy, Department of Classics, Harvard University); and, most recently, a monograph on the life and work of Gerald FitzGerald, Third Earl of Desmond, a fourteenth-century Hiberno-Norman magnate believed to have originated the practice of courtly love poetry in Irish (Gaelic), in *Oghma 2*, 1990.

Collected poetry in Irish, *An Cion go dTí Seo*, Dublin, Sáirséal Ó Marcaigh, 1987; in contemplation from the same publisher, a selection of her poetry in Irish with English translations; from Fortnight Press, Belfast, 1997, *Trasládáil*, a selection of favourite Irish poetry, spanning the classical modern period, with English verse translations of her own; *Shoah agus Dánta Eile*, Sáirséal Ó Marcaigh, 1999; and from Cló IarChonnachta, 2001, a conjectural novella about Pierce Ferriter, *A Bhean Óg Ón ...*

A translation into Irish (Gaelic), recently completed, of Rainer Maria Rilke's *Duino Elegies*, all ten of which have appeared in various literary periodicals and collections.

Editor of *Poetry Ireland Review*, Nos.31–33.

Believed to be the oldest living poet publishing in Irish (Gaelic).

Distinctions: Awarded a D.Litt Celt *honoris causa* by the National University of Ireland, 1992; winner of the O'Shaughnessy Poetry Award of the Irish-American Cultural Institute, 1988; Elected to Aosdána, 1996 – subsequently resigning on principle; member of the Register of Peers of the Australia Council for the Arts; Honorary Member of the Irish Translators' Association, 1999.

LETTER TO THE AUTHOR FROM PROFESSOR GREGORY NAGY

DEPARTMENT OF THE CLASSICS

319 Boylston Hall
Cambridge, Massachusetts 02138

8 Dec. 1993

Dear Dr. Mhac an tSaoi,

Please forgive me for not replying
sooner! I found your genial
article in Studia Hibernica, for which
I thank you warmly, very important
for my own work.

To reciprocate, I send you the
enclosed offprint, which I hope
you will find interesting. I also
have some other recent things that
you might find useful for your work.
Please let me know if you would like
for me to send them to you! Yours, with admiration,
Gregory Nagy

INDEX